Reaching Key Financial Reporting Decisions

How Directors and Auditors Interact

Vivien Beattie

University of Glasgow

Stella Fearnley

University of Bournemouth

Tony Hines

University of Portsmouth

Foreword by Peter Wyman CBE

Based on research funded by
the ICAEW's charitable trusts

A John Wiley and Sons, Ltd., Publication

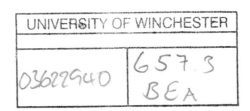
This edition first published 2011
© 2011 John Wiley & Sons, Ltd

Registered office
John Wiley & Sons Ltd, The Atrium, Southern Gate, Chichester, West Sussex, PO19 8SQ, United Kingdom

For details of our global editorial offices, for customer services and for information about how to apply for permission to reuse the copyright material in this book please see our website at www.wiley.com.

Library of Congress Cataloging-in-Publication Data

Fearnley, Stella.
   Reaching Key Financial Reporting Decisions : How Directors and Auditors Interact / Stella Fearnley, Vivien Beattie, Tony Hines.
      p. cm
   Includes bibliographical references and index.
   ISBN 978-0-470-74874-9 (hardback)
   1. Financial statements–Great Britain.   2. Corporate governance–Great Britain.   I. Beattie, Vivien (Vivien A.)
II. Hines, Tony.   III. Title.
   HF5681.B2F34 2011
   657′.30941–dc22

                                                                                    2010050391

A catalogue record for this book is available from the British Library.

ISBN 978-0-470-74874-9 (hardback) ISBN 978-1-119-99329-2 (ebk)
ISBN 978-1-119-97375-1 (ebk) ISBN 978-1-119-97376-8 (ebk)

Typeset in 11/13pt Times by Aptara Inc., New Delhi, India
Printed in Great Britain by CPI Antony Rowe, Chippenham and Eastbourne

Contents

List of Figures   xiii

List of Tables   xiv

Foreword by Peter Wyman   xv

Preface   xix

Acknowledgements   xx

Abbreviations   xxi

PART I   THE BACKGROUND   1

1 Introduction and Background   3
   1.1   What This Book is About   3
   1.2   Recent Regulatory Changes   3
   1.3   Contribution of This Book in the 2010/2011 Regulatory
         Environment   4
   1.4   Research Approach   6
   1.5   Outline of Book   6
   1.6   Key Findings and Conclusions   8

2 Review of Relevant Literature   11
   2.1   Overview   11
   2.2   Regulation   11
         2.2.1 Regulation Theory   11
         2.2.2 Regulatory Policy and Structures   12
         2.2.3 International Standards on Auditing (ISAs)   13
         2.2.4 Ethical Standards for Auditors   13
   2.3   IFRS   14
         2.3.1 Rules versus Principles Debate   15

        2.3.2 Complexity Debate   16
        2.3.3 New Business Reporting Models   17
    2.4 Audit Quality   18
        2.4.1 Definition of Audit Quality   18
        2.4.2 Audit Quality Research   19
        2.4.3 Non-Audit Services   20
        2.4.4 Auditor Tenure   21
        2.4.5 Individual Audit Partner Effects   21
        2.4.6 Survey Research   23
    2.5 Enforcement   24
        2.5.1 The FRRP   24
        2.5.2 Audit Firm Review and Inspection   25
    2.6 Corporate Governance and the Role of the Audit Committee   26
        2.6.1 General Evolution of Audit Committees   26
        2.6.2 The UK Corporate Governance System   27
    2.7 Interactions and Negotiation in Non-Audit Settings   28
        2.7.1 Theory   28
        2.7.2 Empirical Studies   29
    2.8 Interactions and Negotiation in Audit Settings   30
        2.8.1 The Audit Setting   31
        2.8.2 Archival Studies Using Public Data   31
        2.8.3 Experimental Studies   32
        2.8.4 Questionnaire Studies   33
        2.8.5 Interview Studies   34
        2.8.6 Link Between Audit Committee and Financial Reporting
               Quality   40

3   The Survey   43
    3.1 Overview   43
    3.2 Methods   43
    3.3 Findings   44
        3.3.1 Background Characteristics of the Companies   44
        3.3.2 Audit Committees Characteristics   44
    3.4 Interaction Issues   45
    3.5 Financial Statement Changes   48
    3.6 Summary   49

PART II   THE CASE STUDIES   51

4   Case Studies   53
    4.1 Introduction to the Case Studies   53
    4.2 How the Case Companies were Selected and Approached   53
    4.3 Broad Approach to the Grounded Theory Analysis   55

4.4 Writing Up Each Case (Matched Set of Interviews) — The Stories   57
4.5 Preliminary Within-Case Analysis: Attaching Labels to the Key
Categories   58
    4.5.1 Labelling the Concepts Described in the Stories   58
    4.5.2 Preliminary Analysis of Context   59
    4.5.3 The Interactions   59
    4.5.4 The Outcomes   60
4.6 Within-case Analysis   60
4.7 Tabular Summary of Cases   60

5 Case 1 — Sandpiper plc   **69**
5.1 Background to the Case   69
5.2 Corporate Governance   69
    5.2.1 Attendees at the Audit Committee   69
    5.2.2 Cycle of Meetings   71
    5.2.3 The Chairman's Management of the Audit Committee and
    Key Relationships   73
    5.2.4 The Nature of the Relationship   75
    5.2.5 Satisfaction with Auditors and Partner Changes   77
5.3 Key Interactions Between Stuart, Duncan and Patrick   78
    5.3.1 Audit Fees   79
    5.3.2 The Accounting Treatment of Costs Associated with a Major
    Change in the Company's Computer System   82
    5.3.3 Re-Organization Costs   85
    5.3.4 Inventory Provisions   87
    5.3.5 Dividends from Subsidiaries   89
    5.3.6 Pension Liabilities   91
5.4 Contextual Factors and Analysis of the Interactions   93
    5.4.1 Audit Related Interaction: Fee Negotiation   95
    5.4.2 Financial Reporting Interaction: the Accounting Treatment
    of Costs Associated with a Major Change in the Company's
    Accounting System   95
    5.4.3 Financial Reporting Interaction: Re-Organization Costs   96
    5.4.4 Financial Reporting Interaction: Inventory Provisions   96
    5.4.5 Financial Reporting Interaction: Accounting for Dividends
    from Subsidiaries   97
    5.4.6 Financial Reporting Interaction: Pension Liabilities   97
5.5 Conclusions   97

6 Case 2 — Kestrel plc   **99**
6.1 Background to the Case   99
6.2 Corporate Governance   99

6.2.1 Audit Committee Attendees	99
6.2.2 Cycle of Meetings	100
6.2.3 Chairman's Management of the Audit Committee and Key Relationships	103
6.2.4 The Nature of the Relationship with the Auditor	105
6.3 Key Interactions Between Philip, Guy and Barry	107
6.3.1 Valuation of Intangibles on Acquisition	107
6.3.2 Impairment Reviews	112
6.3.3 Financial Instruments — Treatment of Preference Shares	115
6.3.4 Financial Instruments — Hedging	117
6.3.5 Restructuring Costs	119
6.3.6 Fraud and Illegal Acts	121
6.4 Contextual Factors and Analysis of the Interactions	122
6.4.1 Financial Reporting Interaction: Fair Value on Acquisition	122
6.4.2 Financial Reporting Interaction: Impairment Reviews	124
6.4.3 Financial Reporting Interaction: Financial Instruments — Treatment of Preference Shares	125
6.4.4 Financial Reporting Interaction: Financial Instruments — Hedging	125
6.4.5 Financial Reporting Interaction: Restructuring Costs	126
6.4.6 Corporate Governance Issue: Fraud and Illegal Acts	126
6.5 Conclusions	126
7 Case 3 — Mallard plc	**129**
7.1 Background to the Case	129
7.2 Corporate Governance	129
7.2.1 Attendees at Audit Committee	129
7.2.2 Cycle of Meetings and Issues Discussed	130
7.2.3 The Chair's Management of the Audit Committee and Key Relationships	132
7.2.4 Nature of the Relationship with the Auditor	134
7.3 Key Interactions Between Jack, Paul and Gerald	134
7.3.1 Audit Fee	135
7.3.2 Accounting for a Complex Transaction	135
7.3.3 Business Review	137
7.3.4 Financial Instruments — Hedging	138
7.3.5 Going Concern	140
7.3.6 Impairment of Assets	141
7.4 Contextual Factors and Analysis of the Interactions	141
7.4.1 Audit Fee	143
7.4.2 Financial Reporting Interaction: Accounting for a Complex Transaction	143

7.4.3 Financial Reporting Interaction: Business Review   143
7.4.4 Financial Reporting Interaction: Financial Instruments —
      Hedging   143
7.4.5 Financial Reporting Interaction: Going Concern   144
7.4.6 Financial Reporting Interaction: Impairment of Assets   144
7.5 Conclusions   144

8 Case 4 — Finch plc   **145**
8.1 Background to the Case   145
8.2 Corporate Governance   146
    8.2.1 Attendees at Audit Committee   146
    8.2.2 Cycle of Meetings   148
    8.2.3 The Chair's Management of the Audit Committee and Key
          Relationships   148
    8.2.4 Tendering   150
    8.2.5 Nature of the Relationship   151
8.3 Key Interactions Between Ben, Robert and Damien   151
    8.3.1 Audit Fees Following a Tender   152
    8.3.2 Notional Interest on Unwinding of Deferred Consideration   153
    8.3.3 Earnings Per Share   154
    8.3.4 Share-based Payments   155
    8.3.5 Treatment of Tax Credits on Exercise of Options   157
    8.3.6 Revenue Recognition and Provisioning on Contracts   158
    8.3.7 Valuation of Intangible Assets on Acquisition   160
    8.3.8 Segmental Reporting   162
    8.3.9 Business Review   164
8.4 Contextual Factors and Analysis of the Interactions   164
    8.4.1 Audit Related Interaction: Audit Fees Following a Tender   166
    8.4.2 Financial Reporting Interaction: Notional Interest on
          Unwinding of Deferred Consideration   166
    8.4.3 Financial Reporting Interaction: Earnings Per Share   167
    8.4.4 Financial Reporting Interaction: Share-based Payments   168
    8.4.5 Financial Reporting Interaction: Treatment of Tax Credits on
          Exercise of Options   168
    8.4.6 Financial Reporting Interaction: Revenue Recognition and
          Provisioning on Contracts   169
    8.4.7 Financial Reporting Interaction: Valuation of Intangible
          Assets on Acquisition   169
    8.4.8 Financial Reporting Interactions: Segmental Reporting   170
    8.4.9 Financial Reporting Interaction: Business Review   170
8.5 Conclusions   170

9 Case 5 — Cormorant plc **173**
 9.1 Background to the Case 173
 9.2 Corporate Governance 173
   9.2.1 Attendees at Audit Committee 174
   9.2.2 Cycle of Meetings and Issues Discussed 175
   9.2.3 The Chair's Management of the Audit Committee and Key
     Relationships 176
 9.3 Key Interactions Between William, Dave and Simon 179
   9.3.1 Identification of Intangibles on Acquisition of Eagle 179
   9.3.2 Impairment of Goodwill on Acquisition of Eagle 182
   9.3.3 Deferred Tax Asset Resulting from Eagle Losses 184
   9.3.4 Provision on Inventories 185
   9.3.5 Business Review 186
   9.3.6 Misreporting in Eagle 187
 9.4 Contextual Factors and Analysis of the Interactions 188
   9.4.1 Financial Reporting Interaction: Identification of
     Intangibles on Acquisition of Eagle 190
   9.4.2 Financial Reporting Interaction: Impairment of Goodwill
     on Acquisition of Eagle 190
   9.4.3 Financial Reporting Interaction: Deferred Tax Asset
     Resulting from Eagle Losses 191
   9.4.4 Financial Reporting Interaction: Provision on Inventories 191
   9.4.5 Financial Reporting Interaction: Business Review 191
   9.4.6 Corporate Governance Interaction: Misreporting in Eagle 191
 9.5 Conclusions 192

10 Case 6 — Pochard plc **193**
 10.1 Background to the Case 193
 10.2 Corporate Governance 193
   10.2.1 Attendees at Audit Committee 194
   10.2.2 Cycle of Meetings 195
   10.2.3 The Chair's Management of the Audit Committee and Key
     Relationships 196
 10.3 Key Interactions Between Peter, Alan and Henry 197
   10.3.1 Presentation of Cash Flow Statement Under IFRS 198
   10.3.2 Inventory Valuation 200
   10.3.3 Contingent Liabilities 200
   10.3.4 Fair Value on Acquisition 203
   10.3.5 Restructuring Costs 205
   10.3.6 Segmental Reporting 206
   10.3.7 Control Weakness 207
 10.4 Contextual Factors and Analysis of the Interactions 208

10.4.1 Financial Reporting Interaction: Presentation of Cash
Flow Statement   208
10.4.2 Financial Reporting Interaction: Inventory Valuation   210
10.4.3 Financial Reporting Interaction: Contingent Liabilities 210
10.4.4 Financial Reporting Interaction: Fair Value on Acquisition 210
10.4.5 Financial Reporting Interaction: Restructuring Costs   211
10.4.6 Financial Reporting Interaction: Segmental Reporting   211
10.4.7 Corporate Governance Interaction: Control Weakness   211
10.5 Conclusions   211

11 Case 7 — Woodpecker plc   213
11.1 Background to the Case   213
11.2 Corporate Governance   214
11.2.1 Attendees at the Audit Committee   214
11.2.2 Cycle of Meetings   214
11.2.3 The Chair's Management of the Audit Committee and Key
Relationships   216
11.2.4 Tendering   217
11.2.5 Nature of the Relationship with the Auditor   218
11.3 Key Interactions Between Richard, Horace and Edward   219
11.3.1 Inventory Valuation   219
11.3.2 Breach of Internal Controls in an Overseas Subsidiary 221
11.3.3 Valuation of Intangible Assets on Acquisition of a
Subsidiary   222
11.4 Contextual Factors and Analysis of the Interactions   224
11.4.1 Financial Reporting Related Interaction: Inventory
Valuation   224
11.4.2 Corporate Governance Related Interaction: Breach of
Internal Controls in an Overseas Subsidiary   224
11.4.3 Financial Reporting Related Interaction: Valuation of
Intangible Assets on Acquisition of a Subsidiary   226
11.5 Conclusions   226

12 Case 8 — Raven plc   229
12.1 Background to the Case   229
12.2 Corporate Governance   229
12.2.1 Cycle of Meetings and Attendees   229
12.2.2 The Chair's Management of the Audit Committee   230
12.2.3 Communication with the Auditors   232
12.2.4 Nature of the Auditor-Client Relationship   232
12.2.5 Satisfaction with Auditors and Partner Changes/Tendering 233

12.3 Key Interactions Between Trevor, Norman and Ivan   233
    12.3.1 Accounting for a Complex Transaction   234
    12.3.2 Disclosures Relating to Potential Future Losses in a
           Subsidiary, Chestnut   235
    12.3.3 Business Review Disclosures   235
12.4 Contextual Factors and Analysis of the Interactions   236
    12.4.1 Financial Reporting Interaction: Accounting for a
           Complex Transaction   236
    12.4.2 Financial Reporting Interaction: Disclosures Relating to
           Potential Future Losses in a Subsidiary, Chestnut   238
    12.4.3 Financial Reporting Issue: Business Review   238
12.5 Conclusions   239

13 Case 9 — Ostrich plc   241
13.1 Background to the Case   241
13.2 Corporate Governance   241
13.3 Key Interactions Between Matthew, Victor and Luke   241
13.4 Contextual Factors and Analysis of the Interactions   242
    13.4.1 Financial Reporting Interaction: Valuation of Intangibles
           on Acquisition   242
    13.4.2 Financial Reporting Interaction: Share-based Payments   244
    13.4.3 Financial Reporting Interaction: Business Review   244
    13.4.4 Financial Reporting Interaction: Segmental Reporting   245
13.5 Conclusions   245

PART III CROSS-CASE ANALYSIS AND CONCLUSIONS   247

14 Views of Interviewees on the Regulatory Framework   249
14.1 Introduction   249
14.2 Financial Reporting Issues   249
    14.2.1 International Financial Reporting Standards (IFRS)   250
    14.2.2 Other Regulation Relating to Disclosures in the Annual
           Report   256
    14.2.3 Financial Reporting Review Panel (FRRP)   256
14.3 Auditing Issues   258
    14.3.1 Ethical Standards   258
    14.3.2 International Standards of Auditing (ISAs)   260
    14.3.3 Audit Inspection Unit (AIU)   262
14.4 Corporate Governance   264
    14.4.1 Audit Committees   265
    14.4.2 Other Aspects of Corporate Governance   266
14.5 Summary   267

15 Attributes and Procedures of the Audit Committee and the Audit Committee Chair: Evidence   **271**
    15.1 Overview   271
    15.2 The Audit Committee   271
          15.2.1 Membership and Attendance   271
          15.2.2 Financial Experience and Understanding   272
          15.2.3 Interviewees' Views on IFRS   272
    15.3 The Role of the Audit Committee Chair   273
          15.3.1 Dealing with Accounting Problems   273
          15.3.2 Level of Engagement   273
    15.4 Issues Discussed at Audit Committee Meetings   274
          15.4.1 Range of Issues   274
          15.4.2 Audit Planning   274
          15.4.3 Audit Fees   275
    15.5 Conclusions and Contribution to the Academic Literature   275

16 Cross-case Analysis and Theory Development   **279**
    16.1 Introduction   279
    16.2 Summary of Interaction Attributes   279
    16.3 Summary of Cross-case Analysis   282
    16.4 A Revised Grounded Theory of Financial Reporting
          Interactions — Overview   283
    16.5 General Company/Audit Firm Context   304
          16.5.1 Quality of Primary Relationships   304
          16.5.2 Company Circumstances   305
          16.5.3 Audit Firm Circumstances   306
          16.5.4 Company Buyer Types   307
    16.6 Specific Context   307
          16.6.1 Interaction Issues   307
          16.6.2 Goals and Objectives of Parties   308
          16.6.3 Third Parties   308
          16.6.4 Other Specific Contextual Factors   309
    16.7 International Regulatory Regime   309
    16.8 National Regulatory Regime   310
    16.9 Interactions (Core Category)   311
          16.9.1 Interaction Events   311
          16.9.2 Interaction Tactics and Strategies   311
          16.9.3 Interaction Outcome   312
          16.9.4 Interaction Consequences   312
    16.10 Outcome Determinants   313
    16.11 Comparison with Extant Literature   318
          16.11.1 Beattie *et al.* (2001)   318
          16.11.2 Other Literature   321

17 Conclusions   **325**
   17.1   Overview   325
   17.2   The Regulatory Setting   325
   17.3   Evidential Base and Structure of Findings   325
   17.4   The Nature of Financial Reporting Interactions Between FDs,
       ACCs and AEPs   326
   17.5   The Interaction Process   326
   17.6   Interaction Outcomes   329
   17.7   The Regulatory Framework   331
   17.8   The ACC and the Audit Committee   333
   17.9   Policy Implications   333
   17.10 Limitations and Implications for Future Research and
       Regulatory Interest   335

References   **337**

Index   **349**

List of Figures

2.1	The grounded theory model of Beattie, Fearnley and Brandt (2001)	35
5.1	Sandpiper – General context for interactions	94
6.1	Kestrel – General context for interactions	123
7.1	Mallard – General context for interactions	142
8.1	Finch – General context for interactions	165
9.1	Cormorant – General context for interactions	189
10.1	Pochard – General context for interactions	209
11.1	Woodpecker – General context for interactions	225
12.1	Raven – General context for interactions	237
13.1	Ostrich – General context for interactions	243
16.1	Principal analytical categories in the revised grounded theory of financial reporting interactions	283
16.2	Key interaction parties, characteristics and impact of regulatory change	306
16.3	Visual representation of financial reporting interaction outcomes in two dimensions	313
16.4	Relationships between influence categories and outcome characteristics	317
16.5	The shrinking interaction outcome domain between 1997 and 2007	320

List of Tables

2.1   The categories, concepts and dimensions in the grounded theory
model of Beattie, Fearnley and Brandt (2001)   36

3.1   Audit committee members with recent and relevant financial
experience   45

3.2   Top ten discussion issues   46

3.3   Top ten negotiation issues   47

3.4   Top ten issues resulting in change to the accounting numbers   49

3.5   Top ten issues resulting in change to the disclosures   50

4.1   Overview of cases: general context and interactions   62

16.1   Analysis of financial reporting interactions by issue type, interaction
type and decision type ($n = 45$)   280

16.2   Analysis of decision type by interaction type   282

16.3   Cross-case analysis of interactions   284

Foreword

This book examines the findings from academic research carried out by the authors into the functioning of the governance of financial reporting and auditing following reforms introduced in the UK in the wake of the Enron and other scandals which rocked the world at the start of the 21st Century. I have a very personal interest in these findings since I became President of the Institute of Chartered Accountants in England and Wales (ICAEW) on 12th June 2002 having spent the previous 6 months co-ordinating the UK Profession's response to these scandals. Law makers and regulators from countries as far away as Australia and as close to home as London and Brussels were considering what steps to take. Much of the debate was emotional and political, and while this was understandable given the scale of the failure at Enron, good policy outcomes are achieved from careful analysis of evidence, not from decisions made in the heat of the moment based on hearsay and prejudice. In an attempt to get an informed debate in the UK my first Council meeting as President approved a number of changes to our existing regulations and proposed a number of areas for further consideration by the relevant authorities. These measures, all of which had been developed from detailed discussions with people with great experience of corporate governance, corporate reporting and auditing, including the authors of this book, and following a careful study of all the available academic literature, formed the basis of the profession's 2002 reform agenda. The measures were also later adopted almost in their entirety by the UK Government in the review conducted by the Co-ordinating Group on Accounting and Auditing (CGAA), on which I sat as an observer.

On 26 June 2002, just two weeks after I had become President, I woke to the news that Worldcom, a major US corporation, had announced that it had overstated its profits by $4bn as a result of fraudulent accounting irregularities. This scandal transformed the political environment for financial reporting and auditing at a stroke. What may well have been fairly modest reforms in America were transmogrified within the space of a couple of weeks into the Sarbanes-Oxley Act (Sarbox) with dramatic changes for companies and auditors there. The Act also made one change which would have worldwide repercussions – the creation of an independent (of the profession) audit regulator. It became immediately clear to me that the self-regulatory model we had in the UK (and, indeed, in most of the rest of the world) would no longer be acceptable even though it had not failed. I began to talk privately to the Government about the changes we might make while at the same time beginning a dialogue with a far from persuaded profession. Although it took a further six months to play out, the result was the creation of the "new" Financial Reporting Council (FRC) as the independent regulator and the setting up of the Audit Inspection Unit (AIU) under it. The Financial Reporting Review Panel (FRRP), which also sat under the FRC, was strengthened and developed from a body which simply reacted to complaints to one which pro-actively investigated.

Today, policy makers and regulators are again looking at corporate governance, corporate reporting and auditing, this time in light of the global financial crisis that began in 2008. The consensus is that auditors did not cause the crisis, nor could have prevented it. Yet, in both the UK and in Europe there is a sense that "something must be done". Leaving aside the inconvenient fact that there is no reason why anything should be done (and there are certainly other far more pressing and significant areas policy makers should be devoting their energies), any changes should only be introduced if there is clear evidence they will not have unintended consequences. To borrow from the Hippocratic Oath, "first do no harm". The research in this book should be compulsory reading for all law makers and regulators considering reform since it provides both insight into how the financial reporting chain actually works (as opposed to how people want to imagine it works) and a compelling commentary on the impact of the reforms we introduced following Enron.

The first wave of changes were announced by me immediately after the ICAEW Council meeting at a lunch attended by a wide range of politicians, civil servants, regulators, academics and leading members of the accounting profession. My speech included the following "This morning Council took a number of decisions to strengthen auditor independence. Audit partners will now be subject to a two year cooling off period before they are allowed to join their audit client as an employee or director". Secondly, the audit partner rotation rules will be tightened and, thirdly, the framework on threats and safeguards concerning the provision of non-audit services will also be tightened. I know full well that these proposals are not universally welcomed either by the audit firms or by business. However, I believe the advantage outweighs the undoubted inconvenience and disruption that these changes will cause. Elsewhere in my speech I had said "We must resist any move to restrict unduly the scope of services able to be offered by auditors to their audit clients." In other words, I was looking for a proportionate response to the issue of auditor independence, bearing in mind that there was no evidence to show that auditors providing non-audit services to their audit clients compromised audit quality, but recognising there was a perception issue which needed to be addressed. In the intervening time the restrictions on the provision of non-audit services has gone much further than I wanted, and the research shows the current approach is counter-productive. It narrows the experience of auditors and reduces the extent to which auditors can help their clients, something which smaller companies in particular need from time to time, while there is no evidence to show that audit quality is in any way improved as a result of these restrictions. The book demonstrates beyond doubt that there is no appetite from anyone involved in the financial reporting process for any further restrictions.

The "tightening" of the audit partner rotation rules referred to above reduced the rotation period from seven years to five. This followed the Sarbox rule. I expected the European Union and, in due course, much of the rest of the world to move to a five year rotation period. This did not happen, and there is now a widely, although not universally, held view, supported by a number of those interviewed in the research, that the shorter rotation period was a mistake. At the very least, it is clear from this research that five years is the absolute shortest rotation period that can be accepted without risk to audit quality and that in complex audits a period of handover in addition to the five years will add to the effectiveness of the audit.

I went on to say that "at the top of our international agenda is the desire to see the adoption of International Accounting Standards, which are at least as good as the standards we currently have in the UK. I firmly believe that the adoption of International Accounting Standards will greatly improve the quality, and indeed usefulness of, financial reporting available to investors in a global economy. In addition to International Accounting Standards, we need global auditing standards and a framework of principles of corporate governance to be developed and adopted worldwide."

Almost without exception, interviewees were critical of aspects of International Accounting Standards (IFRS) and, to a lesser extent, International Auditing Standards (ISAs). Both were criticised for their complexity. IFRS was frequently seen as producing inappropriate and potentially misleading reported financial results while ISAs were seen as too bureaucratic leading to a rules-driven approach. This is not to say we were wrong to push for international standards, since the principle of a single set of global standards is broadly supported. It may be that IFRS was adopted too early, although I suspect that without a rigid timetable the debate would have continued for longer without necessarily producing a better outcome. Certainly, though, the research is compelling in demonstrating that significant further work is necessary before IFRS can be said to be totally fit for purpose.

The learning outcome from the research for ISAs is different. Regulatory pressure has driven much of the rules driven approach in ISAs. Regulators find a rules driven approach much easier to understand and much easier to monitor and report against. While the evidence does not make a compelling case for a root and branch reform of the standards it does suggest to me that the greater involvement of regulators in the standard setting process, at the expense of expert involvement of practitioners, has been counter-productive.

Looking to other measures that would be needed to restore public confidence I said "I suggest we now need an enhanced role for audit committees, including a clearly defined role in setting policies for the awarding of non-audit work to the auditors, and not only recommending the appointment of the auditors each year, but also agreeing their remuneration. As a result, auditors will come to regard the Audit Committee as being just as much the client as the executive management."

A large part of the research in this book centres on nine in depth case studies which shine light on how the relationships between the Executive Directors, the Non-Executive Directors and the Auditors work in practice. The case studies demonstrate that the outcomes I was seeking from enhancing the role of audit committees have been achieved, and it is clear that of all the reforms that have been introduced over the past decade this is the change that has been the most significant force for good. Audit regulators who have been concerned that there are insufficient showdowns at audit committees between auditors and finance directors will see that these conflicts are avoided by a tri-partite working relationship designed to identify and resolve issues as early as possible, a system which undoubtedly produces better outcomes than would be achieved if the audit was set up to be adversarial. None of this is to suggest that the auditor is in any way less objective or less rigorous; indeed, the case studies show the auditor stands his ground when necessary. They also show that right minded finance directors and audit committee chairmen are equally keen to have compliant accounts.

The research which is reported in this book reveals some fascinating, although for those involved with the financial reporting process unsurprising, insights on the impact of the "new" regulatory regime in the UK. There is considerable support for the FRRP, which is seen as an independent expert body whose views are taken with great seriousness by all concerned. The same cannot be said for the AIU which is seen as concentrating on those things that can be inspected easily rather than on more substantive but more judgmental matters. However, the seriousness with which an adverse AIU finding is regarded demonstrates the value of independent inspection. Indeed, in my view, of all the changes made in recent years independent audit inspection has been the greatest regulatory benefit.

The research provides much of the evidence which should inform future policy. It demonstrates that much of what some strident voices are calling for are not necessary and would, in fact, be harmful to audit quality. The case studies demonstrate how good audit committees function in practice, and show that calls for having more regulatory rules for audit committees simply miss the point – it is not about ticking more boxes but allowing responsible people to behave responsibly. Finally, the research demonstrates the continuing dissatisfaction with aspects of IFRS while recognising the benefits of a set of global standards that can be used around the world. No-one should propose any reform to financial reporting or auditing until they have read and understood this excellent work.

Peter Wyman CBE FCA

Preface

Recent changes in the UK regulatory framework have resulted in financial reporting and auditing becoming increasingly complex and highly regulated activities. A key regulatory change is that a company audit committee is now expected to play a significant role in agreeing the contents of the financial statements and overseeing the activities of the auditors. This book presents the results of a research study exploring the high level process of interactions between the Chief Financial Officer (CFO), Audit Committee Chair (ACC) and Audit Engagement Partner (AEP). This vital process is unobservable to third parties but significantly leads to the agreement of the numbers and disclosures which are published in the financial statements and to the issuing of the auditor's report which accompanies them. The book reports survey findings which identify the issues that CFOs, ACCs and AEPs discussed and negotiated. This is followed by rigorous analysis of case-study interviews with the CFO, ACC and AEP in nine listed companies, where the interactions and the influences on their outcomes are explored in depth, providing new insights into the process and the effectiveness of the changed regime. This evidence is highly relevant to current debates in the UK, EU and internationally concerning the value of audit, IFRS and the relative merit of rules-based versus principles-based accounting standards in relation to professional judgement and compliance.

Acknowledgements

We thank the Institute of Chartered Accountants in England and Wales' Charitable Trusts for their financial support of this project, without which this book would not have been possible. We thank the auditors and company directors who assisted us in the development of the questionnaire and the audit firms who gave their support. In addition, thanks are due to the 498 individuals who completed the questionnaire, the results of which are summarized in Chapter 3. We are especially grateful to the 26 individuals who agreed to be interviewed for the case studies and whose experiences lie at the heart of this book. Finally we thank Peter Wyman CBE for his perceptive Foreword and Robert Hodgkinson, Chris Humphrey, Martyn Jones and Shyam Sunder for their endorsements of our work.

Abbreviations

AADB	Accountancy and Actuarial Discipline Board
ACC	Audit Committee Chair
AEP	Audit Engagement Partner
AIU	Audit Inspection Unit
APB	Auditing Practices Board
ASB	Accounting Standards Board
CCAB	Combined Committee of Accounting Bodies
CEO	Chief Executive Officer
CFO	Chief Financial Officer
CGAA	Co-ordinating Group on Audit and Accounting Issues
DTI	Department of Trade and Industry
EBR	Enhanced Business Review
EC	European Commission
EFRAG	European Financial Reporting Advisory Group
EPS	Earnings per Share
ES	Ethical Standard
EU	European Union
FASB	Financial Accounting Standards Board
FRC	Financial Reporting Council
FRRP	Financial Reporting Review Panel
FSA	Financial Services Authority
IAASB	International Auditing and Assurance Standards Board
IAS	International Accounting Standard
ICAEW	Institute of Chartered Accountants in England and Wales
ICAS	Institute of Chartered Accountants of Scotland
IFAC	International Federation of Accountants
IFIAR	International Forum of Independent Audit Regulators
IFRS	International Financial Reporting Standard
ISA	International Standard on Auditing
KPI	Key Performance Indicator

NAS   Non-audit Services
OFR   Operating and Financial Review
POB   Public Oversight Board
SEC   Securities and Exchange Commission
SOX   Sarbanes-Oxley Act

Part I
The Background

1

Introduction and Background

1.1 WHAT THIS BOOK IS ABOUT

This book offers important and unique insights into how the largely unobservable financial reporting and auditing process in UK listed companies actually works in the current UK regulatory environment, which has undergone significant change in the last eight years. It explores how finance directors (i.e. Chief Financial Officers (CFOs)), Audit Committee Chairs (ACCs) and Audit Engagement Partners (AEPs) interact with each other to reach agreement on key financial reporting issues as the financial statements are finalized. It also examines how the new regulatory regime is being implemented, by exploring corporate governance practices relating to financial reporting and auditing issues — part of the context within which these interactions take place. The governance practices mainly relate to the role of the audit committee and the audit committee chair.

By means of a wide ranging questionnaire survey and nine company case studies, we identify and analyse the interaction process involving these three principal parties in (a) discussing and negotiating financial reporting issues and (b) reaching the agreed financial reporting outcome of each interaction that took place. We also explore the key influences on the interaction outcomes. Key findings and conclusions are briefly summarized at the end of this chapter. The survey and company case studies were carried out in the UK in 2007/8. The changes to the UK's financial reporting, auditing and corporate governance regulatory frameworks were introduced in the UK in 2003/4 by the UK government (CGAA, 2003) after the collapse in 2002 of the US company Enron and the audit firm Andersen and the passing of the US Sarbanes-Oxley Act (SOX) (2002).

1.2 RECENT REGULATORY CHANGES

The UK-initiated post-Enron reforms include:

• The setting up of a new body, the Audit Inspection Unit (AIU), under the aegis of an expanded and reformed Financial Reporting Council (FRC),[1] to inspect public interest audits and issue public reports on their findings.

---

[1] The Financial Reporting Council was previously responsible only for the setting and enforcement of UK Accounting Standards. Following the CGAA reforms responsibility for setting auditing standards and auditing ethical standards was passed to the FRC, as was oversight of the accountancy professional bodies.

- Changes to the UK Corporate Governance Code (previously known as the Combined Code for Corporate Governance)[2] now require audit committees to engage with the audit and financial reporting process in a more formalized way (FRC, 2005)
- Change to the operations of the Financial Reporting Review Panel (FRRP),[3] the UK's financial reporting enforcement body, from reactively responding to complaints and concerns about companies' accounts to a pro-active role of systematically reviewing public interest company accounts and other outputs.
- Transferring the Auditing Practices Board (APB), the UK auditing standard setting body, to the FRC and giving it the additional responsibility for setting auditors' ethical standards. The APB then adopted International Standards on Auditing (ISAs) amended for use in the UK (APB, 2004a) for 2005 year ends. These are based on ISAs set by the International Auditing and Assurance Standards Board (IAASB) and include ISA 260 (APB, 2004b) which requires the auditor to engage with the client's audit committee on audit and accounting related matters. The APB also issued a suite of Ethical Standards (ES) (APB, 2004c) which restrict the supply of non-audit services (APB, 2004c, ES 5) and require audit engagement partners to rotate off listed company audit every five years (APB, 2004c, ES 3).

There was also a major change at European level. A European Union (EU) Regulation (2002) required EU listed companies to adopt International Financial Reporting Standards (IFRS), set by the International Accounting Standards Board (IASB), for their group accounts for December 2005 year-ends onwards. A major influence on the IASB standard-setting process has been the planned convergence of IASB standards with those of the US Financial Accounting Standards Board (FASB), (FASB and IASB, 2006). This convergence process commenced in 2002. The change to IFRS and the convergence plans have been subject to much criticism with concerns about convergence, the complexity of accounts prepared under IFRS (FRC, 2008a), the accounting model itself, particularly the fair value or mark-to-market principle, convergence with US GAAP and the rules-based nature of the standards (Fearnley and Sunder, 2007; Page and Whittington, 2007; Isaac, 2009, Beattie, Fearnley and Hines, 2009a).

1.3   CONTRIBUTION OF THIS BOOK IN THE 2010/2011 REGULATORY ENVIRONMENT

The insights from this book will be useful for policy makers in the development of the UK regulatory framework. The global financial crisis that hit in 2008[4] is the latest

---

[2] As the UK Corporate Governance Code was known as the Combined Code for Corporate Governance at the time this study was carried out, we have used term Combined Code throughout.

[3] The FRRP has powers to apply to the court to force a company to restate its accounts if the directors refuse to do so voluntarily.

[4] This crisis followed on from the subprime mortgage problems in the US that emerged from mid-2007.

economic event to raise intense interest globally in financial reporting and auditing quality and further changes to the framework are under consideration. In its report on the banking crisis which sparked this global financial crisis, the UK Treasury Committee (2009) expressed concerns about the role of audit (based on the bank audits with 2007 year-ends). They concluded that audit was in danger of being 'lost in a sea of detail and regulatory disclosures' and identified this as a possible unintended consequence of the changed regulatory regime. The Committee also questioned the value of audit. In June 2010 the UK Financial Services Authority (FSA) and Financial Reporting Council (FRC) issued a joint discussion paper suggesting that auditors should be more sceptical and challenge management more (FSA and FRC, 2010). This was followed by an APB (2010a) discussion paper on the same topic. The Future of Banking Commission (Which, 2010) has questioned the erosion of judgement in favour of a rules-based approach in the UK and calls for a restatement in law of the 'true and fair view' principle.

At the EU level, a green paper on the role of auditors has been published (EC, 2010). The objective of this green paper is to initiate a debate on the role and governance of auditors. The commissioner responsible, Michel Barnier, said 'While the role of the main economic and financial actors (banks, hedge funds, credit rating agencies etc.) were immediately called into question following the financial crisis, the role of the auditors has not really been questioned until now'. Interest in financial reporting quality has, however, been ongoing for many years. This book will provide insights into a vital process which is normally inaccessible to all but its participants.

This book is a successor to *Behind Closed Doors: What Company Audit is Really About* by Beattie, Fearnley and Brandt, which was published in 2001 by Palgrave (Beattie, Fearnley and Brandt, 2001). *Behind Closed Doors* explored, for the first time, how finance directors and audit partners of UK listed companies interacted with each other in agreeing the contents of the company's financial statements. The analysis was based on six matched interviews with company finance directors and their audit partners. The authors were called in 2002 to give evidence based on the book to the Treasury Select Committee on the Financial Regulation of Public Limited Companies. The researchers received the prestigious Deloitte/American Accounting Association Wildman Medal in 2007 for the book. The Wildman Medal is awarded for research which is judged to have made the most significant contribution to the advancement of the practice of accounting. The researchers were the first non-US research team to receive this award.

A key change for financial reporting and audit quality since *Behind Closed Doors* was published is the enhanced engagement of the company's audit committee, particularly the audit committee chair, with the auditing and financial reporting process. Our main reason for writing a new book in this area is that our research results reveal that the process for reaching agreement on financial reporting outcomes has changed significantly under the revised UK framework. In a book we can offer readers both an analysis of behaviour in the recent pre-financial crisis environment and compare it to the previous research, thus providing insights into the impact of the changed environment. Given the ongoing pressures for further changes emanating from the current economic climate, this will be highly topical and policy-relevant.

1.4   RESEARCH APPROACH

The book reports on two unique datasets, using a mixed methods research design (Creswell, 2009). First, we report on the results of the 2007 survey of finance directors, audit committee chairs and audit partners of UK listed companies. The survey asked which financial reporting issues the three parties had discussed and negotiated. It also asked about the functioning of the audit committee and sought views on the effectiveness of the UK regulatory framework relating to audit quality. An exceptionally high response rate for surveys to these groups of 36% was achieved, making the results authoritative. This large-scale survey allows the extent, nature and outcome of interactions to be assessed for the population as a whole. A summary of the findings from this stage is presented in Chapter 3.

The major part of the book consists of nine company case studies where the researchers conducted face to face interviews with CFOs, ACCs and AEPs of companies with different attributes including size, industry sector and ownership structure. The researchers' reputation enabled them to obtain unprecedented access, hold frank and open discussions with the interviewees and record all the interviews verbatim. The interviews explored the financial reporting and auditing interactions which had taken place and how each party perceived his or her role in the resolution of the issue. The analysis of individual case studies and the cross-case analysis will provide the only publicly available evidence of how financial reporting outcomes are achieved in the recent UK regulatory environment. The comparative analysis in *Behind Closed Doors* offers a unique opportunity to review the differences between two regulatory environments. This will enable the researchers to draw valuable conclusions about the overall impact of the recent changes (1996–2007) on the quality of financial reporting and auditing in the UK and the implications for public policy going forward.

Although the cases relate to a particular point in time, and hence a specific economic and regulatory environment, some of the issues that emerge, such as inventory valuation, are shown to be generic and insensitive to the passage of time, while others, such as financial instruments and intangibles, are a product of the prevailing regulatory setting.

1.5   OUTLINE OF BOOK

This book has been organized in three parts, as follows.

Part I comprises Chapters 1–3. Chapter 1 provides an introduction and background to the accounting regulatory framework in the UK. Chapter 2 reviews the relevant academic literature relating to the auditor–client relationship. Specific areas covered are: regulation theory; IFRS; audit quality; enforcement; corporate governance and the role of the audit committee; interactions and negotiation in non-audit settings; and interactions and negotiation in audit settings, including the grounded theory model developed in *Behind Closed Doors*. Chapter 3 summarizes the results of the questionnaire which provided the introduction to the nine case companies. This first stage of the study shows the frequency of discussion of 35 accounting issues; the frequency of negotiation about these issues; and the frequency of resulting changes to the accounting numbers and disclosures.

Part II comprises Chapters 4–13. Chapter 4 begins by explaining how the case companies were selected and approached, and the interview techniques employed. The broad approach taken to the analysis is then set out, including a brief explanation of grounded theory and how we use it on the cases, together with details of how each case was written up. This is followed by a description of the preliminary within-case analysis, and a tabular summary of the general context and the interaction issues in each of the nine cases.

Chapters 5–13 present the findings from the interviews. These nine chapters tell the story of each case as described by the interviewees, including numerous direct quotations for seven of the cases. Each case is presented using the same structure, beginning with an overview of the background setting in which the interactions take place. This is followed by the interviewees' perceptions of the corporate governance structures and processes relating to financial reporting and auditing which are in place within the case company. The third main section introduces the key interaction issues to emerge before each is considered in depth. The process of interaction and resolution for each issue, seen from the perspective of each party, is documented. The fourth section presents the within-case analysis, beginning with the key contextual factors and moving on to identify and discuss the key influences, parties and strategies adopted, in each of the interaction issues. The concluding section offers a brief summary of what the case tells us about the audit, financial reporting and governance process in the case company.

Part III comprises four chapters. Chapter 14 offers a description and analysis of the comments made by the interviewees about the regulatory framework generally. Chapter 15 reviews the attributes and activities of the audit committee and ACC which emerge from the survey and the nine case studies. Chapter 16 begins by summarizing the financial reporting interaction attributes and the cross-case analysis, using a tabulated analysis of the 45 interactions as a key analytical tool. The revised grounded theory is then presented which shows that new concepts have emerged, the significance of established concepts has changed and relationships have altered. Finally, a comparison of the findings of this study with those of the extant literature is made, particularly the previous UK study of Beattie *et al.* (2001). Finally, Chapter 17 summarizes the findings and conclusions, and offers implications for policy and suggestions for future research.

1.6   KEY FINDINGS AND CONCLUSIONS

The key findings from this study are outlined here. Further discussion and additional findings are presented in Chapter 17.

- *Nature of financial reporting interactions between CFOs, ACCs and AEPs*. A total of 45 financial reporting interactions were identified across the nine case companies and it is likely that the high level can be partly attributed to the (then) recent implementation of IFRS. Some specific issues occurred in several cases, notably identification/valuation of intangible assets on acquisition (five cases), inventories (four cases) and Business Review (five cases). While 69% of the decision types were categorized as judgements and only 11% were pure compliance, the latter were more likely to result in an interaction between key parties escalating into a negotiation. In some cases this negotiation arose because of disagreement with the principles involved. The overall frequency of negotiation is lower than in the Beattie *et al.* (2001) study.
- *Engagement of ACC and audit committee.* The study provides evidence that ACCs are fully engaged with the financial reporting process. They act as filters to, and managers of, the audit committee. Members of audit committees who do not have an accounting qualification and IFRS experience find the complexity of IFRS challenging — this has become the *de facto* benchmark for 'recent and relevant financial experience'. Consequently, the ACC (generally the most financially literate audit committee member) personally takes on much of the monitoring role formally assigned to the audit committee, while the audit committee most often fulfils a ceremonial role (i.e. reviewing decisions and judgements already sanctioned by the ACC).
- *Goals and objectives of key parties.* There is now a shared general objective to comply with the rules and the processes underpinning judgements in standards in order to keep out of trouble with the regulatory enforcement bodies. The CFO and AEP are keen to take an agreed position to the ACC so that there is no loss of face and damage to personal reputation. The ACC wants no surprises at the audit committee. All three parties seek to take an agreed position to the audit committee, again so there is no loss of face in a forum where senior executive directors and senior managers are also present. Neither the ACC nor the audit committee is keen to act as arbiter.
- *Interaction process*. The corporate governance changes relating to the role of the audit committee and the ACC served to shift the predominant dynamic in financial reporting interactions of a dyad relationship between the CFO and the AEP to a triad relationship where both the CFO and AEP are accountable to the ACC, who manages the AC. Consequently, interactions now tend to be characterized by problem-solving behaviour and rarely by disagreement and confrontation. The complexity of judgements introduced by IFRS into a number of accounting areas (e.g. intangible valuations), combined with the more detailed auditing standards and the strong enforcement regime, meant that more attention was given to the process

underpinning a judgement. Thus, auditors sought to ensure that judgements made would comply with the process and evidence for a decision was documented. At times this could take precedence over the quality of the decision itself.

- *Power.* Corporate governance changes, combined with the strength of the enforcement bodies, have changed the power relations between the key parties. The ACC (and audit committee) have gained power on accounting and auditing matters at the expense of the CFO and AEP. IFRS complexity has delivered more power into the hands of the technical departments of the audit firms.

- *Influences on financial reporting outcomes.* The strongest influence on the interactions is the national enforcement regime (i.e. FRRP and AIU) which has been strengthened post-Enron and greatly increases the risk of cases of non-compliance being discovered with adverse consequences for those involved. It has changed behaviour and reduced the extent to which key parties are prepared to negotiate.

- *Change in influences since Beattie et al. (2001).* Characteristics that had been an important influence on the interactions in the previous study were now of peripheral or no importance. Features such as the quality of primary relationships, company circumstances, reporting style, audit partner type and company buyer type all fell into this category. The increased relationship complexity has tended to reduce the impact of such factors as personality differences. The compliance culture has removed other influences such as audit partner type. Also, certain negotiation strategies (e.g. ingratiation and reciprocity-based strategies) were no longer observed as they could have been exposed by the enforcement regime.

- *Quality of financial reporting outcomes.* This is one dimension of the interaction outcomes. The outcome of all the compliance issues was classified as compliant. While it was not possible to evaluate the quality of a judgement issue, it was classified as either acceptable or unacceptable in terms of compliance with the process of reaching the judgement. All the judgement outcomes were classified as acceptable. While the good news is that there are no unacceptable outcomes as a consequence of the strong compliance culture, the undermining of the true and fair view and the loss of the principles of substance over form and prudence mean that some of the highest quality outcomes are no longer achievable. The only significant influence on the quality of financial reporting was the regulatory framework.

- *Ease of outcomes.* The ease of agreement, the other dimension of the interaction outcomes, was also strongly affected by the regulatory framework. The existence of accounting standards which are more rules-based often made agreement easier. The enhanced role of the audit committee made it more difficult for other executive directors to get heavily involved in decisions. However, other factors could also be significant. Agreement was more difficult where the regulatory framework was unclear, where primary relationships were less good, where individuals had a face-saving agenda, or where the CFO was prepared to challenge the rationale of the relevant accounting standard.

- *Quality of IFRS*. Interviewees did not believe that the introduction of IFRS had improved the quality of UK financial reporting, due to excessive complexity, high disclosure volume and increased emphasis on rules rather than principles. Some standards were considered to produce dysfunctional results and to require costly information collection that was subsequently ignored by users (e.g. intangibles in business combinations).

- *Quality of ISAs.* Although ISAs were a less prominent feature of the cases, views were expressed that they, like IFRS, were overly detailed and prescriptive.
- *Quality of auditors' ethical standards.* Some aspects of audit ethical standards were considered to be problematic. The five year rotation period for AEPs was a concern, particularly for more complex clients and where CFOs and ACCs had also changed. The restrictions on non-audit service provision presented some challenges, particularly for small cap companies with fewer accounting resources who were no longer able to obtain accounting and business advice from their auditor.
- *Effectiveness of enforcement.* The FRRP was considered to be an effective financial reporting enforcement body and all key parties have strong incentives to comply with standards. The procedures of the AIU (the enforcement body for auditing standards) were considered to be process-driven and based on box-ticking; however, it was still considered a formidable regulator in enforcing ISAs and AEPs were most anxious to avoid adverse reports. Although the AIU has reduced drastically the scope for poor quality audit, the nature of the procedures may, in conjunction with other aspects of the regulatory framework, have helped to reduce the scope for very high quality audit as well. Thus, the boundaries within which audit quality and compliance can be measured are narrower.
- *Relationship between standards and enforcement and between audit quality and financial reporting quality.* Under an effective enforcement regime, it is the quality of the standards and regulations being enforced that will determine the quality of the final outcomes. The quality of the mainly international accounting and auditing standards being enforced by the national regulators has been subject to criticism. High quality financial reporting requires *both* high quality accounting standards and high quality audit. High quality audit is, therefore, a necessary but not sufficient condition for high quality financial reporting as audit is only one piece of the financial reporting jigsaw. The auditing and financial reporting outcomes that arise from the unique UK regulatory nexus formed by IFRS and ISAs (sets of standards with perceived deficiencies), a robust financial reporting enforcement regime, and a robust auditing standards enforcement regime will themselves be deficient in some respects. It may be appropriate to move towards a more *de facto*, principles-based set of standards — one that would perhaps reinstate the substance over form principle and the true and fair view override. This would avoid some of the undesirable (and unintended) consequences of the detailed, complex, rules-based, process-driven nature of IFRS and ISAs (and consequently enforcement procedures).

2

Review of Relevant Literature

2.1 OVERVIEW

The overall quality of financial reporting represents the outcome from a highly complex, interdependent set of structures and processes operating at the supranational, national, company and individual levels. The quality of the applicable accounting and auditing standards, together with the quality of enforcement, provides the broad regulatory setting for all companies. National regulatory bodies are increasingly interconnected with supranational private sector regulatory bodies at the global level (i.e. the IASB, IFAC and the International Forum of Independent Audit Regulators (IFIAR)) and governmental regulatory bodies at the European level (i.e. the EU and EFRAG) (Cooper and Robson, 2006, p. 430). The context of individual companies, in particular the quality of their corporate governance, provides the organizational setting for interactions. The audit firm and the quality of audit provided also influences financial reporting quality. Finally, the personal characteristics of the key individuals involved will affect financial reporting outcomes.

In this chapter, we look at relevant literature on each of these aspects in turn. Section 2.2 examines regulation, covering regulation theory, regulation policy and structures, ISAs and ethical standards for auditors. Section 2.3 considers, in broad terms, the accounting standards applicable to the case companies — IFRS — and the various debates associated with the introduction of the standards framework. These debates are the principles versus rules debate, the complexity debate and the debate on new business reporting models. Section 2.4 examines the issue of audit quality. Regulatory enforcement, which has changed significantly in recent years, is covered in section 2.5. Corporate governance and the role of the audit committee are examined in section 2.6. Finally, interactions and negotiation in non-audit settings are covered in section 2.7 while those in audit settings, including the grounded theory model developed in *Behind Closed Doors*, are considered in section 2.8.

2.2 REGULATION

2.2.1 Regulation Theory

Regulation research uses a range of theoretical lenses. The most commonly applied lens is economic, in particular regulatory economics and public policy economics. Market failure arguments are used to justify the need for regulation on social welfare grounds. Frequently, regulatory impact analysis is undertaken to demonstrate the net beneficial effect of introducing regulation. Such analysis, however, often fails

UNIVERSITY OF WINCHESTER
LIBRARY

to adequately capture the unintended consequences (often undesirable) of regulatory intervention (Beattie, Fearnley and Hines, 2010).

The fundamental mode of regulation selected — either self-regulation or government regulation — offers a trade-off between expertise and independence. Regulatory economics argues that potential efficiency gains from self-regulation arise, due to the producers' superior knowledge of the issues, their greater ability to adapt to changing institutional conditions and the lower transaction costs of the regulatory process. The trade-off is the risk of self-interested participation in the process (Grajzl and Murrell, 2007). The government model is not, however, completely free from the risk of loss of independence, as regulatory capture is a danger (Dal Bo, 2006). In addition to the nature of the regulatory body, options exist regarding monitoring and enforcement systems. For example, self-reporting is an alternative to traditional direct monitoring of violations and inspection regimes.

Financial regulation covers the setting of mandatory rules and the establishment of best practice guidelines in relation to the financial information reported and the behaviour of parties involved in the reporting process. Another lens used in regulation research draws on the discipline of psychology. Hirshleifer (2008, p. 2) argues that 'certain beliefs about regulation are especially good at exploiting psychological biases to attract attention and support'. This irrationality, especially of the proponents of regulation, pervades the political discourse of regulation and strengthens the case for *laissez-faire*. A range of social and psychological processes are identified which can result in detrimental regulation. The Enron scandal and the subsequent enactment of Sarbanes-Oxley are used to illustrate salience and vividness effects (i.e. events that draw attention), the violation of fairness and reciprocity norms, scapegoating and the availability heuristic amplified by media attention.

Consistent with Hirshleifer's scapegoating thesis, Guénin-Paracini and Gendron (2010) use the ideas of Girard, a French anthropologist, to argue that auditors are often the sacrificial victims in the aftermath of corporate scandals. Importantly, however, the way in which they are condemned strengthens the legitimacy of the audit function.

As would be expected, financial regulation involves the professional accountancy associations, standard-setting bodies and regulatory agencies. The professional firms, in particular the global Big Four, are an increasingly important 'node in the network of institutions through which regulatory and professional processes operate' (e.g. Cooper and Robson, 2006, p. 417). These writers argue, further supporting Hirshleifer's (2008) scapegoat bias argument, that regulation has been used to restore trust. The impact of the financial crisis on the international financial architecture has been characterized by Humphrey, Loft and Woods (2009) as strengthening Wade's (2007) 'standards-surveillance-compliance' system based on transparency and calculable standards and outcomes.

2.2.2   Regulatory Policy and Structures

The 1980s heralded in a period of de-regulation in the US (consistent with governmental policy of competition and market forces). However, the Enron scandal in 2002 prompted a global shift to re-regulation (Kinney, 2005). In the US, the Sarbanes-Oxley Act (2002) introduced major changes to the US audit, financial reporting and corporate governance regimes designed to restore confidence. Due to the global nature of capital markets and following further scandals in Europe (e.g. Parmalat), Sarbanes-Oxley style reforms were adopted throughout Europe and elsewhere (Coffee, 2006; Oxley, 2007; Quick, Turley and Willekens, 2007; Lennox, 2009).

In the UK, specific regulatory changes followed the Enron crisis (CGAA, 2003). The review by the Co-ordinating Group on Audit and Accounting Issues (CGAA) resulted in the existing oversight body (the Accountancy Foundation) being replaced by a restructured Financial Reporting Council (FRC), with several new operating bodies. The FRC's remit when it was established in 1992 had been to set and enforce accounting standards (via the Accounting Standards Board (ASB) and the Financial Reporting Review Panel (FRRP)) and to maintain the Combined Code for Corporate Governance (renamed the UK Corporate Governance Code in 2010). Its responsibilities were extended to include control of the Auditing Practices Board (APB), the Accountancy and Actuarial Discipline Board (AADB) and general oversight via the Professional Oversight Board (POB). Inspection of public interest audits fell under the POB.

2.2.3   International Standards on Auditing (ISAs)

The APB adopted International Standards on Auditing (ISAs) with minor adaptations to take into account the specifics of the UK environment (APB, 2004a). These ISAs became mandatory for all UK audits from December 2005 year-ends onwards. In early 2009, the International Auditing and Assurance Standards Board (IAASB) completed its five year long 'clarity project', intended to ensure that all 36 ISAs were in a form which would enhance understanding and implementation.

One ISA of particular relevance to the study reported here is ISA (UK and Ireland) 260 (APB, 2004b) *Communication of Audit Matters with those Charged with Governance*, since it concerns the audit committee–external auditor relationship. The standard requires the auditor to communicate in a timely manner to the relevant parties in the company about audit matters, including: issues arising from the audit of the financial statements; auditor independence; the engagement terms; audit planning and scope; and audit findings. While these requirements mirror some of the provisions in the UK Combined Code for Corporate Governance, they make compliance mandatory for auditors.

2.2.4   Ethical Standards for Auditors

In addition to its existing duties of setting auditing standards, the APB took responsibility for setting ethical standards for auditors. The five ethical standards jointly cover a range of issues concerning auditor integrity, objectivity and independence. Key provisions of the ethical standards, reflecting the EC's fundamental principles for auditor independence (EC, 2002), were introduced in 2004. In particular, mandatory rotation of all partners on each listed company audit, with the audit engagement partner rotating every five years, was required under Ethical Standard 3. Extensive restrictions on the provision of non-audit services by the incumbent auditor were put in place by Ethical Standard 5 (APB, 2004c). In 2008, after the research for this study had been undertaken, the ethical standards were amended to ensure consistency with changes in the law which arose from the implementation of the European Union (EU) revised 8th Statutory Audit Directive (APB, 2007). Subsequently, it was proposed that limited existing flexibility to increase the term of the audit engagement partner from five to seven years be extended to a wider range of situations, with the approval of the audit committee to 'strike the right balance between auditor objectivity and relevant knowledge and experience' (APB, 2009b, para. 2.2). This revision was implemented in October 2009 (APB, 2009a). In 2008 IFAC approved changes to the independence requirements in its Code of Ethics for Professional Accountants.

2.3 IFRS

International Financial Reporting Standards (IFRS) were introduced into the EU (EU, 2002) for the group accounts of listed companies for accounting periods commencing on or after 1 January 2005. They are promulgated by the International Accounting Standards Board (IASB). UK GAAP remains an option for other companies including subsidiaries of listed companies. Planned convergence of IFRS with US GAAP was announced in 2002 (FASB and IASB, 2002) after the Enron scandal which created the widespread perception that US accounting had been deficient (Bhimani, 2008, p. 448). In 2007 the US Securities and Exchange Commission (SEC) announced that foreign registrants would no longer be required to file a reconciliation statement to US GAAP with the SEC if their accounts were prepared under IFRS (SEC, 2007). The prospect of one set of global standards from these events has encouraged the adoption of IFRS in many countries outside the EU. The SEC issued a roadmap in November 2008 (SEC, 2008) which set out plans for full scale adoption of IFRS in the US with a final decision being taken in 2011. There remains, however, some uncertainty regarding the adoption of IFRS in the US.

A significant change was that the overriding UK principle of 'true and fair view' was replaced by a 'present fairly' requirement in IFRS (Evans, 2003). There has been considerable debate regarding whether the two requirements are equivalent. The initial view was that they did not mean the same and, until the relevant provisions of the 2006 Companies Act came into force in 2008, there was no requirement for directors to ensure that the financial statements gave a true and fair view (Nobes, 2009, p. 416). Thereafter, official guidance deems both concepts to be effectively equivalent. After detailed consideration, however, Nobes concludes that the arguments to support this conclusion are weak.

Other key differences between UK GAAP and IFRS are that IFRSs do not clearly state the 'substance over form' principle of FRS 5 *Reporting the Substance of*

Transactions (ASB, 1994) and that IFRS seek to limit managers' accounting choices, relative to UK GAAP.

Whilst there is widespread support for the principle of common global accounting standards and the benefits to the UK of adopting IFRS (e.g. Broadley, 2007; United Nations Conference on Trade and Development (UNCTAD), 2008), specific standards have been criticized by both practitioners and academics. There was criticism of the IFRS fair value accounting model before the development of the current economic crisis (e.g. Plantin, Sapra and Shin, 2005; Ball, 2006; Penman, 2007). As the crisis deepened, more criticism emerged (e.g. Fearnley and Sunder, 2007; Bush, 2009; Isaac, 2009). In 2009, US policy makers began to show less enthusiasm for the US GAAP/IFRS convergence project (Millman, 2009) and European regulators are expressing reservations about the accounting model (e.g. McCreevy, 2009; Turner, 2009). Beattie, Fearnley and Hines (2009a) report many criticisms from UK preparers and auditors about the quality of the IFRS standards. Preparers and auditors criticize IFRS for: complexity and irrationality; the risks inherent in the accounting model; detachment from business activity; unreliability of fair value; US GAAP convergence; and the demotivating effect of working with IFRS. These respondents also believe that IFRS has undermined the integrity of UK reporting (Beattie, Fearnley and Hines, 2008a).

In empirical accounting research, the general concept of accounting quality is associated with increased value relevance, reduced earnings smoothing and timely loss recognition (Barth, Landsman and Lang, 2008). It has recently been shown that IFRS increased value relevance, that is, the ability of financial statement information (specifically, earnings and book value of equity) to capture information that affects share prices (Devalle, Onali and Magarini, 2010). In an interesting study of 707 true and fair view overrides invoked by UK companies during 1998–2002 (i.e. pre-IFRS), Livne and McNichols (2009) find that quantified overrides increase profit and equity significantly, suggesting that UK companies have taken advantage of the override to mask unfavorable financial performance or financial position. They suggest that this provides evidence against a principles-based approach to accounting standard-setting (see next section), since the true and fair view qualitative criterion is generally taken to be the cornerstone principle of such a system.

It is of interest that, since the introduction of IFRS in 2005, the incidence of invocation of the override has dramatically reduced. Only three cases of override have occurred — two involving pension accounting and one involving the recognition of unauthorized trading losses (Livne and McNichols, 2009, p. 422).

2.3.1   Rules versus Principles Debate

Approaches to regulation can be characterized as principles-based or rules-based. Principles-based regulation relies on high level rules or principles and requires the application of judgement, while rules-based regulation involves detailed prescription and less scope for judgement. US GAAP is widely considered to be rules-based whereas IFRS seeks to be more principles-based. Since the Enron scandal, many commentators have argued strongly in favour of a principles-based set of standards (e.g. ICAS, 2006; Black, Hopper and Band, 2007).

It is increasingly being recognized, however, that the choice between these two systems is not black and white. Conceptually, a hierarchy of rules exists and principles sit at the top of this hierarchy. There are trade-offs between the levels within the hierarchy, in terms of ease of application, congruence, certainty and scope for creative compliance (Black *et al.*, 2007). Schipper (2005), a leading US academic with experience working for the FASB, argues that the extensive implementation guidance in IFRS amounts to *de facto* rules. Similarly, Benston, Bromwich and Wagenhofer (2006) take the view that the more judgement an accounting principle requires, the more difficult it is to cast into a standard without extensive guidance. Bennett, Bradbury and Pragnell (2006) argue that the only useful distinction to exist between the systems relates to the *degree* of judgement required. They conclude that a relatively more principles-based system requires professional judgement at both the transaction level (substance over form) and at the financial statement level (true and fair view override).

Sunder (2010) puts forward a more general argument against the pursuit of uniform written reporting standards (whether rules-based or more principles-based), claiming that judgement and personal responsibility are the hallmarks of a learned profession. In his view, a balance must be struck between written standards and unwritten social norms.

2.3.2   Complexity Debate

Since the adoption of IFRS in various jurisdictions, evidence is emerging that the transition from national GAAPs to IFRS was costly and burdensome and some consider the new standards to be excessively complex, adding many pages to the financial statements (e.g. Pickering, Aisbitt, Gray and Morris, 2007; Dunne, Fifield, Finningham, Fox, Hannah, Helliar, Power and Veneziani, 2008; Jermakowicz and Gornik-Tomaszewski 2006; ICAEW, 2007; Buthe and Mattli, 2008).

In 2008 the UK FRC set up a working group to review the complexity and relevance of financial reporting (FRC, 2008a) and has recently issued a consultation paper on reducing complexity (FRC, 2009a). This consultation paper identifies, from a survey and 51 interviews with preparers, users and auditors, sources of complexity in the UK. These are: acquisition accounting; capitalization of research and development costs; accounting choices; research and development costs; discontinued operations; embedded derivatives; fair value; financial instruments; financial instruments risk and reporting disclosures; hedge accounting; the proliferation of interpretive guidance; segmental reporting; and share-based payments.

Further impetus to reduce complexity came from the House of Commons Treasury Select Committee report into the banking crisis (May 2009). The Committee noted that lengthy annual reports fail to tell a 'story'. Subsequently, ICAS (2010a) has developed an illustrative proforma Short Form Annual Report and Results and both FASB and The European Financial Reporting Advisory Group (EFRAG) have initiated Disclosure Framework projects aimed at developing more useful, organized and consistent disclosures.

2.3.3   New Business Reporting Models

For the last 15 years or so, there have been calls for a new business reporting model. The Jenkins Report, published by the American Institute of Certified Public Accountants (AICPA, 1994), has been particularly influential in this respect. The concern has been that the so-called 'traditional' model needs to evolve to cope with the changing business environment, especially the claimed rise in importance of intangible assets and the need for more forward looking information (for representative literature on this topic, see RSA, 1998; ICAS, 1999; Lev, 2001; ICAEW 1997; Tomorrow's Company, 2007; and, most recently, ICAEW, 2009). Proposals have tended to focus on the provision of additional narrative disclosure outside the financial statements, to include management's explanation of performance and financial position, forward-looking information relating to plans, risks and opportunities and non-financial performance indicators.

Traditionally, narrative reporting in the UK has been mainly voluntary. A limited legal requirement was established by section 235 of the Companies Act 1985 which called for 'a fair review of the development of the business of the company and its subsidiaries during the financial year and of their position at the end of it …'. Best practice guidance existed in the form of the Operating and Financial Review (OFR) Statement, originally introduced into the UK in 1993 (ASB, 1993).

A revised OFR Statement was introduced in 2003 to reflect improvements in narrative reporting (ASB, 2003). Contemporaneously, in a wide-ranging review of company law, the government issued a White Paper recommending that the OFR should be mandatory for listed and very large private companies (DTI, 2002; 2004). The stated function of the revised OFR was to 'set out the directors' analysis of the business, in order to provide to investors a historical and prospective analysis of the reporting entity "through the eyes of management"' (para. 2).

In May 2005, the ASB issued Reporting Standard 1: Operating and Financial Review, which was intended to become mandatory for all UK quoted companies (ASB, 2005). Compliance with the standard would constitute compliance with the requirements of the Companies Act 1985 (Operating and Financial Review and Directors' Report etc.) Regulations 2005 (HMSO, 2005). The standard was principles-based. However, a few months later, the UK government unexpectedly repealed the OFR legislation and withdrew the mandatory OFR requirement from the draft Company Law Reform Bill. Reporting Standard 1 was quickly converted to a best practice Reporting Statement (ASB, 2006), with changes being limited to those required to make the language consistent with a voluntary statement. The mandatory OFR was replaced with legislation (s. 234ZZB Companies Act 1985) requiring an enhanced business review (EBR) to be included in the directors' report to meet the minimum narrative reporting requirements of the 2003 EU Accounts Modernization Directive. This review must disclose information that is material to understanding the development, performance and position of the company, and the principal risks and uncertainties facing it, and in so doing must include financial and, where appropriate, non-financial key performance indicators (including those specifically relating to environmental and employee issues) (DTI, 2005). Compliance with the OFR Reporting Statement will more than meet the legal requirements for the EBR.

More recently, the Companies Act 2006 (section 417) contains new requirements to extend the EBR requirements for quoted companies. For periods commencing on or after 1 October 2007, the additional requirements were for: the main trends and factors likely to affect the future development, performance and position of the company's business; information about the environment, employees and social and community issues; and information on significant contractual or other arrangements which are critical to the business.

Most recently, the change of government in the UK in 2010 heralds the reinstatement of an OFR and a consultation is underway to consider the future of narrative reporting (BIS, 2010).

2.4   AUDIT QUALITY

This section begins by looking at what is meant by audit quality (sub-section 2.4.1), before setting out the broad scope and nature of empirical audit quality research (sub-section 2.4.2). Thereafter, several specific issues impacting audit quality are considered — non-audit service provision, auditor tenure and individual audit partner effects (sub-sections 2.2.3–2.2.5). (The monitoring and enforcement of audit quality is dealt with in section 2.5, which covers the enforcement of financial reporting quality in addition to audit quality. The role of the audit committee is covered in section 2.6.) A final sub-section looks at findings of survey studies concerning auditor independence and audit quality.

2.4.1   Definition of Audit Quality

DeAngelo's (1981) seminal economic analysis defines audit quality as the 'market-assessed joint probability that a given auditor will both (a) discover a breach in the client's accounting system and (b) report the breach'. Subsequently, however, researchers have recognized that these two characteristics of competence and independence do not represent the whole spectrum of audit quality attributes, with the effectiveness of the regulatory framework, service quality and responsiveness also being important aspects. Francis conceptualizes audit quality as 'a theoretical continuum ranging from very low to very high' (2004, p. 346).

The FRC (2006b), having identified the lack of a clear agreed definition of audit quality, cites the definition used by the Audit Inspection Unit (AIU) (p. 19):

> Undertaking a quality audit involves obtaining sufficient and appropriate audit evidence to support the conclusions on which the audit report is based and making objective and

appropriate audit judgements. A quality audit [also] involves appropriate and complete reporting by the auditors which enables the Audit Committee and the Board properly to discharge their responsibilities.

In considering how to promote audit quality, the FRC promotes its Audit Quality Framework (FRC, 2008c) which identifies five drivers of audit quality. These are: the culture within an audit firm; the skills and personal qualities of audit partners and staff; the effectiveness of the audit process; the reliability and usefulness of audit reporting; and factors outside the control of auditors affecting audit quality.

Recently, following on from the UK Treasury Committee (2009) report on banks and audit quality, the issue of auditor scepticism has come to the fore. A joint discussion paper suggesting that auditors should be more sceptical and challenge management more has been issued by UK regulators (FSA and FRC, 2010, p. 8). This was quickly followed by adverse comment in the annual report of the Audit Inspection Unit (2010) (see sub-section 2.5.2 below) and an APB (2010a) discussion paper on the same topic.

2.4.2 Audit Quality Research

As the audit process is unobservable, public confidence in the value of audit depends on both the appearance of audit quality and the fact of audit quality. DeAngelo (1981) refers to the former as the 'market-assessed' probability of breach detection and reporting. This has produced two main lines of research. First, quantitative archival empirical research into audit quality uses various observable outcomes to proxy for the unobservable fact of audit quality. Common proxies are audit opinions; auditor selection and change decisions; financial statement outcomes, especially earnings management; and analysts' forecasts. Second, surveys investigate the perceptions of interested parties regarding the factors affecting audit quality.

Francis (2004) reviews 25 years of empirical audit quality research, concluding that a lot has been learned. He claims that the most significant development in audit quality research is grounded in the assumption that audit quality differences exist and can be inferred by comparing different groups of auditors. The main basis of differentiation is between large and small auditors (recently the Big Four versus the non-Big Four). Large audit firms are argued to be less dependent on any single client and also to have incentives to protect their brand name. Research has shown that there is demand for quality-differentiated audits and that the top tier audit firms are higher quality (have lower thresholds for issuing modified audit reports and more effectively curtail aggressive earnings management). By contrast, Humphrey's (2008) review of auditing research argues that the dominant use of 'scientifically rigorous' archival and experimental research methods has meant that we know very little about audit practice. He calls for more qualitative and critical research, grounded in observations of actual practice.

A great deal of research focuses on specific factors believed to influence auditor independence, especially non-audit services provided by the incumbent auditor and auditor tenure (and the related issue of audit firm and audit partner rotation). Each of these is briefly considered in the following sub-sections.

2.4.3   Non-Audit Services (NAS)

Regulatory concern regarding the growing significance of non-audit service provision by the incumbent auditor was exacerbated by the Enron case, where Andersens were reported to have received $25m in audit fees and $27m in non-audit fees. The concern is that such provision threatens auditor independence. The five threats are: making management decisions (which is prohibited); self-review; advocacy; trust (i.e. familiarity); and intimidation. Joint service provision can, however, make economic sense, insofar as economies of scope are generated, in particular knowledge spillovers, which result in cost savings which may or may not be passed on to the client company.

Beattie and Fearnley (2002) undertake a review of the theoretical and empirical literature on the impact of non-audit service provision by the incumbent auditor on auditor independence. The empirical studies adopt a range of methods, such as questionnaires, interviews, case studies, experiments and regression analysis using publicly available datasets. It is concluded that 'there is little clear support for the view that joint provision impairs independence in fact' but there 'is a reasonable consensus' that 'joint provision adversely affects perceptions of auditor independence' (p. 62). Reviews by US academics reach the same conclusions (Francis, 2006; Schneider, Church and Ely, 2006).

In the UK, at the time of Enron, companies were required to disclose the amount of NAS fees paid to their auditor and the auditor independence framework gave guidance as to which NAS an audit firm could provide, with appropriate safeguards, without compromising independence. In the wake of Enron, tougher safeguards were put in place by independent setting of auditors' ethical standards and an enhanced role for the audit committee in overseeing auditor independence and NAS provision. Ethical Standard 5 addresses NAS provision, using a threats and safeguards approach, similar to that in the EC (2002) recommendations on auditor independence. The general tone is that insufficient safeguards are likely to be possible for the following services: preparing accounting records and financial statements (prohibited for public interest entities); design and installation of financial IT systems; valuation services; internal audit; acting for a client in a legal dispute; senior management recruitment; and corporate finance activities.

Beattie, Fearnley and Hines (2009b) explore the impact of post-Enron regulatory changes to the NAS regime in the UK. They report that, for the top UK listed companies, NAS fees as a percentage of audit fees decreased dramatically from a peak of 300% in 2001 to 75% in 2008, with companies changing service suppliers due to the regulatory changes. Based on data from a survey conducted in 2007, they conclude that there have been four main drivers of this change: the enhanced role of the audit committee in developing a NAS policy; concern regarding adverse publicity and shareholder challenge in the face of high NAS levels; the limitations on provision placed on auditors by ES 5; and the strong enforcement of ES 5 via the audit inspection regime (see section 2.5 below).

Most recently, the issue of NAS provision has been raised again in the context of the recent banking crisis. The report of the Treasury Select Committee into this crisis (UK

Treasury Committee, 2009) concluded that, although there was 'very little evidence that auditors failed to fulfil their duties' (para. 221), 'investor confidence, and trust in audit would be enhanced by a prohibition on audit firms conducting non-audit work for the same company' (para. 237). The FRC (via the APB) was charged with consulting on this proposal and the outcome of this consultation is awaited, although responses indicate that there is no appetite for an outright ban on all services (APB, 2010a). The main conclusion of a working group set up by ICAS (2010b) was that a complete ban is not desirable; rather, greater transparency and additional disclosure is sufficient.

2.4.4 Auditor Tenure

Long audit firm tenure can have both positive and negative effects. The positive effect arises from the depth of knowledge and understanding of the client company's business that is developed over time, enhancing audit quality. The negative effect arises from the potential for an overly 'cosy' relationship to form between the auditor and the client company management, threatening auditor independence. Mandatory audit firm rotation remedies the negative effect. Empirical studies of the link between audit quality proxies and tenure do not generally provide any evidence that actual audit quality is impaired by long tenure (see Myers, Myers and Omar, 2003; Jackson, Moldrich and Roebuck, 2008; and Jenkins and Velury, 2008 for support; contrary evidence is provided by Li (2010) in the case of less important clients); rather, there is evidence of impairment in the early years of incumbency (Johnson, Khurana and Reynolds, 2002; Fargher, Lee and Mande, 2008). Nevertheless, the perception of impairment may exist (Boone, Khurana and Raman, 2010).

Audit *partner* rotation is a less radical intervention. Many jurisdictions introduced a five year rotation period post-Enron (e.g. in the US, SEC, 2003). The limited evidence regarding the consequences is somewhat mixed. Studies set in Australia have shown that audit quality improves upon audit partner rotation (Fargher *et al.*, 2008), whereas recent German evidence shows no association between mandatory audit engagement partner rotation and audit quality, but does find that audit quality declines upon the rotation of the audit review partner (Watrin, Lindscheid and Pott, 2009). The situation in the UK was set out in sub-section 2.2.4 above — the APB recently extended the circumstances in which the rotation period for audit engagement partners could be increased from five to seven years. This extension is permitted *only if* the audit committee determine that it is necessary to safeguard audit quality, with disclosure to the shareholders (APB, 2009a, §16–17). The period for engagement quality control reviewers and key partners is seven years (§19).

2.4.5 Individual Audit Partner Effects

This line of research moves away from relying solely on rational, economic models to explain behaviour in the audit setting. In particular, psychology, especially social psychology, is used to investigate auditor behaviour. Kleinman and Palmon (2001) develop a multi-level model of auditor independence behaviour which comprises the individual level, the audit firm level and the environment. The individual audit partner factors impacting auditor independence are: personality factors; values; motivation; stage of career; and aspiration level.

Beattie *et al.* (2001, pp. 275–278) develop a taxonomy of audit partner types based on case studies of auditor–client relationships. These 'seller' types map onto an AEP quality scale. The highest quality partner is the 'crusader', who has extremely high professional and personal integrity and is fully prepared to escalate an issue. Next highest is the 'safe hands' partner who exhibits high professional integrity, identifies closely with the client and is prepared to escalate an issue. Next is the 'accommodator', who has moderate professional integrity and will knowingly bend the rules under pressure. The lowest quality partner observed in the case studies was characterized as the 'truster', who has moderate professional integrity and may, unknowingly, permit rules to be bent because he or she is not sufficiently sceptical. Two other, lower quality categories were considered to exist in theory — the 'incompetent' and the 'rogue'.

Building on these ideas, van Buuren (2009) argues that differences in individual audit partners impact audit quality. He presents a model of the audit partner effect which results in three audit partner archetypes — high quality, conservative and liberal (p. 53). In the model, these archetypes arise due to differences in audit risk preferences and hence materiality assessments. The consequent audit judgement differences influence the usefulness of financial statements in terms of their value relevance. The high quality audit partner specializes in high quality audits, with consequently high audit fees, that maximize the usefulness of financial statements. The conservative audit partner specialises in low budget auditing which can be achieved by minimizing risk in the financial statements to minimize audit risk. The liberal audit partner specializes in high risk audits and charges a relatively high audit fee to enable audit risk to be reduced to an acceptable level. Van Buuren empirically tests his model on a sample of European listed companies for the period 1997–2005 and finds that there is considerable heterogeneity of audit quality within large audit firms, suggesting that the firms' internal control and governance policies are of limited effectiveness in relation to audit quality. It is worth noting, however, that the empirical evidence is based on practices before IFRS became mandatory, and common auditing standards are not mandated across EU countries.

Other individual auditor characteristics to be examined in the academic literature include gender and mood. Gold, Hunton and Goman (2009) examine the impact of client representative gender and auditor gender on auditors' judgements by means of an experiment. It is found that both male and female auditors are more persuaded by a male rather than female client representative to change their position regarding a valuation adjustment. Moreover, this effect was stronger for female auditors. Cianci and Bierstaker (2009) experimentally explore the impact of auditors' mood on their ethical judgement. In line with the predictions of psychology research, they find a positive relationship between positive mood and more ethical decisions. Chung,

Cohen and Monroe (2008) find that positive mood is associated with less conservative and more dispersed stock valuation judgements by auditors. Nelson (2009) provides a model of professional scepticism in auditing. It is shown, based on prior literature, that sceptical judgement is influenced by the individual auditor characteristics of traits (including ethical predisposition) and knowledge. These combine and interact with incentives, experience and training and audit evidence.

Finally, Gendron, Suddaby and Lam (2006) survey Canadian professional accountants to explore how changing work conditions have altered individual accountants' commitment to the core professional value of auditor independence. They find that auditor independence, once viewed mainly as a moral-ethical position, is today increasingly seen as an object to be regulated and verified through inspection systems.

2.4.6 Survey Research

There have been relatively few surveys about attitudes and beliefs about audit quality and what the key dimensions are. An advantage of this direct research approach is that the relative importance of a range of factors can be assessed. Carcello, Hermanson and McGrath (1992) survey preparers, auditors and users in the US and find that important factors are: knowledge of the client; industry expertise; responsiveness; and compliance with auditing standards. Post-SOX, 82% of 253 US audit committee members surveyed believe that audit quality has improved (Center for Audit Quality, 2008). The reasons for improvement were identified as being: increased audit committee oversight; requirements regarding internal controls; better communication with audit committees; CEO/CFO sign-off on financial statements; increased emphasis on quality of auditors; more rigorous audits; and audit committee oversight of auditors. Interview evidence from US company directors indicates that new regulation on the management–external auditor–audit committee relationship has improved audit quality, although there are suggestions that this benefit has involved costly compliance (Cohen *et al.*, 2009). In Australia, interviews with key stakeholders reveal that the introduction of legally enforceable Australian Auditing Standards has not increased perceived audit quality (Hecimovic, Martinov-Bennie and Roebuck, 2009).

In the UK, Beattie, Fearnley and Brandt (1998, 1999) find that the factors that audit partners, finance directors and financial journalists most believed to enhance auditor independence in the pre-Enron environment were: existence of an audit committee; risk of referral to the FRRP; and risk to the audit firm of loss of Registered Auditor Status. Duff (2004) distinguishes between technical quality and service quality in a survey carried out in 2001–2002 before the post-Enron changes were implemented. It is found that technical quality is characterized by status, independence and knowledge, while service quality is characterized by responsiveness, non-audit services and understanding of the client. In a UK investor survey about independence threats, Dart (2009) finds economic dependence in general and non-audit service provision in particular to be the most serious threats.

Most recently, in a survey of UK listed company chief financial officers (CFOs), audit committee chairs (ACCs) and audit partners (APs) conducted in 2007, Beattie *et al.* (2010) obtain views on the impact of 36 economic and regulatory factors on audit quality. This set of factors is reduced to nine uncorrelated dimensions using factor analysis. In descending order of importance these were: economic risk; audit committee activities; risk of regulatory action; audit firm ethics; economic independence of auditor; audit partner rotation; risk of client loss; audit firm size; and, lastly, International Standards on Auditing (ISAs) and audit inspection.

2.5 ENFORCEMENT

Two primary enforcement bodies exist in the UK — one for financial reporting (the Financial Reporting Review Panel (FRRP)) and one for audit (the Audit Inspection Unit (AIU)).

2.5.1 The FRRP

The, FRRP was established in 1990 as part the Financial Reporting Council. The Panel seeks to ensure that the provision of financial information by public and large private companies complies with relevant accounting requirements. Since April 2006 the Panel also reviews directors' reports. In 2004, the Panel changed its model from reacting to complaints and publicly available information to pro-active monitoring of the financial statements of public interest entities. Since April 2006 the Panel also reviews directors' reports. The Panel now selects accounts for review (i) via discussion with the FSA to identify industry sectors under strain or likely to give rise to difficult accounting issues; (ii) based on outcomes from its own risk model; (iii) by identifying topical accounting issues; and (iv) as a response to complaints from the public, the press and the City.

The Panel puts concerns to the company directors, encouraging them to consult their auditors, to involve their audit committee and to take any other advice they feel they need. If satisfied by the company's explanations, the case is closed and the fact that an enquiry was made remains confidential. Where the directors agree to take remedial action the Panel issues a press notice.

Research into the activities of this innovative body is limited. Brandt, Fearnley, Hines and Beattie (1997) provide a useful description of activity and outcomes in the early years of the operation of the FRRP. The FRRP deals directly with directors but not auditors. Hines, McBride, Fearnley and Brandt (2001) engage in discussions with key members of the FRRP and conduct semi-structured interviews with company directors and audit firm partners who had direct experience of dealing with the FRRP. Drawing on institutional theory, they conclude that the FRRP has engaged in 'myth building' by pursuing cases that involved rather less serious issues than their public statements might suggest. Further analysis of this interview evidence reveals that the FRRP's activities, even prior to the enhancement of its role in 2004, incentivized auditors to focus more on accounting compliance (Fearnley, Hines, Brandt and McBride (2002)).

2.5.2 Audit Firm Review and Inspection

The AIU is part of the POB, the body responsible for the inspection of public interest audits and the publication of the results of the inspections. Firms which audit more than ten entities within the AIU's scope are subject to full scope AIU inspections and there are currently nine such firms (FRC, 2009b). The AIU reviews these major firms' policies and procedures in a range of areas, such as: performance evaluation, promotions and remuneration; client risk assessment and acceptance/continuance; audit quality monitoring; independence and ethics; and audit methodology. Reviews of individual audits place emphasis on the appropriateness of significant audit judgements exercised in reaching the audit opinion, as well as the sufficiency and appropriateness of the audit evidence obtained. The AIU does not carry out a detailed technical review of the financial statements, as this is the responsibility of the FRRP. If the AIU considers there is sufficient doubt as to whether an accounting treatment adopted and/or disclosures provided comply with the applicable accounting framework, it may draw the matter to the attention of the FRRP.

In its most recent Annual Review, the AIU reveals 11% of audits carried out by larger firms and 55% of those carried out by smaller firms require 'significant improvement' (AIU, 2010). The report also concludes that, where judgements are required, firms sometimes look for evidence that corroborates the client company's view, rather than challenging it. The specific issues where greater scepticism is called for are fair values and the impairment of goodwill and other intangibles and future cash flows relevant to the consideration of going concern. The AIU evidence relates directly to the auditor scepticism debate that emerged in the UK in 2010 (FSA/FRC, 2010; APB, 2010b).

In many countries outside the UK, systems of audit firm review and inspection have changed significantly in recent years and research on the effects of these changes is beginning to appear. From 1988 until 2002, audit firms operating in the US with SEC clients were subject to mandatory peer review every three years, with the results of this review being publicly disclosed. Hilary and Lennox (2005) find that audit firms gained clients following receipt of a clean opinion and lost clients following receipt of an adverse opinion, suggesting that the process credibly signalled audit quality, a conclusion confirmed by Casterella, Jensen and Knechel (2009).

Following SOX, this model was replaced by independent inspections carried out by the PCAOB. Lennox and Pittman (2010) find that audit firms' market shares are not sensitive to these reports, suggesting that the new regulatory regime is not viewed as an effective signal of audit quality. This may be because the inspectors are not seen to possess adequate technical knowledge and/or because the PCAOB reports are less informative that the peer review reports (as they do not disclose quality control problems). However, as DeFond (2010) rightly points out, this conclusion must be tempered by consideration of several related issues: (i) a lack of information value does not necessarily mean that the inspections are ineffective; (ii) the new regime may be effective in providing *ex ante* incentives for audit quality to improve, by applying stricter standards and/or imposing more severe penalties; (iii) the quality of financial reporting may have improved post-SOX. Gilbertson and Herron (2009) find that, during the first three years of PCAOB enforcements, disciplined firms tend to have fewer partners, consistent with previous research relating auditor size to measures of audit quality. In contrast to Lennox and Pittman's findings in the US, Van de Poel, Opijnen, Maijoor and Vanstraelen (2009) conclude that independent inspections are effective in detecting audit quality in the Dutch setting.

2.6 CORPORATE GOVERNANCE AND THE ROLE OF THE AUDIT COMMITTEE

Interest in audit committees has increased rapidly in recent years (e.g. Cohen, Gaynor, Krishnamoorthy and Wright, 2007; DeZoort, Hermanson and Houston, 2008; Beasley, Carcello, Hermanson and Neal, 2009), due to SOX-style reforms which have significantly strengthened their role. There is wide recognition that the nature of the auditor-company relationship and the role and effectiveness of the audit committee has changed as a consequence of these reforms (e.g. Sabia and Goodfellow, 2005; Audit Committee Chair Forum, 2006a; b; 2007; KPMG, 2006). This section begins by outlining the general evolution of audit committees (sub-section 2.6.1), before going on to detail specific UK developments (sub-section 2.6.2). Consideration of the empirical evidence regarding the role and impact of the audit committee is deferred until section 2.8.

2.6.1 General Evolution of Audit Committees

Sabia and Goodfellow (2005), writing from a Canadian perspective, offer a useful review of the evolution of audit committees. They observe that, in addition to the board of directors, corporate reporting involves three key players: management, the external auditor and the audit committee. Traditionally, audit committees have operated within a hierarchical, linear corporate governance model. In this model, the external auditor interacted with management, who interacted with the audit committee, who interacted with the main board. The more recent model of corporate governance has all four parties interacting with each other in a more dynamic and interdependent way. In this model, the importance of relationships between the parties and of continuous communication (in addition to structures and mere compliance) has become paramount (2005, pp. 6–11).

There are, however, subtle differences between the unitary board structures that prevail in the US and Canada and those of the UK. Both forms of unitary board comprise a combination of executive directors, with intimate knowledge of the business, and outside, non-executive directors, with a broader perspective. However, the US model typically has a majority of non-executive directors and is chaired by the chief executive, whereas the UK model often has more executive directors and is chaired by a non-executive Chairman (Wyman, 2002).

Sabia and Goodfellow (2005) observe that, traditionally, audit committees have been reluctant to participate in resolving conflicts between the auditor and management. They argue, however, that participation by the audit committee can serve to avoid the escalation of a disagreement to crisis proportions (p. 223).

In his analysis of recent scandals and the role of the professions (gatekeepers), Coffee (2006) highlights the crucial role played by the audit committee. He argues that it is necessary to restore a strong principal–agent relationship in the case of the auditor. However, he concludes that, as 'an ideal principal is not easily identified', 'the audit committee may be the best available' (p. 343).

2.6.2   The UK Corporate Governance System

In the UK, it was the financial scandals of the early 1990s that led to the emergence of a formal corporate governance framework, in the form of the Cadbury Report (1992). Subsequent reviews (Hampel Report, 1998; Smith Committee, 2003) resulted in the Combined Code for Corporate Governance and subsequent revisions to it (FRC, 1998; 2003; 2006a; 2008b; 2010). The FRC is responsible for maintaining the Code; renamed the UK Corporate Governance Code in 2010.

The UK system of business regulation is described as a 'market-based approach' which emphasizes the company–shareholder relationship (FRC, 2006c). This carries through to the corporate governance framework which operates on a 'comply or explain' basis. The FSA, the market regulator, requires listed companies to provide a 'comply or explain' statement in their annual report which explains how the Code has been applied by the company (FRC, 2006c, p. 7; ICAEW, 2006a, p. 18). The Code provisions are in five parts, dealing with: directors; remuneration; accountability and audit; relations with shareholders; and institutional shareholders (FRC, 2006a; 2008b). The key Code provisions relating to audit committees are provision C3.1 and C3.2.

Provision C3.1 states:

> The board should establish an audit committee of at least three or in the case of smaller companies two, members, who shall all be independent non-executive directors. The board should satisfy itself that at least one member of the audit committee has recent and relevant financial experience.

Provision C3.2 sets out the main role and responsibilities of the audit committee and this includes 'to monitor the integrity of the financial statements of the company . . . reviewing significant financial reporting judgements contained in them'.

The Smith Report (2003) reviewed the role of the audit committee and produced guidance to assist company boards in making suitable arrangements for their audit committees (FRC, 2005). This guidance sets out in more detail the role and responsibilities of the audit committee with regard to financial reporting (paragraphs 4.1–4.4) and the external audit process (paragraphs 4.16–4.38). In particular, it is recommended that:

> The audit committee should review, with the external auditors, the findings of their work. In the course of its review, the audit committee should:
>
> - Discuss with the external auditor major issues that arose during the course of the audit and have subsequently been resolved and those issues that have been left unresolved;
> - Review key accounting and audit judgements; and
> - Review levels of errors identified during the audit, obtaining explanations from management and, where necessary the external auditors, as to why certain errors might remain unadjusted (para. 4.35).

Updated guidance was issued in 2008 (FRC, 2008b). Most recently, in the wake of the Walker Report (2009) on the governance of banks and other financial institutions triggered by the 2008–2009 financial crisis, the FRC brought forward the regular Code review scheduled for 2010 so that corporate governance in other listed companies could be assessed at the same time. The revised Code, renamed the UK Corporate Governance Code, was issued in 2010. The five sections of the Code provisions have been slightly reorganized into: leadership; effectiveness; accountability; remuneration and relations with shareholders. Provision C3.1 is more specific:

> The board should establish an audit committee of at least three, or in the case of smaller companies two, independent non-executive directors. In smaller companies the company chairman may be a member of, but not chair, the committee in addition to the independent non-executive directors, provided he or she was considered independent on appointment as chairman. The board should satisfy itself that at least one member of the audit committee has recent and relevant financial experience.

Since the early 1990s, the significance and remit of the audit committee as a corporate governance mechanism has clearly increased significantly. Their role in the US was significantly strengthened under Sarbanes-Oxley reforms and this has had a major international influence, changing the nature of the auditor–company relationship and the role and effectiveness of the audit committee. The audit committee now has a primary role in communications between the company and the auditor. Significant emphasis is now placed on such communication in the relevant auditing standard (ISA (UK&I) 260) (see sub-section 2.2.3 above).

2.7 INTERACTIONS AND NEGOTIATION IN NON-AUDIT SETTINGS

2.7.1 Theory

Negotiation is a generic process which has been investigated in many specific settings, resulting in the development of a new interdisciplinary field of study. The negotiation process has been defined as 'interaction between disputing parties whereby, without compulsion by a third party adjudicator, they endeavour to come to an interdependent, *joint decision* concerning the terms of agreement on the issues between them' (Gulliver, 1979, p. 79, emphasis in original).

The negotiator's problem is that of 'being interdependent while having interests which are in contrast to those of the other party' (Mastenbroek, 1989, p. 56). In addition, negotiating presumes a certain symmetry in the balance of power, that is, the ability of one actor to overcome resistance in achieving a desired result (Mastenbroek, 1989, p. 63; Brass and Burkhardt, 1993).

A useful general purpose model of the negotiation process, developed from actual cases which span a wide range of social, cultural and economic contexts, is provided by Gulliver (1979). This model captures economic, social and psychological aspects of the negotiation process. It is a non-game model that identifies two distinct, interconnected processes — a cyclical process and a developmental process.

The cyclical process involves the ongoing exchange of information between the parties and may incorporate information from third parties. The information exchanged may relate to procedural rules, appeals to norms, factual information, threats and promises. Upon receiving information a party will first evaluate it, then adjust their own preference set and their expectations of the other party, revise their overall strategy and finally make a tactical decision about what information to pass to the other party. Tactics include: obtaining further information; changing the subject matter of the information exchange when a current issue seems threatening; focusing on the affective tone of the relationship; matching the behaviour of the other party; offering opposing behaviour to that of the other party; and making concessions (Gulliver, 1979, pp. 109–111).

Successive iterations of this cyclical process form the developmental process, which drives the negotiation through several overlapping phases. The factors causing convergence and the nature of the outcome can often be explained in terms of appeals to norms and other sources of power.

2.7.2 Empirical Studies

Many empirical studies of negotiation focus on outcomes and contextual factors, leaving the actual negotiation process as a black box. Kipnis and Schmidt (1983) review early studies that look inside this black box and investigate the exercise of tactical actions. Kipnis, Schmidt and Wilkinson (1980) empirically investigate managerial use of 58 tactics using a questionnaire. The factor analysed responses reveal seven dimensions of influence: reason — the use of facts and data to support the development of a logical argument; coalition — the mobilization of other people in the organization; ingratiation — the use of impression management, flattery and the creation of goodwill; bargaining — the use of negotiation through the exchange of benefits or favours; assertiveness — the use of a direct and forceful approach; higher authority — gaining the support of higher levels in the organization to back-up requests; and sanctions — the use of organizationally derived rewards and punishments.

In her recent review of 25 years of negotiation research, Menkel-Meadow (2009) concludes that hopes for a universal and simple theory of negotiation have not been fulfilled — rather, the literature indicates increasing 'complexification' of theory and practice. One size will not fit all. The basic aspects, such as tactics and outcome, of negotiation that have added to the complexity include, *inter alia*, number of parties, layers of hierarchies, negotiator continuity, authority to commit, relationships, trust, intertemporal commitments, formal legal requirements, ethics (formal and moral), accountability, discourse strategies and conflict resolution strategies. Moreover, negotiation theory and behaviour is conditioned upon context, culture and gender. The range of disciplines drawn upon has expanded from the early economic, game-theoretic and psychological work to include political science, sociology and anthropology. Menkel-Meadow identifies a number of fruitful lines of research, including how the move from two to three parties might lead to coalitional behaviour.

Leary (2004) and Putnam (2004) discuss the concept of critical moments and transformation in negotiation. Transformation refers to moments in the negotiation process in which the parties involved reach new understandings of the situation which redefine the problem or relationships. Such moments are more likely to occur under conditions of frustration, curiosity, connection between the parties and building recognition and trust.

As stated above, ethics is one of the aspects of negotiation that has received increased attention in recent years. A useful review of the empirical ethical decision-making literature is provided by O'Fallon and Butterfield (2005). They note that the dependent variable can be one of four steps in the ethical decision-making process: awareness (of an ethical issue); judgement; intent; or behaviour. Influencing factors are grouped into individual, organizational and moral intensity (i.e. magnitude of consequences and social consensus), with much of this work drawing upon Rest's (1986) moral development theory. Based on a detailed analysis of over a hundred studies published between 1996 and 2003, they conclude that: where gender has an influence at all, females are more ethical than males; education, employment, cognitive and moral development, religion, internal locus of control and idealism are positively related to ethical decision-making; external locus of control and the personality trait of Machiavellianism are negatively related to ethical decision-making; nationality seems to have an influence but the nature remains unclear due to limited research.

2.8 INTERACTIONS AND NEGOTIATION IN AUDIT SETTINGS

This section begins by outlining the specific characteristics of the audit negotiation setting (sub-section 2.8.1). The next four sections look at the findings from empirical studies of audit interactions. Indirect archival research (sub-section 2.8.2) uses financial statement and audit outcomes to make inferences about the effect of potential conflicts of interest in audit interactions. Although real-world decisions are used, the causal connection between the variables of interest is not clear-cut. To investigate interactions using direct methods, it is necessary to open the black box of high level audit interactions. Experimental research is a useful alternative because it allows strong causal inferences to be made; however, the number of variables that can be examined is strictly limited and the setting is artificial (sub-section 2.8.2). Research using survey methods (i.e. questionnaires and interviews) (covered in sub-sections 2.8.4 and 2.8.5) can overcome some of the problems with both of the above approaches, but it does not generally explore the influence of audit committees.

A principal area of interest in relation to audit interactions concerns the quality of the outcome of the interaction process, in terms of audit quality and overall financial reporting quality. The link between audit committees and financial reporting quality is considered in sub-section 2.8.6.

2.8.1   The Audit Setting

The audit setting has specific features that are likely to have a significant impact upon the process and outcome of interactions. In particular, the activity involved is highly regulated and the interaction process (and often the outcome) is unobservable. In the event of failure to reach agreement in the audit context, the auditor may qualify the audit report, communicate with shareholders and/or either not seek reappointment or resign.

As a result of regulatory changes, new variables have emerged that are likely to influence auditor–client interactions. In particular, the audit committee and the audit committee chair have emerged as key influences in the financial reporting process. Thus, additional parties are now routinely involved in audit interactions. The main points of contact for the AEP within the client company are the CFO and ACC. Interaction issues at this senior level can comprise a simple sharing of information, discussion between the parties to find a solution to a problem or negotiation to resolve a conflict. The issues can be raised by any one of the three parties. In their review of auditor–client interaction research, Nelson and Tan (2005, p. 58) call for research that recognizes that practice has changed 'to involve audit committees and various forms of regulatory oversight to a greater extent'.

2.8.2   Archival Studies Using Public Data

Nelson (2005) provides an excellent summary of archival conflicts-of-interest research. Observable audit opinions, auditor changes and earnings management are used to explore the effects of incentives to withstand pressure from the client company. For example, Frankel, Johnson and Nelson (2002) find a positive association between the absolute magnitude of abnormal accruals and the ratio of non-audit to total audit fees paid to the incumbent auditor. This finding is used to infer that non-audit fees provide an incentive for auditors to permit aggressive reporting by the client company.

2.8.3 Experimental Studies

Early game-theoretic models have generally been tested using experimental methods. For example, Fisher, Schatzberg and Shapiro (1996) test the Fellingham and Newman (1985) model, and find that the model generally fails to predict a significant proportion of observed auditor and client behaviour, with the observed behaviour involving mutual cooperation. These models are acknowledged to be 'highly stylized and abstract away from some of the important and interesting features in the extant auditing environment' (Fisher *et al.*, 1996, p. 157).

More recent experimental research into audit interactions adopts a psychological perspective and has focussed on negotiation strategies and tactics. Bame-Aldred and Kida (2007) compare the initial negotiation position and tactics of auditors and clients in a revenue recognition conflict, finding that clients were more flexible and more likely to use tactics such as bid high/concede later and trade-off one reporting issue for another. Sanchez, Agoglia and Hatfield (2007) and Hatfield, Agoglia and Sanchez (2008) explore the effect of auditors' use of a reciprocity-based strategy on auditor–client negotiations in a post-SOX environment. This strategy of concession involves the transparent waiving of inconsequential audit adjustments by the auditor in order to secure a significant income decreasing adjustment. Sanchez *et al.* (2007) find that client management are more willing to post significant adjustments under the reciprocity strategy than under a no-concession strategy. This approach also results in greater client satisfaction and retention. Hatfield *et al.* (2008) find that auditors are more likely to use such a strategy when management's negotiating style is competitive and client retention risk is high. Brown and Johnstone (2009) investigate the impact of auditor experience and engagement risk on negotiation process and outcome. They find that auditors with higher negotiation experience use a less concessionary strategy, achieve a more conservative reporting outcome and are more confident that the achieved outcome complies with US GAAP compared to auditors with lower negotiation experience. The experienced auditors' behaviour is unaffected by client risk, whereas less experienced auditors bent under client pressure.

Wang and Tuttle (2009) find that auditors subject to mandatory audit firm rotation adopt less cooperative negotiation strategies and are involved in more regulation impasses. Auditor rank is found to be associated with pre-negotiation positions, with partners taking a harder stand than managers (Trotman, Wright and Wright, 2009), in line with the experience influence found by Brown and Johnstone (2009).

While most studies focus on the auditor–CFO dyad, a few studies explore the influence of audit committees on negotiation using experimental methods. Pomeroy (2010) examines audit committee members' investigation of accounting decisions when they are (or are not) informed that an auditor–client negotiation took place and when a decision results in an aggressive versus conservative financial reporting outcome. It is found that negotiation knowledge has no effect on audit committee investigation (the asking of probing questions) and that investigation becomes more extensive as the proposed accounting becomes more aggressive.

DeZoort, Hermanson and Houston (2008) investigate audit committee member support for auditor-proposed adjustments by means of an experiment involving 241 US audit committee members. Based on comparison with a previous study conducted in the pre-SOX era (DeZoort, Hermanson and Houston, 2003), they find that support is significantly higher in the post-SOX era, with this result being driven by members who are CPAs. Follow-up survey questions to participants showed that, post-SOX, audit committee members feel more responsible for resolving the accounting issue, are more conservative and believe that they have more power.

2.8.4   Questionnaire Studies

One of the first experiential questionnaires was undertaken in the UK in 1995 by Beattie, Fearnley and Brandt (2000). Comparable questionnaires were sent to the CFOs and AEPs of listed companies, eliciting the frequency with which, over a three year period, a set of 46 financial statement and audit-related issues was discussed, negotiated and resulted in a change to either the accounting numbers or disclosures.

A similar survey was undertaken in the Canadian context two years later (in 1997) by Gibbins, Salterio and Webb (2001), who asked AEPs about the frequency of negotiation and then asked them to identify a specific example and, in a series of structured questions, describe its features. Ninety-three experienced Canadian public accounting firm partners responded in the context of a specific negotiation example selected from their experience; client perceptions were not surveyed. They concluded that negotiation is important, frequent and context-sensitive. Agreement was reported to have been reached somewhere between both parties' original positions in 41% of cases, on the auditor's original position in 32% of cases, and on the client's original position in 4% of cases, with a new solution being generated in 16% of cases. The two factors said to be of most importance to the negotiation were 'accounting and disclosure standards' and 'audit firms' accounting expertise'.

Gibbins, McCracken and Salterio (2007) surveyed 101 Canadian CFOs at a later date (mid 2002). The majority of CFOs (81%) had experienced negotiation, which was viewed as arising from change (in accounting standards, in personnel on either side or in business). The main negotiation issues were revenue recognition, capitalization of expenditure, extent of disclosure, business combinations and asset write-downs. The CFOs did not involve the audit committee early in the negotiation process, often informing them when the issue was resolved. Gibbins McCracken and Salterio (2005) compare the congruency of responses from both groups and find substantial consistency in responses from both sides.

Research has shown that trust is negatively related to professional scepticism (Rose, 2007). Rennie, Kopp and Lemon (2010) use an experiential questionnaire to Canadian auditors to explore the impact of auditor's trust of a client representative on the auditor–client relationship. They find that, during a disagreement, trust is increased by the client representative's openness of communication during the disagreement and demonstration of concern towards the auditor. Both of these behaviours are, therefore, deemed to be trust-attracting.

2.8.5   Interview Studies

An alternative direct approach to the exploration of audit interactions has been the use of qualitative interviews.

Some of this research adopts an explicitly interpretative, sociological perspective on auditing. An important early study by Pentland (1993) identified 'comfort production' as the key objective of audit activity. This activity is seen as ritualistic, reflecting the emotional dimension as well as the cognitive dimension of judgement. Power (1999, p. 40) develops this view by emphasizing that 'the production of comfort is negotiated'. The important role of comfort has also been identified by Beattie and Fearnley (1998, p. 20 and p. 44) who identify a 'comfort chain' linking the various parties and hierarchical levels and the 'comfort-seeker' as a distinct buyer type. More recently, Carrington and Catasús (2007) explore the comfort production process in interviews with 20 Swedish audit seniors. Drawing upon comfort theory developed in the field of nursing, they identify three dimensions of audit comfort: comfort as state, comfort as relief and comfort as renewal.

In a groundbreaking study, Beattie *et al.* (2001) conduct in-depth, matched interviews with the CFOs and AEPs of six major UK listed companies. From this evidence, covering 24 distinct interaction issues, a grounded theory model is developed of the negotiation process and the factors that influence the nature of the outcome of interactions. This model is also presented, in summary form, in Beattie, Fearnley and Brandt (2004). Grounded theory involves the coding of data, initially looking for concepts which can be grouped into categories. These categories have associated dimensions. Figure 2.1 shows the principal analytical categories in this model, arranged in five groups around the core category — the interaction itself. The most distant group of influences was the global regulatory climate, followed by the external national trading and regulatory climate, general contextual factors, specific contextual factors and the interaction itself. Each category within these five groups is listed in Table 2.1, along with the associated concepts and dimensions.

General contextual factors comprised the quality of the primary relationship, company circumstances, audit firm characteristics and the company buyer type. The specific interaction context covered, in particular, the substantive issue that was the subject of the interaction, the objectives of the parties and the identity and role of key third parties. Categories associated with the interaction itself were events, strategies, outcome and consequences.

Company buyer type (a general contextual factor) is a concept introduced by Beattie and Fearnley (1998). Based on questionnaire and interview evidence, they inductively derive four audit buyer types: the grudger; the status-seeker the comfort-seeker and the resource-seeker. These buyer types capture the diversity observed in relation to what the client company wants from their auditor. The grudger sees little value in audit,

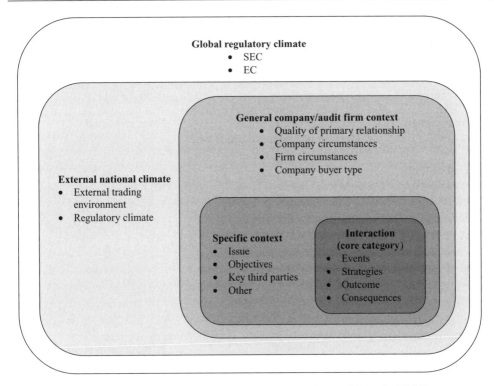

Figure 2.1   The grounded theory model of Beattie, Fearnley and Brandt (2001)

Source: Behind Closed Doors: What Company Audit is Really About, Vivien Beattie, Stella Fearnley and Richard Brandt, 2001, Palgrave, reproduced with permission, Palgrave Macmillan.

and hence seeks to minimize audit fees and is generally unhelpful to the auditor. The status-seeker sees limited value in audit but wishes to gain credibility and reputation by associating with an audit firm of high status. The comfort-seeker sees significant value in audit and wants assurance that controls are operating effectively and the financial statements are of high quality. Finally, the resource-seeker, who also sees significant value in audit, wants technical financial reporting advice, business ideas and non-audit services. However, this type of advice and additional service is no longer permitted under the ethical standards for auditors.

This approach has since been replicated in the Canadian context with broadly similar results (McCracken, Salterio and Gibbins, 2008). Eight matched interviews, conducted in late 2001, elicited five accounts of common issues and five issues discussed by one party in the dyad only. McCracken *et al.* (2008) interpret their findings using the lens of social positioning negotiation research (Kolb and Williams, 2000), whereby negotiation occurs at two levels — the substantive issue and a shadow negotiation that defined (and continually redefines) the roles of the parties and the relationship between them. They conclude that it is the CFOs who define the relationship and the roles. Some CFOs initiate a proactive relationship, where the CFO seeks to consult

Table 2.1   The categories, concepts and dimensions in the grounded theory model of Beattie, Fearnley and Brandt (2001)

Category	Underlying concepts	Associated dimensions
Global regulatory climate	SEC EC	None identified
National climate	Trading environment Regulatory regime (UK GAAP, FRRP, governance)	None identified
General context:		
Quality of primary relationship	• Mutual objectives • Mutual trust and respect • Compatible personalities • Experience/competence • Commensurate level of professional integrity • Age gap • Previous employment • Length of relationship	High to low
Company circumstances	• Company size • Ownership structure • Reporting style • Professional integrity of CFO • Effectiveness of audit committee • Financial position • Growth position • Bid risk • Level of technical accounting expertise within company	• Importance of the company to the client portfolio • Client audit risk • Level of technical support required
Audit firm circumstances	• Support & monitoring infrastructure • Partner incentives • Professional integrity of AEP • Personal integrity of AEP	None identified

Company buyer type	• Grudger
	• Status-seeker
	• Comfort-seeker
	• Resource-seeker
		• Perceived value of audit
		• Importance of:
		  ○ auditor integrity
		  ○ auditor's acceptability to third parties
		  ○ quality of working relationships with auditor
		  ○ non-audit services

Table 2.1   (*Continued*)

Category	Underlying concepts	Associated dimensions
Specific interaction context:		
Issue	• Fundamental principle • Recognition • Measurement/valuation • Classification • Disclosure • Corporate governance • Audit-related	• Fact versus judgement • One-off versus continuing • Visible versus not visible • Materiality
Objectives of parties	• Minimize effect/visibility • Revenge • Face-saving • Secrecy • Keep out of trouble • Avoid escalation • Avoid confrontation	None identified
Third parties	• Chairman • Individual NED • CEO • Main board • Audit committee • Senior management (below main board) • Second partner • Technical partner/department • Regulator • Specialist advisor • Shareholders • Analysts • Lenders	• Affiliation • Direct or indirect influence • Active versus passive involvement • Nature of involvement
Other	• Party raising issue • Agreement issue needs addressed • Extent of time pressure • History of issue • Impact of other issues • Impact on future accounting periods	None identified

(*Continued*)

Table 2.1   (*Continued*)

Category	Underlying concepts	Associated dimensions
Interaction:		
Events	• Information provision • Information withholding • Third party opinion sought • Search for solution • Change of position • Acknowledgment of mistake	None identified
Strategy	• Assertiveness • Sanction • Ingratiation • Reasoning • Coalesce • Higher authority • Conditional acceptance	None identified
Outcome	• Quality of accounting • Ease of agreement	• High-low • Compliant/not compliant • Very easy/difficult
Consequences	Impact on: • Other accounting interactions • Future accounting periods • Fee negotiations • Quality of primary relationship • Third parties	None identified

the audit partner at an early stage to ensure high quality financial reporting. This role of 'expert advisor' was considered to be ideal by audit partners. Other CFOs did not consult at an early stage, viewing the financial statements as theirs; consequently, the audit partner was cast in the role of police officer and negotiations were more difficult because issues arose only once the CFO had adopted an entrenched position. Irrespective of the role implicitly assigned to the audit partner, both parties worked together to find a resolution to the issue and in both situations the audit partner had responsibility for managing the relationship (i.e. keeping the client happy).

As stated above, however, these lines of research do not explore the influence of audit committees. Other interview studies explore audit committee processes without looking specifically at the role of the committee in interactions. However, there exists only a limited amount of research into audit committee *processes*, with most research relating audit committee inputs (structural indicators) to financial reporting outputs (outcomes) (e.g. Larcker, Richardson and Tuna, 2007; Turley and Zaman, 2007, p. 67). The few studies that do focus on process tend to use interview or case study methods. Gendron (2009) calls for further qualitative positivist research in accounting and corporate governance research.

Beasley, Carcello, Hermanson and Neal (2009) explore the audit committee oversight process in the post-SOX era by interviewing 42 US audit committee members. They find evidence of both substantive monitoring (consistent with agency theory) and ceremonial action (consistent with institutional theory). Revenue recognition was the financial reporting risk area most frequently reviewed by the audit committee (45%). Of the interviewees, 57% claimed to be involved in discussion of the specific judgements/estimates/assumptions concerned with implementing an accounting policy and 67% discussed alternative accounting treatments available under GAAP (p. 49). Members with accounting expertise were significantly more likely to state that their audit committee: drives the content of the information packet; discusses specific judgements/estimates/assumptions concerned with implementing an accounting policy; and discusses alternative accounting treatments under GAAP.

Cohen, Krishnamoorthy and Wright (2008) interview 30 audit managers and partners from three of the Big Four audit firms in the US to explore their experiences in interacting with management and audit committees in the post-SOX era. Comparisons are made with a similar pre-SOX study (Cohen, Krishnamoorthy and Wright, 2002). It is found that audit committees are believed to have become significantly more active and diligent, and to possess greater expertise and power. There were indications, however, that audit committees play a passive role in helping to resolve disputes, with the auditor and management usually seeking to resolve issues before they come to the audit committee's attention. This is similar to the Canadian findings of Gendron and Bédard (2006) and the US audit committee member evidence of Beasley *et al.* (2009).

Gendron and Bédard (2006) explore, via interviews in three large Canadian companies, the meaning of audit committee effectiveness. They find that each audit committee attendee's sense of meaning comprises a different and diverse mix of emotions (such as confidence, hopefulness, anxiety) about the committee's formal duties. Interestingly, these meanings are constructed around a range of minor events and actions surrounding audit committee activity, rather than through major conflict resolution situations.

In a longitudinal series of case studies, LeBlanc and Gillies (2005) interview 194 directors and attend the board and audit committee meetings of 21 Canadian organizations. Drawing from this rich dataset, they identify several director types, some of which are functional (change agents, consensus-builders, counsellors and challengers) and some of which are dysfunctional (controllers, conformists, cheerleaders and critics). Two types of chair (a role with crucial influence) are also identified — the functional conductor chair and the dysfunctional caretaker chair. Effective boards and committees require a balance of functional director types and a conductor chair, together with the alignment of director competencies, behavioural characteristics and corporate strategy.

In a case study of a UK FTSE 100 financial services company, Turley and Zaman (2007) examine interactions among key corporate governance actors. Interviews were conducted with, *inter alia*, the ACC but not with either of the other two audit committee members. The year in which the evidence was collected is not reported. Both formal and informal audit committee processes are explored, in addition to the power relationships surrounding the audit committee. They conclude that: the most significant effects of the audit committee on governance outcomes occur outside the formal structures and processes; the audit committee has a significant influence on power relations between key organizational participants; and the audit committee may be used as a threat, ally or arbiter in resolving issues and conflicts.

2.8.6   Link Between Audit Committee and Financial Reporting Quality

Many of these studies focus on the relationship between audit committee characteristics and proxy measures for the level of earnings management. Agrawal and Chadha (2005) analyse a US dataset of audit committee and other corporate governance characteristics in relation to earnings misstatements. They find that the independence of audit committees did not influence the frequency of restatements, although the presence of an independent director with financial expertise did reduce the frequency of restatements. Based on a meta-analysis of 20 (mainly US) studies that investigate the impact of audit committees on earnings management, Lin and Hwang (2010) conclude that there is a clear negative relationship between the level of earnings management and the audit committee's independence, size, expertise and the number of meetings. No UK studies are included in the set of studies considered.

Literature review studies have yielded interesting generalized insights into the link between corporate governance and financial reporting. DeZoort, Hermanson, Archambeault and Reed (2002) review the empirical audit committee literature on audit committee effectiveness (output variable), focusing on audit committee composition, authority, resources and diligence (the former three being input variables and diligence being a process factor). They call for further research on process variables. More recently, Bédard and Gendron (2010) review the results of studies published between 1994 and 2008 which examine the relationship between certain audit committee characteristics and measures of audit committee effectiveness in terms of strengthening financial reporting. They conclude that audit committee existence, members' independence and members' competence have generally been found to positively influence effectiveness, whereas the number of meetings and the size of the committee generally have no effect. They note a paucity of research using either psychological or sociological perspectives or conducted outside the US, ending with a plea for research into the dynamics of audit committee processes.

Cohen, Krishnamoorthy and Wright (2004) review research literature into the relationship between broad aspects of corporate governance and financial reporting quality and conclude that corporate governance is best viewed as a 'mosaic' of interactions among actors and institutions (p. 88). Pomeroy and Thornton (2008) conduct a meta-analysis of the association between audit committee independence and financial reporting quality. They conclude that financial statement quality and audit quality are complementary contributors to financial reporting quality. Audit committees are found to be more effective at enhancing audit quality than financial statement quality.

Finally, and of particular relevance to the present study, Cohen, Gaynor, Krishnamoorthy and Wright (2007) review recent research into auditor communications with the audit committee and the board of directors. The review is structured around the discussion questions posed by the Public Company Accounting Oversight Board (PCAOB) in the US (PCAOB, 2004, cited in Cohen *et al.*, 2007). In relation to financial reporting quality, it is concluded that communications between the auditor and the audit committee should include discussions of areas susceptible to earnings management and also factors that may drive management to make aggressive accounting choices.

3

The Survey

3.1 OVERVIEW

In this chapter, we present a summary of the relevant aspects of the questionnaire stage of our study. CFOs, ACCs and AEPs reported on audit committee characteristics and the frequency with which 35 financial statement issues were discussed, negotiated and resulted in a change to the accounting numbers and/or disclosures. First, the methods used are outlined, then the results are summarized and discussed. Where relevant reference is made to a previous study carried out by Beattie, Fearnley and Brandt (2000).

3.2 METHODS

A questionnaire was sent to three samples in June 2007: CFOs, ACCs and AEPs of domestic, officially listed UK companies (excluding AIM companies and investment trusts). The sample covered the top 250 qualifying companies by market capitalization (as at 5 February 2007) and a systematic sample of 250 from the remaining qualifying companies. Questionnaires to CFOs and ACCs were sent to the same companies. To eliminate multiple selections of ACCs, the final sample sent out to this group was reduced to 446 as it was felt that an ACC would not be prepared to fill in more than one survey. To identify suitable AEPs acting for qualifying companies and facilitate the distribution of the questionnaire, we were assisted by 11 large audit firms. As listed company audit partners could not be publicly identified at the time, the firms identified 439 listed company AEPs to whom questionnaires were sent and returned direct to us. The AEPs were asked to complete the survey with reference to their largest listed company client within the scope of the study. The useable response rates obtained were: CFOs 149 (30%); ACCs 130 (29%); AEPs 219 (50%). This represents an overall response of 498 (36%).

The questionnaire asked (among other matters) about key company characteristics such as size and industry sector, the composition and functioning of the audit committee and also the impact of the changes to the regulations regarding the provision of non-audit services by the auditor. It then proceeded to ask about recent experiences of discussions and negotiations between the parties on 35 financial statement issues. In relation to the financial statement issues discussed and negotiated respondents were asked: which parties were involved in the *discussion* (defined as: matters raised by one or more participants and considered in speech or writing); whether the discussion became a *negotiation* (defined as: the process of reconciling conflicting views advanced in discussion, by concessions by one, two or all participants); and whether the discussions or negotiations resulted in a change to the proposed accounting numbers or disclosures.

Further details of the results from the non-audit services responses are reported in Beattie, Fearnley and Hines (2009b) and further details of the discussion and negotiation responses are reported in Beattie, Fearnley and Hines (2008b).

3.3 FINDINGS

3.3.1 Background Characteristics of the Companies

Several background characteristics of the companies with which the respondents were associated are of interest. Of the combined set of 498 respondents, 26% were FTSE 100, 39% were FTSE 250, 31% were FTSE Small-Cap and 4% were Fledgling. A total of 10% had a US listing. Broad industry sectors were: 18% financials; 13% consumer goods; 33% services; 20% industrials; 12% resources; and 4% utilities. Audit firm size was Big Four in 88% of cases and non-Big Four in the remaining 12% of cases, reflecting the dominance of the Big Four in the listed company market. The overall results show a good spread of respondents from different company sizes and industry sectors.

3.3.2 Audit Committees Characteristics

The average reported number of audit committee meetings per year was four and 53% stated that e-mail contact among audit committee members was used to resolve issues outside of meetings. The auditor discussed the audit plan for the year with the audit committee in 96% of cases, discussed specific audit-related issues in 97% of cases and discussed closing issues at the end of the audit in 100% of cases. The external auditor attended, on average, 3.6 audit committee meetings. In 90% of cases the external auditor met with the full audit committee at least once a year when the executives were not present; in 7% of cases such a meeting took place with only the ACC and in the remaining 3% of cases no such meeting took place.

Asked whether the audit committee structure changed after revision to the Combined Code in 2003 recommended an enhanced role for audit committees, 46% said 'yes'. On average, each audit committee included 0.6 members who were former auditors and 1.3 members holding recognized accounting qualifications. When asked 'how many audit committee members have "recent and relevant financial experience"?', the mean response was 1.7, 1.7 and 1.5 from the CFOs, ACCs and AEPs, respectively. The distribution of responses is shown in Table 3.1. It can be seen that a small number of respondents did not consider that *any* audit committee member had such experience. This occurred disproportionately more in companies in the Small-Cap and Fledgling stock market indices.

The survey also asked about the impact of regulations restricting the provision of non-audit services (NAS) by the incumbent auditor. In total, 54% of respondents

Table 3.1 Audit committee members with recent and relevant financial experience

No. of members	CFOs % (N = 149)	ACCs % (N = 130)	AEPS % (n = 219)
0	5	1	5
1	42	48	51
2	39	34	34
3	10	12	10
4 or more	4	5	0
Total	100	100	100

reported that regulatory change has prevented or discouraged NAS purchase. The percentage was highest for the CFO group (62%) and similar for the other two groups. The services most frequently cited as being affected were tax advice and accounting/disclosure assistance.

We also asked questions about the attendance at the audit committee meetings. One question asked 'who *from the company* normally attends your audit committee meetings?' It was clear from the responses received that, while the average number of members might be 3.4, the number of people attending could be far in excess of this. The CEO was reported to attend by 75% of respondents, the CFO was reported to attend by 94% of respondents and the internal auditor was reported to attend by 65% of respondents. Other frequent attendees included the company secretary, the financial controller, the head of risk and the head of compliance.

As audit committee composition is a subject of considerable interest, we gathered additional information about audit committee and board characteristics from the annual reports of the 228 companies where the CFO, the ACC or both responded to our survey. The average (mean) size of the company main board was 9.1, comprising 3.8 executive directors and 5.3 non-executive directors. Board size ranged from 3 to 21. The average size of the audit committee was 3.4 members, with committee size overall ranging from two to six members. Only three companies had executive directors as full members of the audit committee. These members were the CFO, the executive chairman or another executive director. Across 15 companies a total of 16 non-executive directors who were not independent of the company were audit committee members. The ACC was an independent non-executive director in all but two companies both of which were small cap companies. The composition of the audit committee and the attendance at meetings is discussed further in Chapter 15.

3.4   INTERACTION ISSUES

The ten top ranking discussion issues cited by respondents are presented in Table 3.2. Importantly, the level of discussion reported to take place by each group indicates

Table 3.2   Top ten discussion issues

Issue	% indicating discussion took place (n=)			Rank		
	CFO (149)	ACC (130)	AEP (219)	CFO	ACC	AEP
Intangible assets/ goodwill	62.4	58.5	59.4	1	1	3
Issues in subsidiary undertakings	61.1	53.1	71.2	2	8	1
Segmental reporting	57.7	49.2	54.8	3	9	5=
Deferred tax assets/ liabilities	56.4	43.8	51.1	4	[12]	9
Presentation of the primary financial statements	55.7	57.7	63.9	5=	2=	2
Business Review	55.7	53.8	55.3	5=	6=	4
Revenue recognition	53.0	53.8	54.3	7=	6=	7
Exceptional items	53.0	57.7	49.3	7=	2=	10=
Fair value on acquisition	49.0	57.7	49.3	9=	2=	10=
Liabilities/provisions	49.0	55.4	53.0	9=	5	8
Share-based payments	44.3	42.3	54.8	[12]	[13=]	5=
Financial instruments	38.9	45.4	43.4	[13]	10=	[12]
Directors' remuneration report	37.6	45.4	40.6	[14]	10=	[14]

Source: Reproduced from Briefing: *Auditor/Company Interactions in the 2007 UK Regulatory Environment*, Vivien Beattie, Stella Fearnley and Tony Hines, 2008, with kind permission ICAEW.
Note: Table is ordered on the CFO group; issues ranked outside the top ten are shown in square brackets.

that ACCs are equally as aware of discussion issues as the other two groups. For the combined group of respondents a mean of 11.3 discussion issues are reported by each respondent.

The three groups appear broadly to agree on the most frequent issues for discussion. Three issues relating to business combinations feature high in the list. This may be attributed to a new requirement in IFRS 3 that the difference between what was paid for the acquisition and the fair value of the assets acquired must be allocated to the various identifiable intangible components, such as brands, customer lists and goodwill. A study conducted on behalf of the EC found that many companies fail to provide a description of these components, doubting that the costs involved are justified (ICAEW, 2007).

Presentation of primary statements was ranked second by two out of the three respondent groups, while exceptional items ranked within the top ten for all three groups. IAS 1 leaves flexibility in the presentation. The FRRP has pronounced that

Table 3.3   Top ten negotiation issues

Issue	% indicating negotiation took place (n=)			Rank		
	CFO (149)	ACC (130)	AEP (219)	CFO	ACC	AEP
Presentation of the primary financial statements	12.1	6.9	14.6	1	4=	6
Exceptional items	9.4	9.2	16.9	2	2	2
Issues in subsidiary undertakings	8.1	6.9	19.2	3=	4=	1
Revenue recognition	8.1	5.4	13.7	3=	6=	8
Segmental reporting	7.4	4.6	12.8	5=	8=	9
Liabilities/provisions	7.4	5.4	15.5	5=	6=	4=
Intangible assets/goodwill	6.7	7.7	16.4	7	3	3
Financial instruments	6.0	3.1	7.8	8=	[13=]	[12=]
Deferred tax assets/liabilities	6.0	1.5	14.2	8=	[21=]	7
Fair value on acquisition	5.4	10.0	15.5	10=	1	4=
Business Review	5.4	2.3	10.0	10=	[19=]	10
Inventories	3.4	4.6	4.6	[14=]	8=	[17=]
Identification of pre/post acquisition expenses	0.7	4.6	2.7	[25=]	8=	[22=]

Source: Reproduced from Briefing: *Auditor/Company Interactions in the UK Regulatory Environment*; Vivien Beattie, Stella Fearnley and Tony Hines, 2008, with kind permission ICAEW.
Note: Table is ordered on the CFO group; issues ranked outside the top ten are shown in square brackets.

additional income statement line items are permitted when deemed necessary to explain elements of financial performance (FRRP, 2006).

The top 10 negotiation issues are presented in Table 3.3. A mean of 1.71 issues negotiated is reported, much lower than the mean figure for issues discussed. One financial statement issue (presentation of the primary financial statements) is cited by at least 10% of CFOs and one issue (fair value on acquisition) is cited by at least 10% of ACCs. However, AEPs report a markedly higher incidence of negotiation than either of the preparer groups. A total of ten issues are cited by at least 10% of AEPs. This difference in incidence also emerged in the earlier study by Beattie *et al.* (2000), who considered that AEPs may have different levels of recall because the audit is their main contact with the company.

The issues most often negotiated are similar to the issues most frequently discussed for all three groups. Notably, ACCs rank inventories and identification of pre-/post-acquisition expenses in the top ten, well above the other respondents. Financial instruments are ranked in the top ten by CFOs only, despite the fact that the IFRS standards relating to this issue have received widespread criticism. However, most of our respondents were not from the financial sector and would be less affected by the financial instrument standards.

As there are differences in research design and the accounting regime is significantly different, detailed line by line comparisons with the earlier study by Beattie *et al.* (2000) is not possible. However, high level review of the two studies shows a decline in the probability that a discussion evolves into a negotiation. This is discussed further in Chapter 16.

3.5 FINANCIAL STATEMENT CHANGES

Changes to the financial statements were not necessarily preceded by a negotiation interaction; many changes occurred following a discussion interaction. Similarly to the negotiation issues, AEPs tended to report higher levels of change to the financial statements than either CFOs or ACCs. This was also found in Beattie *et al.* (2000).

The top ten issues to create a change to the accounting numbers are presented in Table 3.4 with a mean of 1.45 for each respondent. Four issues appear which did not feature in either of the previous tables which focused on interaction frequency. These four issues are: share-based payments (introduced for the first time by IFRS 2): retirement or other employee benefits; prior year adjustments; and associates/joint ventures. Deferred taxation, an area of ongoing subjectivity, is first in the CFO rankings, while ACCs rank fair value on acquisition top and AEPs rank issues in subsidiary undertakings top. Research has shown that deferred tax had caused more restatements than any other issue in the transition to IFRS (ICAEW, 2007).

The top ten issues resulting in change to the disclosures are presented in Table 3.5 with a mean of 2.35 for each respondent. The issue to appear for the first time in this table is directors' remuneration report, which is always a sensitive issue. Segmental reporting emerges as the second ranking issue for two groups. This is likely to be because greater disclosure of segment assets and liabilities is required under IAS 14 than under SSAP 25 (the UK equivalent). Also the early adoption of the new international standard (IFRS 8) by some companies may have prompted changes. The Enhanced Business Review, mandated for year-ends beginning after 1 October 2007, was anticipated by many companies and led to discussion with the auditors.

Beattie *et al.* (2000) also find in the earlier regime that new regulatory requirements dominate the discussion and negotiation issues between CFOs and AEPs relating to financial reporting. Some of the top ten topics which are discussed and negotiated in Beattie *et al.* (2000) arise in the top ten subjects in the current study, although the accounting treatments under IFRS are different. These topics are: fair value on acquisition; re-organization costs; inventories; directors' remuneration disclosures and deferred tax. This reflects the continuing level of activity in these subjects. However, in Beattie *et al.* (2000) there were more discussions which evolved into negotiations.

Table 3.4 Top ten issues resulting in change to the accounting numbers

Issue	% indicating change to the accounting numbers took place (n=)			Rank		
	CFO (149)	ACC (130)	AEP (219)	CFO	ACC	AEP
Deferred tax assets/ liabilities	7.4	4.6	13.7	1=	[13=]	4=
Share-based payments	7.4	6.9	7.3	1=	5	9
Exceptional items	6.7	6.2	12.8	3	6=	7
Revenue recognition	6.0	8.5	15.1	4=	2=	3
Intangible assets/ goodwill	6.0	7.7	13.7	4=	4	4=
Issues in subsidiary undertakings	5.4	6.2	26.9	6=	6=	1
Retirement or other employee benefits (e.g. pension schemes)	5.4	5.4	5.9	6=	9=	10=
Financial instruments	5.4	5.4	9.6	6=	9=	8
Liabilities/provisions	4.7	5.4	13.7	9=	9=	4=
Prior year adjustments	4.7	6.2	4.6	9=	6=	[14=]
Fair value on acquisition	4.0	10.0	18.7	[11=]	1	2
Issues in associates or joint ventures	4.0	8.5	2.7	[11=]	2=	[19=]
Presentation of the primary financial statements	2.7	5.4	5.5	[14=]	9=	[12=]
Segmental reporting	2.7	2.3	5.9	[14=]	[18]	10=

Source: Reproduced from Briefing: *Auditor/Company Interactions in the UK Regulatory Environment*; Vivien Beattie, Stella Fearnley and Tony Hines, 2008, with kind permission ICAEW.
Note: Table is ordered on the CFO group; issues ranked outside the top ten are shown in square brackets.

3.6 SUMMARY

The survey and the additional data gathered about audit committees reveal some interesting findings. The external auditor is heavily engaged with the audit committee, attending most audit committee meetings. Almost all auditors meet with the non-executives when the executives are not present. There is a very high level of interaction on planning and audit-related issues and all the respondents confirmed that the auditor attended the final closedown meeting. Only three small companies report that no member of the audit committee has recent and relevant financial experience. Of the respondents, 54% also indicate that regulatory change has influenced the purchase and supply of non-audit services.

Table 3.5   Top ten issues resulting in change to the disclosures

Issue	% indicating change to the disclosures took place (n=)			Rank		
	CFO (149)	ACC (130)	AEP (219)	CFO	ACC	AEP
Presentation of the primary financial statements	17.4	9.2	31.5	1	2=	1
Segmental reporting	16.8	9.2	21.0	2	2=	4
Business Review	15.4	9.2	24.2	3	2=	2
Issues in subsidiary undertakings	12.1	6.9	23.7	4	9=	3
Exceptional items	11.4	10.0	16.9	5	1	6
Intangible assets/ goodwill	9.4	8.5	16.4	6	5=	7=
Financial instruments	8.1	7.7	15.5	7	7=	10
Deferred tax assets/ liabilities	7.4	3.8	16.4	8=	[16=]	7=
Directors' remuneration report	7.4	5.4	16.0	8=	[11]	9
Liabilities/provisions	6.7	4.6	11.0	10=	[12=]	[14]
Retirement or other employee benefits (e.g. pension schemes)	6.7	4.6	13.2	10=	[12=]	[12]
Issues in associates or joint ventures	6.0	7.7	5.0	[12=]	7=	[19=]
Fair value on acquisition	4.7	8.5	18.7	[14=]	5=	5

Source: Reproduced from Briefing: *Auditor/Company Interactions in the UK Regulatory Environment*; Vivien Beattie, Stella Fearnley and Tony Hines, 2008, with kind permission ICAEW.
Note: Table is ordered on the CFO group; issues ranked outside the top ten are shown in square brackets.

In terms of financial reporting interactions, there is a high level of interaction between all three parties on specific financial statement issues. Respondents report that an average of 11.4 issues are discussed and 1.7 are negotiated. On average, 1.45 issues led to change to the numbers and 2.45 led to change to the disclosures. There is also considerable agreement among respondents on the issues which have most frequently been discussed/negotiated/caused changes to the financial statements. The high frequency interaction issues relate to IFRS standards which have introduced significant change. These include goodwill and intangibles, deferred taxation and presentation of primary statements.

These findings are reviewed in Chapter 16 in relation to the evidence from the interviews.

Part II
The Case Studies

4

Case Studies

4.1 INTRODUCTION TO THE CASE STUDIES

In this chapter we describe the research methods used for the matched interview stage of the study. We first describe how the nine case companies were selected and approached and also the interview techniques employed and the process for agreeing the stories with the interviewees. Section 4.3 sets out the broad approach taken to the analysis, including a brief explanation of grounded theory and how this theory is applied to the cases. Details of how each case story was written up are provided in section 4.4. This is followed in sections 4.5 and 4.6 by a description of the preliminary within-case analysis. Finally, we include a tabular summary of the general local context and the interaction issues in each of the nine cases (section 4.7).

4.2 HOW THE CASE COMPANIES WERE SELECTED AND APPROACHED

The cases were identified from the questionnaire study. The results of the questionnaire which are relevant to the specific objectives of this study are in Chapter 3. As part of the questionnaire, respondents were asked 'Would you be willing to be interviewed by one of the researchers, at a time convenient to you, to enable the issues to be explored in more detail?' A total of 39 CFOs, 33 ACCs and 78 AEPs agreed in principle to be interviewed. It had been decided initially to include ten cases within the project, in line with suggested norms for case study research in the literature (Eisenhardt, 1989).

As we needed permission from the directors of the company to speak to their AEP, it was necessary to approach the directors first. Of those who agreed to be interviewed in the questionnaire responses, there was only one company where both the CFO and ACC had agreed. We therefore selected the target companies we would like to interview from those where either the CFO or the ACC had agreed to be interviewed, with the intention of persuading the other party to agree. The target companies were carefully chosen to reflect different sizes, industry sectors and audit firms, including all the Big Four firms and some other organizations. Before approaching the companies, we agreed with the audit firms that we could approach their AEPs, subject to client consent. It was also agreed by the firms that we could assure the AEPs that we had the audit firm's permission to interview them but, in order to protect their personal confidentiality, they were under no obligation to inform the firm about the interview unless they wished to do so.

The individuals who had agreed to be interviewed were approached personally and the case study project was explained, including our requirement to interview all three parties and unconditional assurances of confidentiality were offered. We obtained permission to approach the CFO, ACC and AEP in nine companies. However, after the first interview, one ACC withheld permission for us to speak to the CFO and AEP, thus this interview and the case was lost and the number of cases was reduced to eight. We took a different approach with the final target company as, although we already had one case audited by a non-Big Four audit firm, we ideally sought another one. We identified a survey company audited by a major non-Big Four firm where only one out of the CFO and ACC had returned the questionnaire and this person had not agreed to an interview. We approached the head of audit in the audit firm concerned and asked for introductions to the CFO and ACC. The introductions were most helpfully provided.

At each interview, permission was sought and obtained to record the interview. Assurances were re-iterated that neither the company nor the interviewee would be identified or identifiable in any subsequent publication, nor would we disclose the identity of the companies beyond the research team. We also undertook to contact the interviewees when we had written up the results of the interviews to give them the opportunity to comment in order to ensure that the company could not be identified from the story. It was our intention to interview all the parties separately but in one case all three interviewees decided just before the scheduled meetings that they wished to be interviewed together rather than individually. In another case, after many attempts by the researchers to make contact, the ACC did not respond to our requests to be interviewed and so one case is based on two interviews only.

All the interviews were jointly conducted by two of the principal researchers to ensure consistency of approach. As well as being experienced academics in qualitative research, both researchers also had experience of auditing listed companies and were, therefore, conversant with the process and issues being discussed. In preparation for each meeting, the company's annual report for the period covered by the questionnaire was obtained and studied. This enabled us to become familiar with the nature of the company and its activities, its approach to corporate governance and accounting issues that appeared to be significant. We also reviewed relevant questionnaire responses, where available, to form an agenda for the interviews. In cases where interviewees had completed a questionnaire, a copy was given to them at the interview so it could act as an *aide memoire*. When the interviewee had not completed a questionnaire, a blank one was given to them to act as a focus for the discussion. In some cases, at the request of the interviewee, we sent copies of the questionnaires, completed or blank, before the interview.

There was no fixed series of interview questions as the issues arising in each case were different. Interviewees were first asked to describe how the relationship between the three parties and the audit committee worked in practice in their company (or client). Then they were asked to talk about the issues that had given rise to interactions (discussions or negotiations) with either of the other two parties and how they viewed the progress of the issue to its final resolution. Not all interviewees from the same company commented on the same issues. They were encouraged to raise any other issues they wanted to and, if there was time, we also asked for their overall views on the recent changes in the regulatory framework. (These views are reported in Chapter 14.)

The interviews employed both neutral, conversational prompts and a laddering technique. This technique requires that the interviewer keeps asking for further clarification, working backwards to antecedent conditions and forwards to anticipated effects (Brown, 1992, p. 293). Examples of prompts used were:

- Who first raised the issue?
- What form did the discussions take?
- Was the ACC involved? At what stage?
- What role did the audit committee play?
- Were any threats or promises made?
- Were you happy with the outcome?
- Did the outcome affect subsequent relations?

We were very careful not to give any indications to the interviewees of what the others had said about the issues. Where appropriate, reference was made to the company's annual report for a confirmation of the reliability of the evidence collected (Yin, 2008). No inconsistencies were found between the annual report and the interviews. All the interviews were recorded and fully transcribed and lasted between one and three hours. With the exception of two interviews, which were carried out in hired private office rooms at the ICAEW premises, all interviews took place at the client's premises, wherever located. The interviews were carried out between December 2007 and April 2008. However, the interviews for each case company were held as close together as possible and companies were approached in succession.

4.3   BROAD APPROACH TO THE GROUNDED THEORY ANALYSIS

The approach to the analysis follows that adopted in *Behind Closed Doors*. This employed a four stage process:

- describing the stories in each case;
- within-case analysis based on existing grounded theory;
- cross-case analysis; and
- testing and modifying theory from cross-case analysis.

This is consistent with the grounded theory methodology of Corbin and Strauss (2008). Grounded theory refers to the process of building theory inductively from the analysis of data. The approach focuses on a core phenomenon or incident and seeks to understand it, by constantly comparing the data at different levels of abstraction. This is done by coding key features in each text and grouping these into concepts that apply across cases. Similar concepts are further grouped into categories and the relationships between these categories form the final grounded theory.[1] In the type of grounded theory applied in the present study, researchers are permitted to be open to prior theory and the analytical procedures are well-defined.

The research question being addressed in relation to the financial reporting interactions can be stated as follows:

How do companies and their auditors resolve important financial reporting issues?

The interaction is thus the core phenomenon. In exploring this phenomenon, theoretical sensitivity emerged primarily from our systematic review of the relevant theoretical literature (Chapter 2). This allowed us to maintain an awareness of the subtleties of meaning of data and suggested concepts and relationships that were assessed against the data collected. In addition, the rigorous procedures and techniques used in the analytical process, similar to those followed in Beattie *et al.* (2001), were expressly designed to test and modify the grounded theory of Beattie *et al.* (2001). However, whereas the Beattie *et al.* study (2001) was *generating* grounded theory, the present one seeks to *test* and if necessary *modify* that theory. Grounded theories are evaluated in terms of their fit, relevance, workability and modifiability (Glaser and Strauss, 1967). Therefore, we did systematically test the existing grounded theory concepts against the present data to ascertain which of these concepts still had influence and whether the influence had changed. We also sought to identify new concepts evident in the data, some of which may exist in the prior literature. In examining and re-examining each interaction, we were looking for causal conditions, context, intervening conditions, action strategies and consequences (Kelle, 2005).

Chapters 4 to 13 and Chapter 16 include the final versions of the tables, diagrams and notes that emerged during the within-case and cross-case analysis. With the

---

[1] The analytical process was described in Beattie *et al.* (2001, p. 254) as follows: 'The analytical process involved coding of various forms, as the data was read and reread. This went far beyond the mere descriptive summarization of data. Three types of coding were used. First, open coding, in which concepts were identified, labelled and categorized. Concepts are the basic unit of analysis in grounded theory — it is a name that represents a phenomenon and therefore can be used at a higher level of generality than the raw data. Concepts were identified by asking questions of the raw data and by comparing phenomena so that like phenomena are given the same name. Once concepts began to emerge from this coding, we began to group concepts that appeared to relate to the same phenomenon, thus forming categories. These categories were also labelled, using higher-level names than those of the concepts grouped under it. In order to identify and understand the relationships between categories in the later stages of analysis, it was necessary to establish the attributes of the categories (i.e., their properties) and also the dimensions of these properties. Whereas open coding focused on the breaking down of data, the second type of coding, axial coding, focused on putting the data back together again in a different way, by making connections between each category and its sub-categories. This process allowed categories to be developed beyond their properties and dimensions. Elements of this type of coding inevitably creep into open coding, for as the data is broken apart it is natural to begin to put it back together in a relational form. The third and final type of coding, selective coding, concerns the final theory development phase of analysis. It involved the selection of a core category, followed by a process of systematically relating all other categories to it at a high level of generality. As the data was read and reread, all three types of coding took place, although open coding dominated early coding sessions while axial and selective coding dominated later sessions. Moreover, all early coding was viewed as provisional, as concepts and categories evolved and changed as new data was read and compared. Many iterations were required before a stable set of concepts and categories emerged.'

inclusion of these materials, the reader will be able to see how we bridged the 'huge chasm' that separates the data from the final conclusions (Eisenhardt, 1989, p. 539).

4.4   WRITING UP EACH CASE (MATCHED SET OF INTERVIEWS) — THE STORIES

Each interview transcript was printed out and then coded. The coding scheme for each case was developed from the matched interviews based on identified themes, which emerged from repeated reading of the material and from the existing grounded theory of Beattie *et al.* (2001). These themes focussed on: (a) corporate governance practices, reported in Chapter 15; (b) views of the regulatory framework (where interview time had permitted), reported in Chapter 14; and (c) the key processes and events associated with each interaction and its outcome.

The drafts of the stories were written up to include a brief overview of the companies followed by the interviewees' descriptions of how the relationships between them and the audit committee worked in practice. In these initial two sections of the stories, some distinguishing features of the companies and their governance have been disguised by making minor changes to the context to protect the identity of the companies. These changes did not compromise the integrity of the story. For example, the nature of the company's activities may have been changed. Also, two of our interviewees were female but, given the relative paucity of women in CFO, ACC and AEP roles in the listed company sector, it was decided with regret that describing these interviewees as female could lead to identification of the company. Similarly, one of our interviewees was from an ethnic minority and this has not been disclosed. Thus, interesting issues to do with the effect of gender (see Kolb, 2009) and ethnicity on negotiations cannot be explored in detail within the cases presented.

In addition to these essential changes, certain aspects of the stories have been omitted for the same ethical reasons. Some of our companies had a US listing and, therefore, were required to engage with and comply with the requirements of the US regulatory framework. As so few UK companies are US listed we have omitted any reference to this in the write up of the interactions and also from the context. Also, some companies referred to having had queries about specific interactions from the FRRP. Although the FRRP rarely issues company-specific press notices, this information has been omitted as it could lead to identification of the company by its industry sector. In some cases we limited the detail of an interaction as, if it was specific to a sector, this could also lead to identification. Changes to data driven by ethical considerations have been made in similar field-based accounting research projects (e.g. Beattie *et al.*, 2001; Anderson-Gough, Grey and Robson, 1999).

Following these initial two sections, the main interactions were written up individually as a chronological story reflecting the different perceptions of the interviewees who commented on the specific issues (Hansen and Kahnweiler, 1993).

In all cases, once we felt we had an acceptable draft of the stories which were consistent with each other in style and format, we made contact again with the interviewees as we had undertaken to do. This contact occurred approximately two years after the interviews took place. We offered the interviewees the story which emerged from the interviews including verbatim quotes, but not our analysis and comments on the story. We were aware that some of the material in the stories could be sensitive to the company circumstances and some could also be sensitive to the individuals in terms of what they had said about each other. As we felt it was essential to avoid damaging continuing business relationships, we first contacted the AEP for a view on the sensitivity of the story, before passing it on to the CFO and ACC with any amendments suggested by the AEP. We took the view that criticism of the AEP by the client could be helpful to the individual and the audit firm, but criticism of the ACC or the CFO by the AEP or criticism by the ACC and CFO of each other could be damaging.

The AEPs' view of the story's sensitivity varied. Although some had rotated off, all the AEPs were very helpful, except in one case where the company had been taken over and there was no interest in engaging with it. In this case, we had the same reaction from the former ACC and CFO. All the AEPs recalled the interviews but some of the ACCs and CFOs did not and we had to remind them of the research.

The interviewees' reactions to the stories ranged from contentment for us to tell it as it was, provided the company was not identifiable, to great sensitivity either about the relationships or the risk of identification. This led to several rewrites of some of the stories to satisfy the concerns of the three parties involved. In some cases, final approval was given by the company chairman or the audit committee itself. Agreement of some individual stories took up to four months and nine iterations to achieve.

In one case (Ostrich) the CFO and ACC did not want the detailed story to be included in the study and in this case we have included a brief outline and the analysis of the transactions. In another case (Raven) a wish was expressed not to report the interviews verbatim so the story is reported in third party narrative form.

4.5   PRELIMINARY WITHIN-CASE ANALYSIS: ATTACHING LABELS TO THE KEY CATEGORIES

Once agreement of the contents of the stories had been obtained from the interviewees, and following the approach of Beattie *et al.* (2001), we recognized that to perform the analysis of the stories a classification system had to be developed by which common labels could be attached to the key concepts identified in each case.

4.5.1   Labelling the Concepts Described in the Stories

The first stage was to consider the concepts discussed by our interviewees. These could be divided into either descriptive or interactive. The descriptive concepts provide background information about the nature of the company's activities, the role and function of the audit committee and the ACC and how the three interviewees viewed their roles in the governance process. The interactive concepts, which describe the discussions and negotiations which took place, have been labelled interactions. The results of the interactions have been labelled outcomes.

4.5.2   Preliminary Analysis of Context

Drawing upon the work of Beattie *et al.* (2001), we identified a number of contextual factors that might influence the nature and outcome of the interactions:

- the size of the company (large listed or small listed);
- the size of the audit firm (Big Four or non-Big Four);
- the quality of the relationships between CFO, ACC and the AEP (graded poor to good);
- the attributes of the audit committee (e.g. number of members, other attendees, financial literacy of ACC, number of meetings per year, degree of contact outside the meetings); and
- the company reporting style, classified in terms of compliant/non-compliant and conservative/aggressive. As it transpired all the case reporting styles were compliant.

As explained above, confidentiality constraints have restricted the amount of information we have been able to disclose on company size and audit firms in some cases.

4.5.3   The Interactions

Interactions are classified according to their form — either as a discussion or, where conflicting views are reconciled, a negotiation (see section 3.2 in Chapter 3 for a full definition).

The subject of the interactions is divided into three broad categories — financial reporting, audit and corporate governance. In all there were 50 interactions of which 45 were financial reporting interactions. As only the financial reporting interactions would have a direct impact on the company financial statements we have referred to the others as context to the cases. The 45 financial reporting interactions have been further sub-classified using the same scheme as that adopted by Beattie *et al.* (2001). *Recognition* concerns the boundaries of an entity as reported in its financial statements. *Measurement* concerns the value to be attached to an asset or liability. *Classification* refers to the location where accounting numbers are disclosed in a primary statement. *Disclosure* relates to the information content of the financial statements over and above the primary statements. *Fundamental accounting principle* covers such issues as going concern or materiality.

Having established the interaction issue type, we have used two additional descriptive labels for the decision type. The first, *compliance*, refers to interactions where the regulatory framework prescribes how the issue should be treated in the accounts. The other, *judgement*, is used for matters like valuations where no prescriptive pronouncements can be made although a process for making the judgement may be set out in the

relevant accounting standards. Sometimes an interaction can have elements of both of these. For example, if an accounting standard requires that an item is recognized in the balance sheet, that is a compliance issue, but the valuation attached to it must be a matter of judgement. The precise wording of a mandated disclosure will also involve judgement.

4.5.4   The Outcomes

The outcomes of those financial reporting interactions which are compliance issues have been classified as compliant or non-compliant. This classification has been assigned according to whether the outcome complies fully with the regulatory framework ruling at the time of the relevant transaction *and does not make any judgement as to the quality of that framework*. This is the same classification basis as was used in Beattie *et al.* (2001). Where an outcome is a matter of judgement it is not possible to evaluate the quality of the judgement but it is possible to consider it in terms of compliance with the process of reaching the judgement.

4.6   WITHIN-CASE ANALYSIS

Having established a basic set of categories and labels to use for the local contexts, interactions and outcomes, we were able to proceed with the in-depth, within-case analyses. For each case we identified the local contextual factors that appeared to influence the nature and outcome of all the interactions. These are both described in the text and are summarized in diagrammatic form in each case chapter.

In the fourth section of each case chapter, local contextual factors are identified and commented upon and each interaction that occurred is analysed separately and appropriate labels attached to its type and outcome. This within-case analysis looks for local context, causal conditions, intervening conditions, tactics and strategies and consequences associated with each interaction. This allows the fit of the existing grounded theory to each interaction to be assessed.

A concluding fifth section to each chapter summarizes the main issues that emerge from the case.

4.7   TABULAR SUMMARY OF CASES

To provide a preliminary overview of the key features of each case we present the general local context and interaction issues in each of the nine cases in Table 4.1. Certain aspects of the table only emerged during the analysis stage. Each case is titled using a changed company name, with these fictitious names themed on bird species. The names of the key individuals in each case have also been changed.

Table 4.1   Overview of cases: general context and interactions

Case name & no.	Co. size	Audit firm type[1]	Quality of relationships	Audit committee attributes[2]
Sandpiper, Case 1	Large	B4	CFO/AEP poor ACC/AEP satisfactory ACC/CFO good	4 members; 3+ meetings/yr; no pre-meeting but regular contact; Meet without execs present; Others attending: CEO, CFO, Chair, other execs, auditor welcome; ACC financially literate but not CCAB
Kestrel, Case 2	Large	B4	Good	3 members; 4+ meetings/yr; pre-meetings; Meet without execs present; Others attending: CEO, CFO, Chair; ACC financially literate (CCAB); others financially literate with business experience
Mallard, Case 3	Large	B4	Good; improved since risk profile went down	5 members; 6+ meetings/yr; informal pre-meeting Meet without execs present Others attending: CEO, CFO, DFD,[5] auditors, internal auditors, others as needed;[6] Chair;[7] ACC financially literate (CCAB plus one other); others less financial expertise but business knowledge
Finch, Case 4	Small	B4	Good	3 members; 3 meetings/yr; pre-meetings; Meet without execs present; Others attending: CEO, CFO; ACC financially literate (CCAB); others less financial expertise but business knowledge

Reporting style	Key interaction issues	Interaction attributes		
		Interaction type[3]	Issue type[4]	Decision type[8]
Compliant but don't like aspects of IFRS	S1. Audit fees	N	A	n/a
	S2. Accounting treatment of costs associated with a major change in the company's computer system	N	M	C/J
	S3. Re-organization costs	N	CL	J
	S4. Inventory provisions	N	M	J
	S5. Dividends from subsidiaries	D	CL	C
	S6. Pension liabilities	N	M	J
Compliant but don't like aspects of IFRS	K1. Valuation of intangibles on acquisition	N	R/M	C/J
	K2. Impairment reviews	N	M/DI	J
	K3. Financial instruments — treatment of preference shares	N	CL	C
	K4 Financial instruments — hedging	D	R/M	C/J
	K5. Re-organization costs	D	CL	J
	K6. Fraud and illegal acts	D	A	n/a
Conservative but don't like aspects of IFRS	M1. Audit fee	N	A	n/a
	M2. Accounting for a complex transaction	N	R/M	J
	M3. Business Review	D	DI	J
	M4. Financial instruments — hedging	N	R/M	C/J
	M5. Going concern	D	FP	J
	M6. Impairment of assets	D	M	J
Compliant but don't like aspects of IFRS	F1. Audit fees following a tender	N	A	n/a
	F2. Notional interest on unwinding of deferred consideration	N	M/DI	C/J
	F3. Earnings per share	D	DI	C
	F4. Share-based payments	N	R	C
	F5. Treatment of tax credits on exercise of options	N	M/DI	C
	F6. Revenue recognition and provisioning on contracts	D	R/M	J
	F7. Valuation of intangible assets on acquisition	D	R/M	C/J
	F8. Segmental reporting	D	DI	J
	F9. Business Review	D	DI	J

(*Continued*)

Table 4.1   (*Continued*)

Case name & no.	Co. size	Audit firm type[1]	Quality of relationships	Audit committee attributes[2]
Cormorant, Case 5	Small	NB4	CFO/ACC satisfactory/ Others good	3 members; 3+ meetings/yr; pre-meetings and regular contact; Meet without execs present; Others attending: CEO, CFO, Chair; ACC financially literate (CCAB); others less financial expertise but business knowledge
Pochard, Case 6	Large	B4	Good	3 members; 3 meetings/yr; pre-meetings; Meet without execs present; Others attending: CFO, Chairman; ACC financially literate (CCAB); others less financial expertise but business knowledge
Woodpecker, Case 7	Small	NB4	Good	3 members; 3 meetings/yr; pre-meetings; Meet without execs present; Others attending: CFO, Group FD; ACC CCAB qualified; others financially literate and business knowledge
Raven, Case 8	Large	B4	Good	3 members; 6+ meetings/yr; pre-meetings; Meet without execs present; Others attending: CFO, internal auditors, head of compliance; financial controller, others as necessary; ACC financially literate (CCAB); others with a range of business experience

Reporting style	Key interaction issues	Interaction attributes		
		Interaction type[3]	Issue type[4]	Decision type[8]
Conservative but don't like aspects of IFRS	C1. Identification of intangibles on acquisition	D	R/M	C/J
	C2. Impairment goodwill on acquisition	D	M	J
	C3. Deferred tax asset resulting from losses in subsidiary	D	M	J
	C4. Provision on inventories	D	M	J
	C5. Business Review	D	DI	J
	C6. Misreporting in subsidiary	D	M/CG	J
Compliant but don't like aspects of IFRS	P1. Presentation of cash flow statement	N	CL	J
	P2. Inventory valuation	D	M	J
	P3. Contingent liabilities	D	DI	J
	P4. Fair value of lease on acquisition	D	M	J
	P5. Re-organization costs	D	CL	J
	P6. Segmental reporting	D	DI	J
	P7. Control weakness	D	CG/DI	J
Conservative as wish to protect brand; don't like aspects of IFRS	W1. Inventory valuation	D	M	J
	W2. Breach of internal controls in overseas subsidiary	D	CG	n/a
	W3. Valuation of intangibles on acquisition	D	R/M	C/J
Compliant but don't like aspects of IFRS	R1. Accounting for a complex transaction	N	R/M	J
	R2. Disclosures relating to potential future losses in a subsidiary	N	R/M/DI	J
	R3. Business Review	D	DI	J

(*Continued*)

Table 4.1   (*Continued*)

Case name & no.	Co. size	Audit firm type[1]	Quality of relationships	Audit committee attributes[2]
Ostrich, Case 9	Small	Not disclosed	Good but strained by late adjustment	3 + meetings/yr; Others attending: CEO, CFO & AEP attend all AC meetings; ACC financially literate (CCAB)

Notes:
1. B4 = Big Four auditor; NB4 = Non-Big Four auditor.
2. CCAB denotes that the ACC holds an accounting qualification recognised by the Consultative Committee of Accountancy Bodies.
3. D = discussion; N=negotiation.
4. FP = fundamental principle; R = recognition; M = measurement; CL = classification in a primary statement; DI = disclosure; CG = corporate governance; and A = audit.

Reporting style	Key interaction issues	Interaction attributes		
		Interaction type[3]	Issue type[4]	Decision type[8]
Compliant but don't like aspects of IFRS	D1. Identification of intangibles on acquisition	N	R/M	C/J
	D2. Share-based payments	D	R/M	J
	D3. Business Review	D	DI	J
	D4. Segmental reporting	D	DI	J

5. DFD = deputy finance director.
6. Others include internal auditor, risk manager.
7. O = occasionally attends.
8. C = compliance related outcome; J = judgement related outcome.

Case 1 — Sandpiper plc

The partner is technically very competent. I think it is the presentation of the issues which he hasn't been crisp enough about *(Duncan, audit committee chair)*

5.1 BACKGROUND TO THE CASE

Sandpiper plc is a listed retail company with a wide ranging global market. Sales had been declining in the UK and there had recently been a change of finance director following the early retirement of the previous incumbent.

Duncan, the chair of the audit committee has a wide range of experience in the financial sector in the City and is a well respected figure outside the company. He is not an accountant. He runs the audit committee effectively. The new finance director, Stuart is a new broom intent on establishing himself and improving the company's systems and reporting effectiveness. The audit partner, Patrick, from a Big Four firm, had been in post for some time and was soon due to rotate off. Stuart found Patrick a bit difficult to work with although this was not considered to be an obstacle to the quality of the accounting.

A key issue for the group was a structural re-organization to make it more cost effective and this was accompanied by the introduction of a major new IT system which had cost a lot more than the board had expected. There was a strong culture in the company to contain costs, including audit fees.

5.2 CORPORATE GOVERNANCE

According to the relevant financial statements the board consisted of four executive directors and four non-executive directors. There were no disclosures which indicated that the company did not comply fully with the Combined Code. All non-executive directors were members of the audit committee which met at least three times a year and dealt with risk management as well as financial reporting and internal control, including internal financial control. Stuart, Duncan and Patrick talked at length about how the process worked.

5.2.1 Attendees at the Audit Committee

Some changes to audit committee attendance had been made to ensure all directors were fully informed about what was happening. Parties other than the members of the audit committee attended the audit committee meetings. Duncan explained the need to ensure all non-executives were members of the audit committee:

> The four independent directors are all members of the committee and turn up for the meetings. For a period of two years we only had three of the four independents on the audit committee but we decided it was better to have all of them on. So that all board members had the same level of information about auditing matters. (**Duncan**)

A number of others also attended the meetings at Duncan's request:

> The chairman also attends but is not a member. When I took over the chair I said I expected the two executive directors, the CEO and the finance director, to attend because otherwise we found that the finance people were talking to each other without the management. And we also have the company secretary who is the secretary of the committee. Where relevant the head of internal audit and, at all bar one meeting, the external auditor and often his manager. The meeting is also attended, I should have said, by the financial controller. (**Duncan**)

Prior to this change Patrick also had concerns about the way the audit committee worked:

> Now all the non-execs are members of the audit committee, but there was a time when some were on the remuneration committee and some were not and you found that everyone was milling around, so they joined you and they listened from the corner. The non-execs became more and more involved in the decision-making. And one of the conversations I had with the previous chairman was that he needed to change the … relative numbers of non-execs and execs on the board, because we were getting overwhelmed by the sheer number of questions that were emerging there. You were sitting there more in a supervisory nature. (**Patrick**)

Duncan considered it was normal for others to be present at the audit committee meetings:

> But I would think that is normal. I mean the other audit committee that I sit on, which is [company name], has the same sort of attendance with the external auditors, financial controller, finance director, the chief executive, the chairman and the non-executive directors. (**Duncan**)

He reflected on the dynamics of the meetings when there are a number of non-member attendees:

> When I was chairman of a company, I definitely took the view that I wanted to attend the audit committee so that I knew what was going on. Yes, it will change the dynamics to some extent. A meeting with ten people around the table is going to be different than a meeting with four people around the table but nevertheless I think that all the non-executive directors wished them to be present. So, while it may marginally change the dynamics, the important thing is to have the right people round the table. (**Duncan**)

Patrick referred to his engagement with the audit committee:

> It works as you would expect for a company of this size. It is quite formal, it meets up to six times a year, I typically attend three of those meetings. (**Patrick**)

Stuart took comfort from the fact that part of the audit committee meeting took place without executives present:

> What they do have is a session with the auditors without management and that is their opportunity to raise anything. I think it is fair to say that, from Duncan, I have never got any feedback on that. It implies that there wasn't anything that had come to light. (**Stuart**)

Patrick also referred to this as a safety measure:

> We also have at the end of it obviously an opportunity where the company executives have left the room, and if there is anything particular that we wish to raise with them, so we have that opportunity to have a discussion. (**Patrick**)

5.2.2 Cycle of Meetings

There was a pre-determined cycle of meetings for the year. Stuart described the schedule:

> We have three or four audit committee meetings and we have nine board meetings. We have one at the half year, one at the full year, one in July and one in February. All but one of those are at the same time as the board, on the same day. (**Stuart**)

Risk was taken very seriously in the company and discussed with the auditor. The company had very open processes and Patrick was welcome to attend any audit committee he wished to. He also had meetings with the chief executive. Regular contact was maintained with Patrick throughout the year at different levels within the company.

The first meeting in the annual cycle was the risk assessment meeting which Patrick normally attended because of its implications for the audit going forward:

> The cycle starts in July where they have almost a full day ... it is a meeting to consider business risks, in the wider sense. Risk is not formally delegated to the audit committee because it is a board matter but, nevertheless, at a practical level the audit committee do it because there are a number of internal forms which are completed. I attend that because at the tail end of that meeting we then consider its implications for the audit and the scoping for the current year. (**Patrick**)

Patrick's firm had also encouraged the company to address risks, in particular fraud risk:

> We have also encouraged them to think about risks, including fraud risks and [are] asking them to document why they think these are properly managed. (**Patrick**)

Duncan also referred to the risk analysis being presented to the main board:

> We go through the full works in relation to the risk map and whether the audit committee think we have the risks in the right pockets, whether we think the risk processes are adequate, and we talk about the internal audit and all those things, assurance generally and we report back to the board for the board to consider the major risks which we have reduced to four or five with the auditor present . . . We are talking about all risks. **(Duncan)**

Patrick revealed that planning for the next audit begins very soon after the end of the previous one with the production of a workplan and strategy document. These are initially agreed with Stuart:

> Yes, I would review it and before it goes the audit partner and I would have talked about it, had our input. So that is what generally happens . . . and the strategy goes to the audit committee. There is generally not a lot of input on the strategy. **(Stuart)**

Duncan discussed his role in the process:

> They write to us. They produce a document which sets out what they think the key issues are likely to be in the audit which they come and talk to me about and they present to the audit committee. They say this year we are going to look at a, b, c, d, e and f because we think those are the key issues and then after the audit we get a letter saying . . . what had turned up out of the audit, what are the key matters that have arisen. **(Duncan)**

Patrick knew he would be able to attend any meeting and before each meeting he had a discussion with Duncan about the agenda:

> I could attend all the meetings, if I chose to. What typically happens is that when there is a meeting Duncan will call me and just confirm that either I am attending or seek my agreement that there is no particular reason for me to attend. Typically the late January, early February one I wouldn't attend and probably have a very short discussion with Duncan to confirm that that is appropriate. **(Patrick)**

However, in the current year Patrick planned to attend this meeting:

> This particular year, because they were looking at their treatment of both [revenue recognition] and pension accounting, and doing something internally to try and manage pension costs. They had been in discussion with the trustee, so I will be attending, but usually I wouldn't go to a meeting such as that. **(Patrick)**

The most important meeting for Patrick was, unsurprisingly, the meeting to agree the financial statements:

> The main meeting is essentially the end of May, which is the annual report just prior to the announcement. Typically end of May, early June. It tends to play across a pretty orderly cycle. **(Patrick)**

5.2.3   The Chairman's Management of the Audit Committee and Key Relationships

Duncan was an experienced and financially knowledgeable chairman. He managed the audit committee and its relationship with the auditors to ensure that he was in control and informed of all developments.

Duncan referred to his own style in managing issues. He also commented on recent contact with audit committee members:

> I spoke to two members of the committee on the telephone in the last 24 hours. I am not in touch with them every 24 hours but it so happens that I have today. If there are any contentious issues I would talk to them. I normally talk to the one who is the accountant before the meeting to make sure that he hasn't got any issues that trouble him having read the papers. (**Duncan**)

The internal auditor was required to contact him about weak reports:

> In the last week the internal auditor rang me up. Unusually there was a weak internal audit assessment which was in fact to do with an IT system in [country] and I am due to ring him back about it. But it is a standing requirement that he has to get in touch with me if there is a weak audit report. (**Duncan**)

He also had a standing arrangement with Patrick:

> The audit partner, he comes to see me before the six month and full year results and goes through his management letter with me. ... The sort of things that they talk to me about, they bring to the committee. But if they didn't one would ask them to do so. (**Duncan**)

Duncan effectively acted as a filter for the audit committee:

> So, yes, if either the internal auditor or the external auditor or the finance director or any of the members has issues they would be in touch with me. I tend to deal with them myself, yes. But I am obviously conscious of them at the meeting and I make sure that if they are relevant they are aired. (**Duncan**)

He also made sure that the chief executive is involved where necessary:

> And I as chair make sure that if there are issues that affect the running of the company that we get a response from the chief executive not just from the finance director. (**Duncan**)

Stuart referred to his relationship with the audit committee. He did not wish to take disagreements with the auditors to the audit committee:

> Generally, if it is about the year-end issues, it has all come through before. My aim is that when I'm going with something, the auditors are fine with it, otherwise it is a red flag for the audit committee. That is always the aim unless there is something current that comes up at the audit committee. **(Stuart)**

He also described his relationship with Duncan as audit committee chair. Matters are dealt with as they go along via the board meetings:

> It is issue driven ... as and when there are issues that come up. I see him at board meetings so, if there are issues that I have got or he has got we raise it there at that point. Yes, so anything he has got a concern with he'll make me aware and we discuss what we are going to do about it. **(Stuart)**

Patrick did not attend main board meetings but had contact with the chief executive and the chairman through the audit committee:

> I don't go to the board meetings. The board meetings typically follow the audit committee meetings. But at the audit committee all the board members, even if they are not members of the audit committee are present, so in effect I know all the board members. **(Patrick)**

He also met with the chief executive and the chairman on separate occasions, not always about financial reporting issues:

> Typically I would see the chief executive three times, obviously for the two halves, plus I had a meeting with him recently, in January where we talked about the business, but unrelated to the financial reporting sense. He was interested in having another view and I got one of my colleagues who is a specialist in that area to join me for that meeting. Then I would typically see the chairman in connection with the annual process. So, there is actually interaction outside of the formal meetings. **(Patrick)**

However, Patrick did want to make sure that when major issues were coming up, Duncan was alerted to them. There was obviously much more contact with Duncan when major issues arose. Patrick referred specifically to the IFRS conversion.

> If there is a particular issue he wants to talk to me about, he will call me. During the IFRS conversion process, which is a very technical one, there were one or two conversations which were largely to inform him of things that were developing, as opposed to seeking his opinion on these matters, because obviously, in due course, the company would prepare papers which they would circulate for discussion. **(Patrick)**

Patrick also kept in regular phone contact with Stuart and the financial controller:

> Every alternate month I have a regular call with Stuart and the group financial controller and we talk about things that have emerged. **(Patrick)**

Duncan believed the company processes were open:

> But it is very open, which I think is absolutely critical in any company ... and there has
> never been any suggestion that any information is held back from the audit committee.
> **(Duncan)**

Patrick agreed that the company had an open style and wanted to do the right thing:

> It is actually an organization that at all levels, not just the audit committee, has a pretty
> open discussion on all things. It isn't the sort of organization where the objective is —
> what is the minimum we can do? It is the sort of organization that looks for the right
> thing that they should do. Then the only thing is — have we the right issues getting to
> the table? And that is where the responsibility is essentially shared. **(Patrick)**

Duncan believed that little has changed in the process for some time:

> I think it has been, by memory, much like this for a long time — since 2000. **(Duncan)**

5.2.4   The Nature of the Relationship

Stuart believed overall that the nature of the relationship had changed because of the
increased complexity of the reporting regime, and that Patrick's authority had been
undermined because of his increased dependence on his firm's technical department.
Patrick explained how he believed the relationship worked:

> I think there is very heavy reliance on me to summarize for the non executives. If anything
> goes awry then they can blame you. I think there is that, and I think there is quite a lot
> of reliance on the group financial controller to get things done in the first instance, and
> then for us to do our bit in the next instance. I think that is the primary. ... On the other
> hand, when issues have surfaced or been raised, discussed, they are discussed in a pretty
> objective manner. **(Patrick)**

He thought that quality of staff was a key concern for Stuart and Duncan:

> Competence of staff. They talk mainly about the people. It is a small head office and they
> want to make sure ... but actually we have had fairly good continuity on their account
> from year to year. **(Patrick)**

He believed that reliance on the auditor had generally increased, because of the
increased complexity of the regulatory environment, particularly the accounting:

> More reliance on auditors. Yes, absolutely. You would say it is a high key fact, a very
> important fact. **(Patrick)**

Stuart, however, felt that Patrick placed too much reliance on his firm's technical
department:

> So I have definitely seen that going to the technical department has grown since IFRS
> ... seems to be the way. **(Stuart)**

Patrick acknowledged that he had to make use of his firm's technical department and things had changed considerably:

> Our technical departments are infinitely more specialist than they were 10, 15, 20 years ago. Twenty years ago every partner would say to you — I can probably get the right answer by using my business experience, today most partners will say, on retirement — thank God that that is at least something I won't have to do. **(Patrick)**

He attributed the change to added volumes of material and the complexity which they had to deal with:

> It has changed it in the sense that I seek their involvement more than I might have in the past simply because of the volume of material . . . that is one issue. If the only thing that I ever did was read technical material, I could absorb it in the timeframe. It is a shorthand, involving specialists at the right time, at one level. And on the other hand, it is also difference of view. If you are already starting from the position that this is all terribly complicated, you can understand why. **(Patrick)**

Stuart felt that audit partners no longer had authority:

> But now there is a certain amount that the audit partner can agree himself, which I think in reality is pretty small, pretty routine stuff. The big stuff, they immediately go to the technical department. I would never have dreamt ten years ago of asking the audit partner if he had authority. **(Stuart)**

Furthermore, he believed that auditors did not like to be challenged on their lack of authority:

> They don't like that question. They don't want to acknowledge it. They are trying to do a job and we are reliant on them, but it is very important to know when you are having a discussion with someone whether they do have the authority or not, because you want to know whether he makes this decision or am I briefing him on an issue which he is then going to brief internally. **(Stuart)**

Stuart felt that the regime under IFRS was very different than it had been before:

> It is IFRS because it seems much more rules-based than principles. So therefore the scope for looking at the principles and making an all round decision seems to be much less . . . I don't understand every IFRS and I don't think our partner does. No-one in the technical department knows it all, but they obviously have elements which know in depth in each area, and that is the way it is. **(Stuart)**

He thought that the audit inspection regime had also changed auditor behaviour and they were more cautious:

> I think given the scrutiny that they get from external bodies . . . they feel that they have to go through the right process; they feel they need to document what goes on, etc, etc. That means that there is an element of process that they have to do, that they have to be seen to document. **(Stuart)**

Stuart felt that the relationship worked better at the auditors' head office level but there was too much focus on trivia and not on the big issues:

> The head office team, in terms of the team that does the work, and the team here, that works really well. What maybe doesn't work ... the tensions tend to be around this balance between the big issues and, what are seen by us to be, small issues. How much of that is down to the individuals on their side and how much is down to the new world we live in is a good question. (**Stuart**)

He felt that some of the difficulties related to the regulatory regime:

> There is a nervousness at the back of their minds about whether they ... not only did make the right decision, did they ask all the right people? There are no prizes for them, particularly for making a call on stuff. That is the sense I get from them. (**Stuart**)

Stuart reflected further on the role of audit partners under the existing regulatory framework:

> My view on the role of the audit partner is that it has changed quite a bit and I think they are probably as busy, if not busier than they ever were, and probably financially doing as well as they ever were, but in terms of the job satisfaction? I have a friend who is a partner in one of the big firms and that is what he says, he has never been busier, never made more money, but the satisfaction of the work has gone down. And the tension that there can be between the client and him has gone up. (**Stuart**)

5.2.5   Satisfaction with Auditors and Partner Changes

Both Duncan and Stuart referred to the importance of a good relationship with their auditor and considered it was their prerogative to ask for a change of partner if they were not satisfied with the incumbent. Stuart then explained a problem in an overseas country where they had changed the audit partner:

> It is the relationship. In [foreign country] [there was] an issue so we have had to send the financial controller out in the last few years to resolve the issue. We did actually decide to change the partner in one place but I would hasten to add that it was 50/50 between their issue and our issue. We have done that, but generally things work pretty well. (**Stuart**)

Duncan was not entirely satisfied with Patrick's performance in presenting information to the audit committee, although Duncan considered him to be technically competent.

> I think they are all technically very competent and I think the partner is technically very competent. I think it is the presentation of the issues which he hasn't been crisp enough about. (**Duncan**)

Duncan too considered partner change to be the company's prerogative:

> I think that by not being very crisp about things they are making it a less efficient process than it should be and I think we are going to have a debate about whether we ask them to change the audit partner before the end of the five years. **(Duncan)**

Both Duncan and Stuart explained that, as a matter of course, an auditor appraisal process was carried out within the company each year:

> Every year, after the audit, we send out a questionnaire to each of the people involved on our side and we get them to give feedback and score. Generally the score out of five is two and a half, so it is OK. Some areas are higher some are down at the one and a half, two level. But overall the feedback is OK. I doubt that many companies would say their auditors were fine. You have to be realistic. **(Stuart)**

Duncan explained the source of the assessment questionnaire:

> As it happens the questionnaire is based on something I have been given by [name of audit firm] so it seems quite a sensible questionnaire. **(Duncan)**

Duncan explained his role in the assessment process:

> Well, every year we have an assessment of the performance of the external auditors and that is done by the finance director who gets in touch with the heads of the finance departments round the world and they are given a little questionnaire and they respond. The group financial controller does a note for the audit committee saying what the overall assessment is and we discuss it at the audit committee and then we talk to the external auditors. I speak directly to the partner of the audit firm about it. **(Duncan)**

He also thought that a company should be able to choose its audit partner and not just be given one by the firm, which had happened with Patrick's appointment before he became audit committee chair:

> And I didn't chair the audit committee when the current partner was appointed and I think we were only given one other person to talk to when the previous partner rolled over. I think elsewhere, and nowadays, always one would wish to see at least two people, not just be given one, to choose from. **(Duncan)**

Duncan thought that audit partner character was very important:

> Usually I think a lot of it, as always, is personality, not necessarily how good they are technically, which one will discover later, but how commercial and how strong their personality is. **(Duncan)**

5.3   KEY INTERACTIONS BETWEEN STUART, DUNCAN AND PATRICK

During the course of the audit a number of issues prompted interactions between the interviewees. Of the six interactions reported below, the first interaction was audit related and was about fee negotiations and the other five related to financial reporting issues.

1. Audit fees.
2. The accounting treatment of costs associated with a major change in the company's accounting system.
3. Re-organization costs.
4. Inventory provisions.
5. Accounting for dividends from subsidiaries.
6. Pension liabilities and the accompanying assumptions.

5.3.1 Audit Fees

Because the audit committee was not entirely happy with Patrick as their engagement partner, they were considering holding a tender for the audit when his five year term was up. The same concerns also meant that agreement of the audit fee caused friction.

Duncan asserted that the company was cost conscious:

> We are concerned about cost, as all companies are, and we need to be persuaded that it has been done in the most efficient way. (**Duncan**)

Patrick explained that because the company had many overseas operations setting the fees was done at local levels:

> Because most of the countries around the world are all statutory audits, therefore it is a local matter. Obviously, there are some countries either where there is some service issue or alternatively an increase does look unusual and ... their group controller will have prior discussions. But once it is settled locally it comes up, and the end result is not gigantically different. (**Patrick**)

He explained the need to get agreement at local level for overseas fees:

> But the emphasis is — please settle this locally, because we do not want to waste a lot of time at the centre having to agree it. And I certainly don't want to be in a position where I agree one group fee and then I just allocate, because you just end up with service issues everywhere. History tells you that. (**Patrick**)

Duncan described how fees were linked to how many overseas operations were visited and how additional costs could be incurred in some countries:

> We agree with the auditor each year which particular countries they will visit, ... and the audit partner will visit ... One additional expense is in [European Country] as their response to Enron is to require all companies to produce statutory quarterly accounts, audited, so we have to spend an extra £X thousand or something a year getting local accounts audited which otherwise we wouldn't do in terms of materiality. (**Duncan**)

It was Stuart's role to negotiate a fee with Patrick and make a recommendation to the audit committee:

> Well, it goes to the audit committee as a recommendation or not as the case may be. I am not in a position to agree the audit fee but clearly in terms of all the discussion and negotiation going up to it, then, that is done with me. **(Stuart)**

In Stuart's second year in the company, he was not entirely comfortable with the fee proposed by Patrick and couldn't get him to move on it, so he took a proposal he didn't fully support to the audit committee:

> Well, I've done two. They agreed with the first. With the second one I had got to a point with the auditor ... I wasn't particularly happy with what he was proposing ... and I thought I had pushed him as far as I could, so, I needed some extra support. So the last proposal wasn't fully endorsed by me. The first one was. I have never had a fee that I recommended that hasn't been agreed. But I didn't particularly agree this last one. **(Stuart)**

Stuart was concerned that the audit committee would not accept the fee as they were cost conscious:

> I thought it was a bit too high. I didn't think the audit committee would agree to it. They are preoccupied by fees. Ask Duncan. **(Stuart)**

Patrick explained that what had happened was unusual:

> This year was a little different. This is where it is unusual. The audit committee was asking Stuart to effectively renegotiate with us, because a new member of the committee was of the view that the fees were high. **(Patrick)**

He did not understand that Stuart had instigated the review and found it unusual that the audit committee appeared to be interfering:

> To me it was quite curious because normally audit committees are supervisory organizations and therefore not directing executive members ... Stuart was clearly embarrassed by the whole thing. It was presented to me as — I'm only doing what I have been asked to do, which is a little different. **(Patrick)**

Duncan did not consider the auditors' fee calculation process was transparent enough for the company:

> I think it is a rather 'cost plus' mentality in the audit firms and it is quite difficult to pin down exactly what is going on. It is all broken down between totals and percentage increases as against the previous year, and explanations for them, and a total increase on a comparable basis and a total increase on a special basis if there were any special jobs in one year as against the other year. There is always a reason for it but you are never quite sure whether there has been a change in the breakdown between partner work and manager and non-manager work. **(Duncan)**

He was also unhappy that he had been unable to establish what the salary inflation rate used was:

> We weren't actually told ... what their salary inflation level was and because of competition you can't tell, but I did find out at [another company] what the salary inflation level was, so you do the best you can. **(Duncan)**

Both sides benchmarked their fees against competitors. Patrick believed that the fee was relatively low:

> So, what we do, in the end, is catalogue a pile of other (similar) companies and it comes out that this is pretty much a bottom quartile, which is what I know. It is a very tight fee that we do ... I sent the information back to them and that is the end of the matter. Next year is another one. **(Patrick)**

Duncan indicated what the audit committee did to benchmark:

> We look at what [competitor company] are paying and the people round the table will have their own experience of what they are paying elsewhere and the relative complexities of the companies. **(Duncan)**

Duncan had been irritated by an earlier attempt by Patrick to charge for the additional costs of meeting the requirements of the FRC Audit Inspection Unit:

> Two or three years, they wished to charge us an extra £15,000 for the trouble of dealing with the AIU. I said that the reason that they are doing that is because of deficiencies in the accounting profession. Can't possibly expect us to pay. **(Duncan)**

Stuart was also aware of the firm's attempts to charge more because of additional regulatory requirements:

> You certainly hear that in fee discussions and them justifying their higher fees and all the rest of it. Because they have to not only do the process but document it because they get hauled up and all the rest of it. **(Stuart)**

Duncan's dissatisfaction with the fee was linked to his misgivings about the relationship:

> The finance team has spent a lot of time sort of grinding down the figures to something like a 5.5% increase but we have expressed our unhappiness about the [name of Patrick's firm] relationship. **(Duncan)**

He suggested that a different tactic should be taken with the auditors:

> I suggested that instead of us saying — will you just knock off £10,000 or something — we should say to them — your position is a bit rocky, you'd better consider what you really wish to charge us. **(Duncan)**

The audit committee was considering holding a tender when Patrick rotated off the audit:

> We may well feel at the end of this period or conceivably before the end that we wanted to have a tender. **(Duncan)**

Patrick appeared not to be aware of the level of dissatisfaction with the relationship:

> We also, in the last summer, had done a client service review, so there were one or two things that came out of that, but they were quite at the margins, in terms of better communication and so on. **(Patrick)**

A recently appointed audit committee member had been pushing for a tender based on his experience in another company:

> We had a discussion about this at the last audit committee and a new member who is a CEO of another company said that they had recently had a tender and while he and the finance director had been against it they had done. And it had been very worthwhile and the costs had come down quite materially and they were generally pleased with the outcome. **(Duncan)**

Duncan also felt that a tender would settle the market level for the fee:

> It certainly would resolve the issue of whether the fee is high or not. It would either confirm that it is not . . . because it is quite difficult in our mind to answer that question. **(Duncan)**

Stuart was not entirely comfortable with the prospect of an audit tender:

> I am not rushing to do it because they are time consuming. If you change your auditors, that is very time consuming. But we do the benchmarks, if the fee is the same percentage of revenue as us, but you know, if you see the benefit then you should do it. If you look at our fee as a percentage of revenue with other client companies our fee doesn't look fantastic or terrible. **(Stuart)**

However Stuart recognized, as Duncan did, that the only way to find out was to hold a tender:

> They tell us that we have one of the lowest recovery rates so often that we think it is true, so that is another bit of data, but you never know until you do the tender. **(Stuart)**

Despite this, the plan to go out to tender was dropped, but the fee was reduced.

5.3.2   The Accounting Treatment of Costs Associated with a Major Change in the Company's Computer System

The company had made a decision some years earlier to introduce a major change in its IT systems. The system adopted was intended to provide both a core financial system and a transactional system. It was being installed in all locations. Some difficulties arose about the accounting treatment of the costs associated with the project which were much higher than had been expected.[1] A key purpose of installing the new system was to reduce the cost base and create efficiencies going forward. Duncan gave some justification for it:

> For the whole of their European business, it is one IT platform so they have complete visibility of how much stock there is and so on. (**Duncan**)

When Stuart joined the company he found that the costs had greatly exceeded the original proposal:

> Started off end of the last decade so it has gone on for a long time. I found the investment proposal for that which said it would be done in two years and cost [£x] million quid. It actually took us eight years and cost about [£8x] million quid. (**Stuart**)

Duncan and the audit committee were concerned about accounting for the costs:

> And we, the committee, were obviously concerned about the extent to which these costs were being capitalized. (**Duncan**)

Stuart was also concerned about what should be capitalized:

> The thing took longer and cost much more than we would have thought and then there was an issue as time went on primarily around what should we capitalize and what should we write off. And the concern was that it had taken so long, cost so much, we shouldn't capitalize inefficiency ... when we looked at the system we had about [£3x] million sitting on the balance sheet. (**Stuart**)

The audit committee had taken the view that a cap should be imposed on the total spend in each location:

> And we looked very carefully at what we thought the benefits were and we set caps because we were concerned about levels of inefficiency in the spend. We did all that and actually I think that was very sensible because some of these caps bit and what might otherwise have been capitalized was written off against profits. (**Duncan**)

The caps were agreed between the finance director and the audit committee with little input from the auditor, but the audit committee did not automatically accept the recommendations of the finance director and the financial controller:

> I don't think we accepted things just off the face of the finance director's paper and we would have said what sort of caps we thought were appropriate but I don't think we were being pushed by the auditors. I think it was more between the audit committee and the finance director. And the auditors saying that that was an acceptable approach. (**Duncan**)

---

[1] IAS 16 *Plant, Property and Equipment* (PPE) states that PPE should be recognized when the cost of the asset can be reliably measured and it is probable that the entity will obtain future economic benefits from the asset. PPE is measured initially at cost. Cost includes the fair value of the consideration given to acquire the asset and any directly attributable cost of bringing the asset to working condition for its intended use.

As the system went live Stuart considered that the issue of write off[2] became more pressing:

> The question was should we maintain that investment or should we actually write it down because what was clear was that the direct benefits from the system were not going to be as great as we had originally thought. **(Stuart)**

According to Stuart the audit committee were divided on how to treat the level of write off. Some were concerned that writing it all off would indicate that the previous carry forward was over-valued, although it wasn't an issue for him as he had joined the company later:

> Certain members of the audit committee were keen to write it down. It's taken too long, There's an opportunity here just to get rid of the whole thing. Others were very nervous about that in terms of the message that would be sent ... Well, basically if you write something off you are saying that it isn't worth what you said it was. So you've botched it up and they weren't keen to do that. I didn't have quite the same concern. So there was a lot of tension within the audit committee on it. **(Stuart)**

Stuart explained the two accounting treatments being considered:

> Should you support it by direct benefits from the system because if you did then you should write the thing down or do you say it is an intrinsic part of the business and therefore you can support it on the cash flows of the whole business. In the end we went with the latter and therefore we held it. But there was a huge amount of discussion. **(Stuart)**

There was concern from Stuart that in the past they had not received clear advice from the auditors on what the correct accounting treatment should be:

> But what had been happening in the previous few years was that there had been a big push, not quite sure who from, but it was either the audit committee or the auditor or both, to say that you have really got to support this asset by the benefits. So huge exercises went in to see what benefits we were going to get from the system, huge job creation. When I looked at it I thought that was all fine, but actually it had nothing to do with accounting. The accounting is there in the cash flows and the business can support them, so it is fine. So there we are. **(Stuart)**

---

[2] IAS 36 *Impairment of Assets* states that an asset may not be carried on the balance sheet above its recoverable amount. Recoverable amount is defined as the higher of the asset's fair value less costs to sell and its value in use. Value in use is ascertained by estimating future cash flows to be derived from the asset discounted by a pre-tax market rate which takes account of the time value of money and asset specific risk. If the carrying value exceeds the recoverable amount it is considered impaired and the loss is recognized in the profit or loss. While recoverable amount is generally calculated for individual assets, an asset seldom generates cash flows independently of other assets. Therefore, most assets are tested for impairment in groups of assets known as cash generating units (CGUs) (PwC, 2009).

Stuart felt a lot of time had been wasted because of the auditors' requests for information:

> It was a pointless exercise, there was a lot of discussion and quite a lot of friction between me and the auditors because I thought they were leading us down the garden path for a few years making us do this. (**Stuart**)

Duncan was also aware that the auditors had given advice which had not been quite clear:

> But I think it subsequently transpired that we had probably not been precisely complying with the standard and that our treatment was more conservative than the standard. Because the standard says that if something is integral to the whole you just look at the business as a whole so long as . . . etc., etc . . . So some people thought at the end of that process that we hadn't had the clearest advice from the auditors on the standard, but no harm done. (**Duncan**)

Patrick acknowledged that there had been a lot of interaction with the audit committee chair about the issue but did not refer to the possibility that the company may have been misdirected over the accounting treatment:

> Several years ago when we had the project which was costing them a very significant amount of money, we had very many conversations . . . the non-execs became more and more involved in the decision-making. Now that it is out of the way, it is less business critical so we tend to have fewer calls. (**Patrick**)

5.3.3   Re-Organization Costs

Three years earlier the company had committed to taking £Xm out of its cost base by segmenting its customers into different groups and targeting the groups specifically as their needs were different. This was made possible by the new computer system. There would be some upfront costs to do this and some complexity in how the results were presented in the income statements. Stuart described the strategy change:

> When we announced our new strategy about two and a half years ago we said we would do three things, we would have a customer segmentation strategy where we focused on [two] types of customers — and we said we would take about £X million out of the cost base, there would be some one-off costs to get the £X million out and we would do that over a three year period. (**Stuart**)

Duncan explained the issue in more detail:

> They reported one segment. But increasingly in their analyst conversations they talked about [a new business] and that made further disclosure more necessary. (**Duncan**)

He described his concerns about possible analyst reaction:

> But anyway, they present this to the analysts and the point I had been making to them [was] that it was a matter of time before the analysts were going to turn round and

say 'Well, has this strategy worked? Can you show us what the sales growth has been as a result of this?' So they need to start measuring this. So no decisions as yet, but it was really drawing attention to the fact that their strategy was changing and their management reporting was keeping up with it. **(Duncan)**

Stuart wanted to find a way of presenting this change in the accounts:[3]

When I came in, I said that what I wanted to do was to take account of the £X million, to strip that out of the core profit, and that was quite tricky. So after quite a bit of negotiation in the prior year, we came through to this concept where we have profit before tax and something we call headline profit, and the difference between the two is the cost to implement that £X million. **(Stuart)**

Stuart explained Patrick's view:

There was quite a bit of pushback from the auditors on that. In fact they didn't really like it. They didn't want us to do it. They then came up with — you can't call it that — he wanted to call it adjusted profit or something but I said, no, that sounds a bit dodgy to me, I don't like it. I wanted something like underlying profit, he said it's got to be adjusted. **(Stuart)**

Patrick explained his position:

Well, it is what they call headline earnings. So what we try to do is to get them to understand if they are going to do that, they are going to have to do it consistently. What we have now got is ... additional disclosure ... If you look at the primary statements there is now further information to help somebody ... guide somebody towards headline profits. If you then link it back to the analyst presentations you will see where you are. **(Patrick)**

However, Stuart found a way out by talking to another client of Patrick's firm where this treatment had been allowed:

The previous finance director here said he had exactly the same issue with another firm where he is on the audit committee and they were with [same audit firm] and they say if you call it headline that will be fine. So I went to the partner and said I don't like adjusted earnings. You are not prepared to go with underlying. Let's call it headline, and by the way there is another corporate client and they do it, so why are you pushing back on me? **(Stuart)**

Stuart was annoyed by this as he felt another client was being favoured:

I was quite annoyed. I felt that they were doing one thing for another client, why were they not doing it for us. Why did I have to go and embarrass him to do it? It was fortuitous that I happened to bump into [the previous finance director] and talk about the issue and

---

[3] IAS 1 *Presentation of Financial Statements* states that although there is no prescribed format for the financial statements, there are minimum required disclosures. Additional disclosures should be made when they are relevant to an understanding of an entity's financial performance. The nature and amount of income and expense should be disclosed separately where they are material. Disclosure may be in the statement or in the notes. Restructuring costs are cited as an example.

he gave me the example, and I could see that this was not what they were doing with another client and I just did not think that was fair. **(Stuart)**

Patrick referred to the separate issue of how the write offs were presented in the income statement, and how the company was justifying it under headline earnings:

> One of the things is that they have a lot of money they have spent on the implementation [of the new computer system] and they have been trying to explain to people that this is one off, not core. They also made some promises on cost reduction and on the revenue generation. So we have talked about the revenue piece and their strategy. On costs it was like — they are going to take £X million out of our cost base and so they have been spending money to achieve it. **(Patrick)**

5.3.4 Inventory Provisions

As a result of legislative change a number of the items the company was selling could no longer be sold to all customers but could still be made available for some customers engaged in certain types of work. It was therefore necessary to make provisions against this stock.[4] A negotiation arose between Stuart and Patrick when it emerged in year two that the provision may have been too high.
Patrick explained the position:

> This standard which has come in, in Europe, [means that] all their products have to be compliant. Now of course they have got non compliant stock, which you think surely you can just send it back to the suppliers, not with this. So, that is why we have got a provision for it. If they can't sell it, there is a cost of scrapping it. **(Patrick)**

Stuart set out how he approached the issue:

> Anyway this came along. We hadn't really had that kind of change before so we recognized we had a lot of stock which ... was effectively non-compliant stock which we could continue to sell to some customers. So we did a lot of work. We recognized there would be some kind of extraordinary provision that we would need to make because our normal provisions didn't account for this. So we did ... we looked at our crystal ball and we basically took some assumptions in terms of demand over time because we reckoned it would hold up for a while, the first six months, and then it would tail off and then, hopefully after a year, there would be no demand. **(Stuart)**

---

[4] IAS 2 *Inventories* requires cost to be valued at the lower of cost and net realizable value. Cost is defined as 'all costs of purchase, costs of conversion and other costs incurred in bringing the inventories to their present location and condition'. It also requires the cost for items that are not interchangeable to be determined on an individual item basis. Paragraph 28 states that cost may not be recoverable if inventories are damaged, if they have become wholly or partially obsolete, or if their selling prices have declined. The practice of writing inventories down below cost to net realizable value is consistent with the view that assets should not be carried in excess of amounts expected to be realized from their sale or use.

Having prepared an estimate of the necessary provision Stuart cleared it with the audit committee and the auditors:

> That went through the audit committee. It was difficult for the auditors to audit it because it was based on assumptions that were our best guesses at the time. They were no more than that which sort of made it difficult. But actually made it quite easy in a way because you didn't have any history so you could just use our judgement and that was as good as anything else. Nothing had happened before. So that was there and we announced it as did quite a number of others in industry. **(Stuart)**

Duncan referred to the matter going through the audit committee:

> So we had a paper from the finance director on the subject and we put in a provision. **(Duncan)**

The following year, however, matters became a little more problematic for Stuart as his original estimate of the provision was too high:

> The next year we actually had more of a challenge because we had some history and what we had found. What had happened was that we hadn't had the rate of decline in these products that we had planned for the first nine months. So, basically we were off, it looked like we had provided too much. That was the auditor's view. **(Stuart)**

Patrick referred rather vaguely to this issue:

> And they found it quite difficult to manage because on top of that they have got a web site and people are coming on the web site and looking at stock; this is compliant stock and this is non-compliant stock. So, the complexity of ordering rises dramatically. **(Patrick)**

Stuart took a robust line on not wishing to write back the provision:

> Our view was that we would end up at the same point, possibly over a longer period, but we would see a slight decline then a dropping off. And we'll end up with the same provision. We still felt, gut feel, that we probably would end up with a write off but it would maybe take us two years to get there rather than a year which is what we had assumed. So we re-cut our numbers basically ending up at the same point over a longer period. And that was quite difficult to deal with because they had a bit of history, and we hadn't done what we had said, and we were basically supporting the same number. We just said it would take longer. **(Stuart)**

Stuart reinforced his position by getting external evidence:

> We had various arguments about why it would take longer. We had some customer feed back to say what it was, but ultimately people will move away from these products and they will have to be scrapped at the end of the day. And I guess that was a discussion that we had with auditors. In the end they got themselves into a place where they said — I think we can live with it. They were not that happy with it but they can live with it. They don't know any more than we know and we had some other supporting evidence. **(Stuart)**

Patrick made reference to this:

> It comes down to customers. If the customer is merely replacing under a repair then he can continue to buy it, but of course behaviour begins to change pretty quickly — why don't we just use a compliant one? You could, theoretically, take it to another part of the world where [legal change] is not yet in. But one of the interesting things is the speed with which this kind of legislation is being picked up in other parts of the world. People are saying — we don't want your non-compliant stuff. It is quite interesting. (**Patrick**)

Stuart believed that he won the argument with Patrick by producing convincing evidence:

> His only proposal was that we were off the plan, so we're going to have to write back a couple of million. It was the evidence that we produced. He said — it doesn't feel right but you do your work — and we came up with a case and it worked. The quality of the work that we did and the argument won through. But clearly we had a difficult case because what we said the year before hadn't come to pass, but that was no surprise it was no better than finger in the air, and we didn't say it was anything else either. (**Stuart**)

Interestingly, Stuart reports that there was no evidence of conflict by the time it got to the audit committee:

> It wasn't really an issue because we just said we were on this line here. We are now on that line and we are still confident that we will get hit at the end of the day. We've done a lot of analysis. We are comfortable with the analysis that we have done and it all stacks up. It was raised but it wasn't a debate. But that was an example where, if we hadn't done the work, it would have been a massive debate. (**Stuart**)

Duncan had no idea that there had been a conflict:

> I don't think there was any negotiation. They would have satisfied themselves that it was reasonable and I suspect that one of them talked to me before the audit committee so it is not as though we are unreasonable. (**Duncan**)

An interesting final word on this comes from Stuart:

> And it is always difficult for the auditor when there is an element of doubt not to go with the people who are closest to the coal face . . . He lived with it. (**Stuart**)

5.3.5 Dividends from Subsidiaries

The group had committed itself to maintaining its dividend and, therefore, availability of distributable reserves[5] was vital. At a late stage Patrick realized that there was a

---

[5] Companies Act 2005 (in force at the time) defined distributable reserves as accumulated, realized profits, so far not previously utilized by distribution or capitalization, less its accumulated, realized losses, so far as not previously written off in a reduction or reorganization of capital. Public limited companies are subject to an additional restriction in that distributable profits are to be further reduced by any net unrealized losses.

deficiency in one of the subsidiaries paying its dividend up to the holding company. Patrick explained why he had been watchful over distributable reserves:

> Because we had been concerned, because for the last three or four years the dividend has been uncovered, and they had committed themselves to a pretty high dividend . . . whereas their after tax income was less. **(Patrick)**

Stuart explained further:

> We do have distributable reserves but . . . what we want to make sure is that the holding company and the principal subsidiaries . . . are in a net current asset position and actually one of them was very close; it had very low net current assets and one initially had net current liabilities. So the auditor picked that up. **(Stuart)**

Patrick realized the issue was material:

> There was £X million involved, quite a lot of money, that needed to be put into the right box. **(Patrick)**

Patrick thought that individual company issues had been overlooked:

> We had talked about distributable reserves many times, but like all of these things until you get down to look at individual financial statements you don't understand them. This is one of the problems if you are always looking at consolidated information. These are issues that are relevant to individual [company] financial reporting, and simultaneously, you obviously do the subsidiaries they have invested in at head office and make a review of that. They paid out a dividend, how has it been treated in the plc, and if that is an intercompany transfer, well that is not realizable. **(Patrick)**

He also recognized that both sides had overlooked the matter as more junior people had been involved in the work:

> And what also tends to happen is the group controller's attention is all on the consolidated and not the companies which is done by more junior people — and inevitably our side is also more junior because that is just some holding company isn't it . . . You can trip up on company law and dividends because of that. **(Patrick)**

Initially there were concerns that they might have to raise more funding to support the dividend:

> How did they react? I think that once they recognized there was an issue then it was just, how? Because they had to get, potentially, some banking arrangements in place to ensure that they could get the funds, i.e. the company that was paying the funds could actually borrow the money to pay it out, all of this had to be done pretty quickly and it was pretty quickly resolved. **(Patrick)**

Stuart was initially very worried about it as it had come up so late but fortunately the solution was relatively straightforward:

> So that was raised. It was one of those issues where we thought, oh my God, that is going to be a big problem . . . When we looked at it we had actually incorrectly classified

some liabilities between due within one year and due over one year, so actually once we made the correct adjustment we did have net current assets. They brought this issue up because when you get into issues about going concerns, you have to support them. They picked it up; very good point; it was late in the day; we then did quite a lot of work and realized that we had made some incorrect classifications. **(Stuart)**

They all had to move very quickly and Duncan was informed:

I discovered it on Friday and then had to do something over the weekend and Monday. By Tuesday it was resolved as to how we were going to treat it . . . in the meantime Stuart had spoken to Duncan so he was in the loop as to what the issue was. **(Patrick)**

Stuart acknowledged that it had been hot for a short time:

We looked into it and thought we could change that and we were OK. It was an issue quite rightly raised; we worked it through; it was pretty hot for a while but by the time we got to the audit committee it was fine. We have a bit more work to do for the next year and we've done that. **(Stuart)**

Patrick believed some tidying up was needed in the subsidiaries which had been done:

Allied to that you start saying how can I make sure the cash is in the right place. I have got all these strange balances; let us tidy them all up . . . to make it clear what is a funding balance and what is a temporary settlement balance. **(Patrick)**

Duncan had little to say on the matter as it had been satisfactorily resolved before it reached the audit committee:

Dividends from subsidiaries, again, we have had a paper on that. It was brought to the audit committee; it was a pretty straight forward decision. **(Duncan)**

Stuart was not quite so sanguine:

By the time we got to the audit committee we had resolved the issue but we had a bit of a white knuckle ride. One, we hadn't seen it as an issue and point two, initially we didn't know how we were going to find our way through the issue. **(Stuart)**

5.3.6   Pension Liabilities

The UK operation had a significant pensions deficit.[6] There was considerable debate about the mortality assumptions relating to the scheme as they appeared to be out of line with Patrick's firm's expectations. A major problem had emerged in the previous year.

---

[6] IAS 19 *Employee Benefits* required that defined benefit pension plans should recognize a liability in the balance sheet equal to the net of: The present value of the defined benefit obligation (which will incorporate a suitable mortality rate); Deferred actuarial gains and losses and deferred past service costs; and The fair value of any plan assets at the balance sheet date.

Patrick recognized that the main issue lay in the UK:

> They have got a small scheme in country X and country Y which is effectively . . .
> a money purchase. It is really the UK . . . where the majority of the employees are.
> **(Patrick)**

Patrick also believed the pensions issue was important:

> Pensions is a big one because they have got a large pensions deficit, . . . which they then
> reported as a reduction at the half year. **(Patrick)**

Stuart explained that Patrick's firm had a database against which they benchmarked
individual client's pension liabilities:

> Pension has come up on the radar screen for everyone. Auditors and companies alike . . .
> the prior year we had a right ding dong with the auditors on pension scheme assumptions
> which I don't think we had ever had before. They have got this wonderful database which
> plots your assumptions versus the market so you say 'oh right, you are here and the
> market is there' and there are a couple of assumptions that they felt were pretty aggressive
> versus the market, the mortality for example. We weren't assuming people were living
> as long as their benchmark showed. **(Stuart)**

Stuart felt he had been caught out the previous year:

> We didn't think it would be an issue so we didn't focus and so they came back with
> a whole load of questions relative to their database. We didn't even know they had a
> database. So then we had to scurry around getting our arguments and support. At the
> end they were OK with it. It was late in the day. We were surprised. We hadn't realized
> how high it would be on their agenda. **(Stuart)**

Duncan was more circumspect about the 'ding dong':

> We have had, yes, we have certainly had discussions about the appropriate assumptions
> on inflation rates largely because auditors tend to look at the difference between a straight
> bond and an indexed bond and that is not necessarily a correct measure of future inflation
> but it is that sort of discussion and, yes, all the usual things that you talk about, mortality
> rates. **(Duncan)**

Stuart felt that they had been able to address Patrick's previous concerns about
their mortality assumptions by drawing on data local to the company's main
location:

> We had provided a lot of specific data about our scheme because a lot of our people are
> based in [one] area and, if you look at the mortality tables, that is a poor mortality area.
> So, we said that is why. It is not surprising that we are different than the country because
> most of our people are in this poorer mortality area. We had a lot of debate on this; we
> didn't move our numbers; they were OK with it but it took a lot of justification. We were
> right in the process. **(Stuart)**

Duncan also commented on this:

> It so happens that the main operation at [location] is populated by people from the [specific] industry and their mortality is higher than normal. The question is, is that a continual feature or a running-off feature? So we have those discussions. (**Duncan**)

Stuart said the auditors had not recognized the specific mortality issues relating to the location of their main plant:

> We shared all the mortality tables for location and all that . . . No, they didn't know that initially. So we went away and supported our position with the data. So that is what we did the year before. (**Stuart**)

Stuart did not have high regard for actuaries:

> Yes, they got their pension expert to have a look at it . . . Oh, yes, but to get two actuaries to agree on which way is north is impossible at times. (**Stuart**)

Patrick had accepted the arguments about mortality rates:

> Alter some of the life expectancy risks and so on. (**Patrick**)

Stuart was determined not to have another major disagreement on pensions for the current year:

> This year we said that we were not having this merry dance again. Actually, this is stuff we can pre-agree upfront. So what we arranged was that our pension manager and their pension expert would sit down in January and February to go through the assumptions and make sure they were comfortable and that the whole thing was OK. From being an issue it became not an issue because we had done the pre-work. We realized it was going to be a hot button for them. In the prior year we had under estimated their interest in it. (**Stuart**)

Patrick expressed an interesting view about over management of pensions issues:

> And also my experience is that wherever people have forced the issue it has been made much more expensive than if they had kept it under watch and attempted to manage it. (**Patrick**)

5.4 CONTEXTUAL FACTORS AND ANALYSIS OF THE INTERACTIONS

The general contextual factors in Sandpiper are drawn together in Figure 5.1. As can be seen from the diagram, the company was well managed and had a strong and financially literate audit committee chair, Duncan, and a new and assertive finance director, Stuart, who was technically very competent. The audit partner, Patrick, was also competent, reliant to some extent on his firm's technical department and rather

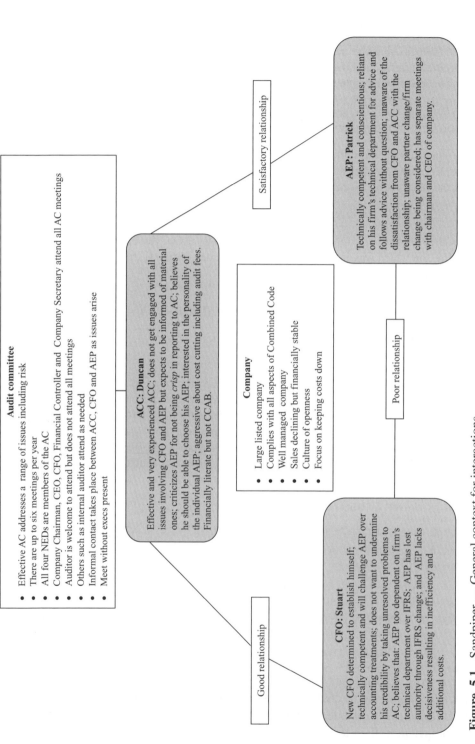

Audit committee

- Effective AC addresses a range of issues including risk
- There are up to six meetings per year
- All four NEDs are members of the AC
- Company Chairman, CEO, CFO, Financial Controller and Company Secretary attend all AC meetings
- Auditor is welcome to attend but does not attend all meetings
- Others such as internal auditor attend as needed
- Informal contact takes place between ACC, CFO and AEP as issues arise
- Meet without execs present

ACC: Duncan

Effective and very experienced ACC; does not get engaged with all issues involving CFO and AEP but expects to be informed of material ones; criticizes AEP for not being *crisp* in reporting to AC; believes he should be able to choose his AEP; interested in the personality of the individual AEP, aggressive about cost cutting including audit fees. Financially literate but not CCAB.

Company

- Large listed company
- Complies with all aspects of Combined Code
- Well managed company
- Sales declining but financially stable
- Culture of openness
- Focus on keeping costs down

AEP: Patrick

Technically competent and conscientious; reliant on his firm's technical department for advice and follows advice without question; unaware of the dissatisfaction from CFO and ACC with the relationship; unaware partner change/firm change being considered; has separate meetings with chairman and CEO of company.

CFO: Stuart

New CFO determined to establish himself; technically competent and will challenge AEP over accounting treatments; does not want to undermine his credibility by taking unresolved problems to AC; believes that: AEP too dependent on firm's technical department over IFRS; AEP has lost authority through IFRS change; and AEP lacks decisiveness resulting in inefficiency and additional costs.

Satisfactory relationship

Poor relationship

Good relationship

Figure 5.1   Sandpiper — General context for interactions

inflexible in setting out technical interpretations to his client. He was not aware that his client was not happy with the relationship.

Duncan did not expect to resolve issues for the auditor or the finance director but wished to have significant problems reported to him as they progressed. He did not want surprises at the audit committee and wanted all relevant parties to be present at the audit committee meetings to ensure that they were informed about what was happening in the company. The auditor, Patrick, was invited to all audit committee meetings but did necessarily not attend every one.

Stuart, the finance director, regarded it as a personal failure if he took an unresolved issue to the audit committee for them to decide. He saw it as his responsibility to sort things out with the auditor before they were reported to the committee and his technical expertise enabled him to challenge Patrick's technical interpretations of IFRS. The auditor, Patrick, was technically competent but reliant to some extent on his firm's technical department. Stuart saw this as a weakening of partner authority.

5.4.1 Audit Related Interaction: Fee Negotiation

Stuart knew that Duncan was cost conscious and had been particularly irritated by Patrick's firm trying to increase fees in a previous year because of the additional costs of the audit inspection regime. Duncan expected Stuart to agree the fee with Patrick and submit it to the audit committee for approval. In his second year at Sandpiper, Stuart was not able by himself to get Patrick to reduce the fee to a level he believed that Duncan and the audit committee would accept. He did not want to propose an unacceptably high fee to the audit committee as it would reflect poorly on him. As he did not want to take unresolved problems to the audit committee, he decided to take the proposal to the audit committee and say he did not support it. Thus, he escalated the issue to the audit committee to get support for his view.

As Stuart expected, Duncan and the audit committee took a hard line. Duncan suggested that Stuart should threaten Patrick with a tender unless he lowered the fee. The fee was rejected by the audit committee and referred back to Patrick, who was told that the objection came from the audit committee not from Stuart. Stuart, therefore, successfully saved face with Patrick by saying that the fee challenge came from the audit committee.

The factors that particularly influenced this outcome were Stuart's desire not to lose face with the audit committee by proposing an unrealistic fee and Duncan's strong resistance to high audit fees. The lack of respect for Patrick arising from the poor quality of the relationship also comes out in the way both Duncan and Stuart behave towards him. Stuart was prepared to misrepresent the position to Patrick and Duncan was prepared to threaten a tender to get his own way.

5.4.2 Financial Reporting Interaction: the Accounting Treatment of Costs Associated with a Major Change in the Company's Accounting System

This interaction was mainly a matter between Stuart, Duncan and the audit committee. The increasing cost for the IT system was a problem before Stuart arrived and the numbers were getting bigger. Before Stuart joined the company, they had been advised by Patrick that each year they needed to value the direct benefits accruing to the company from the system to establish the value of it. This had taken a lot of time and effort to work out and Stuart suggested an alternative methodology could be used based on the cash flows of the whole business. The audit committee was concerned to get the accounting treatment right but also they did not want to show a write off which the investors might interpret as mismanagement of the project. Stuart convinced the audit committee to adopt his view of it. This was a simpler and more pragmatic view of the situation and also more beneficial to the company.

The factors that influenced this outcome were the audit committee's desire not to look as if they had mismanaged the project and Stuart's wish to do the best for the company. Stuart and Duncan both considered they had not had the best advice from Patrick in the past as he had not considered alternative treatments. This had cost them a lot of time and led them to be over prudent in their original valuations. Duncan and Stuart both felt let down, thus undermining respect for Patrick. The interaction was an IFRS interpretation issue combined with judgement as to the valuation.

5.4.3   Financial Reporting Interaction: Re-Organization Costs

This was a disclosure issue which related both to the write off of costs for the computer system and a commitment to their analyst following to reduce their cost base. Patrick had advised that their disclosure plan was not acceptable. Stuart then challenged Patrick's view, initially without success, until he found out from another source that Patrick's firm had allowed another company to do what Stuart was proposing. Stuart was again annoyed by Patrick's initial advice.

This outcome was again influenced by Stuart's wish to do his best for the company and by Patrick's inflexibility in his advice. It shows how Stuart got his own way by a different means — that of finding out another client of Patrick's firm had been allowed to disclose the re-organization costs in the way he wanted to. Patrick, therefore, had to give way. This issue also brings out the flexibility of IFRS in this area of disclosure and was an interpretation issue.

5.4.4   Financial Reporting Interaction: Inventory Provisions

This interaction was about what appeared to be an overprovision on some potentially obsolete inventory for the previous year. Patrick originally wanted Stuart to write it back. Although acknowledging that it was an overprovision, Stuart argued that the total provision was needed but would spread over a longer period of time.

In order to convince Patrick that he did not need to write the provision back, Stuart did a lot of analysis justifying that the overall provision was at the appropriate level and was needed. Patrick accepted this on the basis of the analysis that had been produced.

This interaction shows that another mechanism a finance director can use is to provide strong evidence to justify what he wants to do to the auditor. Inventory valuation is a judgemental area and is not specific to the IFRS environment.

This outcome was again influenced by Stuart's determination to do his best for the company. Interestingly, Duncan was not informed about this as it was resolved satisfactorily between Stuart and Patrick and was not material enough to require a debate at the audit committee.

5.4.5   Financial Reporting Interaction: Accounting for Dividends from Subsidiaries

A mistake was discovered by Patrick at a late stage when he did an overall review of the consolidation and found that the assets available in one of the subsidiaries to pay a dividend up to the holding company were insufficient. Both Stuart and the audit team had missed it. Fortunately, a resolution was found in time which was not difficult to achieve. As this was a potentially serious issue, it was reported to Duncan when it arose in accordance with his expectation that he would be informed about any important issues as they came up.

In this case Patrick helpfully suggested afterwards that a tidying up of the subsidiaries should be carried out to avoid this happening again. Stuart was determined not to have this happen again. Stuart acknowledged that Patrick had found the problem and thus had been helpful to the company. Duncan was not aware how much effort had been involved in resolving it.

The interaction was about an error which had been made which was picked up by the auditor and then put right.

5.4.6   Financial Reporting Interaction: Pension Liabilities

The interaction in this case arose from Patrick's firm's pensions database which checked the company's assumptions against the market norms. This resulted in a challenge to the mortality assumptions in Sandpiper's UK pension fund, which appeared to be out of line. There had been a 'ding dong' the year before and Stuart determined to avoid this in the current year by addressing the problem at an early stage. He then provided evidence to support the assumptions that had been made and agreement was reached.

This interaction was resolved without too much difficulty as Stuart determined to allow plenty of time to deal with it and gathered evidence. It was influenced by Stuart's desire to do the best for the company. This was a judgement issue.

5.5   CONCLUSIONS

The interactions in this case have some interesting features. Patrick was initially inflexible in putting over his (or his technical department's) interpretation of how accounting issues should be treated. He was faced with an assertive and up-to-date finance director who was also determined to make the right impression with the audit committee and not take unresolved issues to them. He also wanted to do the best for the company. This led to a relationship which was confrontational at times.

In two cases (IT system and re-organization costs) Patrick had to back off his original proposal because Stuart came up with legitimate alternatives which were more beneficial to the company. In one case Stuart used as a negotiating tool the evidence of Patrick's firm having allowed another client to do what he wanted to do.

In two other cases (inventory provisions and pension liabilities) which were challenged by Patrick, Stuart produced sufficient strong evidence to justify his position. In order to avoid a last minute problem, Stuart resolved to sort the pensions issue out well before the year-end, thus avoiding a last minute problem. Both these issues were resolved in favour of the company.

In the fifth case Patrick had found an error relating to dividends which had been missed and they all worked together to resolve it.

Apart from the dividend error, all the accounting issues which came up were of a judgemental or interpretational nature. Some interactions were specifically associated with IFRS requirements (IT system, re-organization costs and pension liabilities). Others related to accounting issues which are not unique to IFRS, either errors (dividend problem) or inventory valuation. All outcomes, however, complied with IFRS.

Duncan discharged his role as audit committee chair very competently. Duncan's concerns about audit fee levels enabled Stuart to cover his own position about not having got the fee down enough in his own negotiations with Patrick as he knew that Duncan would support him at the audit committee, whose members were also cost conscious. Duncan was quite aggressive about audit fees, a position which not all audit committee chairs adopt.

This chapter has presented the interesting scenario of a strong and cost conscious audit committee chair combined with an assertive and technically competent finance director standing up to an auditor on technical interpretation of IFRS. In combination, they obtained a better result for the company and also a reduced audit fee, whilst remaining compliant with the accounting requirements.

6

Case 2 — Kestrel plc

So you know when you are dealing with the auditors that not only are they trying to
obviously do the job they are required to do on your audit, but they are also making sure
that they cross all the t's and dot all the i's for when they get that inspection *(Philip,
finance director)*

6.1 BACKGROUND TO THE CASE

Kestrel plc is a manufacturing group which has a number of overseas subsidiaries.
Recent results have been adversely affected by the recession allied with the higher
raw material and energy prices. Because of the nature of the group's activities there
is considerable disposal and acquisition activity.

The Kestrel Group is not tightly controlled centrally and individual subsidiaries
have freedom to set their own procedures.

The finance director is Philip (aged in his 50s), a qualified accountant with experience in a large firm of accountants. He also served as a director in other multinational
companies before joining the board of Kestrel. The audit committee chair is Guy
(also in his 50s) is a qualified accountant who holds a number of other non-executive
directorships and has recent experience of serving as chairman for a PLC. Previously
he has acted as finance director for a major company and has also worked in public
practice. He joined the board of Kestrel relatively recently. Barry (in his 40s), the
audit partner, is a senior audit partner in a Big Four Firm.

6.2 CORPORATE GOVERNANCE

The board of Kestrel has more non-executive directors than directors. Three of the
non-executives serve on the audit committee. No cases of non compliance with the
provisions of the Combined Code are reported in the company's report of corporate
governance.

6.2.1 Audit Committee Attendees

Barry's evaluation of the audit committee was positive:

> They have a very good audit committee . . . It has evolved slightly. They have gone from
> some very experienced audit committee members . . . and they have now replaced them
> with guys who are chief executives or finance directors who are in business. So, they
> are a very knowledgeable audit committee and you have a discussion about things like

impairment or classification or whatever they will immediately resonate with problems they have come across themselves. So, you can end up with discussions on the topic which are outside of Kestrel, sort of industry type discussions. **(Barry)**

Guy was strongly of the view that the other members of the audit committee, who did not necessarily have the same level of financial expertise as he did, made a valuable contribution:

> They won't be involved in all the consultations, but they will listen to the output of those consultations and to some extent they are the general businessman ears and eyes who say that they hear that you technical chaps have gathered in a cluster and come up with this, but actually we don't see it like that, so tell us why you are right ... If you have got all these experts around, what do the other non-execs do who aren't experts? And I think it is that they have got to keep their feet on the ground and listen and say does it make sense. **(Guy)**

He added that the chairman, who attends by invitation, has financial expertise as he is also a qualified accountant.

> [Name of chairman] is quite mischievous. He loves throwing little bombs on the table for people to sort out ... I won't say he is not enjoyable, but he is quite troublesome. You have to be quite firm with him sometimes and say 'Hang on! We're not doing that, we're doing this!' Otherwise he would drag it off somewhere and you don't want that. All these things are very tightly timetabled. **(Guy)**

Barry, who confirmed that he attends, was positive about the attendance of non-members at the audit committee:

> Interestingly, at Kestrel, the chief executive will generally attend all the audit committee meetings by invitation. And indeed the chairman will probably attend. They are not members. And that allows us to have a very good discussion if there is a particular commercial issue that we are discussing ... It raises the tone. **(Barry)**

6.2.2   Cycle of Meetings

Guy considered that the Smith Report had been useful in that it provided a check list which was helpful in setting the agenda:

> There is a bit of a myth that audit committee chairs drive the agenda. The company secretary drives the agenda, so it is them sending the agenda out ... You can go through and give to the company secretary and make sure that during the year I cover all these items ... I'll say 'When was the last time we looked at whistle blowing? When was the last time we looked at fraud?' ... So it is those things that you do intermittently that you have to check on. **(Guy)**

Philip outlined the normal audit planning process at Kestrel:

> Their normal starting point is the previous year, what other stuff do they have to do? What can come of it? ... Typically they would produce a document which is their

scope of work. That will get agreed with the company and then they come along and present it as part of their overall presentation to the audit committee. It is fairly detailed process they go through, but the document that is produced to the audit committee is a summary document. The audit committee typically will say they presume it has been discussed in detail with the management. So we don't trawl through in detail with the audit committee, they delegate the process to the management and the comfort that they get is that the auditor says to the audit committee if we do this work, that is what we need to do to support our opinion. They would normally ask the audit committee if there is anything particular outside of this that they want them to do. **(Philip)**

Guy agreed that the audit committee took on a supervisory role regarding audit and observed that overseeing this could be a fairly onerous task:

> We read it, we are talking about forty odd pages of audit plan . . . One of the bugbears of all the non-execs is the amount of reading we have to do. Because these things land on your desk normally at the same time as the QC report and the board papers so you end up with a big read. **(Guy)**

Philip stated that a similar approach was adopted for agreeing the audit fee and that he was primarily responsible for negotiating with the audit partner:

> On setting fees, I don't know whether this is the experience with other companies, but the audit committees that I have worked with have not wanted to have a discussion about fees. That is for the management to sort out with the auditors, they will authorize it. And when you present them with information they might raise questions about it, but then they will authorize. In my experience it is unusual for any negotiation to take place at the audit committee. **(Philip)**

Guy confirmed this to be the case and described how he perceived the role of audit committee chair in the process:

> Formally we have to agree it, but my role as audit committee chair . . . is the antithesis of my role as a director. My role as audit committee chair is to make sure that the auditors feel their fee is big enough for them to do a proper audit. My job as a director is to minimise the audit fee. So, actually in the audit committee I will be saying to the auditors 'Have you got a good enough fee here? If you are telling me you have been constrained on the fee and you can't do a proper audit as audit committee chair that is a primary concern to me' and I would take that to the board. **(Guy)**

Philip described the information provided to the audit committee:

> We have what is called an accounting and reporting commentary that is produced by the head of financial reporting and it is a continuing document in that down the left hand side there are various issues and down the right hand issue is whether that issue has changed during the quarter . . . So every three months the audit committee is being updated on issues. **(Philip)**

Philip provided some examples of how the accounting and reporting commentary is used:

> Included in there are things like new accounting standards, whether we need to take any action. There will be issues like, for instance, if there is any litigation against the group, is there a need for a provision, if there isn't why there isn't ... When an acquisition is made, it appears on the list and it will appear saying, acquisitions made, when, and fair value still to be determined — because obviously you don't know. Then the following quarter what progress you have made on determining fair value. **(Philip)**

Philip noted that the auditors also supplied the audit committee with a document of their own:

> They tended to refer to this document (the accounting and reporting commentary) ... so that it made their document, I would hesitate to say this, somewhat redundant ... because they didn't have any issues to report to the audit committee over and above the issues that had already been covered by this document. And they have the normal schedule of unadjusted errors because clearly you have to go through that process. **(Philip)**

Barry, while acknowledging that management produced high quality information, did not accept that the papers produced by the auditors were superfluous:

> They get good papers. The management will give them ... I think it is a pretty comprehensive paper. You will also have a paper from us which, whilst we don't repeat what management have, if there is an issue that needs more explanation, if it is a big issue ... we would probably repeat them in full so that rather than reading a tract over time, we would give a summary of it as it was, with our recommendation of where to go. They have those in advance, in time to read them. And do read them actually ... Our paper is independent, we write that from scratch. **(Barry)**

Barry dismissed the possibility of conflicting papers going to the audit committee:

> We would have an executive meeting ... But actually ... because the audit committee now is such a big event in the reporting cycle, the whole audit effort is directed towards the audit committee meeting rather than the close meeting with the finance team and the finance director. **(Barry)**

Barry was very aware that general practice had evolved:

> But of course if you ... wind the clock back maybe five or ten years it was the meeting with the finance director that was the definitive meeting and then the audit committee was a bit of a run through in under an hour. Whereas now your average audit committee meeting is maybe two to three hours. **(Barry)**

6.2.3   Chairman's Management of the Audit Committee and Key Relationships

Philip explained that providing the audit committee with high quality information was essential for enabling problems to be resolved at an early stage:

> The process Kestrel goes though, which I think is a fairly good process, is one which I believe that very few issues should ever get to the audit committee unresolved. In fact I can probably list on one hand the number of issues that have ever had any real serious discussion at the audit committee because that communication process means that the issues invariably get resolved before they ever get to the audit committee . . . If I go back to when I first joined Kestrel and I look at the quality of the papers that were submitted to the audit committee before I joined, it is barely an agenda and nothing else. **(Philip)**

Barry shared this perspective on how the audit committee should operate:

> I tend to try to get to the issue early so that I can say 'Have you thought about this and this and whatever?' So, therefore, hopefully there is no need to have a dig in or punch up and you don't sort of fall out. Now having said that, we have had some reasonably robust discussions on acquisition fair values and employment matters . . . I would like to think that in most cases by the time it gets to the audit committee meeting, with historic issues, it is done. And occasionally we will be there trying to make sure that the audit committee members understand what the key assumptions were. **(Barry)**

Guy also believed that it was important to pick up problems at an early stage because it was easier to find a solution given time:

> The job, as I see it, is to pick that up early and to force it back and also to anticipate. I think that as audit committee chair I sit down with the finance director and with the audit partner separately and I say 'What problems do we have and what problems can you foresee?' because they are the ones that we should tackle before we get there. If we put all the problems on the table and say we are going to resolve them in the next two weeks we are probably going to have an argument, if we can say we have got three years, then we can find a way through. **(Guy)**

He thought that the audit partner was particularly well placed to provide insights on future developments:

> They are far more up to date than any of us are on the practical side. If you can look out into this stuff and say the way you do things now is fine but I think you will find that in a couple years time, there is something happening with real estate in America that is going to mean that so and so . . . then you can move your way out of it beforehand. **(Guy)**

While Philip did not contact Guy particularly frequently, he did contact Guy in advance of each audit committee meeting:

> Normally that would only happen a couple of weeks before . . . the meeting where I would ring him up and say that there are some issues or there aren't any issues . . . Typically the discussion would be that there aren't any issues. (**Philip**)

Philip would also meet Barry:

> He would have a meeting with myself, ahead of the audit committee, once they have concluded much of their work and he would tell me the things that he is then going to tell the audit committee chair about. And of course, I will make sure that I have also had a conversation with the audit committee chair. Generally speaking there will be two or three things. (**Philip**)

In recognition of the importance of the audit committee Barry always met Guy in advance:

> I will always meet with the audit committee chair in advance; we would either meet or have a telephone call. So, he is aware of the tone of exactly what we are saying. And if there is any disconnect in the tone he will spot that and will come back to you . . . And it is also for him, he may have something he wants to bounce of me that he has picked up along the way . . . So by the time you get to the audit committee the facts are out on the table . . . It is all just a question of understanding what the issues are. And most times we aim to get them dealt with before the meeting. (**Barry**)

Despite the increased importance of the audit committee Barry was in no doubt that Philip was still his principal point of contact, but was able to identify other members of the management team with whom he was likely to have contact:

> I mean there are three people, maybe four, that I would communicate with on issues, actually there are five. The issues will be tax related in which case it is with the tax director and then I will have the tax partner helping me . . . The other people are their VP of finance, their VP financial reporting who is based in London . . . then there is an operational finance director, commercial finance director who is based in [name of foreign country] and is the finance director for their largest division. These are the people who, if there are issues, I will have direct contact with them. (**Barry**)

Barry reflected more generally on the nature of the relationship between audit partners and finance directors:

> I think it is . . . quite a complex relationship which I don't think that regulators really appreciate. Because they are assuming that the audit partners communicate with management and that is wining and dining, sure you are doing that, but that is to get the relationship to work, it is not cosying up to them. It is a very odd relationship. You are friendly but then you can have quite an adversarial position on negotiating fees . . . You have some accounting policy change or some practice that you are not quite comfortable with that you want to move back on and get it to happen slightly differently. (**Barry**)

As far as Kestrel was concerned Barry thought the relationship was generally strong:

> We have a good team, I think. We have had a few issues in [name of foreign country] relating to chemistry with a previous audit partner who has now rotated off, as it happens . . . I think they felt he was occasionally too picky on points that didn't really matter or that they had under control and were getting fixed . . . You occasionally get the discussion as to . . . 'Should I be talking to your technical director who will be taking a decision on that?' **(Barry)**

Guy gave his views on the three-way relationship between the finance director, audit committee chair and audit partner:

> We are a threesome working together, we have got a common objective which is truth and fairness and all the rest of it. Some of the literature sort of talks as though you are spies on each other, trying to catch each other out. I don't believe that, I think we are there trying to help each other, trying to resolve problems before they get there, as I say, not working against each other at all. **(Guy)**

But he was convinced that the audit committee made a difference to audit quality:

> We sit there as an appeals court to some extent, but the mere existence of us means that it is not necessary. **(Guy)**

While Guy acknowledged that the additional responsibility now given to audit committees was a consequence of the Smith Report he believed that there was a key omission from the Report:

> The issue with Smith is that he set out what we should do as a tick list, but, he hasn't set out an objective so, if you say . . . 'What is the objective of the audit committee?' No one can answer that . . . Do we succeed or fail? — Who knows? Because we don't know what our purpose is . . . You certainly know when it goes wrong. **(Guy)**

6.2.4   The Nature of the Relationship with the Auditor

Guy was clear in the qualities he wanted from an audit partner:

> Partners who desire not to lose status by losing a key client . . . that would be my fear as an audit committee chair . . . As long as the partner is doing his job, he's independent, he's secure and knowledgeable about the company and prepared to state his mind whatever it is . . . Barry is a big enough guy to do that. It is a very nice client for them but it is not a be all and end all client for them . . . You need somebody who can say well, if Kestrel don't like it, well we can live with that. **(Guy)**

While as chair of the audit committee Guy was required by the Combined Code to review and monitor the effectiveness of the audit process, he admitted that he was

unlikely to notice any technical shortcomings in the audit partner but believed they might still be exposed by interactions with a large client:

> If the Big Four aren't technically competent then I am not going to notice it. The subject of technical competence of the audit partner ... It would come up because there had been a dispute about a technical item. Companies like Kestrel have technical experts so sometimes they find themselves at odds with the auditors. **(Guy)**

Philip expressed satisfaction with the quality of work undertaken by the auditors:

> Generally speaking everyone was happy with the quality of the work that was done and the people involved ... Generally speaking the relationship is very good. **(Philip)**

Philip was adamant that his relationship with the auditors needed to be based on a principle of openness:

> I am a great believer in transparency. The thing that always horrifies me in any organization that I have been involved with is if anybody ever says that we can't tell the auditors. You are required to tell them everything. **(Philip)**

He also believed that it was important to take the initiative in dealing with difficult issues:

> I have always taken the view when dealing with auditors that it is most important not to ask them what they think of something, but it is actually to say that this is the issue and this is what we are doing about it and then you have the opportunity to discuss the solution rather than giving them the opportunity to come to it. **(Philip)**

Philip believed this approach was even more necessary given the recent changes to ethical standards[1] with respect to auditors supplying non-audit services in the form of accounting advice:

> Of course with the transition of responsibilities and the legal position with auditors and their unwillingness to get involved when you are preparing accounts ... if you went in and said 'How do you think we should treat this?', they would say 'How do you think you should treat it? And we will tell you what we think of your solution.' Years ago you didn't do that. They came along and gave their recommendation, whereas now they regard that as preparing the accounts, which of course they can't do. **(Philip)**

While accepting the new style of relationship Philip believed that audit partners overreacted when the tighter regulation first took effect:

> I actually think that what happened with the audit firms, I think they went too far in the direction of — no, we can't be helpful. It almost got to the stage where they became

---

[1] ES 5 *Non-audit Services Provided to Audited Entities* (APB, 2004) provides requirements and guidance on specific circumstances arising from the provision of non-audit services by an audit firm to entities audited by them, which may create threats to the auditor's objectivity or perceived loss of independence. It provides examples of safeguards to eliminate or reduce the threat to acceptable levels. Where it is not possible to do this the auditor should either withdraw from the audit or the provision of non-audit services. Some non-audit services are effectively prohibited.

unhelpful, they were feeling their way ... They backed off from the relationship that finance directors once commonly valued with partners in the audit firm. **(Philip)**

He also considered audit inspection regimes had a strong influence on auditors' behaviour:

> And the other thing that has impacted the way auditors behave ... is the existence of the Audit Inspection [Unit]. So you know when you are dealing with the auditors that not only are they trying to obviously do the job they are required to do on your audit, but they are also making sure that they cross all the t's and dot all the i's for when they get that inspection. **(Philip)**

Guy conceded that the requirement to rotate audit partners could have a major impact on the key relationships:

> It was Barry's first year when I joined the board and I think previous to that there had been a bit of friction between Philip and the previous audit partner. When I assumed the chair Philip talked to me about whether we should go out to tender or not. I have done one tender and I have to say it is an awful lot of work. And it seems to me that the Big Four are all much of a muchness, they don't like me saying that, but they are. **(Guy)**

6.3 KEY INTERACTIONS BETWEEN PHILIP, GUY AND BARRY

During the course of the audit the following issues prompted interactions between Philip, Guy and Barry.

1. Valuation of intangibles on acquisition.
2. Impairment reviews.
3. Financial instruments — treatment of preference shares.
4. Financial instruments — hedging.
5. Restructuring costs.
6. Fraud and illegal acts.

6.3.1   Valuation of Intangibles on Acquisition

This issue was raised by Philip and Barry but not Guy. Barry outlined the problem which had its origins in IFRS 3:[2]

> The question at issue really was where there was a change with IFRS, where there was a much more significant recognition of intangibles and goodwill in particular. Parcelling

---

[2] IFRS 3 *Business Combinations* requires that all identifiable assets should be recognized in the balance sheet at fair value. This includes all intangible assets that meet the definition of an intangible asset in IAS 38 *Intangible Assets* and whose fair value can be measured reliably. The excess of the cost of the business combination over the acquirer's interest in the net fair value of the identifiable assets, liabilities and contingent liabilities is recognized as goodwill (IASB, 2004, paras. 36–37; 45; 51). The rules are far more stringent than UK GAAP was in requiring intangible assets to be recognized rather than being subsumed into goodwill.

up goodwill into customer relationships, etc., etc. There was initially a reluctance to do that simply on the basis that there wasn't much technical merit in the intangible asset, it didn't really mean a lot, very subjective as to how you calculated it. And consequently there was a desire just to leave it as goodwill. **(Barry)**

Philip was dismissive of the standard:

Clearly the accounting standard is getting into the realms of dancing on pinheads and we found that from a practical perspective, that is just not the way you would look at the business ... We think all of this is a load of nonsense. How can you possibly attribute values to particular elements of the intangible? **(Philip)**

He elaborated further on why he thought it inappropriate in the context of Kestrel's business:

Kestrel is a very value focused business and there is an awful lot of credibility attached to looking at the intrinsic value of the business and when an acquisition is made, the valuation is made on the basis of forward cash flows. Our view was always that what you paid for a business was a reflection of its economic value. That economic value is a product of human resources, intellectual capital, route to market, customers ... and no one of those is capable of individual valuation. That was our starting point. One of the reasons why we were concerned about saying that you should try to recognize individual elements of it was that what does the residual represent? Does it represent goodwill? You can't attribute it to anything else. Our assessment was, it's what you pay for the business, that's the value and that's the end of it. **(Philip)**

Furthermore, he did not believe that there was any demand for the information from users:

Most analysts ignore it anyway and we had that discussion with the auditors. Go and talk to the analysts, they ignore it, they don't take it into account. It's a technical nonsense in terms of accounting. **(Philip)**

Although Barry was keen to ensure that Kestrel fully complied with IFRS 3 *Business Combinations* he admitted that he too had reservations about the requirement to show identifiable intangibles on the balance sheet:

It is a very problematic area. The difficulty you have is that you actually put values on things you acquire, whereas all the existing business, you ignore. So if you have got a company that has grown through acquisition you will end up with shed loads of intangibles on your balance sheet. If you have grown organically or you have been around since the accounting standards changed you don't have any of that on the balance sheet. And that is a very difficult thing to explain. **(Barry)**

The whole issue was brought to a head when Kestrel made an acquisition in the first year of IFRS:

And interestingly it wasn't a particularly large acquisition. But I knew that if I didn't have the discussion on the first time it came up then, with a large acquisition, you've got the initial reaction of 'You haven't done this the previous time, why are you insisting on this now?' ... It was a principle that we had to get right and it was really an IFRS presentation issue. **(Barry)**

Philip explained how the area of disagreement gradually emerged:

When the issue was first raised by [Barry's firm] they were basically putting their marker down saying that you just have to do these things ... Of course their assessment was that we had to disaggregate it and come up with all these various bits ... So they got a push back from us on that particular point. **(Philip)**

Philip's perception was that the auditors suspected them of refusing to reclassify goodwill as individual intangible assets (which are required to be amortized over their expected useful life) because of the potentially favourable impact on the income statement:[3]

If it is all intangible goodwill you don't amortize it, but if it is an element of an intangible like a customer list or whatever you do amortize it. And the auditors thought that we were trying to take a position where you come up with goodwill, and because we have called it goodwill, we don't see the charge going through the income statement. And that is rubbish because we separately identify the intangible write off in the accounts. **(Philip)**

However, the process of resolving the problem did not follow the normal pattern:

That, unfortunately, we did actually resolve at the audit committee ... We didn't go to the audit committee with a decision. I knew what the outcome of the meeting would be, I think Philip did as well; ... I think he just wanted to have that discussion with his fellow directors present. **(Barry)**

Philip confirmed that bringing an unresolved issue to the audit committee was unusual:

It isn't the job of the audit committee to decide these things. You bring these things to the audit committee to tell them the issues that you have faced and dealt with and how you dealt with them but don't bring them issues where you have a disagreement with the auditors ... In my experience it is unusual for any negotiation to take place at the audit committee. **(Philip)**

Philip made it clear that this was the culmination of a long debate on the subject with the auditors:

For the 2005 yearend there had been an awful lot of debate with the auditors ahead of it ever getting to the audit committee and there had also been a lot of time energy gone

---

[3] IAS 38 *Intangible Assets* classifies intangible assets as either having a finite life (with a limited period of benefit to the entity) or an indefinite life (with no foreseeable limit to the period over which the asset is expected to generate net cash flows for the entity). The cost of an intangible with a finite useful life is amortized over that life, although impairment testing (in accordance with IAS 36 *Impairment of Assets*) is required whenever there is an indication that the carrying amount exceeds the recoverable amount of the intangible asset. Intangible assets with an indefinite useful life are not amortized but must be tested for impairment at each reporting date. IFRS 3 *Business Combinations* requires that goodwill should not be amortized but should be tested for impairment at each reporting date.

into it, lots of calculations, and so on and so forth. I think that really the process that we went through, probably with hindsight, should have reached a conclusion before it got to the audit committee. **(Philip)**

Philip outlined the structure of the debate at the audit committee:

The discussion at the audit committee was a fairly protracted one about me questioning the application of fair values to a customer list and the auditors effectively taking a very technical position on this. Their preference was for Kestrel to use an external valuer and we didn't want to do that because we felt it was pandering to the development of an industry, fiddling about with numbers that did not mean very much. And we said that we had the internal capability to calculate it ourselves, which we did. **(Philip)**

They also had different perceptions as to the value of the customer list:

We were coming at it from the point of view that the customer really had little value and that most of the premium over the asset value we had paid for the acquisition was typical goodwill associated with the view of cash flows going forward in the future, discounting them back that gave you a value and compared to book value this was goodwill. And of course the auditor wanted us to be more precise in the sense of actually complying with the technical accounting. **(Philip)**

Barry's recollection was that the agreed solution did not result in an adjustment to the financial statements:

On that particular acquisition it was pretty de minimis. I would need to check it. I don't think we made any adjustment but I think we did have an adjustment on our adjustment schedule. And the clear agreement was that the way to deal with this going forward is — we do this exercise. **(Barry)**

Philip remembered the outcome differently:

Of course the ironic thing is, as it happened, we did have to attribute a value to the customer list but as time progressed the list didn't perform as we had hoped it would perform. So you could argue that that intangible may well be potentially impaired. **(Philip)**

Philip accepted that a refusal to value and recognize identifiable intangible assets was unlikely to produce a solution:

Well, the important point was that we were never ever going to succeed by taking that extreme position. That was clearly apparent. **(Philip)**

However, he was also convinced that the auditors would not have issued Kestrel with a modified audit report over this issue:

I don't think that the auditors ever get to the stage of saying 'Oh well, we'll qualify'. Clearly on that kind of issue they wouldn't have done it because it was irrelevant to our position ... They have to, in a way, work with the management, to get the management to recognize that maybe they are right in terms of the commercial aspects of it, but we do have to comply with the accounting requirements and you have to show willing and all this sort of stuff . . . It wasn't something that you really wanted to be falling out about. **(Philip)**

Reflecting on his strategy, Philip refuted the suggestion that he never had any possibility of persuading the auditors to accept his position:

> I have always taken the position in the past that if there is an issue which I consider to be a technical issue but not one that would give rise to an audit qualification I will push it as far as I can because I don't see why the auditors should just get their way on technical accounting issues when I don't actually agree with them that technical accounting makes sense . . . But we wouldn't just keep on pushing. Because at the end of the day, you know, we've all got a business to run and a job to do and the more time you spend trying to deal with these issues the less time you have got to deal with things that actually create value. **(Philip)**

Even when Philip accepted that the customer list would have to be valued there were still difficult exchanges with the auditors:

> We did recognize customer lists and then we would say — if we recognize customer lists and then they would say 'How do you think you should do it?' So we would then come up with a methodology which, when we presented them . . . they would say 'We don't like that methodology.' So then we would say 'We asked you in the first place how we should do it and you wouldn't tell us. Now we've done it and you don't like it.' So there was that sort of thing. Would you call that a negotiation? **(Philip)**

Although he may not have won the main argument, Philip believed that the company gained some benefit from the discussion process:

> I think the only negotiation, if it was negotiation, was getting them to accept eventually that you just can't apply the letter of the law. We are dealing with principles rather than rules . . . They eventually moved themselves so that we got what I think was a very sensible solution . . . It was happening in the first year of transition to IFRS . . . So their natural tendency was to focus on a rule that you had to do something rather than the principles of whether it made sense. It even got to what I regard as a rather silly situation with the auditors where they were agreeing that it didn't make sense but that is what the accounting standard said therefore that is what you have to do. And I think that is where you are moving into that rules versus principles environment and we had those discussions. **(Philip)**

Although Philip had clearly disagreed with Barry this did not appear to have adversely affected their relationship and he clearly felt others in the audit firm bore greater responsibility for the protracted discussions:

> He was very sympathetic . . . He was probably more pragmatic than for instance the guy in [foreign country], because bear in mind this was an issue that arose in [foreign country]. And the [foreign country] do tend to be rules rather than principles, so the partner in the [foreign country], he dug his heels in for a while on this particular issue. Eventually common sense prevailed because there was a discussion that went on internally within [Barry's firm] with Barry trying to deal with this with an experienced, mature, pragmatic

approach. Because the other thing within the audit firm, you do get the involvement of these technical groups and they take a particular position on matters. **(Philip)**

Barry considered that the value of the debate was to establish a future principle:

> And subsequently we have had a number of acquisitions that would have been problematic but actually it has been relatively straightforward ... We are now reasonably confident we are in the place that we need to be, where the company does the analysis ... which we can review and generally agree with. **(Barry)**

Philip also accepted that the issue had been largely clarified for subsequent years:

> What was agreed for the 2005 yearend was that for future acquisitions we would have to do a better job of documenting the thought processes that we had gone through. And we thought we had done a good job the previous year as it happens ... For 2006 the only reason it came up again was that there had been some more acquisitions and they were still a little bit concerned that we weren't using external valuation, but they confirmed that if effectively we had gone through a good process and that they were then happy with the valuation we were attributing to intangibles. **(Philip)**

6.3.2   Impairment Reviews

This issue was raised by all three interviewees. Barry raised the general question of impairment reviews on acquisitions covering not only goodwill but tangible and intangible assets as well.[4] He was well aware that the company might be sensitive to the issue:

> Because I think companies are concerned that if they make a goodwill impairment that people will say two things at least. One is — you overpaid for it so bad commercial judgement, so you are at fault. And the other is — what does that do to my forecast going out? Does that mean your business isn't performing very well and therefore it has a problem going forward? So there is a reluctance to deal with it in this big lump ... I think once companies get used to this and analysts get used to it, I think they just put it to one side and ignore it. But again it is difficult; it adds a level of edge, I suppose, to discussions when the number you are talking about could be relatively large ... And the other problem is once you make an impairment you are removing all the headroom so therefore, if your forecasts are off at all after that, you end up with another write down, so it gets doubly sensitive. **(Barry)**

---

[4] IAS 36 *Impairment of Assets* states that an asset may not be carried on the balance sheet above its recoverable amount. Recoverable amount is defined as the higher of the asset's fair value less costs to sell and its value in use. Value in use is ascertained by estimating future cash flows to be derived from the asset discounted by a pre-tax market rate which takes account of the time value of money and asset specific risk. If the carrying value exceeds the recoverable amount it is considered impaired and the loss is recognized in the profit or loss. While recoverable amount is generally calculated for individual assets, an asset seldom generates cash flows independently of other assets. Therefore, most assets are tested for impairment in groups of assets known as cash generating units (CGUs) (PwC, 2009).

Barry was also acutely aware of another problem in applying the relevant standard:

> And of course the whole thing is very subjective. With your best endeavour, if the three
> of us sat down given all the same information we would probably come up with three
> different numbers. That is always the difficulty. (**Barry**)

Kestrel performs regular impairment reviews, a process that is linked to their annual
planning exercise which raises a further sensitivity:

> That then forms the basis of the profit bonus pools for each of the businesses, so, it is
> quite an important thing. It gets finalized towards the end of the year. They actually look
> at the full value of the business so, whether the goodwill is on the balance sheet or not,
> it actually gets addressed and it is quite a sensitive issue. (**Barry**)

Guy agreed that the executive incentive scheme could be an issue when considering
impairment, particularly as the shape of remuneration packages had changed in the
recent past:

> If you look at the remuneration these guys get ... We had a very good salary, we had
> a pension scheme and we got a little bit of bonus and we were alright. Now there is no
> pension scheme ... Well, pretty much by comparison ... but huge bonuses and long
> term incentives and so their eyes are naturally towards that ... I would say there has
> been a change in behaviour ... I would say it makes them more aggressive in terms of
> striving for performance. Not necessarily trying to corrupt the numbers but in striving
> for financial performance. (**Guy**)

Barry identified a problem with the approach taken on impairment reviews:

> But unfortunately the way they do it doesn't quite fit with the standard so, actually it is
> getting recognition of that fact, and then getting the exercise done in accordance with
> the standard, you get a slightly different answer. (**Barry**)

Guy's focus was one particular acquisition:

> The debate item ... was around an acquisition that was made, probably two years ago,
> in a subsidiary ... It contains significant goodwill ... the actuals were tracking behind
> the business case ... This isn't quite as good as we thought but — then the markets hit
> the bottom and then it became more arduous ... So the issue was, was there evidence of
> impairment? (**Guy**)

Philip considered this to be a long standing issue:

> For 2007 there has been an ongoing discussion about the potential impairment of good-
> will associated with one of the acquisitions that Kestrel made in 2002. (**Philip**)

Guy outlined the shape of discussion on the matter before it reached the audit committee. He agreed that Barry and Philip would have been involved:

> They would have gone through it. More particularly, it would have been Philip's subor-
> dinates. I think they would have discussed it with Barry's audit team. On the whole, my
> experience of these things is you don't want your audit partner and your finance director

to start discussing this cold. You want the ground rules of the discussion well rehearsed and ideally that subordinate group to have found out a route forward to put it up to the two wise men so that they can nod it through. **(Guy)**

The auditors and the company had slightly different views on the situation:

The company, not surprisingly, took the view that the business case was as originally projected, was still essentially intact and that if you re-projected it with a pushback to the point at which you got a gross gain then low and behold all the numbers came good. The auditors took the view that it was probably too early to tell yet whether that was the case or not and therefore you are left with this dilemma, what would you do?' **(Guy)**

Guy then became involved:

I would talk to both Philip and to Barry prior to the audit committee meeting to find the views of both. If they were giving me a different view then I would be forcing it back onto them because the last thing I want is a debate between the two of them coming to an audit committee meeting, try and sort it out. In this particular case I think they had pretty much found a way through. **(Guy)**

Guy set out his view of how the options were considered:

To get a better number than the one in the accounts is very difficult because you say — OK let us assume that it is impaired, by how much is it impaired, is it 10% off, or is it all the way out — which to my mind is the only real stopping place, you know to go from 100% to nothing. And so we went through a discussion on this ... We probably tweaked the disclosure up a bit more and I think, my experience on this is that people come last to disclosure as opposed to coming first to it. **(Guy)**

Guy described it as a compromise agreement:

It was — well, we haven't got an impairment value for goodwill but we have got to at least alert the intelligent shareholder — if there is such a thing, and when people look at me, I say 'Well, when this goes belly up we can say actually we did tell you, if you look on page 423, sub-note so and some such, we told you there was a problem here'. **(Guy)**

However, he did not think that on this issue the audit partner was exerting strong pressure for disclosure improvements:

If the company would have said that they were not going to change it I don't think the audit partner would have said 'Well in that case you will get a qualification'. **(Guy)**

He also acknowledged that the subjectivity involved in an impairment review often made it very difficult for auditors to be robust on the issue:

Well, I think the auditors have a discussion but at the end of the day ... When you are desperate as a finance director you look the audit partner in the eye and say — write the qualification down and I'll have a look at it. It is very, very difficult, if you have got undisputable evidence that this is ... of course you haven't, so we have got a half suspicion that there are emerging signs that this thing is not quite worth what it was before, but, on the other hand ... **(Guy)**

Guy expressed the view that this was the sort of judgement where non-executive directors can play a particularly valuable role:

> Because we are sort of more detached, we don't have bonus schemes or anything. One of the things that you will find is that one of the executives has his name on the acquisition which is also part of the problem. **(Guy)**

Philip noted that the issue continued to be kept under review by management and the audit committee:

> A further review took place for the half year and again you will see in the half year report for Kestrel reference to that same issue saying that a review has been performed and there isn't a requirement for impairment at the moment. It will be one of the things that will be reviewed at the closure of 2007. I would say that for 2007 that is the only issue that the audit committee have had any real involvement in. **(Philip)**

Drawing on his general experience with a number of companies, Guy thought that there was a tendency to not acknowledge such problems in a timely fashion:

> You never recognize a loss when it first emerges, you only recognize it when it becomes glaringly apparent to everybody. When you are inside a company you see things emerging and you think well I can smudge that over and colour it in. A good finance director has little bits of tricks he can play and he plays those tricks and so pushes it out a bit so you write these things off at least a period later. **(Guy)**

Overall Guy was not happy with the IFRS requirement that goodwill could not be amortized but had to be subject to impairment review:

> You set up your goodwill and then it stays there and nothing happens to it unless you make an impairment. Personally I prefer the older process ... where you put it in and amortize it, because then at least the problem gets smaller ... The trouble with this one is that we all know the goodwill is not eternal, by definition it can't be, therefore it must have a limited life, therefore sooner or later you are going to have to impair it. And what Tweedie[5] hasn't allowed for is how the hell you do that? And the reality is that companies will impair goodwill at least one accounting period later than they should do. **(Guy)**

6.3.3   Financial Instruments — Treatment of Preference Shares

All three interviewees identified financial instruments as a point of discussion, although they didn't necessarily pick up on precisely the same issue. Philip explained that they and the auditors were trying to make sense of IAS 39 *Financial Instruments:*

---

[5] Sir David Tweedie, Chairman of the IASB.

Recognition and Measurement and that many of the problems originated in the first year of adopting IFRS:

> Kestrel had a preference share which they wanted to have classified as a current liability.[6] Because there was a requirement to redeem, at some stage, part of those shares, and you will see that in the transition year for IFRS ... it was treated in one way in the balance sheet and in the following year it was treated in a completely different way. **(Philip)**

Philip disclosed how the change came about:

> We chose a particular direction that we wanted to go down and initially the auditors agreed with what we wanted to do. And then there was a change of mind from the auditors because we suspect what had happened was that there had been some discussion with the technical people ... We lost the discussion [in 2005] ... Then in 2006 it was treated in the way we initially wanted. They just got it wrong and the following year they held their hands up and said they got it wrong. **(Philip)**

The matter did go to the audit committee in 2005 although by then it had been resolved:

> But we pointed out why we disagreed with it. **(Philip)**

Barry also suggested that the matter had been resolved at that stage in the process:

> That was the audit committee letting off steam. **(Barry)**

He elaborated further:

> It is where the finance team just criticize the end result — but we have to do it this way because that is what the statute says, but it is not the right answer, and you probably get nods around the audit committee table. **(Barry)**

Philip explained how they came to accept the auditors' position:

> We weren't going to win. That is what their technical people said, it had to be treated that way. We presented all the arguments why we didn't think it should be treated that way and they said that is the way it has to be treated. And in fact you could argue that that did have a degree of materiality, in the sense that it was a fairly sizeable number and it was a question of position in the balance sheet. So I suspect, we never actually got to the stage of, if we insisted on treating it the way that we wanted to treat it, whether it would give rise to qualification. I suspect it probably would. **(Philip)**

He also admitted that it was not an issue on which he was prepared to fight to the end:

> I think probably one of the reasons we accepted it was because we didn't really care. The balance sheet, despite what David Tweedie might say ... is not something that

---

[6] IAS 32 *Financial Instruments: Disclosure and Presentation* requires financial instruments to be classified into either debt or equity according to the substance of the contractual arrangement of the instrument. A redeemable preference share, which is economically the same as a bond, is therefore accounted for in the same way as a bond (i.e. as a liability) even though legally it is a share of the issuer (PwC, 2009).

most businesses focus on ... It is a parking lot for costs and revenues that haven't gone through the income statement and the cash flow ... Sure, internally the balance sheet is important in terms of managing working capital and so on. But the statutory balance sheet wasn't a thing that we really focused our energy on. And if [audit firm] were going to take a particular position on a technical accounting issue, which they really didn't fully understand themselves, fine. (**Philip**)

Philip explained that another reason why the treatment of preference shares was not a priority was because of their use of non-GAAP disclosures in the accounts:

They don't exist anymore because they have now all been redeemed or converted, but in Kestrel post-IFRS they were treated as debt and at least subsequently they were treated as long term rather than short term but treated as debt. In the non-GAAP information we basically show net debts excluding preference shares. And then a little reconciliation shows how it relates to net debt that is disclosed in the numbers. And I think what, increasingly, companies will do is if they don't get to a situation where they can present the information in a way that it would sensibly be presented, then they get tied down by all these details, arguably, non sensible rules you'll see a growth of non-GAAP information. (**Philip**)

The final vindication of their original position came when their accounts were reviewed by the Financial Reporting Review Panel:

As it happened the Financial Reporting Review Panel never actually said anything when we changed it back again. (Philip)

Barry did not mention the change in account treatment in the second year.

6.3.4   Financial Instruments — Hedging

All three interviewees referred to another aspect of accounting for financial instruments — hedging. Barry was not impressed with the relevant standard, IAS 39:[7]

Financial instruments, yes, we've had quite a bit of discussion with them on this, actually with IFRS and some of the hedging strategies, because IFRS, the original standard wasn't very well written ... Depending on how you are hedging you can get the wrong result under IAS 39. So whilst commercially they are entirely hedged and appropriately hedged, if your hedging is in different subsidiaries it can fail. It doesn't just sort of aggregate

---

[7] Hedge accounting (recognizing the offsetting effects of fair value changes of both the hedging instrument and the hedged item in the same period's profit or loss) is permitted in certain circumstances by IAS 39 *Financial Instruments: Recognition and Measurement,* provided that the hedging relationship is clearly defined, measurable and actually effective. There are three different types of hedges:
  – fair value hedge: if an entity hedges a change in fair value of a recognized asset or liability, the change in fair values of both the hedging instrument and the hedged item are recognized in the profit or loss when they occur;
  – cash flow hedge: if an entity hedges changes in the future cash flows relating to a recognized asset or liability, then the change in the fair value of the hedging instrument is recognized directly in equity until such time as those future cash flows occur;
  – hedge of a net investment in a foreign entity which is treated as a cash flow hedge (Deloitte, 2007).

and consolidate under IAS 39, so you might have — that works, that doesn't work, that works, so therefore the whole thing doesn't work. We had a bit of that, actually. **(Barry)**

Guy explained the complexity of the problem in broad terms:

> We have a number of complex things on financial instruments I suppose. We report in sterling but are [foreign currency] denominated so we have financial instruments that bounce back and forwards, so if we look at the accounts we have a lot of disclosure on financial instruments ... And of course because of the way the group sits you can have things in [overseas location] that have to go to [foreign currency] because they are owned by [foreign currency] companies before they come back to sterling, so they are going round in circles. **(Guy)**

They had to demonstrate that this was purely an accounting rather than a business issue to get round the problem:

> They changed what they did and that was the right answer ... I could see it was going to be an issue. **(Barry)**

Guy reported that the discussion at the audit committee was fairly low key as expected:

> The discussion was to make sure everyone was happy with the treatment. It didn't give rise to any change so it was just this is what's done, this is what happens, this is why ... My experience is that the audit committee is not going to change much more than one item in any session. If you have more than that, then you have a real problem with your finance director and auditors. They should be doing this beforehand. **(Guy)**

In fact the matter was identified well before the year-end, ensuring that a crisis was averted:

> This was raised in January ... and it got fixed around mid February. So, if you look over the history you can see it in the quarters, it wasn't a yearend issue. They are a large client so you have a lot of dialogue, so, it is quite fortunate. You read management accounts, you look at their internal papers, so hopefully you pick up issues before they become bust up type issues. **(Barry)**

Philip summarized his view on audit committee involvement with the issue:

> The treatment of hedge accounting for IAS 39 was an important issue. It wasn't so much a discussion, more information, bringing the audit committee up to speed. **(Philip)**

6.3.5   Restructuring Costs

This issue was discussed by all three interviewees. Guy explained the background to the discussion:

> We show restructuring costs as exceptionals[8] and the implication is that the restructuring costs are not really part of normal profit which is what we would like the punter to believe. Fortunately in this case the punter isn't wise enough to realize that they have been in there for the last ten years . . . Personally it is not a style that I like, but it is what it is. It is set out, summarized. Some ignore it and some play the game and talk about ongoing profitability. **(Guy)**

He further clarified who he meant by 'the punter':

> The punter in this case is the knowledgeable analyst for the bond side fund manager. The reality is that Kestrel is owned by institutional shareholders . . . which means at least we are talking to professionals, if we believe they are professionals. So, we put this restructuring here. We have done for some time. **(Guy)**

As far as Philip was concerned it was just a means of assisting analysts to perform their jobs more efficiently:

> We always presented what we called adjusted operating profit for Kestrel. It was basically operating profit before restructuring costs, before the amortization of intangibles, because we knew based on the discussions of the analysts, that this was the number they saw as important . . . We didn't hide . . . the amortization of intangibles or the restructuring costs. They were all given equal prominence but the number that was focused on was what we call adjusted operating profit. **(Philip)**

Guy said that there was not a great deal to discuss because IFRS was fairly permissive on this issue, but the matter was still brought to his attention:

> That is the bizarre thing about IFRS because so long as you put it in a box you seem to be able to get away with it . . . Now restructuring during the prior year adjustments were a positive number because we made gains on the disposal of an asset which was bigger than the cost of writing it off. In the year in question the cost of writing it off was bigger than the gain on disposal so it went the other way. **(Guy)**

He was sceptical that the presentation of restructuring costs made any difference the perceptions of users, particularly as the amounts involved were not that large:

> I think it is easy to over emphasize this. I think it is in part management trying to say there are two things we are doing, there are the ongoing businesses and then we have

---

[8] IAS 1 *Presentation of Financial Statements* states that although there is no prescribed format for the financial statements, there are minimum required disclosures. Additional disclosures should be made when they are relevant to an understanding of an entity's financial performance. The nature and amount of income and expense should be disclosed separately where they are material. Disclosure may be in the statement or in the notes. Restructuring costs are cited as an example.

got the projects that are going through which are loss making and then they will return. These things never return because in manufacturing they are always restructuring trying to pull costs down. It is down the slope of the supply curve and you've got keep chasing that down, which is why it is ongoing. **(Guy)**

Having expressed some distaste for the presentation adopted by Kestrel, Guy explained why he was prepared to accept the treatment:

> The job of the audit committee chair is not to try to put the set of accounts up. It is the job of the finance director to put the accounts up, the job of the audit partner to determine if the accounts are true and fair and my job is to try and make sure that the audit partner is independent and encourage them to agree or at least arbitrate if they don't. My job is not to write the accounts. I hold back from that. I have been a finance director and they were my accounts. You might pass side comments to the finance director but not in the audit committee. That is not the job of the audit committee chair. **(Guy)**

Guy also outlined the strategy he would adopt in a case where he considered that an accounting treatment was genuinely wrong:

> In my side discussion prior to the meeting with the audit partner, I would say 'I hear that you are happy with so and so but I am really quite surprised.' Then they can say their technical guys have looked at it. They are entirely happy, so that is fine. **(Guy)**

Barry was more concerned about the nature of the costs to be included under the restructuring cost heading rather than the presentation:

> Their headline numbers are profit before restructuring costs and amortization on acquired intangibles . . . So inevitably . . . what is the restructuring cost? So you have a little bit of debate about that. But of course with IFRS it is almost easier now because you just tie in what you do and as long as you follow that definition it is not a problem. **(Barry)**

As IFRS provided a broader definition than the previous one under UK GAAP, the issue had not been the subject of great debate:

> Not a huge problem . . . probably more initially at subsidiary level where local management wanted to do a bit more than was acceptable . . . It is something that requires policing. There is always a bit of nudging round the edges as you get to finalizing the audit. It is not something we typically have a significant debate about at a group level. **(Barry)**

6.3.6   Fraud and Illegal Acts

Guy explained how the audit committee dealt with frauds:[9]

> One of the functions of an audit committee is to make sure that management have declared all frauds to the auditors and the auditors are familiar with them, you know. **(Guy)**

He also confirmed that the subject was discussed by the audit committee every year:

> That is one of the mandated things. We always do it. We also have this whistle blowing thing . . . Most of the calls are about some illicit affair that is going on in the company . . . We don't get many calls. We have a real worry that we have a whistle blowing system that nobody uses. **(Guy)**

Barry agreed that, in his opinion, fraud was taken very seriously by the audit committee:

> We do have occasionally the odd fraud which is going to happen in any large group like that. Generally, not that large, but they have an absolute zero tolerance on fraud . . . Occasionally we stumble across something, but I would say, they largely pick it up themselves . . . They get a lot of attention actually. You always know that anytime an audit committee has an agenda item related to fraud that it will be a long meeting. There is never any doubt about the topic being discussed . . . From a business perspective they go absolutely frantic about it. They want to get the message out. **(Barry)**

A fraud had occurred during the year under review and Guy provided a brief summary of it:

> We did have a fraud in this year which was just under half a million. In the context of Kestrel it wasn't a big sum of money, but in the context of an individual it is a big sum of money. And it hadn't just happened in the year it was a cumulative thing, apparently . . . Essentially an accounts clerk was booking invoices which were not real invoices and writing cheques for the invoices and making a cheque for her own name to fund a gap . . . It was a classic because she was able to do it. If you look at the control process the controller had stopped doing the strict process which was to check on the cheque run with the first and last cheque tallying with the system . . . She had access to these cheques, she wrote the cheque to herself. **(Guy)**

---

[9] Provision C.3.2 of the Combined Code (FRC, 2008a) sets out the role and responsibilities of the audit committee. These include 'to review the company's internal financial controls, and unless expressly addressed by a separate board risk committee, or by the board itself, to review the company's internal financial control and risk management systems'. Provision C.3.4 requires the audit committee to review arrangements by which staff of the company may, in confidence, raise concerns about possible improprieties in matters of financial reporting and other matters. The audit committee's objective should be to ensure that arrangements are in place for the proportionate and independent investigation of such matters and for appropriate follow up action.

Ultimately the fraud was discovered but this was not the result of control procedures set up by the company:

> It only got picked up because someone in the bank was suspicious because she had paid in this cheque having been the signatory . . . the bank called the company and asked to speak to somebody and that somebody wasn't there and so on. It is always the same; you never go on holiday when you do frauds. (**Guy**)

Guy described the key questions for the audit committee as a consequence of such incidents:

> And so the issue was how did it happen? How did we let it happen? Who should have picked it up? Why wasn't it picked up? Is there a risk that this has been replicated elsewhere in the system? (**Guy**)

6.4 CONTEXTUAL FACTORS AND ANALYSIS OF THE INTERACTIONS

The general contextual factors are shown in Figure 6.1. The company is large, with all three parties interviewed being experienced and capable. The finance director, Philip, does not agree with some of the principles of IFRS and finds it difficult to accept implementation of an accounting model he feels makes no sense. He does not expect to take unresolved issue to the audit committee, but ensures that comprehensive reports are presented to the committee. He feels that the auditors are now less helpful and partly focussed on satisfying the Audit Inspection Unit.

Guy, the audit committee chair, is a former large company finance director and very knowledgeable. He is not aggressive about fees but wants a proper audit done and expects management to negotiate the fee. He does not see his role and that of the audit committee as a decision maker but as an 'appeals court'. He wants early notification of any matters arising.

Barry, the audit partner, is also very experienced and a senior partner in his firm who is confident enough to make pragmatic judgements. Although his main contact is with Philip, he believes the deciding meeting on the accounts is with the audit committee.

An interesting dimension in this case is that the chairman, who has an accounting qualification himself, attends the audit committee meeting and asks awkward questions.

6.4.1 Financial Reporting Interaction: Fair Value on Acquisition

This interaction was between Philip and Barry. Philip objected in principle to the requirements of IFRS 3, the business combinations standard, which required breaking down the intangibles on a small acquisition between intangibles and goodwill. Philip did not see the point of it. The argument was about a customer list being valued as

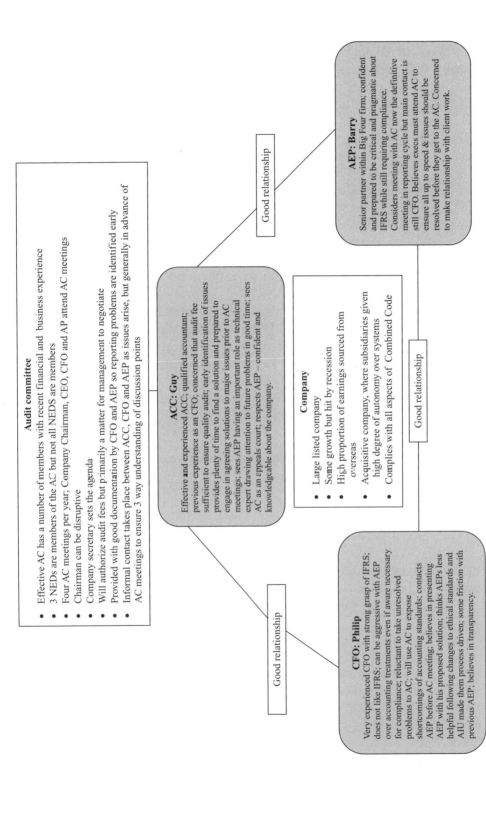

Figure 6.1 Kestrel — General context for interactions

Audit committee

- Effective AC has a number of members with recent financial and business experience
- 3 NEDS are members of the AC but not all NEDS are members
- Four AC meetings per year; Company Chairman, CEO, CFO and AP attend AC meetings
- Chairman can be disruptive
- Company secretary sets the agenda
- Will authorize audit fees but primarily a matter for management to negotiate
- Provided with good documentation by CFO and AEP so reporting problems are identified early
- Informal contact takes place between ACC, CFO and AEP as issues arise, but generally in advance of AC meetings to ensure 3 way understanding of discussion points

ACC: Guy

Effective and experienced ACC; qualified accountant; previous experience as an CFO; concerned that audit fee sufficient to ensure quality audit; early identification of issues provides plenty of time to find a solution and prepared to engage in agreeing solutions to major issues prior to AC meetings; sees AEP having an important role as technical expert drawing attention to future problems in good time; sees AC as an appeals court; respects AEP – confident and knowledgeable about the company.

Company

- Large listed company
- Some growth but hit by recession
- High proportion of earnings sourced from overseas
- Acquisitive company, where subsidiaries given high degree of autonomy over systems
- Complies with all aspects of Combined Code

CFO: Philip

Very experienced CFO with strong grasp of IFRS; does not like IFRS; can be aggressive with AEP over accounting treatments even if aware necessary for compliance; reluctant to take unresolved problems to AC; will use AC to expose shortcomings of accounting standards; contacts AEP before AC meeting; believes in presenting AEP with his proposed solution; thinks AEPs less helpful following changes to ethical standards and AIU made them process driven; some friction with previous AEP; believes in transparency.

AEP: Barry

Senior partner within Big Four firm; confident and prepared to be critical and pragmatic about IFRS while still requiring compliance. Considers meeting with AC now the definitive meeting in reporting cycle but main contact is still CFO. Believes execs must attend AC to ensure all up to speed & issues should be resolved before they get to the AC. Concerned to make relationship with client work.

Good relationship

Good relationship

Good relationship

Good relationship

an intangible. He thought that Barry suspected him of trying to avoid this to improve profits, as goodwill did not have to be amortized every year whereas intangibles did.

Unusually, Philip felt so strongly about the need to do this valuation that he took the issue to the audit committee without resolution to draw it to their attention. He did not follow the auditors' recommendation of employing an external valuer, as he considered it was creating an industry in valuation. Although he knew that in the end they would have to go along with it, he pushed back very hard and insisted that the methodology he had used to do the valuation, even though Barry didn't like it, would hold.

Barry, was quite pragmatic about this but insisted that Kestrel had to comply with the standard, although the valuation itself was a judgement issue and, therefore, imprecise. Barry was concerned to ensure that the principle of valuing intangibles was fundamentally agreed for future acquisitions (of which there were more in the following year) and that Kestrel should document its decision making rather better in future to justify the valuations. Neither Barry nor Philip believed that the accounting requirement made sense.

The main factor that influenced this outcome was the need to comply with IFRS 3, the business combinations standard. Philip made his point very strongly about it not making sense to the extent of taking it as an unresolved issue to the audit committee. Whilst taking a pragmatic view on the valuation methodology rather than just accepting his technical department's line, Barry was determined to get the precedents right for future acquisitions, which he succeeded in doing. This interaction reflects dissatisfaction from all three parties about IFRS 3.

6.4.2   Financial Reporting Interaction: Impairment Reviews

This interaction related to the particularly sensitive and judgemental issue of goodwill impairment reviews, as required by IFRS 3. Key sensitivities referred to by the three interviewees from an external and internal perspective were: a charge to goodwill could be interpreted as having overpaid for an acquisition or that a company is in difficulty; impairment affects the bonus pool for executives; there could be particular sensitivities at boardroom level if an acquisition had been promoted by a particular director; and the valuations are inevitably judgemental. Guy felt that the involvement of non-executives in this matter was particularly important because of executive sensitivities.

Barry was concerned that the company was not doing the impairment reviews quite in accordance with the standard but the difference was not material. All three interviewees were aware of a potential issue and initially it was left to the subordinates in the company and the audit firm to explore possible solutions.

Philip believed there was no need for an impairment as the business case stood up and the auditors were of the view that it might be too early to be sure. Guy discussed it with both sides, outside the audit committee, and found that there was not much difference between them. He did not want a debate at the audit committee about it. A major issue arose about quantifying any impairment that might be needed. In the end, they reached an agreement that, as it was not obvious that an impairment was needed, Kestrel would increase the level of disclosure which would protect them against any future criticism. The impairment review and increased disclosure continued through to the next half year.

Guy particularly felt that the standard was flawed and it would be better if goodwill was amortized over a period so that the judgemental issues year-on-year were removed.

This interaction was a judgemental issue where Philip did not want impairment. Guy, conscious of the executive sensitivities around impairment, listened to both sides and was doubtful if there was a case, but sorted it out with Barry and Philip so it did not go to the audit committee as an open issue because of the sensitivities. The solution was increased disclosure. Guy acknowledged from his experience in other companies that impairments could be delayed until it was absolutely necessary to make them. This interaction also reflects dissatisfaction with IFRS 3 and the problematic and sensitive judgements associated with goodwill impairment, with a preference being expressed for annual amortization.

6.4.3 Financial Reporting Interaction: Financial Instruments — Treatment of Preference Shares

This interaction involved Philip and Barry. This was particularly interesting because in the first year of IFRS implementation, Philip was overruled by Barry as to what the accounting treatment under IAS 39 should be. Philip thought that Barry's firm's technical department had insisted that it should be treated in a certain way.

However Philip, whilst making it clear that he did not agree with Barry's recommendation, thought that a dictate from the technical department had to be followed and could lead to the threat of a qualification if he pushed back. He decided not to push back in any case because as it was a balance sheet classification matter, and he did not think it was sufficiently important.

As it turned out, Barry's firm had got it wrong and Kestrel reverted to Philip's original proposal. Philip rather proudly pointed out that the Financial Reporting Review Panel had reviewed Kestrel's accounts and made no comments. This is an interesting interaction where the auditors' technical department originally made the wrong recommendation, which Philip followed, although he did not agree with it. This shows how strong the influence of an audit firm's technical department can be, even when the advice is wrong.

6.4.4 Financial Reporting Interaction: Financial Instruments — Hedging

This was another IAS 39 interaction which required Kestrel to change the way they dealt with some hedging issues. Barry was particularly critical of IAS 39. However, the problem was recognized early in the year and the proposed solution presented to the audit committee for approval.

This interaction demonstrates the value of the three key parties addressing problem issues well before the end and presenting an agreed position to the audit committee. It also demonstrates that, on matters of significance, the audit committee chair can get involved in reaching agreement.

6.4.5   Financial Reporting Interaction: Restructuring Costs

This was not so much an interaction as a commentary on how the three parties viewed the disclosure of restructuring costs. The core issue was that IAS 1 does not prescribe the layout of disclosure on the income statement so the companies had a lot of flexibility in how to disclose restructuring costs. The key number for the company was described as 'adjusted operating profit'.

Guy did not think that the flexibility in the IAS 1 presentation made any difference to users' perceptions. Barry's view was that as long as it complied with IAS 1 it was fine.

6.4.6   Corporate Governance Issue: Fraud and Illegal Acts

The company had a whistle blowing procedure which produced little response. Guy regards it as important that management disclose all frauds to the audit committee and the company had a zero tolerance attitude to fraud. The audit committee, therefore, took fraud very seriously and, when a fraud did arise, there was an in depth investigation as to how it happened and could have been prevented.

6.5   CONCLUSIONS

The interactions in this case are very interesting. Philip is a knowledgeable and assertive finance director who is seriously annoyed about aspects of IFRS, particularly IFRS 3 about acquisitions and mergers. He is, therefore, hostile to the need to comply with the standards, although he recognizes that in the end he has little choice. Barry is an experienced, confident and pragmatic senior partner in his firm who takes it all in his stride but makes sure that Kestrel does not actually break the rules and run into trouble. Guy is a statesmanlike referee who wishes to be engaged with major issues to ensure that they are satisfactorily resolved before they go to the audit committee. He regards fees as a management issue to be approved by the audit committee.

Two judgemental interactions relate to IFRS 3. The valuation of intangibles on acquisition was not a material issue in the first year of IFRS implementation, but Barry was determined to get a precedent set for the future and Philip knew he could only go so far in objecting to what Barry wanted. The impairment of goodwill was resolved in a situation of uncertainty about the position by all three parties agreeing on further disclosure.

Two issues arose from IAS 39. In the first year, Barry's firm gave an incorrect interpretation of the standard relating to a preference share liability and Philip went along with it under protest but, interestingly, would not challenge Barry's firm's technical department. The error was put right in year two of IFRS implementation. The IAS 39 requirement for hedging was sorted out by the three parties working together to find a resolution to put to the audit committee to pre-empt debate there. Both these interactions related to the interpretation of IAS 39.

The final financial reporting interaction, a judgemental one, related to the disclosure of re-organization costs where IAS 1 was so flexible that the company effectively did what they wanted.

A final point refers to the apparent lack of useful information from the whistle blowing process and the audit committee's zero tolerance to fraud.

Case 3 — Mallard plc

I think the dialogue between the audit committee and auditors is very important. All those things are good news. Do they bring about better quality? They do, actually ... What the best companies have always done is now done everywhere *(Jack, finance director)*

7.1 BACKGROUND TO THE CASE

Mallard is a capital intensive company highly influenced by commodity prices. Turnover and operating profits have shown recent increases due to higher commodity prices and despite a decline in output. Reasons cited for the improvement focus on a higher proportion of fixed price sales contracts which insulated the company from fluctuations in market prices.

The finance director is Jack (aged in his 40s) who was appointed to Mallard a few years ago as he has wide financial experience and had previously been group finance director for another listed FTSE 250 company.

Paul (in his late 50s) is the audit committee chair. He joined the board of Mallard as a non-executive director some years ago. His past experience includes serving on the board of a major listed company (including a spell as chief executive) and he holds a number of other non-executive positions. He is a qualified accountant.

Gerald (in his 40s) is the current audit engagement partner. Another partner, Tom, based in another office, is also involved with the audit, liaising with the main finance function. Gerald has recently been rotated in as audit partner.

7.2 CORPORATE GOVERNANCE

In the company's corporate governance report it is stated that the group considers that it complies with section 1 of the Combined Code. There are five members of the audit committee all of whom are non-executive directors. Both Paul and the deputy chairman of the audit committee are considered to be financial experts. The audit committee meets at least seven times per year.

7.2.1 Attendees at Audit Committee

Jack confirmed that he regularly attended audit committee meetings:

> I go to all the meetings. There is a session at the end of the meeting where both internal and external audit remain behind to see the audit committee members. And basically if no one comes and raps me over the knuckles, we are OK. **(Jack)**

Paul also required the auditors to attend:

> Both the internal and the external auditors attend every meeting. In both cases at my behest ... I don't think in either case it would be politic to say thanks, but no thanks. **(Paul)**

Gerald agreed that the meetings were attended by a number of people who were not members of the audit committee:

> The attendance is always the audit committee members plus quite a number of others. [Chairman] sometimes comes, [chief executive] is almost always there, Martin [deputy finance director] is always there to present the finance papers, I am always there to present the [audit firm] papers ... the head of internal audit is always there to present the internal audit papers and of late the chief risk officer is there to present his report. ... And the head of investor relations is often there when we are talking about any disclosures ... he will be there to present the presentations that go out to analysts and the like. So it is a pretty full meeting. **(Gerald)**

Although the composition of the audit committee included people with a broad range of financial skills, Jack did not consider this to be a problem:

> The way we deal with the results is that we lay them as a paper that goes with the results, that explains what the issues have been, what the debate has been about, the judgement calls. I think anyone reading it can see why we have landed in a certain position and ... a layman, non accountant, would follow the logic. It is written in relatively straightforward language ... One of the things that I do is to ensure that the audit committee has seen the issue ... When one of my team gives a paper on an accounting issue ... I am very keen that members understand where the points are and why we have done certain things. If they are glazing over I will say — the number could have been £x but it is £y because of so and so. It is part of my role to draw these points out. **(Jack)**

Gerald agreed that all the members of the audit committee were able to follow the discussions:

> They are all highly able people and they understand the debate. I have to say there hasn't been much discussion around accounting matters because there simply aren't any. We do talk about going concern, but again you don't need to be an accountant to understand the point about going concern ... I have been on audit committees where, you know, there are people who haven't much idea about what is in there ... But with this audit committee they all interact ... **(Gerald)**

7.2.2   Cycle of Meetings and Issues Discussed

The meetings were timed in conjunction with the main board meetings:

> The meetings will be where the board is. We tend to have two day, day and a half board meetings. Typically the first day is spent on committee business and then we would have a board dinner in the evening, then the board itself would take place usually in the morning of the next day. **(Paul)**

Paul provided an overview of the main content of audit committee meetings in a typical year:

> When it comes to the normal round of agendas, we do a plan for the year and the areas to cover. Some of that is driven by an underlying reporting calendar. We have the half year numbers, the full year numbers. They obviously occupy the same slots each year given the reporting timetable of the company. We also try and get through the other routine items on a regular basis. At least once a year we have a very formal report from internal audit and we do have a quarterly report updating us on progress . . . The chief of internal audit has a plan for the year which he reports against on a quarterly basis and we have an annual wrap up as well. So there is an underlying schedule of issues. **(Paul)**

However, there was scope to include non-routine items on the agenda:

> One off items which the executives want to bring to the committee would be raised with me as part of the agenda setting for each meeting. The company secretary . . . in essence drives the committee meetings . . . The audit committee meets, I suppose, six to eight times a year, depending on non standard business. I would see a draft of the agenda of every meeting and add to or subtract from that draft in consultation with the company secretary. **(Paul)**

Paul described how issues came to be referred to the audit committee from a number of sources:

> We have a series of regular scheduled items which will come from different sources within the executive. So the chief internal auditor's report will come from him and he will report both on a regular basis but also an ad hoc basis . . . They will have specific presentations at the audit committee on individual internal audit reports. Typically we would look through the work that is being done . . . and basically discuss the issues in the schedule. The financial controller would typically raise issues around financial reporting, corporate reporting, half year, full year, accounting policy issues and those sorts of things. The external auditors themselves obviously present a report, not to every committee, but certainly where there is published reporting . . . The group chief risk officer also raises issues of a non financial nature. And of course there is information that comes through the whistle blowing process and they come direct to me as audit committee chair. **(Paul)**

He suggested that the agenda items were mostly initiated by the executive directors:

> The non-execs would rarely raise agenda item issues . . . If non-execs have issues they want to raise they would tend to raise them at the end of the meeting in the private session . . . If they had particular concerns they wouldn't wait that long, they would raise them with me direct. Get it on the agenda or if there were a more appropriate way of doing it. I can't recall non-execs pushing for the inclusion of particular issues that weren't already in the plan for the year. **(Paul)**

The papers made available to members of the audit committee were described by Gerald:

> The company will provide the audit committee with its own accounting paper which will deal with all the same issues that we deal with in our report and so what we tend to do is make reference to the company paper and then provide our own view on the issue . . . What goes into the company paper and what goes into our paper is the negotiation, nothing difficult, just wording. We don't report on some of the things they report on. But they almost always report on the things we report on. **(Gerald)**

Overseeing audit planning was one of the roles of the audit committee and Gerald described the approach adopted by his firm for Mallard:

> There is an audit strategy document that we give to them early in the year. There is a strategy and quality section and . . . there is the planning. They understand our document because it hasn't changed a great deal in a couple of years, and there is the whole process around engagement letters. **(Gerald)**

Gerald would have discussed the audit plan with Jack before it was considered by the audit committee. Paul discussed the approach of the audit committee to the audit plan:

> We go through, not quite line by line, but certainly issue by issue . . . I am sure it is the case that their approach is risk based, there is no sort of verification audit . . . So you tend to focus primarily on what is different than last year. Why are the top ten risks either the same as, or different to, last year? And we talk about resourcing and succession and rotation and all the sorts of issues you would expect . . . It is to some degree formulaic but at least you have to address the issues . . . Somebody has to say something about auditor independence, about the team being of an adequate size. **(Paul)**

Overall Gerald perceived that the main focus of issues under discussion had shifted away from accounting during his tenure as audit partner:

> When I first took it over . . . there was probably an audit committee a month scheduled but we are now down to a lot less than that . . . Now operations and going concern are about the only things we talk about, frankly. And issues coming out of internal audit. **(Gerald)**

7.2.3   The Chair's Management of the Audit Committee and Key Relationships

Gerald gave his perception of the style of a typical meeting:

> The way it tends to work is that Paul chairs it and he has the ownership of the meeting and the individual papers are presented and comments and questions come in from audit committee members, so the others tend to be silent unless it is for them to answer a question. So, most of the questions will be answered by Jack or [deputy finance director], and sometimes if they are talking about technical matters, which we often are these days, then the answer will come in from [chief executive], generally, although often from Jack. **(Gerald)**

Reflecting on the recent regulatory changes that have strengthened the role of the audit committee, Paul believed that there still were practical limitations on how much they should intervene:

> The last thing the audit committee want, even nowadays, is to be cast as arbiter. It is one thing to be involved in the discussion, another to say I would do this. They are poorly placed to make that kind of executive decision ... It doesn't seem like good governance for the audit committee to be effectively cast as decision maker. You might want to influence the outcome by pushing things in a certain direction, that is fair game, but I am not quite sure how you would record a final decision made by an audit committee in the face of opposition by either the finance director or the audit partner ... You are certainly not cast in the role of being the settler of arguments not least because you usually haven't got the ammunition to settle an argument of that sort ... Most of us wouldn't even pretend that we are up to speed with the latest international standards. If the audit committee members are wasting time debating the finer principles you are probably off the track anyway. (**Paul**)

Gerald concurred that the audit committee at Mallard was not used to settle disputes:

> We have never had, whilst I have been in charge of the audit, any need for me to escalate anything to the audit committee because I am not happy with the way things are going. There is no doubt that I can do that and the relationships would be respected, but it is not that sort of problem. (**Gerald**)

Despite this, Paul considered that the audit committee played a very important role:

> It is a question of scrutiny, transparency, visibility reaching down into the organization. And I think also in essence you are a thermometer which tests the temperature of the finance director in particular ... I think the new triangular model, as opposed to the old binary model, where the audit committee come to the party last, is definitely a vast improvement on how things were in the past. (**Paul**)

He continued to explain how he thought the new regulatory approach had altered the typical audit partner's perception of who the client was:

> I think the improvement is a very clear understanding of the role and importance of the audit committee and the need for the audit partner to serve the audit committee first and the executive second. If you ask any audit partner now who he works for, if he has any sense, he will say the audit committee. He may say the board, but he certainly won't say the finance director. Whereas ten or fifteen years ago he would have said the finance director, if you were being honest. (**Paul**)

Jack also reflected on the increased emphasis on the role of the audit committee that had been brought in by the Smith Committee:

> I think the dialogue between the audit committee and auditors is very important. All those things are good news. Do they bring about better quality? They do, actually ... What the best companies have always done is now done everywhere. (**Jack**)

7.2.4   Nature of the Relationship with the Auditor

Jack was very clear that he took his relationship with the auditors very seriously:

> I am very, very keen to be on side with the auditors. I listen very carefully to what the auditors say, what they worry about, and I respond to them. (**Jack**)

Paul outlined the contact he had with the audit partner:

> I meet with the audit partner on my own once a year, as an audit committee we have good informal contact, it is fine. If they have issues they raise them, it does work well. (**Paul**)

At one time there had been some problems in the company and Paul noted that the auditors' assessment was that Mallard was very high risk. This risk profile had significantly affected the behaviour of the partner and the whole relationship with the audit firm:

> If you are a high risk client everything gets double dressed. The audit partner who may be confident enough to go with something suddenly has got somebody behind him saying — you have got a high risk client, don't forget. It is not just you whose neck is on the line. All the rest of these guys back here, we're on the line as well, so for God's sake ... it just makes it very tense, you know. I think everyone's buttocks just tighten up. (**Paul**)

Gerald outlined the rather complex relationships between Mallard and his firm:

> I interact with Jack by and large. I have a partner who interacts with the deputy finance director. The accounting function and the consolidation is done out of [British city] ... I tend to have a relationship with Jack and Paul ... I see Jack, most months. We tend to talk when there is an issue to discuss, there hasn't been much of late. There have been things that have been going on, but in general they tend to be outside the audit now. (**Gerald**)

Gerald provided more detail on his contact with Paul:

> I will generally brief Paul in advance of the main [clearance] meeting and I would always brief him if there was something controversial ... That has fallen into abeyance slightly because the issues at the moment are not the sort of things that are really around financial accounting ... It is much more commercial ... than it is accounting. So, we have a good relationship. I know I can email him, ring him up whenever I want to. (**Gerald**)

7.3   KEY INTERACTIONS BETWEEN JACK, PAUL AND GERALD

During the course of the audit the following issues prompted discussion between Jack, Paul and Gerald:

1. Audit fees.
2. Accounting for a complex transaction.
3. Business Review.

4. Financial instruments — hedging.
5. Going concern.
6. Impairment of assets.

7.3.1   Audit Fee

Gerald outlined the process for setting the audit fee:

> We agree it with management and then put it up for approval at audit committee, and
> Jack is pretty reasonable. **(Gerald)**

Jack confirmed that management were responsible for the initial negotiation:

> We negotiate the fee, one of my team, the deputy finance director, the hard guy. **(Jack)**

Jack's view was that the company always ended up paying marginally more than they
thought they would:

> They would do anything to get a bit more out of us. It is a continual tussle. It is like
> anyone on a time and materials basis. It is like a plumber — it was more difficult than I
> thought replacing that U-bend; same applies to the auditors. **(Jack)**

Paul confirmed that as audit committee chair his perspective on audit fees was slightly
different from that of the executives:

> They are more concerned about cost than we are. The audit committee and the indepen-
> dent non executive directors are concerned only about assurance. So one of the questions
> I always ask, not just in this company but in any company, is 'With this audit fee can I
> get the level of assurance that tells me the control in this company is right?', and if the
> answer is anything other than 'Absolutely', then they should go away and come back
> with another estimate. **(Paul)**

Paul agreed that the audit committee were responsible for final approval:

> We actually approve it. We don't go through the hourly rates of the partners involved. Our
> view is that every pound that we spend has to be pre-approved by the audit committee
> and any change in the estimate has to be pre-approved by the audit committee. Our
> assertion is essentially that we want absolute assurance, we are not interested in any
> cheap thing. **(Paul)**

7.3.2   Accounting for a Complex Transaction

Both Paul and Jack referred to this issue. Gerald was not acting as audit partner when
the transaction took place. There was no clearly prescribed accounting solution for it.
Jack described the issues in broad terms:

> Do we capitalize it or not capitalize it? How do you write it through the P&L? How do
> you deal with at the year-end, cash flow? All those issues were around how you dealt
> with it in such a way that it didn't distort the business report as a result. **(Jack)**

Jack described the approach they had taken to resolve the problem:

> We had [Gerald's firm] as auditors and we had [second firm of accountants] providing advice to the company so that we could debate with [Gerald's firm] about it. Which, I think, is a rather unusual position, but given the complexity of the issues involved our view was that we needed some independent advice. In the end we came to a resolution that everyone agreed to in that technical field, which then allowed us to make a proposition to the audit committee. **(Jack)**

Jack emphasized that the parties involved in trying to solve this problem were members of the firm's technical departments:

> You were outside the realms of an audit partner. This is really very complex technical issues, beyond the boundaries of what had been done before on these things ... so therefore it is the interpretation of it that you have to deal with. So we end up dealing direct. **(Jack)**

The initial proposal for a solution to accounting for the transaction came from the auditors but Jack was not persuaded by it:

> The initial proposition from [audit firm] produced perverse answers ... You ended up with the company performing badly and financial results showing it performing very well. So it was a bizarre situation where the company performs very badly and the actual profits were higher. That struck me as a bit perverse. ... therefore we had to find other solutions. **(Jack)**

Ultimately a satisfactory solution did emerge from the discussions between the company, its auditors and the second accounting firm.
Paul said that, by the time the issue reached the audit committee, it had been settled:

> We weren't being cast in the role of arbiters or final decision makers. **(Paul)**

He also reflected on the decline in the authority of the audit partner at the expense of technical departments on such contentious issues:

> There was a time when if you went to the audit partner and said 'What are we going to do about this?' if he says 'We are going to do this', we knew that he had delivered to you [audit firm's] opinion. Nowadays that is simply not the case ... He would certainly take it away and have a chin wag and then come back and say — this is [audit firm's] view on this. **(Paul)**

7.3.3   Business Review

Both Jack and Paul cited this as a discussion issue although they appeared to have quite different perceptions as to how serious the issue was.[1] For Jack there were no complications:

> This is quite a straightforward business to describe . . . We got ourselves into a pattern. (**Jack**)

Paul considered it a much more exacting exercise:

> We spent a lot of time discussing the verbal narrative positioning of the company because, it is a bit like watching bumble bees fly. Positioning the company is difficult. (**Paul**)

The message and tone of the business review was examined with great care:

> It is gone over with a fine toothcomb. Are we being too optimistic, too pessimistic? . . . It is the executives talking the company down and the non-executives who are talking the company up . . . It tends to be the other way round. It is the non-execs who have less exposure to the cutting edge on a daily basis. (**Paul**)

Gerald did not cite the Business Review as a discussion issue but Paul outlined the extent of the auditor's involvement:

> He had to read through the published numbers and also there is a requirement for it to be congruent. There is no point in saying that the numbers are rubbish, but I'm feeling very up about it . . . And increasingly they will be looking at KPIs to the extent that KPIs are auditable, to make sure that we have the information to measure the KPIs that we present. (**Paul**)

Paul reflected further on the relationship between the Business Review and a set of accounts based on IFRS:

> You come back to the obvious conflict between our desire to have accounting standards and also increasingly the desire to write down how you run this business . . . You will have this body of accounting rules and numerous pages of notes so that it will be very hard to write something which is very different or even looks different to what is in those notes. For a public company, it is very hard for the chief executive or the chairman or the finance director to say in his accounts — this is what I think is important, I would put more store by this. (**Paul**)

He did not feel that the accounting reflected the business activity:

> The KPIs that help us run the business are nothing to the accounting principles of IFRS . . . There is not a single objective that a manager has that is driven by IFRS, apart from

---

[1] The Enhanced Business Review was brought in by the Companies Act 2006, becoming effective for yearend beginning on or after 1 October 2007. Therefore, it did not have a direct impact on the year under discussion in this chapter. It requires companies to include in their annual reports discussion of a number of issues such as a review of the business, objectives and strategies, risks and uncertainties and an analysis using financial and non-financial key performance indicators (KPIs).

the finance director who has got to produce a set of accounts which are compliant . . . to really understand what matters in the business, what the risks are, what the opportunities are, so that we can leverage this business, there is nothing there in IFRS. **(Paul)**

Jack raised a similar point arguing that investors relied on presentations in preference to IFRS-based accounts:

In the world that we live in a lot of work goes into statutory processes but most analysts use figures from presentations that the company gives in their own investor presentations. And what happens in the statutory accounts is a side show . . . Predominately the investor presentations giving the management view of what the numbers really look like and what they mean is what people focus on . . . So you have an anomaly where we spend an inordinate amount of time producing IFRS which is all very interesting but, where do people really look, they look at what management are saying. **(Jack)**

He agreed that there needed to be a clear link between the statutory accounts and the figures used in the presentation:

What I always say to my team is that we need to make sure that there is a very clear path from the statutory numbers to the investor relations presentations, so that you can take people through it . . . No one can accuse you of anything untoward. The statutory numbers on their own are no help at all to investors. **(Jack)**

7.3.4   Financial Instruments — Hedging

Both Gerald and Paul discussed this fairly complex issue. Paul explained his understanding of the problem:[2]

That was just about the treatment of the various instruments we use. Really a trading operation, where in essence we are buying and selling [our product], and whether or not the cover was related to the actual flows in the business or whether it was trading. So the debate was whether the instruments were trading instruments or are they hedges in the normal course of business . . . to hedge underlying flows in the business? So the debate was all about the documentation, how we recorded the transaction. **(Paul)**

Gerald explained why this distinction mattered:

Certain contracts that they have, they have the right to claim own use accounting for, i.e. they don't have to fair value the contracts associated with them, provided they can demonstrate own use, that they are selling their own product. **(Gerald)**

---

[2] Hedge accounting (recognizing the offsetting effects of fair value changes of both the hedging instrument and the hedged item in the same period's profit or loss) is permitted in certain circumstances by IAS 39 *Financial Instruments: Recognition and Measurement,* provided that the hedging relationship is clearly defined, measurable and actually effective. There are three different types of hedges:

– fair value hedge: if an entity hedges a change in fair value of a recognized asset or liability, the change in fair values of both the hedging instrument and the hedged item are recognized in the profit or loss when they occur;

– cash flow hedge: if an entity hedges changes in the future cash flows relating to a recognized asset or liability, then the change in the fair value of the hedging instrument is recognized directly in equity until such time as those future cash flows occur;

– hedge of a net investment in a foreign entity which is treated as a cash flow hedge (Deloitte, 2007).

He made it clear that a move to fair value could potentially have a substantial impact on the accounts, although being dependent on future market prices this could not be predicted. Paul agreed that these discussions were part of a continuing debate and described why the issue was particularly problematic for Mallard:

> It is an ongoing issue because there will always be a debate about the nature of the contract, has it changed at any point? Not least because we all have problems . . . So, you obviously hedge on the basis of what you think you are going to produce and then you can do something completely different. So, there is an ongoing debate about whether a contract is a hedge or not. Because until you deliver the underlying [product] it is very difficult to say whether it is a hedge. So, we obviously say — this is what we could produce, let us take a little bit off for what we have done in the past, and another bit off for comfort and then we will sell the rest. But, we want to sell against a forward price, otherwise we are simply taking small prices all the time . . . **(Paul)**

Gerald confirmed that the nature of the business was instrumental in prompting the accounting debate:

> We have to think quite carefully about whether [Mallard] can continue to take them out of the net for fair value accounting . . . It is an exposure; it is a disclosure issue; it is not yet an adjustment in the financial statements, but it is something . . . the company keeps an eye on and we talk about it at audit committee meetings. **(Gerald)**

Paul gave his view on the tone of the debates:

> I suppose at the margin there may have been some conflict between the auditors and the executive as to what the nature of a particular activity is . . . They both [Jack and Gerald] see the issue. It is not that the finance director is fighting a rear guard action against the accounting standards saying that — this is a hedge and I will say it is a hedge till the day I die . . . As the accounting standards have evolved and our processes have evolved . . . He [Jack] has got to have processes that say — what is this position in such and such a situation and if its nature changes in the course of its life then we have to accept the accounting consequences. Our market risk department is busy writing manuals, processes and recording decisions that are made and why they are made. **(Paul)**

However, Paul consoled himself with the fact that whatever accounting treatment is adopted, it will have no impact on the cash flows of the business:

> You are still going to have the same cash flows over a period of time. All these future contracts are all going to resolve themselves in cash flow terms over the length of the contract. I really can't get too excited about it. **(Paul)**

Paul was not impressed that, not being a financial institution, Mallard had been heavily caught up in the complexities of IAS 39:

> We have got a sledgehammer here to crack a walnut. What is a big issue for banks, as far as the investment banks, in terms of their balance sheets and their activity, is not really such a big issue for trading companies . . . The reason that we do these things is to hedge our positions . . . We don't bring guys on board to use our capital to play the

markets ... Everything we do in trading is basically to manage our underlying position ... We want to cut out the volatility ... Using market instruments to help us hedge it and give us certainty of outcome. But that is not good enough. You have got to get down to an individual contract and say — well, what was in mind when we took this contract on? And if we say — it is to hedge our underlying position, then the next question is — how do you know what your underlying position is, well, I don't actually. So, you are immediately back to — so this is a speculative position. **(Paul)**

Gerald agreed that other contracts needed to be considered in relation to IAS 39:

There are others that we will talk about; we will consider them from the point of IAS 39; whether they are captured or not; how you account for them. It is the toughest, trickiest technical area from an accounting perspective and we have a specialist IAS 39 director who deals with this for me. **(Gerald)**

7.3.5 Going Concern

Going concern was always a discussion issue.[3] Gerald explained how they considered it:

In advance of them issuing a half yearly press release, they put a paper on going concern into the papers for the audit committee, and we comment on it. The principal issue is that there is quite a lot of uncertainty because of the volatility of the [market] price. You can see cash going up and down during the year. So, it is one of the most serious things we have to talk about. **(Gerald)**

Paul agreed that this was an important discussion point but considered that it was less of a concern now than it had been:

Going concern ... not surprisingly there is quite a lot of discussion. There is more certainty on revenues at least. People might default on the contracts, but that is a different issue. Going concern has become simpler because we are not so close to the wire. We look to see if, in x years time, we will be a going concern. **(Paul)**

His view was that, as well as the revenues of the business becoming increasingly predictable, the costs were also relatively easy to forecast. Previously the market conditions left the business more exposed than it was currently:

There wasn't much scope to hedge forward. The market wasn't as liquid then. **(Paul)**

---

[3] IAS 1 *Presentation of Financial Statements* requires management to make an assessment of an enterprise's ability to continue as a going concern. This will involve making a judgement, at a particular point in time, about the future outcome of events or conditions which are inherently uncertain. The auditor's responsibility is to consider the appropriateness of management's use of the going concern assumption in the preparation of the financial statements, and consider whether there are material uncertainties about the entity's ability to continue as a going concern that need to be disclosed in the financial statements (APB, ISA 570).

7.3.6   Impairment of Assets

Gerald explained why he considered impairment of plant and equipment[4] to be a discussion issue:

> We had been debating how you do impairment. This isn't actually resolved yet ... It is all around what is the cash generating unit? **(Gerald)**

He agreed that while this was not really a current issue it still had to be monitored:

> It isn't an issue with the assets at the moment because the values that were placed on them were really quite small, because at the time, the [market] prices were really quite low. Of course, since then, they have moved up quite markedly and so actually the value of the assets is way over what they are stated in the books. **(Gerald)**

Paul emphasized that market price was also a key ingredient in the valuation model and that many uncertainties affected that:

> And that varies from day to day. So you have got to take a view on what the value is going to be ... What we come up with is a view, scenarios, a wind sock of possibilities and you pick something in the middle. It is difficult. We have a well rehearsed model for doing it, and a well rehearsed debate with the auditors. We can and do use third party information. **(Paul)**

7.4   CONTEXTUAL FACTORS AND ANALYSIS OF THE INTERACTIONS

The contextual factors are summarized in Figure 7.1. The diagram shows that the company was well managed with a very strong governance and compliance culture which was partly a legacy of going concern problems in the past which had been satisfactorily resolved. The finance director, Jack, was very experienced and capable and did not want disagreements with his auditors. The audit partner, Gerald, was a senior partner in his firm who had recently taken over the audit on the rotation of his predecessor. Neither Jack nor Gerald expected to take unresolved issues to the audit committee.

The audit committee chair, Paul, was also very experienced and a former finance director of a large company. He saw the audit committee as an 'appeals court' rather than an arbiter between auditor and the finance director. The meetings had a very clear structure and were attended by a range of people including the chairman on occasions

---

[4] IAS 36 *Impairment of Assets* states that an asset may not be carried on the balance sheet above its recoverable amount. Recoverable amount is defined as the higher of the asset's fair value less costs to sell and its value in use. Value in use is ascertained by estimating future cash flows to be derived from the asset discounted by a pre-tax market rate which takes account of the time value of money and asset specific risk. If the carrying value exceeds the recoverable amount it is considered impaired and the loss is recognized in the profit or loss. While recoverable amount is generally calculated for individual assets, an asset seldom generates cash flows independently of other assets. Therefore, most assets are tested for impairment in groups of assets known as cash generating units (CGUs) (PwC, 2009).

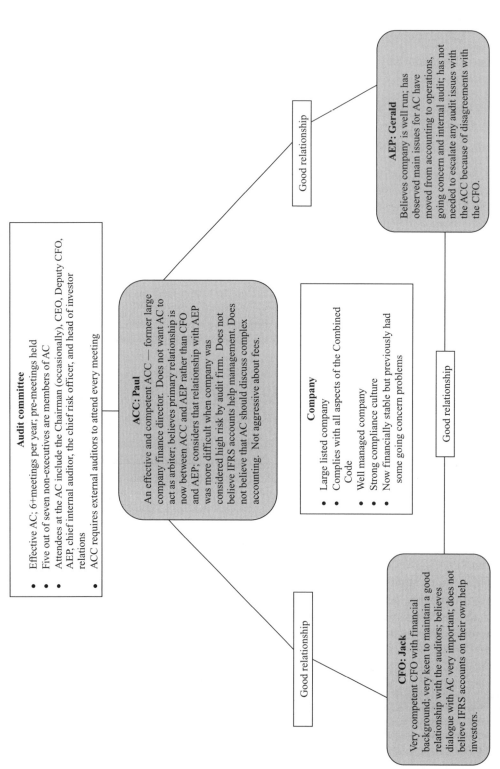

Audit committee

- Effective AC; 6+meetings per year; pre-meetings held
- Five out of seven non-executives are members of AC
- Attendees at the AC include the Chairman (occasionally), CEO, Deputy CFO, AEP, chief internal auditor, the chief risk officer, and head of investor relations
- ACC requires external auditors to attend every meeting

ACC: Paul

An effective and competent ACC — former large company finance director. Does not want AC to act as arbiter; believes primary relationship is now between ACC and AEP rather than CFO and AEP; considers that relationship with AEP was more difficult when company was considered high risk by audit firm. Does not believe IFRS accounts help management. Does not believe that AC should discuss complex accounting. Not aggressive about fees.

Company

- Large listed company
- Complies with all aspects of the Combined Code
- Well managed company
- Strong compliance culture
- Now financially stable but previously had some going concern problems

AEP: Gerald

Believes company is well run; has observed main issues for AC have moved from accounting to operations, going concern and internal audit; has not needed to escalate any audit issues with the ACC because of disagreements with the CFO.

CFO: Jack

Very competent CFO with financial background; very keen to maintain a good relationship with the auditors; believes dialogue with AC very important; does not believe IFRS accounts on their own help investors.

Good relationship

Good relationship

Good relationship

Figure 7.1 Mallard — General context for interactions

and the chief executive. He did not believe in being aggressive about audit fees as his main concern was that the audit should be done to an appropriate standard.

7.4.1   Audit Fee

The comments on fees, which do not have the attributes of an interaction, show that Jack has a different attitude to fees than Paul. Jack feels that Mallard end up paying a bit more than they should, whereas Paul wants to be sure that the fee provides them with the level of assurance that the company needs.

7.4.2   Financial Reporting Interaction: Accounting for a Complex Transaction

In the year before Gerald had been rotated into the audit partner role the company had engaged in an unusual transaction for which there was no prescribed accounting solution. Jack wished to present a proposed solution to the audit committee and he sought advice from another accounting firm to ensure he found the most suitable proposal. In the end, he felt that the interpretation problem of how to account for the transaction was too much for the previous partner, so he dealt direct with the technical department himself. Jack did not like the first proposal from the auditors but in the end they all worked together to find a proposal for the committee as Paul expected. Paul regretted that audit partners had lost authority to their firm's technical departments.

7.4.3   Financial Reporting Interaction: Business Review

The interesting issue in this interaction is that Jack saw it as far less of an issue that Paul was concerned about how the company message was communicated and that the KPIs presented were auditable. Neither Paul nor Jack thought that the IFRS accounts, into which so much resource was invested, offered much to the company or the investors.

7.4.4   Financial Reporting Interaction: Financial Instruments — Hedging

Mallard sold its product mainly by forward contracts and, as there was price volatility, an essential part of their business model was to hedge the transactions. These hedges were caught under IAS 39 and, therefore, they had to put forward a case for each of the hedge instruments not to be fair valued. Jack did not refer to this. Paul knew that Jack accepted the exercise had to be done and Jack had to set processes up to deal with it. They were also writing guidance manuals because the accounting standards said so, but Paul thought it was all necessary and acknowledged that Jack also accepted that it had to be done. Paul thought that there had been some tension between Jack and Gerald over this but there was no question of non-compliance. Gerald saw it as his role to make sure they did comply whilst recognizing that it was tricky and complex. Paul was not enthusiastic about having to go through this exercise as they were not a financial institution and could not get too excited about it as the cash flows were not affected.

7.4.5 Financial Reporting Interaction: Going Concern

Because of previous going concern problems this was taken very seriously by the audit committee and discussed before the half yearly press release went out. Gerald considered going concern to be one of the most serious issues they discussed. Paul believed it was simpler than it had been as the use of forward contracts had made prediction of future revenues a lot easier.

7.4.6 Financial Reporting Interaction: Impairment of Assets

This was an issue that was monitored every year but was not a major problem as the assets were in the records at low values. However, they had a clear process for dealing with the valuations.

7.5 CONCLUSIONS

Mallard was a company with very strong governance and a finance director and an audit committee chair who were both very capable. Although they disapproved of aspects of the IFRS accounting model, there was no inclination from either of them to try to navigate round the system. This is partly driven by previous going concern problems and a desire to keep the company very clean. Paul, as the audit committee chair, does not want to squeeze the audit fee and lose comfort from the audit whereas Jack, as the finance director, feels they always pay a bit too much. Gerald is a mature and experienced partner who ensures that they do get it right.

As the overriding objective has been to get it right in the case of a complex transaction, a second opinion was sought to ensure they did. This was not passed up to Paul until a firm proposal was identified. They were particularly annoyed by IAS 39 requiring them to assess all their hedging contracts, as they regarded hedging future prices as a support for their trading activity, rather than being a financial institution doing trades in financial instruments. The audit committee had some difficulty getting to grips with issues associated with the Business Review and asset impairment also provided some problems in identifying the cash generating unit. Thus, on complex issues, the audit committee does get involved in some debate.

Four issues were judgemental: the complex transaction; going concern; the Business Review; and asset impairment. The hedging issue was an interpretation of IFRS.

Case 4 — Finch plc

Nobody likes prior year adjustments, except the auditors, let's be honest (Damien, audit partner)

8.1 BACKGROUND TO THE CASE

Finch plc is a FTSE — small cap company specializing in the provision of consultancy services to both the private and public sectors. In recent years the group has internationalized beyond its European core by acquiring a number of small consultancies in other countries to attain critical mass.

The company's founder, Matthew, is due to retire as executive chairman. Until recently he also acted as CEO but has now been replaced by Dean.

Ben (aged in his 40s) is the finance director. He is a qualified accountant and has worked for over 20 years in professional services and outsourcing organizations and has experience as finance director for both private and listed companies. He joined the company the previous year.

Robert (also in his 40s) had just given up being audit committee chair, being replaced by Jim. Robert holds an MBA from a prestigious international business school. He has considerable consultancy experience and is on the board and audit committee of a number of private companies. He joined Finch's board as a non-executive director a few years earlier. At the time of the interview he was in the process of becoming non-executive chairman but remaining as a member of the audit committee (although not as chair).

The current audit engagement partner is Damien (in his 40s). Damien's firm won the audit via a tender process from another Big Four Firm the previous year. The change was prompted by the realization that the previous auditors (Firm B) were particularly strong in the IT sector and that Finch wanted to collaborate with them in future bids. This would not be possible if they remained as auditors. A further complication was that Ben had past connections with firm B. As a result of the auditor change, two of the three key players, that is, the finance director and the audit partner responsible for preparing the relevant accounts, were involved with Finch for the first time. One apparent consequence of this was a surprisingly large number of restatements.

The financial reporting culture of the company was described by the audit committee chair as conservative.

8.2   CORPORATE GOVERNANCE

The main board consists of the chairman, the CEO, Ben (CFO), Robert (ACC) and two other non-executive directors. In the company's report on corporate governance for the relevant year it is stated the Group is in compliance with the provisions of the Combined Code except that the chairman for part of the year also acted as chief executive.

8.2.1   Attendees at Audit Committee

The formal membership of the audit committee is the three non-executive directors. Ben provided information about who actually attends:

> Typically the full audit committee meeting is ... typically the chief exec and I will be there and then we will leave and they will have their session but otherwise it tends to be me. The audit committee chair may have other meetings with the auditors without me ... The auditor might bring his tax partner. **(Ben)**

Damien acknowledged that at Finch the meetings had a less formal atmosphere than at some of his other clients where executive directors might not attend. He revealed his strategy for dealing with their attendance:

> When I take on a new client I always say to the audit committee that I think it would be appropriate for there to be a period every meeting where the execs are asked to leave, if I have nothing to say we will spend a couple of minutes talking about the weather and then invite them back. If I have something to say then we don't have to particularly ask for it, it just makes it easier ... And the execs completely understand and they are quite comfortable with it and they all go. **(Damien)**

Nevertheless, Damien believed that there were real advantages of having the executive directors present for at least part of the meeting:

> So in some ways when we are having a discussion about an issue it is slightly bizarre to have the auditors and the non-execs having a discussion about something and the people who understand it better are out of the room. So the advantage of having them there is that they can bring some information to the meeting. And probably give an update from the last time we spoke to them on a subject. **(Damien)**

He added that their presence was particularly valuable with a company like Finch:

> They have got certain perennial contracts where the company will take a view as to what the likely outturn is on those discussions, and they are pretty good on it, actually. So far when they have said — we don't think we are going to get that, we think we are going to have to reduce our fees by that, the outturn has, so far, been very accurate. **(Damien)**

Ben was satisfied with the quality of the audit committee and their ability to keep up with debates:

They are pretty good, I think they more or less glaze over on some of the new accounting issues. But they will be aware of the quality of the finance function. And they will ask some sensible business questions but not get into the technical accounting issues. **(Ben)**

Damien was broadly in agreement with that assessment:

These are all sensible people. I wouldn't want to give the wrong impression, they are just not qualified accountants. And they are sensible people who know quite a lot about what is going on in the business. The management team are pretty good at keeping them up to date. **(Damien)**

Robert was the member of the audit committee with the most recent and relevant financial experience but he refuted suggestions that the audit committee was largely dependent on his financial expertise:

I wouldn't say that is true. I think depending on what we are talking about, if we are talking about some arcane IFRS accounts treatment, maybe, but if we are talking about revenue recognition ... I think the audit committee is quite engaged ... I think that one of our business minded NEDs would probably have a more ... probably the most valid opinion, because he has been conducting business for 25 years. **(Robert)**

Ben had previous experience of a number of different audit committees and had views on the necessary ingredients for success:

I think it is important that you have got people that are experienced in business. Ideally you have actually got some financial stuff as well, who can look at it from outside. It is also quite helpful internally for a CFO if you have got good audit committee chair and you are having some internal discussion at the board ... Your role changes significantly. Your role depends a lot on the mix of the rest of the team. **(Ben)**

Robert had already stepped down from the role of audit committee chair at the time of the interviews and the change of roles meant that the company were in breach of Combined Code provision C.3.1 which requires all audit committee members to be independent:

With [Matthew] leaving, who was the chairman before when I was the chair of the audit committee ... because I have the recent relevant financial experience, therefore we didn't want to make a sudden change to the board, we may do that over time but we didn't want to feel that we were bounced into making a big decision just to fill a gap. Jim [incoming ACC] is chairing the audit committee, I am still sitting on it which although it is technically not compliant ... I understand it is the approach that regulators think small cap companies should take anyway. So I think in time we will either become compliant because we will fix it or because the code changes. But in the near term we felt it made sense for me to stay on and to that extent I will assist Jim if he needs help in any discussions. **(Robert)**

Robert's assessment of the suitability of the new audit committee chair was positive:

He is now involved in a corporate finance business. So he has a degree of financial literacy. **(Robert)**

Damien was less convinced about the sustainability of the new arrangements:

> The guy who is currently audit committee chair is a not a qualified accountant ...
> Robert is the only one who is a qualified accountant. He has now moved up to the
> role of chairman which meant he couldn't be audit committee chair ... If the audit
> committee chair is not at least some way down the line towards understanding some of
> the intricacies of it [i.e. IFRS], he is going to struggle, in terms of being able to challenge
> what is going on ... I think long term they will have to have somebody else on the audit
> committee who is a qualified accountant. **(Damien)**

8.2.2   Cycle of Meetings

Robert described the frequency and main agenda items of audit committee meetings:

> About three meetings a year, two of which are alongside board meetings and one which
> is not alongside a board meeting ... One is to do with the planning of the audit and
> the detailed scope of the audit. The other two broadly cover findings from the audit.
> Any issues that might arise from the audit are brought to our attention, discussion about
> accounting policies and changes, which has generally been as a result of IFRS over the
> last couple of years, and any other matters that arise with the auditors, composition of
> the audit team and any risk areas that emerge. We also carry out a risk study each year
> for the company, but that goes to the board meeting rather than the audit committee.
> **(Robert)**

Ben outlined the audit planning process:

> They will come up with a draft planning document and will speak and meet with
> the audit committee chair separately saying, 'Are there any particular issues that want
> addressing?'; they will talk to me separately with the same thing. Come up with a
> proposal which typically the audit committee chair and myself will go through and then
> that planning document will be circulated to the full audit committee for their approval.
> **(Ben)**

Ben's view was that their agenda was not as broad as some audit committees:

> It is fundamentally twice a year around external reporting, rather than a lot of internal
> auditing function, that side of things is not their focus. **(Ben)**

8.2.3   The Chair's Management of the Audit Committee and Key Relationships

Ben described other meetings that took place before the formal audit committee.
Initial contact on an issue was likely to be between Damien and himself:

> Tomorrow afternoon I will have the first session with the group audit partner, and that
> will be without the audit committee chair, for me to get a bit of a heads up of where we
> will be, some of it is on process as well, precisely where we are up to. Getting a heads
> up of — what do they think of the overseas sites, how have they been, is it better than
> last year, and then Wednesday next week we will actually have the planning meeting,

sitting down with also the chief exec, the audit committee chair and the chief exec and myself and the auditors and then it is Monday week when we have the audit committee itself. **(Ben)**

Damien was adamant that the audit committee should not be used as a forum for decision-making:

Ben doesn't want to go to the audit committee meeting with unresolved issues, we don't. I never want to go to audit committee with unresolved issues ... I've got clients where that happens; it is often where the finance director isn't as strong as we would like and we end up saying — well, I can't decide, so we go to the audit committee. **(Damien)**

Despite this Ben was keen that the audit committee should be kept fully informed about key judgements:

Anything of any sort of substance that either has or hasn't been adjusted for, most of those items that we have made a judgement on, they were flagged up so that the audit committee is aware that these are some of the key things even if they weren't disputed in any way ... Sometimes there is stuff that comes up. Last year in [name of foreign country], they wouldn't be material items but I don't like that, I would rather just put it through if they have spotted something. So adjustments will be made but they will be itemized, so in the auditors' report pack it would talk about the items that have or haven't been adjusted as a result of the audit process. **(Ben)**

Damien described the information that his firm provided in their pack for audit committee meetings:

We ... produce a report for the audit committee which does a scope update, sometimes does some sort of numbers analysis and then we will go through the significant auditing/ accounting issues and the significant control issues. Then there is various stuff at the end, auditor independence, updates on technical standards, always goes at the back. But the key thing is scope, significant issues and significant control issues. And usually the audit committee chair will say to us would we like to talk through the report and we will just go through issue by issue, discussing them and generally the audit committee will ask questions and we will have a discussion. They all participate on the Finch board and we usually have a good discussion. **(Damien)**

His view was that there had been no real divisions at the Finch audit committees:

We haven't had ... anything that was a real point to fall out about ... There are some situations you get with clients where you find yourself with audit committee chair and the finance director against the auditor, which I always find an interesting place for an audit committee chair to be. But we haven't had that at Finch because generally we will be raising issues that we have already dealt with. **(Damien)**

In terms of frequency of meetings outside of the audit committee:

When I was chairing the audit committee I obviously saw Ben at the board meetings and we probably talked once between board meetings, so very rarely ... If Ben has got an issue he will talk to me. As regards Damien, I guess I speak to him every couple of months aside from the audit committee meetings . . . If I haven't spoken to him then I will call him and equally if he has got an issue. But it is not a particularly controversial company. There are no dramas going on. Things are resolved in a sensible fashion. **(Robert)**

Damien admitted that meetings between himself and Robert were often organized by Ben:

I guess my view is that, if I have got something to call the audit committee chair about outside normal, then I will do so. If there is something which the audit committee chair wants to talk to me about it is an open line, but it tends not to be used unless there is something out of the ordinary. **(Damien)**

8.2.4   Tendering

Damien's firm was newly appointed as a result of going out to tender. He was convinced that this was because of Firm B's conflict of interest, but was aware that the previous year, which had seen the implementation of IFRS, had not been easy:

They did have a few issues on the IFRS . . . They delayed their announcement under IFRS on the prelims in the year they did their conversion . . . because they had some issues that had to be sorted out. . . And indeed if you go back to the 2006 accounts you will see that we made a number of adjustments to the 2005 accounts as a result of what we viewed as prior year errors. I think they understood . . . that IFRS was difficult for everybody. They felt their auditors were still learning their way with them. I think that applies to everyone. **(Damien)**

He likened IFRS implementation to dealing with an IPO:

It is a period of intense change, intense work, an opportunity to do a drains up, it inevitably gets stressful because you are trying to do something for the first time and it is quite . . . a difficult process. I am sure that happened in lots of places. **(Damien)**

Ben had reservations about the cost/benefit of that process of going out to tender:

It is always a major pain. You have definitely got to see a big upside, you've always got business issues that are higher up the agenda . . . If you are a bank changing your auditor on a global basis, it is just horrendous. **(Ben)**

Robert described the key attributes that caused them to appoint Damien's firm:

Capability, chemistry of the people, experience in the sector, and you could say fees, but broadly the fees were similar and you could end up negotiating the fees to a level, so that wasn't the key factor. **(Robert)**

He explained the process they went through in reviewing technical competence and personal qualities of the bidding firms:

We took references for the audit partner . . . We spoke to two other companies that he was in and I am not entirely sure but I think Ben may have got a reference for the audit manager . . . One of the issues with the small companies, they just didn't have sufficient depth of similar companies. So if you suddenly find yourself as the largest client they have, that tells you something. (**Robert**)

8.2.5 Nature of the Relationship

Ben was very clear in describing the qualities he considered desirable in an audit partner:

> I want a pretty robust high quality partner, you want people who can stand up and raise issues. (**Ben**)

He was of the opinion that he was more likely to encounter these qualities while being audited by a Big Four firm:

> Partly because they attract decent people and I think they are finding it increasingly hard . . . I think they find it hard when there is so much work out there, both IFRS and Sarbox, and so on. They were definitely having to push their prices up because they were finding it hard to actually get enough people and retain people. That is influenced hugely by the state of the financial markets. (**Ben**)

Robert was positive about the impact of recent regulatory change on audit quality:

> I think a combination of just more expertise, more experience in going through situations . . . If you have more attention on making sure things are done right, people tend to do a better job . . . Companies have to pay more to get their audits done but they probably therefore get more time spent on the audit and probably a better approach. I am sure the audit firms have tightened up their systems and processes and sign offs and that will have contributed as well. (**Robert**)

8.3 KEY INTERACTIONS BETWEEN BEN, ROBERT AND DAMIEN

During the course of the audit the following issues prompted interactions between Ben, Robert and Damien:

1. Audit fees following a tender.
2. Notional interest on unwinding of deferred consideration.
3. Earnings per share.
4. Share-based payments.
5. Treatment of tax credits on exercise of options.
6. Revenue recognition and provisioning on contracts.
7. Valuation of intangible assets on acquisition.
8. Segmental reporting.
9. Business Review.

8.3.1   Audit Fees Following a Tender

In response to the question regarding how the audit fee is negotiated, Ben gave a succinct answer:

> Audit committee chair and myself and the auditors, typically they will come up with something and I will beat them down a bit. **(Ben)**

Damien explained that the fee for his firm's first audit was included in the tender process:

> In this case we pitched, and within the pitch process, we gave them a fee. We fix it, and when we fix it we always say subject to change . . . It is probably fair to say that we start at a lowish level, a bit tight and it is partly because you are pitching for the business, it is partly because you are always too bloody optimistic, you always think it is going to be right and nothing is going to come unstuck. **(Damien)**

Robert also recalled that they negotiated the fee down from the level quoted in the pitch:

> Well, obviously from their original pitch it went down otherwise we would have been incompetent. **(Robert)**

His view was that the original price quoted was probably set with the expectation of further negotiation:

> I imagine they do. Even if you are buying a car the guy who is selling it is obviously trying to get the most he can. But obviously if you are in a process with five people bidding, then you compare them side by side, you have more evidence on the pricing . . . They are all paying each other the same amount so you would not expect to have 100% difference. There is probably 20–25% difference. **(Robert)**

When asked whether he was satisfied that the auditors could deliver a quality audit for the fee, Robert had no doubts:

> Sure. I don't think it is cheap, so yes. **(Robert)**

He then continued to elaborate on his view of the value of audit and the appropriate fee level:

> Value added is relatively indirect to a company; it is not like you were paying a consulting firm to put in an IT system which immediately transforms what you do in business. Obviously it is important to think that the outside world has confidence in your accounts . . . I don't know many firms who go round saying I am quite happy to pay 25% more, you want to pay the going rate, you don't want to pay more and it is up to them to say what they have to do to accomplish, and our role is to benchmark that with other companies and see if we are getting a good deal. **(Robert)**

Damien recalled that they managed to negotiate an increase on the original agreed fee:

We did get it up afterwards and get some more money because that page with all the prior adjustments we felt was some justification ... I am all for avoiding confrontation at heart, so I hate it. I would rather not have to do, it but it is part of the job. So we had an increase on the original fee, it wasn't as much as I would have liked it to be. **(Damien)**

The re-negotiation was with Ben, although the matter was disclosed to the audit committee. Damien considered that fee negotiation with the finance director was the norm:

Occasionally they will use the audit committee chair as a bit of a stick to beat you with ... There are two or three of my clients where the audit committee chair gets heavily involved where really he is the decision maker ... But most finance directors take it as that it is their job and having negotiated the fee; it is reported to the audit committee and the audit committee has the opportunity to say something about it. **(Damien)**

Although the audit committee needs to satisfy itself that the audit can be completed for the agreed fee, in Damien's experience this did not tend to result in adjustments to the audit fee:

I have never had an audit committee chair increase my fees. **(Damien)**

8.3.2   Notional Interest on Unwinding of Deferred Consideration

Both Ben and Robert cited this as an issue. Previously outstanding deferred consideration had not been discounted and this was in breach of IAS 37 'Provisions, Contingent Liabilities and Contingent Assets', which requires the amount recognized as a provision should be the best estimate of the expenditure required to settle the present obligation at the end of the accounting period, measured at the expected cash flows discounted for the time value of money.[1]

Robert's perception of the issue was that a consensus on the appropriate treatment, absent the previous year, had now been reached:

Yes, there was a change in understanding as to how it should be done ... Didn't have a problem. **(Robert)**

He recalled that the issue was raised by the auditors:

Well, the audit committee and the board were aware of it and obviously want to make the right decision on the accounts. So, yes, it is obviously a problem in that you never want to restate your accounts. On the other hand when you have a change of auditors, the old auditors were happy that that was the right way to do it; the new auditor said it wasn't the right way to do it. So that makes you probe very hard as to whether or not there is some ... they are sure in a sense that that is the right way to do it. In terms of

---

[1] IAS 37 *Provisions and Contingencies* states that management must perform an exercise at each balance sheet date to identify the best estimate of the expenditure required to settle the present obligation at the balance sheet date, discounted at the appropriate rate. The increase in provision due to the passage of time is recognized as interest expense.

the material impact on the company, this is not like restating the profits or turnover, it is more a categorization issue. **(Robert)**

Ben's view was that a combination of a new finance director and a new auditor provided the catalyst to correct the treatment:

> No one is feeling that we should have got this right before, so let us get it right now . . . It is [an] utterly bizarre, arcane, economically accurate bit of accounting, but it reflects the fact that we have been buying companies, some of the payments we were making for those companies are in the future, we hadn't put that charge through. It had these really strange effects on net interest charged because actually, real cash interest, we had about 350 thousand coming in that year but there was about a 700 thousand charge going out, so we went from 350 in to 350 out. Leaving us with a cash adjustment. **(Ben)**

The precise form of the presentation of the necessary adjustments was subject to some debate:

> The discussion was more should we make it an adjusted profit item, not whether or not we put it in the main profit and loss . . . the chairman and chief exec who wanted to adjust profit and I just felt let's not have any more adjustments. **(Ben)**

He recalls that analysts had some difficulty in evaluating the significance of the change:

> I end up having to spend far too long explaining to the analysts . . . 'What is this accounting bollocks?' is probably accurate. **(Ben)**

Ben explained that earn outs have a maximum life of three years and, therefore, the impact of discounting on the financial statements was not large. He did, however, concede that the company expected to make many more acquisitions in the near future and for many there was likely to be an element of deferred consideration.

On the question of why it had not been picked up by the previous auditors in the previous year:

> There could have been a reasonable materiality defence in so much as we made two acquisitions in 2006, three acquisitions in 2007, so we had one in January, one in November and one in December, so actually it might not have been a material item. **(Ben)**

8.3.3   Earnings Per Share

Ben explained the nature of the issue which had given rise to a restatement in the accounts:[2]

---

[2] IAS 33 *Earnings per Share* defines basic earnings per share as profit or loss for the period attributable to the equity holders divided by the weighted average number of ordinary shares outstanding. Paragraph 29 states that the effect of a share repurchase at fair value is to reduce the weighted average number of ordinary shares outstanding.

We had acquired ... x% of our shares, most of which we acquired in the previous year. Bought into the Employee Benefit Trust so that we can use them to satisfy obligations under options. So you are not diluting, but you are allowed up to 5% of your shares in these, in the same way as there is a 1% dilution limit. The question was in the EPS calculation should you or shouldn't you include those shares? **(Ben)**

Ben further clarified the rationale for the arrangement from the directors' perspective:

We believed that in this people business you want to have quite a significant share owning incentive. There is an argument that in a lot of these organizations the most natural form of ownership is partnership and you try and recreate that as much as possible ... View was, we think we are going to be growing. The shares are going to be worth more in a year's time, two years time than they were then, therefore let's do this. **(Ben)**

Such a scheme has implications for the way that earnings per share is calculated and the auditors spotted this:

We should have excluded those shares from the base calculation. **(Ben)**

Although the scheme had been in existence in prior years, the matter had not been picked up by the previous auditors:

I think it is probably fair to [Firm B] it wouldn't have been a material item because nearly all the shares were acquired in 2006. That was something that hadn't been picked up. **(Ben)**

Damien, in his only reference to the issue, was less understanding:

And some of these [restatements] were just, they were silly, they were just errors, missing out the Employee Benefit trust in the EPS calculations. **(Damien)**

Once the issue had been raised neither Ben nor the audit committee were inclined to put up any resistance:

Haven't got it right, let us put it right. **(Ben)**

8.3.4   Share-based Payments

This issue was discussed by Ben and Robert. It was relatively straightforward but resulted in a restatement. Ben described the background to the arrangement:

Well, we also had another bizarre bit of accounting in that three of the founders of the company had actually put x% of their own shares ... basically, they said they were going to give them to the senior management team provided the shares get to a certain level. **(Ben)**

Robert emphasized one of the key features of the scheme:

It had nothing to do with the company, there was no dilution, it was not the company's shares, it was entirely a gift from the founders to a group of people. **(Robert)**

Ben was very positive about the innovation:

It was a very sensible move that most organizations wouldn't do and the institutions didn't know anything about that. **(Ben)**

While the objectives of the scheme may have been carefully considered, the accounting implications were less obvious.[3] The issue prompted a number of discussions between key players:

The view of the auditors was that this was a remuneration payment that was targeted affecting the way the executives were paid and had to go to P&L. The view of the board was that whilst the shares were nothing to do with the company, they were given to somebody, why should it go through the P&L and affect our profitability because it had nothing to do with … nobody was suffering any loss. But we had a lengthy debate about it, we examined the standards and how we should interpret them and ultimately we ended up accepting what the auditors were saying and put it through P&L. **(Robert)**

The reaction of the founders who had donated the shares was predictable:

Not very happy. They thought it was a bit crazy that they were giving some of their shares away, and as a result, depressing the profit of the company. It did not seem to be sensible. But nevertheless that was the way it was. **(Robert)**

Despite any misgivings he might have had, Robert was in no doubt as to how the matter should be handled:

When the auditing firm says it has to be disclosed, it has to be disclosed. It clearly needs to be disclosed, it was just a question of what way it needs to be disclosed. So, you know, I suppose we have to do what the rules say. **(Robert)**

Reflecting on the incidence of different interpretations of rules by different companies:

I think there is less scope now because I think it is a lot tighter than it used to be but, you know, they convinced us that this is what the principles say and we had to do it. **(Robert)**

Damien did not comment at length on the accounting treatment for this particular scheme beyond saying:

---

[3] IFRS 2 *Share-based Payment* requires all such transactions involving the entity to be recognized in its financial statements at fair value. Paragraph 3 specifically states that 'A share-based payment transaction may be settled by another group entity (or a shareholder of any group entity) on behalf of the entity receiving or acquiring the goods or services.' For transactions involving employees the entity is required to measure the fair value of the equity instruments granted, because it is typically not possible to estimate reliably the fair value of employee services received. All transactions involving share-based payment are recognized as expenses or assets over any vesting period.

You could probably describe it as a technicality. There was a bit of a discussion about that. **(Damien)**

However, Damien also commented on the way in which the company disclosed share-based payments generally:

What is slightly odd is the way they disclose in these accounts, they are very keen to bring out that they do a big sort of share-based payment out to their employees, and share quite a lot of the profits of the year with their people . . . and they identify it separately on the face [of the income statement], they had already done that before us, and they continue to do it with us on the basis that, actually, you can. You have to box it out, give a slightly difficult looking presentation, every line, before and after share-based payments. **(Damien)**

While not entirely approving of the presentation they saw no reason to discuss the matter at length:

I think we said, 'It looks a mess, do you really need to do it? If you follow it through to this year, does it really make a lot of difference?' Our view was it doesn't. If you want it looking like that there is no reason why not. **(Damien)**

8.3.5   Treatment of Tax Credits on Exercise of Options

Damien also raised another share-based payments matter which resulted in a restatement. The issue was how credits in relation to a tax deduction available through the exercise of a large number of options should be treated and involved applying the transitional rules of IFRS 2 'Share-based payments'.[4] The previous auditors were content that the company should treat these deductions as permanent timing differences and, therefore, the credits were recognized in the income statement. Subsequently, it was agreed that the credits should be recognized directly through equity:[5]

[Firm B] said that was the way to do it. Then we came along and said that we don't believe that is the way to do it and they went back to [Firm B] and they agreed that it was no longer the way to do it but at the time it was. At the time the two firms had disagreement on this issue. [Firm B] have now agreed with the line we took . . . but we said — actually the view hasn't changed, they just got it wrong. **(Damien)**

The disclosure of the restatement in the accounts required suitable compromise wording:

The company is saying that they did what they were told to do at the time and they thought it was right, and now we're telling them that something different was right, we're quite happy to make the change but you can't expect us to say we made a mistake.

---

[4] These share options had been granted before the adoption of IFRS and under the transitional rules it was not necessary to recognize a charge through the income statement in respect of these share options.

[5] Under IAS12 *Income Taxes,* if something is not on the balance sheet but has a tax base (e.g. share-based payments) it is treated as a temporary difference and will result in a deferred tax asset or provision. Under UK GAAP a similar transaction would have been treated as a permanent difference.

Which I think is reasonably legitimate, we try to help everyone out. The wording was nicely put together, and we were all happy with it. **(Damien)**

Robert was fully aware of all the restatements:

Well I don't think any of these were controversial, they were talked through at the audit committee. **(Robert)**

Damien reflected on the company's view of the restatements:

Nobody likes prior year adjustments, except the auditors, let's be honest. I don't recall it being a major problem. We made it clear that we had found them. Most of them were found early on, so they were already aware ... Which meant they weren't surprises, which is always the worst thing. I guess to some extent when you have already got a couple of prior year adjustments it becomes less difficult ... Incoming auditors and finance directors are the ones that don't mind prior year adjustments. **(Damien)**

8.3.6   Revenue Recognition and Provisioning on Contracts

Given that Finch's business consists of a series of consultancy contracts this issue is very important and is, therefore, a standard point for discussion. All three of our interviewees referred to the issue.[6] Damien reiterated the importance of the issue to the business:

Revenue recognition is ... in a sense it is almost the crux of the business, revenue recognition and contracts and debtors. We always have discussions on that and we always have discussion on the levels of contingency set aside for extra costs in a contract, for recoverability fees in a contract, provisions made against fees which have perhaps been booked which is all really about revenue recognition and they are all pretty in depth discussions and they happen at finance director level, they happen at CEO level, they happen at audit committee level with the CEO participating as well. We kind of repeat this discussion. Normally by the time we reach the audit committee we are comfortable with it. **(Damien)**

The issue of recoverability was considered an important topic of discussion by Robert:

We have fixed price contracts ... you often end up with situations where they will have issues with what has been delivered, you have to assess whether or not they are going to pay or you are going to have to do more work to get them to that point. So those are the

---

[6] IAS 18 *Revenue* states that revenue is measured at the fair value of consideration received or receivable. Revenue from the rendering of services is recognized when the outcome of the transaction can be estimated reliably with reference to the stage of completion of the transaction at the balance sheet date. IAS 11 *Construction Contracts* states that where the outcome of the contract can be estimated reliably, revenue and expenses should be recognized using the percentage-of-completion method. This means that revenue and expenses and, therefore, profit are recognized gradually as the contract progresses. When it is probable that total contract costs will exceed contract revenue, the expected loss should be immediately recognized as an expense. The estimate of total contract costs will include the estimated costs of rectification and guarantee work and claims from third parties.

main issues. And so we are discussing those, and I would say that is the most substantive one in most of the audit committee meetings that I have been in, really focusing on the major clients, the top ten in which you will probably record material issues in five. **(Robert)**

Robert acknowledged that the judgements were about provisioning as well as collectability:

Yes, that is the other side because at the end of the day you have got your hours, how many hours you have put in and you have either collected it or it is subject to not being collected in some respect. So we have obviously policies around how we recognize revenue, when it is billed and so on. These are very well understood and we have longstanding board members, myself and [name of another NED] in particular, he knows these issues better than I do. **(Robert)**

The importance and complexity of these contracts was highlighted by Damien:

They have certain big contracts particularly with a couple of local authorities and things like that. They are very big, and complex. There is one where they are effectively a sub-contractor to another business which is effectively a joint venture with the local authority, so it is really quite complex. **(Damien)**

The need to exercise a high level of judgement is often the result of departures from the original contract:

Usually there is a contract in the middle of it all ... but then you find they are doing a whole raft of stuff that isn't in that contract because something different has happened and along the way you have got agreement to do different things, you have even got things ... you have got some fixed contracts which clearly are the most risky and then actually they have some open ended contracts where it says they will do this work, but the client turns round every now and then and says, 'That is jolly interesting, we want to keep you going we have got another twenty millions worth and actually we just don't want to pay you that much, so what are you going to do about it?' And you end up with less because you don't want to lose the relationship. **(Damien)**

Damien admitted that the uncertainties inherent in revenue recognition resulted in lengthy discussions with management:

To me the important thing is that you start off with a client with a sensible position on it all rather than pushing the envelope one way or the other, and so far our view has been that they have taken a pretty sensible approach to it. **(Damien)**

This view of the company's accounting style was shared by Robert:

I would say the company is very conservative. We rarely find that the company is trying to push things through in an aggressive fashion. We go through a lot of these in some detail, and we expect to hear what they have to say about it. **(Robert)**

Robert emphasized that if there were problems with a large contract, the matter would be discussed by the board:

These are issues that because they are so fundamental to the company we would discuss them at board level. . .It is not as though we get a roster of problems that we don't know about through the audit, we knew about them, we may not have known to the same level of detail as we get through the audit, but we are typically quite familiar with what is happening. **(Robert)**

Consequently the distinction between audit committee and main board could become a little blurred:

There are only three non executives and all three of us sit on the audit committee so it is hard to draw a clean line and say whether we had a debate about it at the board or the audit committee? The audit committee is a subset of the board . . . Ultimately it is the audit committee that will make the decision. **(Robert)**

Ben (who had considerable experience of working in businesses with long term contracts) expressed some dissatisfaction with one aspect of the company's revenue recognition policy — treatment of contingencies. This issue had been discussed and was to be changed for the following year:

Before I arrived . . . they took normally 10% on total revenues on a contract, and you only recognize that last element on the earlier of either when you received the cash for the last invoice, or the client has formally signed off . . . Strictly though, that isn't right, just putting it back in the top line, the right way of doing it, which we didn't actually adjust for last year, because it didn't have any materiality. We have put a 10% contingency in costs at the end to deal with the fact that you might get an overrun in trying to finalize at the final bits of the requirement, it is always right at the end, it always takes you longer to wrap up than you think. So there was discussion on the fact that that policy wasn't strictly right, so basically we said — we are not going to adjust it at that time but we will implement through 2007. It is not a change in policy; it doesn't actually make too much difference. **(Ben)**

8.3.7   Valuation of Intangible Assets on Acquisition

All three interviewees discussed this issue. Ben expressed strong views about the IFRS 3 requirements to value separable intangible assets:[7]

I think personally splitting out intangible assets from goodwill is the most meaningless, total waste of time. You really cannot, in most businesses, say what are you going to do with that set of customers or without those people or with that know how. It is rubbish. It really is. The totality of goodwill and intangible, fine. **(Ben)**

---

[7] IFRS 3 *Business Combinations* requires that all identifiable assets should be recognized in the balance sheet at fair value. This includes all intangible assets that meet the definition of an intangible asset in IAS 38 *Intangible Assets* and whose fair value can be measured reliably. The excess of the cost of the business combination over the acquirer's interest in the net fair value of the identifiable assets, liabilities and contingent liabilities is recognized as goodwill (IASB, 2004, paras. 36–37; 45; 51). The rules are far more stringent than UK GAAP was in requiring intangible assets to be recognized rather than being subsumed into goodwill.

He was also unenthusiastic about the move away from amortizing goodwill:[8]

> But it is also illogical to keep your goodwill on the balance sheet forever. In 60 years time, let us assume it carries on growing and it still has these [name of foreign country] acquisitions, it will have this amount of goodwill on the balance sheet. It is much more logical to say it depreciates over time. But what will happen is a business gets into trouble and there is a big write down . . . I don't want a sudden hit of a write down. (**Ben**)

Ben's views were to some extent influenced by his experiences of dealing with analysts:

> Trying to get analysts through pension accounting took years to get them up to speed and it is the same with most of these areas and their knowledge of tax was particularly poor. (**Ben**)

After his general comments about the quality of the standard, Ben explained how it was relevant to Finch:

> We made three new acquisitions therefore we had actually had, interestingly enough we had [Firm B] doing intangible asset valuations on those when [Damien's firm] were auditors. [Damien's firm] weren't allowed to do it. There is a question as to whether you have it done in house or not. This year we have actually done it ourselves, I have done the valuation at [name of previous employer] and so on, so I felt very comfortable with it. (**Ben**)

Ben briefly discussed how the way in which the new acquisitions are structured might impact on the impairment review:[9]

> We have whacked them all in together as just a single business . . . we have created a whole new organization out of those parts. So do we say that bit from that acquisition is impaired? But no, we say, 'Can we support that value? Yes, we can.' (**Ben**)

Robert indicated that Finch's policy of acquisitions had prompted him to ask the auditors to focus on this issue:

> At the audit planning meeting he asked what we would like them specifically to focus on, where do you see major risk? And I said, 'I see this as something I would like you to look at and report'. (**Robert**)

---

[8] IFRS 3 *Business Combinations* states that goodwill and other intangible assets with indefinite lives are not amortized, but they must be tested for impairment at least annually. Previously under UK GAAP amortization was permitted.

[9] IAS 36 *Impairment of Assets* states that an asset may not be carried on the balance sheet above its recoverable amount. Recoverable amount is defined as the higher of the asset's fair value less costs to sell and its value in use. Value in use is ascertained by estimating future cash flows to be derived from the asset discounted by a pre-tax market rate which takes account of the time value of money and asset specific risk. If the carrying value exceeds the recoverable amount it is considered impaired and the loss is recognized in the profit or loss. While recoverable amount is generally calculated for individual assets, an asset seldom generates cash flows independently of other assets. Therefore, most assets are tested for impairment in groups of assets known as cash generating units (CGUs) (PwC, 2009).

Damien referred to the issue but did not consider it to be at all contentious:

> We talked about it, but, yes. I think they got [Firm B] to do a value. Our job is to challenge it, to say does it make sense, and we generally refer to our own valuations people saying, 'These are the assumptions, does this make sense?'. And that was fine. So it wasn't a big issue but we obviously talked about it. It will have been in the board report and again that was going to board as a resolved issue. **(Damien)**

Robert concurred that agreement had been reached without too much difficulty:

> The finance director would take an approach as to how it should be treated and it was discussed with the auditors, the auditors raised it with the audit committee in their report if there was a difference in approach on things. Obviously it was something I would look at and they came back saying, 'This is how it should be done and we concur that the company is doing it the right way'. **(Robert)**

Ben stated that the cost of an external valuation was the prime reason for the move to in-house valuations:

> We spent, I don't know £20–30,000 a pop for each of these things, that is partly why I have done it myself. **(Ben)**

However, the use of an external valuer the previous year has provided a basis for subsequent valuations:

> What I have done this time round is used the same approach, so it is consistent internally. So there was discussion about that. **(Ben)**

8.3.8   Segmental Reporting

Some aspect of this issue was raised by all three interviewees. Ben expressed some general dissatisfaction with IFRS 8 'Operating Segments':[10]

> I personally think there are a whole load of inconsistencies in the accounting standards on this because the new standard says you have got to use what you use internally ... We manage by region, we don't really manage by business line. **(Ben)**

Damien suggested that a discussion on segmental reporting was a fairly routine matter:

> The segmental reporting issue had really been addressed the previous year. Because we were second year IFRS so ... we did talk about segmental because they might have changed the way they reported internally. So they were restructuring their business and that might have led ... **(Damien)**

---

[10] IFRS 8 *Segment Reporting* was issued in November 2006 to replace IAS 14. It was effective for periods beginning after 1 January 2009, but early adoption was permitted. An operating segment is defined as a component of an entity, identified as based on internal reports on each segment that are regularly used by the entity's chief operating decision maker to allocate resources to the segment and to assess its performance. An operating segment becomes a reportable segment if it exceeds pre-determined quantitative thresholds.

With respect to Finch he reflected on the way they structured their business and how this affected the discussions with Ben:

> The [country A] business is essentially one business and because of the way they have been buying companies, they have been buying companies in different areas . . . so effectively they have got eight [country A] businesses in different sectors . . . which makes it easier to integrate, because there is no overlap.. The way that IFRS is set out, it is trying to encourage you to report what you report internally as well. It is not trying to get you to produce new information. There are times when you end up having those discussions because they report in a strange way . . . It is intended that this is a disclosure of information rather than having to create new information. **(Damien)**

Ben highlighted one specific problem:

> Share-based payments we put through in the UK rather than allocate any of that additional cost out to the businesses . . . There aren't that many people who had major share options out of the UK so it wasn't a material planning, we don't bother allocating it out. **(Ben)**

However, the auditors considered segmental reporting worthy of discussion, pointing out that there were people in country A and country B with share options:

> They knew it wasn't a material item. I think they said that as you grow, be aware that this is something that is likely to come up. So that is exactly what we have done . . . this year we have allocated to the individual regions. **(Ben)**

Ben also reflected on another issue that had caused a restatement in the following year's accounts — amortization of acquired intangible assets acquired with a country A subsidiary:

> There might have been some assets . . . I think there was something around tax, some of the [country A] acquisitions, the first ones we made directly from the UK our first acquisition so it didn't sit in the books of the [country A] parent company. Subsequent ones were made by the [country A] parent companies so they did sit in the books, so with one of the acquisitions we had a deferred tax asset sitting in the UK. There was slight adjustment there. **(Ben)**

As the assets relate to the country A subsidiary the charge was reported as part of the country A segment, whereas initially it was reported as part of the European segment. Robert's view was that the serious discussions on segmental reporting related to the previous year:

> We had an issue about whether we needed to disclose one of the regions because we were shutting it down. And so we had to decide whether or not we should be doing that and there was a secondary issue in that . . . the region was so small. **(Robert)**

The auditors had expressed the view that the disclosure should be made. Two counter arguments were put forward by the company:

One is . . . that it wasn't material and the second one was that it was commerciality prejudicial to go and tell one of the customers what margin you are making in this business but anyway that was resolved and the board decided we would disclose. **(Robert)**

8.3.9   Business Review

While Damien perceived that this issue took a reasonable amount of time, neither of the other two interviewees mentioned it:

> Usually it is post-audit committee, I mean it depends how far advanced the accounts are by the time of the audit committee, the good ones have them in good shape . . . My usual kick back on the front end is usually that they use too many non-statutory, non-recognizable numbers and not enough things that you can see in the income statement. **(Damien)**

He questioned whether the audit committee gave the narrative reports quite enough attention:

> They will all look at it but they don't look at it together, so you don't have a debate over it. The process normally works that the audit committee is normally scheduled for about an hour, so you go through the issues, you tend not to go through this. **(Damien)**

A number of revisions have to be dealt with after the audit committee:

> If we feel there is something to be said, we will say — before we finish can we just talk about this, we need a few more minutes, but it isn't often done at audit committee, it tends to be done afterwards, because . . . you come with a draft and everyone will say that we've got to rewrite that. So, it is usually in the last two or three days, sometimes the last two or three hours, that the draft is evolving. **(Damien)**

8.4   CONTEXTUAL FACTORS AND ANALYSIS OF THE INTERACTIONS

The general contextual influences on the interactions between Ben, Damien and Robert are shown diagrammatically in Figure 8.1. As is evident from the diagram, both Ben and Damien were newly appointed to their respective roles following a difficult first year implementing IFRS. Ben was a competent finance director with relevant experience and plenty of views regarding financial reporting. Robert was a financially literate audit committee chair and reasonably engaged, although he had moved on to be chairman during the year and his replacement as audit committee chair did not have the same level of expertise. Damien was also technically competent and robust in his views.

The three way relationship between Ben, Damien and Robert can be described as good. Damien had just been appointed following a tender process. Robert had been involved in that process and had made it clear that, as well as capability and

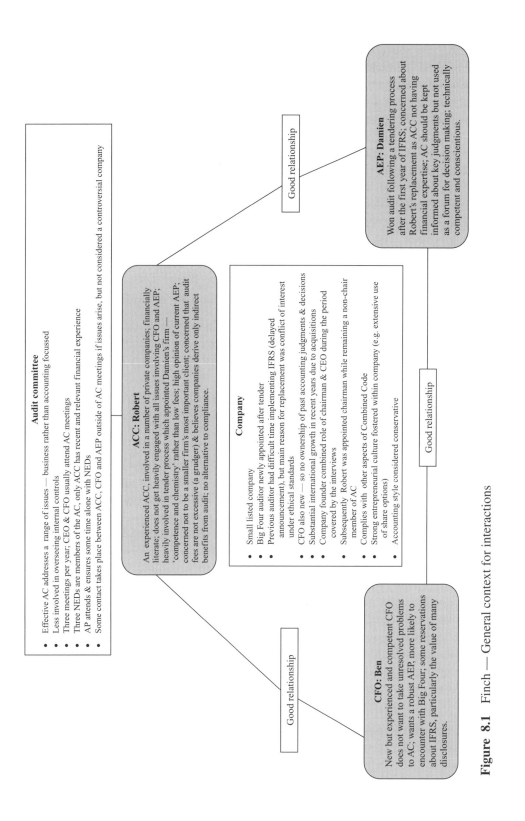

Audit committee

- Effective AC addresses a range of issues — business rather than accounting focussed
- Less involved in overseeing internal controls
- Three meetings per year; CEO & CFO usually attend AC meetings
- Three NEDs are members of the AC, only ACC has recent and relevant financial experience
- AP attends & ensures some time alone with NEDs
- Some contact takes place between ACC, CFO and AEP outside of AC meetings if issues arise, but not considered a controversial company

ACC: Robert

An experienced ACC, involved in a number of private companies; financially literate; does not get heavily engaged with all issues involving CFO and AEP; heavily involved in tender process which appointed Damien's firm — 'competence and chemistry' rather than low fees; high opinion of current AEP; concerned not to be a smaller firm's most important client; concerned that audit fees are not excessive (a grudger) & believes companies derive only indirect benefits from audit; no alternative to compliance.

Company

- Small listed company
- Big Four auditor newly appointed after tender
- Previous auditor had difficult time implementing IFRS (delayed announcement), but main reason for replacement was conflict of interest under ethical standards
- CFO also new — so no ownership of past accounting judgments & decisions
- Substantial international growth in recent years due to acquisitions
- Company founder combined role of chairman & CEO during the period covered by the interviews
- Subsequently Robert was appointed chairman while remaining a non-chair member of AC
- Complies with other aspects of Combined Code
- Strong entrepreneurial culture fostered within company (e.g. extensive use of share options)
- Accounting style considered conservative

AEP: Damien

Won audit following a tendering process after the first year of IFRS; concerned about Robert's replacement as ACC not having financial expertise; AC should be kept informed about key judgments but not used as a forum for decision making; technically competent and conscientious.

CFO: Ben

New but experienced and competent CFO does not want to take unresolved problems to AC; wants a robust AEP, more likely to encounter with Big Four; some reservations about IFRS, particularly the value of many disclosures.

Good relationship

Good relationship

Good relationship

Figure 8.1 Finch — General context for interactions

experience, chemistry was a decisive factor in the final choice of auditor. However, even with good chemistry, Robert was still concerned that the audit fee should be fair.

Robert ran the audit committee meetings, which were very much focussed on external reporting, in a relatively informal manner. There was sometimes a blurring between the audit committee and board because the same people were in attendance. Given the nature and culture of the company, he expected matters to be resolved in a straightforward manner. He was optimistic that recent changes in the regulatory framework had improved the quality of auditing.

Ben was concerned that no unresolved issues should be presented at the audit committee, although they should be made aware of all key judgements. He was keen to have an audit partner who was prepared to challenge. Damien, also competent and conscientious, was prepared to challenge, but was able to differentiate between accounting standard requirements and guidelines.

8.4.1   Audit Related Interaction: Audit Fees Following a Tender

Finch were keen to use their previous auditors to help them on acquisition bids (due to their high level of IT expertise). Under revised ethical standards (APB, 2004a) such activities were no longer compatible with the auditor role, so they needed to appoint a replacement. The problems experienced implementing IFRS may have provided an added incentive for a change. A tender process involving five firms was arranged. Ben had not been appointed at the time of the tendering, although Robert was very much involved in the process.

Damien's firm pitched for the Finch audit quoting a fee, 'subject to change'. The directors noted that the fee variation was not that great (in the range 20–25%) between bidding firms, and that other attributes were seen as more important. The original fee quoted by Damien's firm was negotiated down and they were appointed. Subsequently during the audit Damien was able to re-negotiate an increase in fee with Ben as a consequence of finding so many prior year problems that required a restatement. The re-negotiated fee was disclosed to the audit committee.

Damien considered the original price low due to a mixture of the commercial pressures of pitching for new business and blind optimism. Robert assumed the initial bid included a margin for further negotiation, and rather viewed the process from the perspective of a director rather than ACC. However, he considered the final price was adequate to ensure a quality audit. Damien was pleased that he was able to recoup some of the cost of additional time spent on unanticipated problems, but would have liked a bigger increase. The outcome appears satisfactory as nobody thought they had won or lost.

8.4.2   Financial Reporting Interaction: Notional Interest on Unwinding of Deferred Consideration

The company had made acquisitions in both the first and second years following the adoption of IFRS, where the final purchase price was dependent on the subsequent performance of the acquired entity (earn outs). In the accounts produced for the first year under IFRS, the expected amount payable under such arrangements had not been discounted for the time value of money. This was a clear breach of IAS 37 *Provisions and Contingencies*.

During the audit of the accounts for the subsequent year, the newly appointed auditors identified that the company's treatment of deferred consideration was non-compliant. Damien raised the issue with Ben who was concerned to get the accounting treatment correct for the future and, therefore, readily agreed that an adjustment was required. Even so, Ben was somewhat dismayed at the impact of the adjustment on the reported net interest charge in the accounts. The audit committee and board were also made aware of the issue. Robert had the perception that with the appointment of the new auditors there had been a change in understanding of how earn outs should be treated in the financial statements. Having agreed to the adjustment in principle, discussions then focussed on precisely how it should be presented in the accounts. Ben managed to persuade the chairman and CEO that it was not desirable to make it an 'adjusted profit' item.

The key influence in the outcome was that the correction of past accounting errors was easy because neither Ben nor Damien were involved the previous year and had no reputation or past record to defend. Both were keen to get the right answer and there was no sense of the finance director being on one side of the argument and the audit partner on the other. Robert, the only interviewee who had been involved in the previous year, also wanted to adopt the correct accounting treatment (while expressing regret at the necessity for a prior year adjustment) and was content to comply with the new interpretation. The transactions which caused the interaction were the subject of clear standards, although the precise form of presentation was a matter of judgement. The outcome was compliant; however, Ben was not convinced that this compliant outcome necessarily helped analysts to better understand the business.

8.4.3   Financial Reporting Interaction: Earnings Per Share

During the first year of accounting under IFRS the company had purchased some of its own shares and placed them in the Employee Benefit Trust to permit future obligations under options to be satisfied. IAS 33 *Earnings per share* requires that such shares should be excluded from the EPS calculation, but the company had included them and were, therefore, in breach of the standard.

The auditors picked up what they considered to be a silly error during the subsequent year's audit, although Ben considered that it would have been on the margins of materiality the previous year. Again both Ben and Robert just wanted to put the matter right in the accounts.

Resolution was again easy because both Ben and Damien were engaged in their first set of financial statements for Finch and neither had a reputation to defend. The relevant issue was the subject of a clear accounting standard and the final outcome was compliant.

8.4.4   Financial Reporting Interaction: Share-based Payments

The founders of the company were keen to replicate some of the risks and rewards of a partnership, the legal structure which they felt in some respects to be best suited to a business such as theirs. They therefore decided to gift some of their personal shares to provide performance incentives to senior managers (subject to the subsequent share price exceeding pre-determined targets). The initiative did not dilute the company's shares as they already existed and were held by the founders. It had no other direct impact on the company's share structure. However, despite this, the arrangement was caught by IFRS 2 which requires all share-based remuneration to be reflected in the accounts at fair value.

Damien's view was that regardless of its source, the shares were a remuneration payment which should be charged to the income statement. The Board's initial view was that the share transaction had nothing to do with the company; that this was a private arrangement between the founders of the business and the current senior managers and, therefore, it should not have an adverse impact on the profitability of the company. While Robert's perception was that the issue prompted a lengthy debate and review of standards, it would appear that was largely between the directors and did not apparently involve Damien to any great extent. He admitted to 'a bit of a discussion' but was in absolutely no doubt that the standard was clear and that the transaction needed to be recognized in the accounts. The company accepted that Damien's interpretation of IFRS 2 was correct and that they had to comply. However, the founders were angry that their generosity had resulted in the company's income statement being hit by an additional expense.

Damien had also expressed his preferences about the way in which share-based payments were portrayed in the accounts. The extensive use of boxes was, in his opinion, messy. When he raised the matter with the client, they said that they were satisfied with the existing treatment and did not wish to change. Given that this was not a compliance issue, Damien accepted their position.

The gifting of shares by company founders to current senior managers was a fairly unusual transaction so it would not have been immediately obvious to anyone who was not a technical expert that the transaction would be caught by IFRS 2. However, the standard is clear on the matter and there was relatively little debate on how IFRS 2 should be interpreted. While the rules may have been clear, the board were strongly of the opinion that the result of implementing the standard was counter-intuitive and that it would deter anyone making similar arrangements in future. Therefore, although the outcome was compliant, the reputation of IFRS was damaged in the process.

8.4.5   Financial Reporting Interaction: Treatment of Tax Credits on Exercise of Options

The company had granted a number of options under employee share schemes. Since these options had been granted before the adoption of IFRS under the transitional rules of IFRS 2, no charge had been recognized in the income statement in respect of these. These options were now being exercised resulting in substantial tax credits. On the advice of the previous auditors, the company took the view that these credits were permanent timing differences and were therefore reflected in the income statement for the year.

In the subsequent year, Damien's firm took the view that the previous treatment was wrong under IFRS (although not UK GAAP) and the credits were temporary differences which should be recognized directly through equity. The company went back to the previous auditor who agreed that the previous treatment was no longer the way to deal with the issue, although at the time it was. Damien's view was that the previous approach was always wrong; his firm had disagreed with the previous audit firm at the time. The company had no problems with the principle of restating, but there was some discussion over the wording of the relevant disclosure. A suitable compromise was reached and subsequently considered by the audit committee.

In the first year of IFRS this issue was considered a fairly technical point with no very obvious right answer. To some extent, the company and the auditors were jointly seeking a solution to the problem and the company very much led by auditors' advice. It was apparently discussed at national level by the technical partners of leading audit firms. By the second year of IFRS a consensus had grown on the appropriate accounting treatment and it was clear that the approach adopted by Finch in the previous set of accounts was wrong. Acceptance of this point was made easy as again neither Ben nor Damien was involved the previous year and had no reputation to defend. Furthermore, as a number of other restatements were required, the normal resistance to them had already been broken down. Although the principle of restatement was accepted, the discussion over the precise wording of the disclosure was a more sensitive issue, particularly as the company was reluctant to take responsibility for poor advice. The final outcome was compliant.

8.4.6   Financial Reporting Interaction: Revenue Recognition and Provisioning on Contracts

This was such a fundamental issue for Finch that it was a recurring discussion point not only at the audit committee but also at board level. The interactions are particularly frequent for large contracts and focus on collectability and provisioning. Due to the frequency of interactions, it is not possible to assess the quality of the outcomes, although Damien is satisfied that the company's approach is sensible. However, Ben was able to spot a minor problem with the way the company treated contingencies when recognizing revenue which was subsequently rectified.

8.4.7   Financial Reporting Interaction: Valuation of Intangible Assets on Acquisition

Finch acquired three new companies during the year under discussion and was inevitably caught by the requirement in IFRS 3 to recognize all identifiable assets acquired (including intangibles) at fair value. While Ben disagreed with the standard he accepted that compliance was necessary. The auditors could not undertake the valuations due to restrictions on them supplying non-audit services under the ethical standards. As Ben was reluctant to pay what he regarded as excessive fees to external valuers, the work was actually undertaken in-house. Routine interactions between the key parties resulted in a compliant outcome.

8.4.8   Financial Reporting Interactions: Segmental Reporting

A new standard on segmental reporting (IFRS 8) was being introduced requiring reported segments to be based on segments used for internal purposes. This required existing practice to be reviewed and Damien initiated that discussion. There had been some minor problems in earlier years resulting in yet another restatement. The identification of segments can be considered a matter of judgement and it is difficult to know whether a particular outcome is satisfactory or not.

8.4.9   Financial Reporting Interaction: Business Review

Damien was concerned that there is a general tendency for companies to use non-GAAP measures which have not been reconciled back to the financial statements in their narrative reports. He was also worried that at Finch insufficient time was devoted to their narrative reports both at audit committee and subsequently. While there was no evidence of poor outcomes, the current approach increased the likelihood of them occurring.

8.5   CONCLUSIONS

Many of the financial reporting interactions were restatements to the previous year's figures following a painful time implementing IFRS. This was true of the deferred consideration, earnings per share, treatment of tax credits on exercise of options and part of the segmental reporting issue. These interactions followed a similar pattern: Damien generally raised the problem, Ben agreed that there was an error and that a restatement was desirable and the matter was taken to the audit committee for approval. For two of the issues Robert took the view (possibly sometimes encouraged by the previous auditors) that there had been a change in understanding as to the appropriate treatment. Resolution was easy to achieve because neither Ben nor Damien had any stake in the previous incorrect decisions. Furthermore, the relevant standards were unambiguous on the main points at issue.

In another case (share-based payments) Damien gave a very clear ruling on how the issue was to be treated in the accounts. The board were not happy with the proposed treatment, believed it to be nonsense, but accepted that the relevant standard was clear on what was required.

Revenue recognition and provisioning on contracts was a key judgemental issue in the business. It would appear that the matter was handled in a constructive way by all the key players.

None of our interviewees supported the IFRS 3 requirement to recognize separable intangible assets on acquisition, but they accepted that the standard was clear and, therefore, they should comply. The valuation of the intangibles is fairly judgemental and to avoid incurring excessive costs, this was done in-house and was accepted by all parties.

The majority of the financial reporting issues were a clear cut breach of standards. Furthermore, most were associated with new IFRS requirements. Once discovered, these issues were fairly easy to resolve. Sometimes part of the issue required more judgement (e.g. valuation or disclosure) and although these sometimes took longer to resolve, the approach was constructive.

The audit fee interaction was part of the process of establishing the relationship between auditor and client. Robert was something of a grudger and was concerned to get good value from the auditor. Despite managing to gain a discount on the original quote the number of restatements gave Damien the opportunity to re-negotiate the fee back up. Ultimately nobody considered they had won.

This chapter has illustrated how the complexity of IFRS may have prompted a number of errors in the early years of implementation, and it has also demonstrated how a newly appointed audit partner and finance director are able to identify such issues and then resolve them with a minimum of fuss as no personal reputations are at stake.

Case 5 — Cormorant plc

If we go back to IFRS 3 where we spent four months arguing about what is potentially a misleading statement in the accounts, you question is it achieving anything, is it worth it in the first place? *(William, finance director)*

9.1 BACKGROUND TO THE CASE

Cormorant plc is a small FTSE high quality lingerie manufacturer which has a market both in the UK and in Europe. The company has a number of overseas subsidiaries which supply specialist fabric, including Eagle, which had recently been acquired.

The company was founded by the current Chairman some years ago. It was floated later to finance growth, which had only partially been achieved. The Chairman retains a substantial holding of the ordinary shares of the company. Other members of the family also hold shares which, with the Chairman's holding, represent a significant, but not a majority, stake. This means that the company is not subject to a high level of external pressure from outside investors and potential predators.

The finance director is William (aged in his 40s), a qualified accountant. He had joined Cormorant some years ago as chief accountant and shortly afterwards became finance director. William has limited accounting support within the company particularly as the company is not very profitable and costs have to be controlled.

The audit committee chair, Dave (in his 50s), had been in post for a couple of years. He is also the senior independent non-executive director. Dave is an experienced qualified accountant with a background in public practice and as a finance director of large listed companies. He also chairs the audit committees in a small number of larger companies. The current audit engagement partner is Simon, from a non-Big Four firm. Simon's firm have been the auditors since the company floated. Simon has only recently become involved in the company through partner rotation. His firm has not yet taken over the audit of Eagle as it was a recent acquisition, although they audit all the other subsidiaries.

The culture of the business is for strong regulatory compliance. According to William this was partly internally driven, but also driven by the customer base as they sold their lingerie to major up-market retailers. The main focus of the discussion was the accounts being prepared for the second time under IFRS.

9.2 CORPORATE GOVERNANCE

There are three non-executive directors on the board. In the company's corporate governance disclosures it is stated that the group is not fully compliant with the provisions of the Combined Code (FRC, 2006a), because the chairman does not meet the criteria of independence laid down in the code (A.2.2). The audit committee meets between three and five times per year and deals with effectiveness of external auditors, financial reporting (focusing on accounting policies and compliance) and the effectiveness of internal control procedures. Pre-meetings are held in advance of audit committees at William's request where particular issues are considered worthy of discussion.

9.2.1   Attendees at Audit Committee

The audit committee consists of Dave, who has recent and relevant financial experience, plus two other non-executive directors who do not. William was aware of the limitations that this imposed on their ability to engage fully with the accounting issues:

> Even though the other NEDs have been brought in for specific skills and knowledge of the businesses in which we operate, I think they will be only too willing to admit that they are not accountants and they are not familiar with IFRS. So my understanding is that they very much let Dave lead them on the technical issues. **(William)**

William believed that the non-accountant members of the audit committee had become more detached from the accounting as a result of the introduction of IFRS:

> I think it is scary to . . . the non-accountants who make up the audit committee and makes it feel as though accounting is an even darker art than it really is and it causes them at times to step back more than they did in the old days. **(William)**

Dave shared this perspective on the role of the non-financial NEDs:

> They contribute, they make a lot of contributions but they are not accountants. The more you get into technicalities, the more difficult it is to have non-accountants on audit committees. **(Dave)**

While essentially agreeing with the accounting complexity problem, Simon was very positive about the contribution of the other audit committee members on a range of issues:

> When we start talking about accounting standards then, you know, you have to keep it — the business does this, the standard is trying to achieve this, and therefore you should be led along this path. That is fine as they are very, very bright individuals . . . And they attack. They don't want to talk about financial reporting; they want to talk about the business; they want to talk about the environment; and what choices they have. **(Simon)**

Simon also expressed the view that the Cormorant audit committee took its responsibilities seriously, in fact more seriously than some other larger clients.
William, the CEO and the chairman attended for at least part of every audit committee. Simon recognized that William's knowledge of IFRS made it essential that he was present. He also acknowledged that the CEO brought essential knowledge about the

overseas subsidiaries and the business more generally, but was less convinced about the chairman's presence:

> The chairman is an interesting dynamic . . . I think it gives it a totally different perspective. Ultimately, I suspect if it came down to a vote, he would do the right thing. He would say — I am only here in attendance. I don't know. It has never come to that. But he was certainly a key factor in the half year when we were talking. **(Simon)**

Simon stressed that he had spent some time alone with the non-executive directors who are particularly keen to discover his view on the performance of the executives and the business.

Taking a wider view, William thought that the complexity of IFRS created exposure for Dave as he was the only audit committee member with financial expertise:

> Dave at times is exposed in his role on the committee, and I think that might not be the case in big companies where you have got a number of people on the board who have got similar skills. A small company like ourselves can only really afford to carry one person in that role for compliance reasons and advice. **(William)**

As well as his concern for Dave's exposure, William felt that he could benefit himself, if he could find the time, from a non-executive engagement with another company, to widen his own experience in the current complex environment:

> Having gone through all these issues I sometimes think that I might benefit from being an NED, because it would be nice to see . . . how another finance director actually addresses the process. I wonder how I can create the time with the ever increasing burden that is being placed upon . . . people like myself. I feel that a multi dimensional approach, rather than just being limited to one company would benefit my ability to be able to learn and apply that knowledge in the business. **(William)**

Dave himself felt that the risk/reward balance for non-executive directors was out of line with the executive pay:

> You see the difference between your average FTSE 100 [executive] earnings and your non-exec. The risk profile is always going to be on your mind. **(Dave)**

He was often approached by companies to take on the role of audit committee chair because of his background:

> I've had calls from hundreds and thousands saying 'looking for a non-exec', then they say 'looking for an audit committee chair' . . . Yes, you finish up being on the audit committee and yes, you end up being audit committee chair. **(Dave)**

9.2.2 Cycle of Meetings and Issues Discussed

As well as the formal audit committee meetings some pre-audit committee meetings are held at William's behest:

> I will be the driver. I have to generate all the energy and the commitment to actually run the process so to speak. **(William)**

The financial reporting process effectively began when the interim statement was scrutinized. William discussed with Simon the progress of the business during the year over the latest copy of the management accounts. From this discussion of salient issues the firm then considered its audit strategy:

> We have an audit strategy for the year which basically ticks the boxes just from the standards point of view to make sure that we note all the things that we talk to them about ... There is a document we agree with William which we share with Dave in advance. We go on a no news is good news basis. If he doesn't query anything we presume there isn't an issue. Then I turn up and present it. I literally talk through every paragraph, what it means, why it is there and why they should worry and why they shouldn't worry. (**Simon**)

Dave's view was that they probably discussed audit planning rather more than he had experienced on other audit committees:

> William wants everyone's buy in to this as the approach. (**Dave**)

The question of fees was initially negotiated between William and the audit manager:

> It is like most things. They name a figure. We have a sharp intake of breath. Everybody sits and stares round the table to see whether it is reasonable. (**William**)

William also commented on how costly the IFRS conversion had been for Cormorant:

> Unfortunately we had a huge jump in fees when we changed from UK GAAP to IFRS. It tripled overnight. (**William**)

He added that more time was spent at the audit committee discussing the fees of the firm Cormorant used to provide tax services than his firm's audit fee.
Detailed plans for the audit were discussed at the meeting held before the yearend audit commenced. The group results were then discussed in draft at the next audit committee:

> And we have draft word file annual reports which are then presented to the respective people in the subsidiary boards and also to the audit committee. The audit committee, even though they have all the information, will primarily focus on [one group company] where 90% of the group's trading activities [are] and on the consolidated report. (**William**)

9.2.3   The Chair's Management of the Audit Committee and Key Relationships

Some different views emerged when our interviewees discussed how the audit committee and key relationships worked. Dave's view was that, because the company was relatively small and key issues went straight to the board, there was no necessity for long audit committee meetings:

> I am chair of [other] audit committees and they are all different. There is not a lot that the audit committee in Cormorant needs to discuss. Board meetings are more management meetings than board meetings. A lot of things come up at board meetings, so there isn't a great need for lengthy audit committee meetings. So it really is about planning of the audit, the results of the audit and similar sorts of meetings at either side of the half year . . . IFRS and more technical stuff. **(Dave)**

Dave had regular meetings with William about key issues:

> I do hear from William, I have a fairly regular one on one meeting with him every couple of months. **(Dave)**

Dave explained that William was very keen to get things right with the audit committee:

> He is always keen on understanding what best practice is, what people are including and what people aren't including. What should be in there and what shouldn't be in there . . . But he would like you to see that he has brought it to the audit committee, and there is a debate and an understanding in the audit committee, that this is what we are doing . . . He wants things to be right. **(Dave)**

William considered it important that no information should be withheld from the auditors or the audit committee, and believed this was the way it should be both with the NEDs and the auditors. This was the way the company had developed its relationships over time:

> The NEDs are always on the end of the phone if you want to contact them. That was the arrangement that we have . . . I take a similar approach with the auditors. I just phone up and talk to them . . . I doubt if I go more than five or six weeks without speaking to [Simon's firm] on the telephone. **(William)**

Simon explained that, in complex transactions, William's approach was to present the numbers as dictated by the standards and explain them. In Simon's experience there was a wide range of behaviour from finance directors about how numbers are initially presented:

> The numbers are what the numbers are, and then you have to explain why they are what they are . . . [some] public company finance directors approach it the other way round . . . there is a whole shade of finance directors out there. **(Simon)**

Dave did not believe that IFRS necessarily produced the right results first time round:

> IFRS will prescribe a balance sheet at the end where this is a rule about how you produce every number in the balance sheet and you follow that rule and that is accurate. But I don't think it is, necessarily. **(Dave)**

He preferred not to have to make accounting decisions but have decisions reported to him. He did understand however that his wider commercial experience was a great help to William in some circumstances:

> There are issues . . . where I have had a much more commercial hat on than William has . . . but it is not the audit committee chair's job to decide. **(Dave)**

Although there was a difference in approach Dave did feel that William was competent at what he did:

> He does the job the way he does it and he is competent at doing it . . . it is his way. **(Dave)**

Simon's view was that Dave's interpretation of the role of an audit committee chair was a slightly different dynamic from some others he had experienced:

> It is a very interesting committee . . . Dave would rather that [the auditor] dealt with management and presented to the audit committee a joint position. [In some other companies] if there is an issue, we will have a discussion with the audit committee chair and be told — please, do call me if there is an issue, I want to know about it before the audit committee. Dave's view is a bit more — you should deal with management not the audit committee. So that is interesting, a different dynamic. **(Simon)**

He understood that Dave's experience was with much larger companies where there was a larger management team to run things:

> He is used to dealing with larger corporate . . . in terms of the size of the management team he is dealing with. **(Simon)**

Dave summed it up with his view that the dynamic of how the relationship between finance directors, audit committee chairs and auditors was different in every company:

> To be honest the question is where is the primary communication between audit partner, audit committee chair and finance director, and I think it is different in every situation because it does depend on the personalities and the assessments of their respective strengths and weaknesses. **(Dave)**

William and Dave also commented on their relationship with their auditor. William explained that it was a long-term relationship and the IFRS conversion had been difficult for Cormorant:

> They have been our auditors for a number of years, and there is a definite track record, and we have made it conditional that they don't switch over too many people in the audit team from year to year to keep consistency of performance there. We find that we can have a reasonably open level of communication with them which enables us to discuss a number of issues in depth, which has been very necessary since the introduction of IFRS. IFRS has been designed for big companies and recognizes their needs. There are specific issues that cause conflicts within smaller companies. **(William)**

Partly because of the IFRS change and the limitation on advice which he could get from Simon's firm, William felt that he needed to establish a relationship with another firm as well:

> It was becoming increasingly clear that we needed to develop our associations with more than one firm. Because even though [audit firm] were prepared to get involved with us to discuss, it meant that their independence as auditors was compromised and certainly I think tax is an area where, if you are making an acquisition and you are trading in more than one country and have to take those matters into account. You have to have conversations that enable you to make sure that you have looked at all the options, and at the same time the advisers have made sure that you fully understand the implications of what you can and can't do. (**William**)

Dave felt that Simon's firm was appropriate for Cormorant:

> The Big Four just come over as being more knowledgeable, more competent, more organized, doing all the right things. The opposite side of that is, we probably wouldn't have got to where we have got to with Cormorant if we had used a Big Four firm. They would have taken different views on things and it would have been a much more tricky relationship. But they offer more. (**Dave**)

He also thought that the lack of competition gave the Big Four power over fees:

> I have a concern about how much real competition there is, because there isn't . . . You talk to them and they all know what the fees are and it is — it's a million quid take it or leave it. There is a level of, in terms of fees, comfortable complacency, I think. (**Dave**)

9.3   KEY INTERACTIONS BETWEEN WILLIAM, DAVE AND SIMON

During the course of the audit a number of issues caused interactions between William, Dave and Simon, mostly relating to the acquisition of Eagle in the current accounting period. These included:

1. Identification of intangibles on acquisition of Eagle.
2. Impairment of goodwill on acquisition of Eagle.
3. Deferred tax asset arising from the Eagle losses.
4. Provision on inventories.
5. Business Review.
6. Misreporting in Eagle.

9.3.1   Identification of Intangibles on Acquisition of Eagle

A major interaction involving all three interviewees was a consequence of Cormorant acquiring a new subsidiary. IFRS 3 *Business Combinations* requires that all identifiable assets should be recognized in the balance sheet at fair value. This includes all intangible assets that meet the definition of an intangible asset in IAS 38 *Intangible*

Assets and whose fair value can be measured reliably. The excess of the cost of the business combination over the acquirer's interest in the net fair value of the identifiable assets, liabilities and contingent liabilities is recognized as goodwill (IASB, 2004, paras. 36–37; 45; 51). The rules are far more stringent than UK GAAP was in that it requires intangible assets to be recognized rather than being subsumed into goodwill.

Eagle was well on the way to developing a new fabric which was to be marketed in Eagle's own country as well as being supplied to Cormorant in the UK. However, Eagle had no finance available to develop the product further, so Cormorant purchased the company as something of a speculative investment:

> We purchased the company and we purchased the ... people who were involved in creating and managing the fabric science as it stood at the time of acquisition ... So this company that we purchased had no brand image, no customer base, no real logistical benefits of where it operated at that point in time because obviously it hadn't been trading long enough ... The balance sheet showed negative net assets, in actual fact it was very, very difficult to actually go down the list and actually apply value to any of the intangible items that people normally associate with a valuation. **(William)**

William accepted that when a well established business is purchased it might be possible to value key intangibles such as brands, but he thought the particular circumstances of this case made it impossible to produce a meaningful set of numbers. William insisted that the auditors required them to have a go:

> But we were told by the auditors that we had to do something. **(William)**

Initially William sought independent advice from two Big Four firms who quoted in the region of £20,000 to undertake the work. Ultimately, he decided to use a local independent valuer, who admitted to not having experience of applying IFRS 3, for a fee of £5,000:

> There was no precedent in the market. There isn't a right. There isn't a wrong and why should I spend fifteen thousand for a glossy brochure so people can drive round the country when I could get someone who is down the street. He'll sit with me all day, openly discussing all the issues and thrashing around a way to resolve these problems as soon as possible, which is what we did. **(William)**

Identifying the intangibles acquired on purchasing Eagle was not straightforward for William:

> At the end of the day we agreed that there were two items of value. The product even though it was unpatented, did have value because we wouldn't have bought the company unless we had that product. That was the purpose for buying the product, so we applied value to an unpatented product and we also came to the decision that we wouldn't have paid as much ... if we hadn't had the people who created it and had a knowledge of what to do with it. So we also put a value to know how. **(William)**

William was concerned that the accounting standards did not really fit the circumstances of the Eagle investment:

> I was uncomfortable with the whole concept of how to value it. I am uncomfortable with the concept of just leaving goodwill in the balance sheet anyway. The whole accounting approach to a speculative investment like Eagle was problematic, as far as I could see, from an accounting point of view. (**William**)

Dave had suggested to William that he should deal with it as he was closer to the business than the non-executive directors:

> I bounced it off [Dave], but as [Dave] said we're all in the same situation and when all said and done, I, being the closest to the business, should have as good an idea of what is happening as anybody. So [Dave] very much throws things like this back at me to start the ball rolling ... The energy, the impetus, the driving factor is down to the finance director in small companies. (**William**)

William with various advisors spent a lot of time getting to grips with the logic of the IFRS requirements, to sort the problem out in accordance with IFRS:

> It significantly overstates the value of the investment in the balance sheet rather than understates it, because it literally works it the wrong way round. The more value you put on the asset, the less that actually goes into the balance sheet ... It was actually legally the right way to account for things. It was just so nonsensical. And those discussions that went on before we put them into accounts and what was reasonable to split between goodwill and amortization and all the rest of it and how it reflected in the accounts and how it affected the tax was quite significant. (**William**)

William was initially frustrated by not being able to get advice from his auditors, but then he realized that they were not sure what to do either:

> As auditors they ... do not make decisions but they provided people to speak to, for us to find our own way. Obviously they have to pass judgement on what we then proposed back. They were very reticent in coming forward. In no way did they try and shoehorn us into a particular model, because they didn't know where to go either. When we presented the first cut of what we were trying to report on, [they said] they would have to go and seek advice from their technical department. (**William**)

William valued the expertise of the technical department:

> They had obviously come across companies of varying sizes around the country who had made acquisitions that year and coming to have to report on their acquisition under IFRS. As a consequence ... they were in a position to share considerably more conversations than I would be able to. (**William**)

Dave had a slightly different view of audit firm technical departments:

> In general terms I worry about these guys in technical departments who are sitting with windowless rooms somewhere and never allowed out. I would like it, if there is going

to be a technical issue, somebody to come out and tell me about it, not someone who is hiding behind.... **(Dave)**

The resulting values came before the audit committee for discussion. Dave recalls the initial response of the audit partner who advised about the position going forward:

> Simon said if you prescribe those values, potentially you are digging yourself a hole a couple of years down the line in the way that will be looked at. And have you really thought through those values in relation to how the business is going to run? Let us call time and go away and have a little think about this and perhaps come back with a possible different judgement treatment that might actually be more beneficial for you. **(Dave)**

The problem was that the intangibles valuations appeared to be on the high side which would lead to a higher amortization charged in subsequent years. Dave was also concerned about the position going forward with these future charges:

> It was going to be a potential challenge to the accounts. **(Dave)**

Following discussion, a different split between goodwill, which is subject to impairment review but is not subject to an annual amortization charge, was agreed. Simon was sympathetic towards the initial problem faced by William and the agreed outcome:

> The first time I saw these valuations, I thought 'Oh my gosh, what do we do here?' Hand it over to your own valuation experts internally, they speak to their valuation experts; they speak together in a language that the rest of us couldn't understand. I think this one stands up to that test. It wasn't probably A1 ... it is meant to be good for six years and patents and manufacturing technology for three. With the power of hindsight possibly those life spans are the wrong way round. Possibly, but otherwise the values don't look bad. **(Simon)**

Despite all the debate William still felt uncomfortable at the end of it because he felt he would find it difficult to defend a challenge on it as it was so subjective:

> It left me feeling, after I had prepared the accounts, uncomfortable. Because despite having spent many an hour thinking it through ... no matter what answer I came up with there would always be somebody who could pick that phone up, engage you and challenge you and you would find it difficult to justify what you were saying ... and there would be nothing you could do about it because it was, in all said and done, a very subjective opinion. **(William)**

9.3.2   Impairment of Goodwill on Acquisition of Eagle

This was raised as an issue by both William and Simon, obviously closely related to the previous one. William noted that, while there were very precise rules on how to amortize intangibles, there was relatively little guidance on the subsequent treatment of goodwill.[1] The issue arose after the acquisition when Eagle reported losses:

> Do we impair the goodwill, because we are not getting a 15% return on our investment? Well, we sat and thought about it and we decided that what we had bought was perfectly OK as it does everything that we wanted it to do when we first got it … We came to the conclusion that no, we shouldn't impair, because the potential of our investment is still there. So we prepared some forecasts that we think are quite reasonable and on that basis we justified maintaining the goodwill on the balance sheet. **(William)**

The view of Simon was that, regardless of the forecasts, budgets and other documentation presented and filed it was a judgement matter:

> The judgement comes down to — can you turn a steady state very, very small business into something different? That was a big judgement … The price they paid assumed they could turn it into something that it wasn't. The first thing that they had to do was to get the product to the point where they could sell it and they appear to have done that. The second thing was, if you have got the best product in the world, unless you sell it, it isn't worth anything. And they haven't yet started selling it. **(Simon)**

Simon was content to maintain the value of the goodwill on the basis that if you developed a product that you could sell in [country] market, you would pay a higher price for Eagle than appeared on Cormorant's balance sheet and the fundamentals had not changed as a result of the economic downturn; but it was still an estimate:

> All I can tell you is that if you had six audit partners in the room we would all have a different degree of comfort about it. I can tell you that my view is a reasonable one, don't know if it is the right one. History will tell us that. **(Simon)**

He also expressed the view that a sign of future growth would be necessary to avoid an impairment write down in the following year's accounts.

While satisfied with the outcome, William was troubled by the confused nature of the regulations that he had to apply. He noted that Cormorant had invested strongly in the business:

> So what we have got is goodwill on the balance sheet which represents what we bought, but what we really have is what we have done since. **(William)**

---

[1] IFRS 3 *Business Combinations* requires goodwill to be included in the balance sheet at its original figure, and only adjusted when it becomes impaired. An impairment review is required annually or when there is an indication that the asset might be impaired (e.g. major changes in the relevant market). IAS 36 *Impairment of Assets* states that an asset must not be carried on the balance sheet above its recoverable amount which is defined as the higher of the assets fair value less costs to sale and its value in use. Value in use is ascertained by estimating future cash flows to be derived from the asset discounted by a pre-tax market rate which takes account of the time value of money and asset specific risk. If the carrying value exceeds the recoverable amount it is considered impaired and the loss is recognized in the profit or loss.

9.3.3 Deferred Tax Asset Resulting from Eagle Losses

The losses incurred by Eagle did not only raise questions about the carrying value of goodwill, they also raised questions about the deferred tax balance.[2] The issue was first raised at a pre-audit committee meeting. Essentially, applying the IFRS rules produced a rather curious result in respect of Eagle which all the participants agreed did not make sense.

> Because they had made losses, if you added up the various bits of the balance sheet in respect of Eagle they [would be higher] after buying it, than they were when they bought it, because they made losses and the deferred tax assets [would be] going up quicker than the intangibles were being amortized, which didn't feel desperately right considering that we were debating whether they should be writing things down. (**William**)

The audit committee chair had a similar view:

> I said, 'Fine we shouldn't be doing any impairment, but we have on our balance sheet an asset that is worth more than we paid for it', and I had a problem with that, because it is not performing. We were following the rules, but I don't like that. (**Dave**)

Since following a strict interpretation of IFRS produced something which nobody felt comfortable with, Simon reported that a more pragmatic approach was applied. The solution was initiated by Dave (who seemed particularly concerned by this issue):

> So we adopted a pragmatic response to that which was that we would use four years for our impairment calculations and we would use four years for our deferred tax so everything that we could realize in four years we would recognize. (**Simon**)

The recommendation was then forwarded to the audit committee who confirmed that this was an appropriate course of action.
After all the accounting issues arising from the Eagle transaction, William wondered about the cost-benefit of what had been achieved overall:

> If we go back to IFRS 3 where we spent four months arguing about what is potentially a misleading statement in the accounts, you question is it achieving anything, is it worth it in the first place? If you judge us on the amount of work and effort that went into that, we ought to be ordained. If you judge us on the actual effectiveness of the outcome then we should be executed, so I think it is a peculiar question really, it depends on how you look at it. (**William**)

---

[2] IAS 12 *Income Taxes* states that deferred taxation is based on the temporary differences between the tax base of an asset or liability and its carrying amount in the financial statements. With certain exceptions it should be provided in full based on the tax rates expected to apply when the asset is realized or the liability settled. Management should only recognize deferred tax assets (including unused taxable losses carried forward) to the extent that it is probable that taxable profits will be available against which the deductible temporary difference can be utilized.

9.3.4   Provision on Inventories

While the Eagle acquisition was a one-off in the history of Cormorant and greatly affected by rule changes under IFRS, discussions around the appropriate level of provisions to set against inventories was an annual judgement call which involved all three interviewees.[3]

> So what happens is that we believe that at any level of specification our . . . pants probably have a life of three years so we work out what we think we can sell in the next three years and then we provide for any additional stock holding over and above that. At times that can be a material sum of money . . . That was just a mathematical calculation of reasonableness. **(William)**

Further investigation suggested that one of the problems was with the number of items remaining in stock that had been produced under a major contract for an on-line his and hers matching pants business which had subsequently failed. The company had assumed sales of XX per year, but at that stage no further orders had been received. Simon was concerned about not providing enough against the excess stock:

> So my challenge to them was, 'If you have got no order book and you have got matching pants where you don't know yet where you are going to sell them, is XX a year the right answer?' They went away and I left them to think again. I believe [it] was driven by [the chairman] and the non-execs. **(Simon)**

Opening up the issue for debate gave rise to a range of views:

> William was uncomfortable about changing assumptions that we had gone with in previous years . . . The chairman was excited about the prospect of, dare I say, was he excited about the prospect of smoothing. **(Simon)**

Dave considered it unusual that such a challenge should come from the audit partner:

> It was more going down a business advice route more than I would have expected. **(Dave)**

However, Simon made it clear that there were limits on the extent to which he would assume responsibility:

> I'm not there to tell them what to do. I can't tell them what to do, they are their numbers. They have to say what they believe in and I can give them a view. I can say to them if they say — we might sell X, we might sell Y, I can live with either but I am not going to tell them what the right answer is. **(Simon)**

---

[3] IAS 2 *Inventories* requires inventories to be valued at the lower of cost and net realizable value. Cost includes all directly attributable costs and, where appropriate, a proportion of attributable production overheads. Net realizable value is the estimated selling price in the ordinary course of business less estimated selling expenses.

While William appeared to play a relatively minor role in resolving the appropriate size of the provision, he had his reasons:

> In William's words, 'I don't want to be setting the stock provision because it affects our bonus.' Apparently he had had a meeting with the auditor at the beginning of the process, when we had the meeting afterwards, he said that William wanted me to know that the stock provision affected his bonus, declaring his interest, so I knew that up front, so really this is his whiter than white approach. **(Dave)**

In the event, actual sales in the full year were close to what had been anticipated. The outcome can, therefore, be considered reasonable and Simon thought that it was appropriate to question the provision.

9.3.5   Business Review

William spent considerable time in 2007 attempting to understand fully the implications of the new Business Review requirements brought in under the Companies Act 2006:[4]

> Not just understanding what we have got to write about, but what we have to do in the business to be able to write about it. **(William)**

He was particularly concerned about the specific requirement to produce key performance indicators in a business where they were difficult to define. The response included the implementation of a new accounting system to ensure that information is compatible and can focus on people providing the main services.

> Even having done all this work this year, we still didn't feel that we were in a position to write a Business Review that we could say we were complying with the legislation. We think we will be able to next year. So we have gone for an Operating and Financial Review. But it does place a significant burden on a company of our size to look at all these things in a worthwhile manner that reflects a positive approach. **(William)**

Dave did not think that any of the interactions had been contentious although he was sometimes concerned that the message in the narrative reports was sufficiently mindful of the concerns of external investors:

> The chairman's statement, I think it was written by the managing director rather than William. There was a long paragraph about Joe who was leaving the board, who was the commercial director and Joe has been with the company about fifteen years and left in December, and there was a whole paragraph in the chairman's statement about

---

[4] The Enhanced Business Review was brought in by the Companies Act 2006, becoming effective for yearends beginning on or after 1 October 2007. Therefore, it did not have a direct impact on the year under discussion in this chapter. It requires companies to include in their annual reports discussion of a number of issues such as a review of the business, objectives and strategies, risks and uncertainties and an analysis using financial and non-financial key performance indicators (KPIs).

Joe is leaving, very sad to report he is leaving, commercial director for so many years, be missed by his many friends in the company and was majoring on our [overseas activities], and you know, very big ... going on and on. **(Dave)**

Dave was concerned about reporting the loss of a key director without explaining plans for his replacement:

I am thinking, first of all he wasn't on the plc board, and if you really want to say something like that you have then got to say what you have done about it. Because you can't say this guy, who is very important and has done all this, has left and then silence, he has gone. So is [overseas country] going to fall away? They are a bit like that, family company ... yes. **(Dave)**

William saw another focus for narrative reports:

I think that one has to look at an annual report as more than just reporting to a few shareholders. I think it is very, very important to be used as a powerful sales aid. When we go to overseas countries we always make a point of having our annual report as part of our ... because we actually go out of our way to put certain things in the front of our annual report that make reference to our products and our markets. Such that when we make claims ... they are substantiated by our annual report. **(William)**

9.3.6 Misreporting in Eagle

This issue was not raised by William although both of the other interviewees discussed the problem at some length.[5] Having purchased Eagle, Dave was concerned about the lack of effort by other directors to integrate the new acquisition into the group:

And one of my historic maxims, from say 20 years as finance director, having bought things and been bought and all those sorts of things. You buy something and you engage with it, and you engage with it, yes, you e-mail but you physically get yourself over there. **(Dave)**

His concerns were reinforced when Eagle forecasts were not met and data were not supplied to the board:

There was a lot of trusted expectation, as though they were part of the family, when they weren't part of the family and they had never been part of the family. You have got to make them part of the family. **(Dave)**

William and another board member then visited the overseas subsidiary:

And they found that there were a ... a number of accounting mistakes. They had taken sales that weren't sales ... the directors had loaned money to the company and never recorded it, they needed cash, so they put their own money in. The audit committee

[5] IAS 18 *Revenue* states that revenue is measured at the fair value of consideration received or receivable. Revenue from the rendering of services is recognized when the outcome of the transaction can be estimated reliably with reference to the stage of completion of the transaction at the balance sheet date.

meeting was on Monday morning, I was told about this two minutes before the meeting. To be fair to our audit partner, he didn't blow his top or anything. It was [material]. **(Dave)**

Simon provided a little more detail as to the nature of the problem which resulted in a material write off in the accounts:

> Revenue, basically, being booked on an invoice basis ... You can invoice any time, it doesn't mean you will get paid ... So when they went over and did their work on the half year they found that the revenue number for the last month of the half year had unravelled in front of their eyes. **(Simon)**

Simon thought that Eagle's management had not fully understood the culture in Cormorant:

> I think they were desperately keen to do the right thing. They were told they had to get these results and so ... There is a different culture in [country] as well. **(Simon)**

Dave thought that if Eagle had been audited by Simon's firm, it was likely that they would have picked up on the lack of controls, but he believed that that some responsibility for the problem rested with the board. A similar view was expressed by Simon:

> So we spent a lot of time talking about ... why weren't management more engaged ... They are very trusting, they put processes in place and they make it work. To start with it needs a little bit more than that. **(Simon)**

9.4   CONTEXTUAL FACTORS AND ANALYSIS OF THE INTERACTIONS

The contextual factors are drawn together in Figure 9.1. Cormorant was a small cap company with a family holding but not family controlled. The audit committee chair, Dave, was very experienced both as a former audit partner and large company finance director. He did not expect to resolve accounting issues as audit committee chair but to have solutions which were right for the company reported to him. Dave was the only qualified accountant on the audit committee.

The finance director, William, was very open and honest and wanted the accounts to comply with IFRS. He did not have Dave's wide experience and found IFRS a bit difficult to deal with as there was limited accounting resource in the company to support him. William acknowledged that he would like to find ways of broadening his experience of best practice in the complex regulatory environment but the heavy workload in Cormorant made it difficult for him.

The auditor, Simon, a non-Big Four auditor, had significant listed company experience. Both Simon and William felt constrained that Simon could not offer William extensive advice because of the limits placed on auditors in respect of non-audit services delivery.

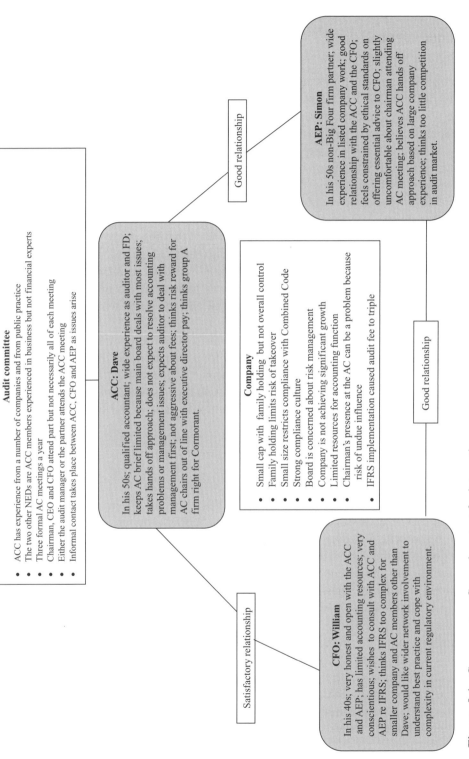

Audit committee

- ACC has experience from a number of companies and from public practice
- The two other NEDs are ACC members experienced in business but not financial experts
- Three formal AC meetings a year
- Chairman, CEO and CFO attend part but not necessarily all of each meeting
- Either the audit manager or the partner attends the ACC meeting
- Informal contact takes place between ACC, CFO and AEP as issues arise

ACC: Dave

In his 50s; qualified accountant; wide experience as auditor and FD; keeps AC brief limited because main board deals with most issues; takes hands off approach; does not expect to resolve accounting problems or management issues; expects auditor to deal with management first; not aggressive about fees; thinks risk reward for AC chairs out of line with executive director pay; thinks group A firm right for Cormorant.

AEP: Simon

In his 50s non-Big Four firm partner; wide experience in listed company work; good relationship with the ACC and the CFO; feels constrained by ethical standards on offering essential advice to CFO; slightly uncomfortable about chairman attending AC meeting; believes ACC hands off approach based on large company experience; thinks too little competition in audit market.

Good relationship

Company

- Small cap with family holding but not overall control
- Family holding limits risk of takeover
- Small size restricts compliance with Combined Code
- Strong compliance culture
- Board is concerned about risk management
- Company is not achieving significant growth
- Limited resources for accounting function
- Chairman's presence at the AC can be a problem because risk of undue influence
- IFRS implementation caused audit fee to triple

Good relationship

Satisfactory relationship

CFO: William

In his 40s; very honest and open with the ACC and AEP; has limited accounting resources; very conscientious; wishes to consult with ACC and AEP re IFRS; thinks IFRS too complex for smaller company and AC members other than Dave; would like wider network involvement to understand best practice and cope with complexity in current regulatory environment.

Figure 9.1 Cormorant — General context for interactions

9.4.1   Financial Reporting Interaction: Identification of Intangibles on Acquisition of Eagle

This interaction was particularly complex because Cormorant had bought a company with negative net assets for its development potential. In these circumstances, William found it difficult to accept the principle that it was necessary to do an IFRS 3 valuation but he was instructed by Simon that it had to be done. As he was not able to seek help from Simon for a valuation, William then got quotes from two Big Four firms which he thought were too expensive, so he employed a local valuer, who was not experienced in IFRS valuation but was less costly. William consulted Dave who told him to sort it out as he (William) was closest to the company. William also turned to Simon for advice. Simon could not tell him what to do and thought Simon's firm were not too sure themselves, as after William's first attempt at the valuation Simon referred it to the technical department. Simon then advised that the valuation of intangibles rather than goodwill might be too high and could lead to a high amortization charge in subsequent years which would not be good for the company. Thus, despite the ethical rules, in these circumstances Simon felt it was appropriate to offer much needed advice. William felt that the valuation was very subjective and would be difficult to defend against a third party challenge.

This outcome was influenced first by William's desire to comply with IFRS and second by his unwillingness to pay a high fee for a valuation. He had not considered the implications for the company of what seemed a steep valuation and it was Simon's intervention which encouraged a rethink in the best interests of the company. This is a slightly unusual position for an auditor to take in the current regulatory environment.

9.4.2   Financial Reporting Interaction: Impairment of Goodwill on Acquisition of Eagle

As Eagle had made losses after the acquisition a further problem arose about impairment of goodwill. William was concerned that there was little guidance in IFRS 3 about goodwill impairment although the rules on amortizing intangibles were precise. William felt that the potential to generate income from Eagle was still there as they had invested in the business and he produced forecasts to justify not impairing the goodwill. Simon knew it was a judgement matter where a wide range of opinion might apply and accepted the evidence that William produced as reasonable, but with hindsight he thought it might be wrong. William thought the standard was confusing as the goodwill in reality represented their post-acquisition investment.

This outcome was entirely judgemental and both William and Simon felt that it was a reasonable guess. Simon accepted the evidence produced by William to support the case. At the same time both parties recognized that it could be wrong and were a bit uncomfortable with having to make such a judgement, William more so than Simon.

9.4.3 Financial Reporting Interaction: Deferred Tax Asset Resulting from Eagle Losses

William identified another anomaly in the IFRS regime which led to the deferred tax asset arising from the losses increasing the overall asset value of Eagle on Cormorant's balance sheet. This was because the deferred tax asset was increasing faster that the intangibles were being amortized. Interestingly, in the end it was Dave who came up with a pragmatic solution to match the deferred tax asset with the amortization of the intangible so the overall balance sheet assets did not increase.

This outcome reflected another problem with international standards. William had produced the numbers according to the IFRS requirements which did not make sense. This time the proposed solution came from Dave.

9.4.4 Financial Reporting Interaction: Provision on Inventories

The company had a policy of applying a formula to inventory provisions. William had followed this policy but in this particular year there was excess stock in one product line. Again it was Simon not William who suggested that this needed to be reviewed as more provisions might be necessary. William demonstrated his own honesty by not wanting to influence the outcome of this interaction as it would affect his bonus.

This outcome was interesting because Simon was again offering some business advice to the company. Dave himself expressed surprise about the business advice Simon was prepared to give, but this was in the best interests of the company.

9.4.5 Financial Reporting Interaction: Business Review

William had found it difficult to meet the requirements of the Business Review in a small company such as Cormorant. Dave, from his wider experience, felt that Cormorant was not targeting its disclosures at the right market, that is, investors, and felt that some disclosures being made were not necessary.

This interaction really related to views expressed on compliance with the Business Review. It shows the gap in experience between William as the finance director and the much more experienced Dave as audit committee chair.

9.4.6 Corporate Governance Interaction: Misreporting in Eagle

This matter arose because of a degree of inexperience among the executives of Eagle in recognizing the need to visit their newly acquired subsidiary quickly, despite Dave's concerns, which arose from his own broader experience of acquisitions. Dave was frustrated that avoidable problems had arisen because the management was too trusting. Simon also felt this to be the case.

This issue again reflects the trusting culture within the executives of Cormorant.

9.5 CONCLUSIONS

This is a particularly interesting case. As a small listed company, Cormorant had limited resources to support its finance director, William. William was transparent and honest and wanted to ensure the financial statements complied with IFRS. He found this difficult because of the lack of resources in the company and the restrictions on the advice that the experienced auditor, Simon, was able to offer because of the non-audit services restrictions. William did not see the point of some IFRS requirements for a company like Cormorant.

Dave who had wide experience as an auditor and a large company finance director did not believe it was the role of the audit committee chair to solve financial reporting problems and expected William to sort things out for himself. However, William had difficulty doing this on his own. Thus, IFRS compliant numbers which did not necessarily reflect the most realistic position for the company were presented to the audit committee. In some cases it was Dave or Simon who found a better solution.

The transactions around the acquisition of Eagle and the valuation of intangibles were judgemental with the exception of the subsequent amortization of the intangible which was prescribed, but this was then adjusted in order to balance with the deferred tax problem. In this case all three parties tried to find an acceptable approach with the final solution to the deferred tax issue being offered by Dave. There was criticism from all three about the accounting requirements and William was concerned about the cost of valuation.

The problem with inventory valuation was also judgemental but this was not an IFRS related issue. In this case the pragmatic solution to changing the established rule for provisions was offered by Simon. William did not want to engage with this because it affected his bonus.

The Business Review issue showed the benefit to the company from having a very experienced audit committee chair like Dave who could point out to the company what was relevant to an investor. The governance about misreporting in Eagle also showed that the company really needed a non-executive director like Dave to bring the benefit of his wider experience to Cormorant.

Interestingly, all the financial reporting outcomes in the end were IFRS compliant. This was achieved by Dave moving away from what he believed the role of an audit committee chair should be and by Simon also moving towards the role of business advisor to help the company. This case is an interesting illustration of how compliance with the current accounting and regulatory regime, particularly the restrictions on non-audit services, can be a real challenge to smaller listed companies.

Case 6 — Pochard plc

It came down to, 'This is our house view', and 'We don't want to do it', and 'It is our house view', then 'We're not doing it!' *(Peter, finance director)*

10.1 BACKGROUND TO THE CASE

Pochard is a manufacturing company. The company operates in the UK and overseas. The UK market is very competitive. Raw materials are subject to a reasonably high degree of price fluctuation which can have a considerable impact on results. In recent years there has been modest growth but pre-tax profits have remained under pressure.

The finance director is Peter (aged in his 40s) who is a qualified accountant. He joined Pochard over ten years ago having had previous experience as finance director in another plc and also in public practice.

The audit committee chair is Alan (in his 60s) who joined the board of Pochard five years ago. He was previously a partner with an accountancy firm and is currently serving on a number of other boards.

The current audit engagement partner is Henry is who is based in the local office of a Big Four firm. He took over the role in the second year after the adoption of IFRS, although many of the issues relevant to the previous year's accounts continued into subsequent years.

In contrast with the other companies who took part in this research study, the three interviewees decided that they would prefer to be interviewed together rather than separately.

10.2 CORPORATE GOVERNANCE

According to the annual report the board consists of three executive directors (including the chairman) and three independent non-executive directors. The company's corporate governance report for the relevant year states that the company complied with the provisions of the version of the Combined Code then in force (FRC, 2006a). The audit committee terms of reference clearly outline its authority and duties which are:

- monitor the integrity of the financial statements of the group;
- review the group's internal financial control and risk management systems;
- monitor and review the effectiveness of the group's internal audit function; and
- oversee the group's relationship with the external auditor.

10.2.1   Attendees at Audit Committee

Apart from Alan, the audit committee consists of two other non-executive directors. Alan was very positive about the contribution these individuals made to the work of the committee:

> He [Non exec A] has a banking, finance background. He has a good understanding of things . . . In fact [Non exec A] is extremely knowledgeable with regard to pension issues. His input on that has been invaluable to the board as well as the audit committee . . . [Non exec B] is also very financially switched on. Both of them have a number of directorships which is always useful. (**Alan**)

Peter's view was that given the breadth of the audit committee's remit it was desirable to have members with a range of experience:

> The audit committee doesn't just cover financial matters. There is the whole risk management side of an audit committee where in particular those guys can really add something as well. (**Peter**)

Despite this, Alan believed it was important that the audit committee should include somebody with recent financial experience and understanding of financial reporting requirements. Even for somebody with Alan's background this was becoming a challenge:

> I think that is becoming quite a problem because your audit committee guys are not, unless you have got a finance director who is a non-exec and he is that audit committee chair, people like me have got to work hard to understand what is going on. (**Alan**)

He then proceeded to outline the ways in which he keeps up to date:

> I do actually find your [talking to Henry] technical papers that come through regularly very helpful and at the time of IFRS . . . I also came in and had a half day with your partner and manager and went through the IFRS stuff and I found that very helpful. This is ridiculous. I have got other roles in public companies as well, as audit committee chair . . . I do my best to keep in touch. (**Alan**)

However, Alan was keen to contrast his role with that of the executive directors:

> I certainly don't think, as the audit committee chair, that I sit and come up with bright spark ideas about issues that Peter should be thinking about, because I think we have a very comprehensive business understanding on the board. Most of the directors have now been on the board for in excess of two years so we have been round several plants, we know the business and we know what the business issues are. (**Alan**)

When asked whether Henry attended all meetings the other two interviewees were keen to answer in the affirmative:

> Yes, you do. I insisted that you have full attendance and that I have private discussion with you on each one. (**Alan**)

Henry himself conceded:

Sometimes, I join by phone. **(Henry)**

Alan noted that the company chairman also took a keen interest in audit related matters:

> He is interested beyond the fee to the actual conduct of the audit, he has got too much time. I do invite the chairman to every audit committee ... He attends most, he attended the most recent one and the previous one he came for half of the time. **(Alan)**

There was an explanation for this surprising level of interest:

> He did start a CA training course and he left the profession disillusioned with the qualification, so there is a bit of a background. **(Alan)**

10.2.2   Cycle of Meetings

The audit committee generally meets three times per year on the morning of the board:

> Year-end numbers; AGM; approval of reappointment, new audit plans and fees; and interim ... And we have interaction in between. **(Alan)**

Alan explained that many issues to be considered by the audit committee emerge out of the board meeting:

> We have pretty formidable board meetings and I would say we cover every issue that the business has to deal with including having a very comprehensive financial report from Peter, which is supported by very comprehensive papers, ... which we get well in advance, and there is a lot of reading to be done. In the course of just normal board meetings, I would say, that is when issues that might have a relevance for the audit committee are more likely to be raised. These things will come through a debate that takes place on business issues or talking about some of the new financial reporting standards and what the impact might be on the business. **(Alan)**

Audit planning is a key responsibility of the audit committee and Henry outlined the timetable for that process:

> Starting point is the debrief from the previous year ... and that starts the planning process which is why we have to have it before the audit committee in May. We then sit down with the team, having agreement from the company, understood what plans there are for the future ... We then sit down with the senior members of the team and devise the plan. That plan is submitted in summary and we also speak to the internal auditors to understand what is happening in that team. We then pull it together, a full audit plan which is submitted to the audit committee for their discussion. **(Henry)**

Henry further explained that the scope of the audit was of interest to the audit committee:

> And we discuss scope with our proposal, if there is a statutory audit requirement. What does that mean? What should be scoped in, scoped out and where are the areas of concern? Where the committee would ask us saying we are a bit nervous about X, Y, Z

we want you to maybe do a bit more there, we are not worried about that. It is a bit of an iterative process. The plan, as submitted to the main audit committee, generally goes through, 90–95% with 5–10% tweaking, refining the scope. **(Henry)**

Alan gave one example of where the audit committee had changed the scope of the audit:

Most recently we have had a discussion about your involvement in the [overseas country] situation and how much work we felt was appropriate there and previously I think, I can't think that we have ever changed the scope other than in that discussion. **(Alan)**

Negotiation of the audit fee is closely linked to audit planning discussions and Alan explained the process:

The fee is discussed with Peter and he will have a friendly conversation with Henry on the subject and will then report to me. **(Alan)**

10.2.3   The Chair's Management of the Audit Committee and Key Relationships

Alan made it clear that much of the work of the audit committee took place outside the formal meeting:

Henry and I have discussions off line before audit committees to make sure that we have understood where we are and what we are talking about . . . then they are discussed formally on line on the audit committee and conclusions would generally be reached prior to the discussion at the audit committee. We would have a pretty good idea of where we are going with these things and we would have checked out the technical aspects of it so that when we finish the audit committee we report back to the full board on our conclusions and our recommendations. That is my perspective. **(Alan)**

Henry agreed that there should be no surprises at the audit committee:

If an issue comes up for the first time at the audit committee then there is something going wrong somewhere in the process. **(Henry)**

Focussing on financial reporting issues, Peter recalled that they had regular meetings with the auditors in the run up to IFRS implementation to assess how each standard was going to affect the company, but the timescale was rather different for subsequent new standards:

On an ongoing basis it would be as a matter arises and of course, with the implementation of new IFRSs being sort of extended now, there is plenty of time in advance to actually look at the fine detail and agree in advance what and how we are going to tackle stuff. **(Peter)**

Henry outlined how he perceived his role:

I think our responsibility in terms of issues is taking an early interpretation of standards and identifying what we think the implications are for our clients and communicating that with Peter and with Alan. **(Henry)**

Peter also found the technical updates issued by Henry's firm useful in anticipating problems well in advance:

> And quite often that prompts a thought, when you read that you think — wait a minute that might affect us. So from that point of view, you wouldn't identify it as a particular issue for me, but it might make me think of an issue. **(Peter)**

Peter then discussed his approach to dealing with identified potential problems:

> We would do our own research on the standards and come up with what we believed was the right way forward. We would then speak to Henry and make sure that he agreed with what we were proposing and if he didn't we would have some sort of discussion and negotiation. If at that point, if we were in discussion and didn't come to an immediate conclusion and I felt that it might become an issue I would talk to Alan . . . just to make sure he was aware of it and it wasn't something that was going to surprise him at some point in the future. But generally speaking, between ourselves and the auditors we would come to a conclusion and then I would speak to Alan outside of the audit committee to make sure that he was aware of the issue and what our thinking was in coming to that conclusion. And then we would report it formally in the audit committee, both what the issue was and what view we took of it, what conclusion we reached. **(Peter)**

Given the work that goes on during the year it is not surprising that the audit tends not to produce new issues for consideration:

> We would very rarely have an accounting issue come up at our year-end audit. We have usually identified them well in advance . . . All the issues on IFRS were identified well in advance. We had one issue this year on pension accounting, but that was just because of the timing of when it arose, not because it was a year-end issue. **(Peter)**

Alan explained the role of the audit committee in respect of the final accounts:

> They are issued to the audit committee in almost final draft form and the audit committee has a week . . . to go through these papers . . . Every single thing I read. **(Alan)**

He then described the way in which the matter was handled in the audit committee meeting:

> But we don't go page by page through it. I expect the audit committee members to read the accounts and to make their own notes. And then Peter and I will have a chat about one or two matters and Peter will prepare a report, section by section, basically on issues that he wants to talk about, that he would like to bring to the attention of the audit committee. **(Alan)**

10.3 KEY INTERACTIONS BETWEEN PETER, ALAN AND HENRY

During the course of the audit the following issues prompted interaction between Peter, Alan and Henry:

1. Cash flow presentation under IFRS.
2. Inventory valuation.
3. Contingent liabilities.
4. Fair value on acquisition.
5. Treatment of restructuring costs.
6. Segmental reporting.
7. Control weakness.

10.3.1   Presentation of Cash Flow Statement Under IFRS

Peter provided an insight into his reaction to the presentational implications of apply-ing IFRS:

> I think when IFRS came in everybody had their ... what do you call the accounts that you do, the specimen accounts, the pro forma, the model. Things like, this is how the cash flow should start and end, and the balance sheet should look like this; and we said that is stupid, we don't like it. **(Peter)**

Henry confirmed that this was a common reaction from finance directors and gave his view of the problems inherent in the first year of IFRS application:

> I think all the accountants were nervous on first time application that we didn't set precedents that were going to cause problems in the future. The aim was to try and get this right from day one, which is very difficult because it is a huge exercise and it is only with a bit of experience, seeing how others have reported and guidance statements coming from the Financial Reporting Council that you get to feel comfortable with what is acceptable. **(Henry)**

Peter was also anxious not to fall foul of the new regulations and despite his reser-vations the company followed them to the letter in the first year of IFRS. However, subsequently they decided to change the format of the cash flow statement:[1]

> I think we were all just dotting the i's and crossing the t's a bit too much at the start to try and absolutely fit into this model. So we changed the format of our cash flow reporting in the second year back to what we were much more comfortable with. We looked at what other people were doing. There were certain things in the pension accounting, like, 'how do you account for net pension financing?', where [Henry's firm] had a house view that you had to separate out the two elements and we said we didn't want to do it. I think we had a discussion up to the wire ... It came down to — 'This is our house view', and 'We don't want to do it', and 'It is our house view', then 'We're not doing it!' **(Peter)**

The proposed approach provided all the required information:

> It was disclosed separately in the notes. **(Peter)**

---

[1] IAS 7 *Cash flow Statements* specifies that certain information must be disclosed in the statement (e.g. operating cash flows, cash flows from investing and financing activities). However, the precise format is not prescribed although illustrative cash flow statements are included in the appendices to the standard.

After initial discussions with Peter, the audit partner raised the matter with the firm's technical department, reporting back to Peter:

> It wasn't a qualification issue, it was more a — so this is what the model accounts look like and the Financial Reporting Review Panel might have an issue with it, and at the end of the day we said we would take our chances. **(Peter)**

Peter's refusal to adopt the recommended approach prompted the audit partner to discuss the matter with Alan:

> The audit partner did speak to me about this because he was nervous about . . . Nervous about how the audit committee would react. So, you know, 'Are you going to qualify?' There are two stages in an audit, in providing advice to the finance team, and, to the audit committee . . . but if it is not a qualification issue but there may well be exposure to a Financial Reporting Review Panel type investigation and criticism if you go ahead, go ahead with your eyes open, but it is not a qualification issue. It is about where you are along that line. **(Alan)**

Peter also sent a report to the audit committee:

> It was one of the matters arising. It said [Henry's firm] would prefer us to do it like this, but we have decided like that. **(Peter)**

Subsequently Henry learned that a number of other companies had adopted the same approach although he was not aware of this at the time of the debate. Reflecting back on this experience and the implementation of IFRS generally, Peter had strong views:

> I think the whole thing got too technical and I think audit firms allowed their technical people to drive it too much. You know, I said to [Henry's predecessor as audit partner] on a couple of occasions — I don't know why I'm asking you, just give me the name and telephone number for your technical guy because his opinion seems to be the one that matters. And I think that was really a first year issue and that has largely disappeared now. I think everybody was a bit nervous. **(Peter)**

Alan's view was that the dominance of audit firm technical departments was likely to be a permanent feature:

> I think the technical departments will always be counselled now on anything slightly out of the ordinary. **(Alan)**

10.3.2   Inventory Valuation

Peter explained that the valuation of the stock[2] of one of the products was a judgemental area as sales were seasonal and it was probably discussed every year at the audit:

> It is a material part of the business but it is a product that we make twenty four hours a day, seven days a week, for fifty weeks of the year. And we sell it all in quite a short selling season, so at times we are holding a lot of stock. Particularly at the yearend, the year-end comes just before the start of the selling season so we have big year-end stocks, but the selling season tends to be March, April so the prices and the sales have not been resolved at the time you sign off the audit. There might be some out of season sales through, but whether that has established the season price, or not, is always a discussion. **(Peter)**

Alan explained the nature of the key judgement required:

> We have to be comfortable that that value is going to be covered. It is a big area of exposure. **(Alan)**

Peter was keen that the valuations would not be considered excessive:

> I think we have, probably what the auditors would regard as a conservative policy in valuing inventory. **(Peter)**

Henry did not disagree with that assertion. The issue was complicated further by climatic variations from one year to the next:

> 2007 it was very wet ... and so we had a very late season, this year has been a much earlier season. So seasonal inventories, it is always a matter for discussion at the year end. **(Peter)**

Henry agreed that although not complex it was an important area for consideration:

> We clearly have to spend hours on it. **(Henry)**

10.3.3   Contingent Liabilities

The main issue under this heading was a European Commission investigation into anti-competitive activities in one of Pochard's operating segments. Peter explained that this was an unexpected development:

> How did they emerge in the first place? Ten European officials knock on your door at eight o' clock one morning and demand entry and access to all your records ... We had never even heard of EU anti-competitive practices before. **(Peter)**

---

[2] IAS 2 *Inventories* requires cost to be valued at the lower of cost and net realizable value. Cost is defined as 'all costs of purchase, costs of conversion and other costs incurred in bringing the inventories to their present location and condition'. Net realizable value is the estimated selling price in the ordinary course of business, less estimated costs of completion and estimated selling expenses.

Such an investigation is usually initiated on the evidence of a whistle blower:

> In this particular case it was a competitor, a salesman was sacked because he had been having dirty weekends with his secretary. He was sacked from the company and complained to the competition authorities that there had been anti-competitive practices going on in his company. And they raided every significant European player in that sector. **(Peter)**

The issue subsequently became rather more complicated:

> We put a compliance programme in place at that time and looked all around the group, and we discovered something else in one of our European businesses that wasn't compliant with the EU legislation so took that to the Commission, so there were actually two investigations running at the same time, they overlapped. The case that we took to them was a much more open and shut case and we provided the evidence to them so they investigated that one first. And they came to a conclusion on that. **(Peter)**

Alan explained the rationale for taking the second case to the European Commission:

> We did get some leniency from them by going forward . . . So from a commercial point of view there was an advantage. **(Alan)**

However, as Peter pointed out, initially this was not certain:

> Once you have blown the whistle leniency is not guaranteed until they make their final judgement. **(Peter)**

Peter explained the accounting problems[3] that arose from such an investigation:

> You can understand that the disclosures that we had to make in terms of contingent liabilities . . . I mean, the whole thing takes five years to resolve of course, these things drag on forever. So we had two different investigations running where the outcome for us could have been very different in both of them where one was a much more serious offence, but it was likely to cost us less. The second one we didn't think there was any particular offence but we were caught up in somebody else's investigation so we spent a lot of time. That was probably the one time that we got lawyers involved in disclosures. **(Peter)**

Peter further outlined how they set about deciding what should be disclosed every six months:

> I don't think you can come up with a figure. I think what you have to say is what is the law. If the law is that you can be fined up to 10% of turnover so that sets a ceiling on it

---

[3] IAS 37 *Provisions and Contingencies* defines contingent liabilities as possible obligations whose existence will be confirmed only on the occurrence or non-occurrence of uncertain future events outside the entity's control, or present obligations that are not recognized because: (a) it is not probable that an outflow of economic benefits will be required to settle the obligation; or (b) the amount cannot be measured reliably. Contingent liabilities are not recognized but are disclosed and described in the notes to the financial statements, including an estimate of their potential financial effect and uncertainties relating to the amount or timing of any outflow, unless the possibility of settlement is remote (PwC, 2009).

and you try and explain as best you can the leniency programme that you are involved in . . . you just set out the parameters and allow people to make their own judgement . . . We tried to explain the whistle blowing policy and the leniency programme so that people would understand. **(Peter)**

Henry's view of the nature of the disclosure was slightly different:

We disclosed the existence of it but in very obscure language. **(Henry)**

He admitted that in the early stages of the case it was impossible to predict the outcome:

And you put a note in the audit report to that effect. **(Peter)**

Given the potential sums of money involved Henry emphasized how seriously the auditors viewed the matter at each year-end:

We actually spent quite a lot of time, in fact there were two others involved, before each audit sign off we spent a few hours with the lawyers just talking about what was happening, we went to a competition specialist so that we were as informed as we could be, as close to the signing off as possible. **(Henry)**

The origins of the case predated Alan's appointment to the board:

I think a lot of it had been bottomed out by the time I came onto the audit committee . . . It was just rolling onwards, there wasn't much change happening as the years went by, until the final year when we started to negotiate. **(Alan)**

Henry agreed that the issue became clearer as the case progressed:

It became a bit clearer as time went on and we felt more comfortable with that position. But you didn't know. **(Henry)**

Eventually both cases were resolved:

We got 100% leniency on the second case and they dropped the first one due to lack of evidence . . . We could have been 25 million euro? Ten percent of group turnover. **(Peter)**

Although a fine had been avoided, the investigation had resulted in the company incurring considerable costs:

Huge amounts, huge amounts. **(Peter)**

Henry was anxious to point out the source of the additional expense:

This was with lawyers, it didn't affect the audit fee. **(Henry)**

10.3.4   Fair Value on Acquisition

Peter explained that they made an acquisition which prompted discussions about how the required fair value exercise[4] should be approached:

> We bought a business in [Country B], so it wasn't reporting under IFRS at the time we bought it, and we, as part of our diligence and planning, looked at the fair value issue and probably at the end of the day the major issue that came out was one on a building lease and ... it was an issue that arose quite late on in the acquisition process. Because of a legal matter in [Country B] we ended up without buying the property, we ended up having to take out a long lease on the property. **(Peter)**

When asked why they had not purchased the property freehold Peter explained the legal complexities:

> We made an offer for the business including the premises but the business that we had bought was embedded, totally embedded within one of their other businesses and in fact the two properties which we occupy are not adjacent to each other, they are on different parts of the site ... They were making the raw material which we use ... It was an American parent. And the transaction was being done by a merchant banker so they put together the sales memorandum basically on an American basis and asked for offers for all the assets of the business including the property. We put our offer in on that basis. It was identified during the discussions that the land would remain with them and we would buy the building. Now that is something that we have done before. **(Peter)**

However, the deal proposed by the bankers encountered a difficulty:

> Now this business was loss making, there was a heavy discount on its assets so in effect we weren't paying anything for the property. So the offer was accepted, we went on to detailed diligence and negotiations and they finally got some [Country B] lawyers involved on the conveyancing side and they said, 'You can't do that under our law, you can't sell a property and lease the land, that is against the law.' So I said, 'That is a problem then'. **(Peter)**

Peter then discussed how the matter was finally resolved:

> So it went back and forward to see whether there was any possibility of restructuring it differently and we just kept coming up against this legal position. So what we said was that we would have to lease the building, we can't buy the land, we didn't want to buy the land because it is on a chemical site and we didn't want to have the environmental issues and anyway under [Country B] law to sub divide the land would have been a long, long process that would have extended it beyond the timescale that we had to do the transaction. So we said — the only other solution was to lease the property from you, but we weren't paying you anything for it in terms of the price, so we are not going to pay you anything for it in terms of the rental ... so it ended up that the lease was basically at a peppercorn rent. **(Peter)**

---

[4] IFRS 3 *Business Combinations* requires that all identifiable assets should be recognized in the balance sheet at fair value.

Peter explained the accounting consequences:[5]

> So we had to fair value that lease. **(Peter)**

Henry pointed out that as the auditors they had been involved in discussions before the deal had been completed:

> Because the important thing is not to sign a deal that ends in something that you trip up over in terms of accounting disclosures. So as the deal was being structured and negotiated there were a number of discussions. So when we were talking about what was likely to come up in terms of fair value there was nothing really new to us ... The process went forward and whether or not there was a requirement to get independent valuers involved at any stage. And that is the biggest concern that has been expressed by other clients is the industry that has grown up around valuing and the costs associated with valuing intangible assets when all you are doing is taking a number and splitting it down, which no one gives a damn about and incurring a load of fees in the process. So there was a lot of discussion about that. **(Henry)**

He also confirmed that they had been in regular contact with their [Country B] partners regarding a number of issues including the approach to lease valuation.
The approach taken by the company in dealing with matters arising from the acquisition was detailed by Peter:

> What we did was that we produced a paper internally setting out all the issues that we thought would arise ... we bought the business in August, and we did that ... round about September, October time? And had a meeting with Henry and basically went through the issues one by one and he more or less agreed with all our points. The lease was identified as the one that we would have to go and do some more work on. **(Peter)**

While Alan was uncertain as to when the audit committee became involved with the transaction, Peter had a clearer recall:

> Alan was involved in that we had discussions ... that we have gone through all the fair value issues and we have agreed on everything, we have this issue with the lease and we have agreed a methodology but we have to go out and get the empirical information and put it together ... I was just keeping Alan up to date with where we had got to. **(Peter)**

Henry expressed approval regarding the way the matter was handled by Pochard:

> If I could see a situation where we would fail to get a resolution I was comfortable that I could call Alan and I would do that but we haven't had that situation. When I spoke to Alan in advance of the audit committee, fair value accounting was on the table to discuss and we discussed our views. **(Henry)**

---

[5] IAS 17 *Leases* (paragraph 4) defines the fair value of a lease as 'the amount for which an asset could be exchanged or a liability settled between knowledgeable, willing parties in an arms length transaction'. It is likely to represent future rewards available to the user of the asset discounted by a risk adjusted rate.

Peter described the company's approach to valuing the lease:

> We went out and looked at similar lease values on similar sites in the area ... because
> there were restrictions on what we could do with the property because it is embedded
> in their site there were quite severe restrictions in terms of sub-leasing it and terms of
> use and also we were reliant on their infra-structure and their utilities and other facilities
> that they provided so ... we applied some discount factors as to what would be regarded
> as a commercial rental in the area to reflect the specific circumstances around the deal.
> **(Peter)**

Henry outlined the response of the auditors:

> The audit team [Country B], we asked them to give their view of the market rental that
> was being ascribed and then when we came to discounts because of restrictions in use,
> sub letting, etc., we took a view based on what we had seen in other companies. This
> was not a big amount of money. **(Henry)**

He expressed the view that on this particular occasion it had not been difficult to reach
an agreement:

> It is an exercise you just have to go through. You have to understand the basis, you need
> to identify the areas where you want to do more work to be comfortable with it. **(Henry)**

When asked about whether an external valuation had been considered Henry was
clear:

> I think the pressure comes on for external valuations when you go for significant
> acquisitions. **(Henry)**

Peter conceded that the acquisition was not particularly significant in terms of the
group accounts and also expressed the view that there was plenty of market-based
information:

> I mean it is a boom town ... there are lots of properties available, there are people
> building properties, there was a lot of third party information available in terms of what
> an appropriate rate would be. **(Peter)**

10.3.5   Restructuring Costs

Given the nature of the changes affecting Pochard's business this item is a recurring
feature of the annual accounts:[6]

> There has never been a year where there have not been at least two or three plants being
> closed or we have shifted stuff from one plant to another and when we do that, we always

---

[6] IAS 1 *Presentation of Financial Statements* states that although there is no prescribed format for the financial
statements, there are minimum required disclosures. Additional disclosures should be made when they are relevant
to an understanding of an entity's financial performance. The nature and amount of income and expense should be
disclosed separately where they are material. Disclosure may be in the statement or in the notes. Restructuring costs
are cited as an example.

incur costs of redundancy on closure, we still disclose it as an exceptional item although we don't describe it as such, we call it restructuring. **(Alan)**

Alan recalled that he became aware of such matters at an early stage in the process:

Because there will be a debate at the board about the commercial viability of closing a plant and what the implications will be and what the costs will be. **(Alan)**

In Peter's view this did not raise any difficult accounting issues:

I think there is just a discussion about how we disclose that and I think probably under IFRS, it is the one thing that it is actually easier to disclose now. There is no option for the company as to what you want to put on the face of the P&L account and what you don't want to. It was an issue but it didn't cause any problems. I think what we do is, if it is not significant we put it in a note and if it is significant we put it on the face. **(Peter)**

Despite this the matter would still be raised with the auditors:

It was one of the things that Peter would call me up to discuss before a public commitment is made regarding disclosures. An ongoing dialogue to make sure that you don't have disagreements. **(Henry)**

Peter recalled that in the year in question he had contacted Henry for specific guidance on the issue of restructuring costs:

We were giving guidance to the City at the end of the year and we were referring to where we were going to be against expectations before and after restructuring costs. So we were actually in the board meeting, and I phoned Henry, and caught him just as he was going to get on a plane, and read out what we were going to say and said, 'Look, is this going to cause us a problem in terms of reporting?', and we changed the wording slightly. **(Peter)**

Henry was keen to stress that his involvement in that episode was limited:

That was something that I had no responsibility for, my name was nowhere near it, but it was something that was going to go into the public domain which if it was going to be significantly different than the stats might raise some questions, so it was that sort of issue. **(Henry)**

10.3.6 Segmental Reporting

Peter viewed this as a problem that arrived with IFRS:[7]

---

[7] IFRS 8 *Segment Reporting* was issued in November 2006 to replace IAS 14. It was effective for periods beginning after 1 January 2009, but early adoption was permitted. An operating segment is defined as a component of an entity, identified as based on internal reports on each segment that are regularly used by the entity's chief operating decision maker to allocate resources to the segment and to assess its performance. An operating segment becomes a reportable segment if it exceeds predetermined quantitative thresholds. The FRRP has more recently expressed concern at the way in which companies have applied the standard (FRRP PN 124, 2010). For example, sometimes companies only identify one segment but they discuss other parts of the business in the narrative reports.

We had never provided segmental information of any kind. We regarded it as — this is our business, and under UK GAAP that was perfectly acceptable. Under IFRS 8, is it? The rules were different. **(Peter)**

Henry gave the benefit of his general experience of how companies applied IFRS 8:

One of the issues that a lot of companies faced under IFRS, the guidance as to what a segment should be is the basis on which you report internally. And so because of that a lot of companies had to impose differing internal financial reporting so that they ended up with something they thought was appropriate for their accounts. **(Henry)**

Peter then discussed the approach they took to the problem at Pochard:

We researched it, we looked at it, we put together an internal paper on what we thought was the correct approach. Basically it was down to, was it a geographical split as the primary split or is it a business sector split as the primary split? And we put all our thinking in place and put a proposal to Henry, a background paper and we sat and discussed and came to an agreement. **(Peter)**

10.3.7 Control Weakness

The next issue of substance to be discussed was a control weakness[8] on the disaster recovery programme which was being implemented. Peter explained the nature of the problem:

The fact that we didn't have a full disaster recovery plan and we had centralized all our IT at one site, it hadn't been an issue up until then as we had disparate systems around the globe it wouldn't have been insurmountable. But during that year we had pulled everything into one site. **(Peter)**

This had certain implications within the programme, which had four stages:

I think by April, by the time we got to the year-end audit, we were not at level one, we were at level two, which incidentally was quite a good programme of success to get to that. It was our view that we should report that in the statement, that there was a minor control area that was receiving attention. **(Alan)**

Peter added further details about the nature of the disclosure:

And what the timetable for getting to the bar level was. It was just a one year disclosure. **(Peter)**

The substantive issue was also discussed at the audit committee:

We had had, at my request, a full report from the IT manager. **(Alan)**

---

[8] Provision C.3.2 of the Combined Code (FRC, 2008a) sets out the role and responsibilities of the audit committee. These include 'to review the company's internal financial controls, and unless expressly addressed by a separate board risk committee, or by the board itself, to review the company's internal financial control and risk management systems'.

10.4 CONTEXTUAL FACTORS AND ANALYSIS OF THE INTERACTIONS

The general contextual factors in Pochard are illustrated in Figure 10.1. The company is fairly large and all the interviewees appear to be competent and conscientious. They also appear to work well together, although to some extent this impression may be the result of interviewing them together.

Peter is an experienced finance director and dislikes the fact that the arrival of IFRS has undermined his knowledge base and reduced judgement in financial reporting. He expects to propose his own solution to accounting problems based on a certain amount of research and this forms the basis of discussions with Henry. Alan is kept informed of major issues to ensure that there are no surprises.

Alan is a knowledgeable and experienced audit committee chair. He values the contribution made by the other members of the committee who do not have recent and relevant financial experience, especially as it adopts a broad view of its remit. While he is familiar with the business and could be described as engaged, he does not believe he should interfere in the finance director's role. He meets with Henry before each audit committee meeting to ensure that they have an agreed conclusion for each agenda item.

Henry, the audit partner, is a senior partner in his firm and may, therefore, be considered experienced. He is concerned to raise impending problems arising from regulatory change with Peter in good time to enable practical solutions to be identified. He too is concerned that there should be no surprises at the audit committee and is in frequent contact with Peter and Alan.

10.4.1 Financial Reporting Interaction: Presentation of Cash Flow Statement

IAS 7 *Cash flow Statements* specifies that certain information must be disclosed in the statement. For example, cash flows from operating, investing and financing activities must be separately reported. However, the precise format of the statement is not prescribed, although illustrative cash flow statements are included in the appendices to IAS 7.

In the first year of implementing IFRS Peter was anxious to be compliant and so based the cash flow statement on the illustrative model in the standard. In the second year of IFRS they had had the opportunity to review what other companies were doing, decided that they did not like the IFRS illustrative example and wanted to change. Henry's firm objected to their proposed revised treatment as it was not in line with their 'house view', particularly with respect to net pension financing. Henry raised the issue with his firm's technical department who suggested that, while it was not a qualification issue, the proposed treatment might interest the FRRP. Peter refused to back down so Henry raised it with Alan. Peter sent a report to the audit committee explaining the decision.

Peter was concerned that the technical departments of audit firms are now driving financial reporting and wanted some space to present accounting information in what

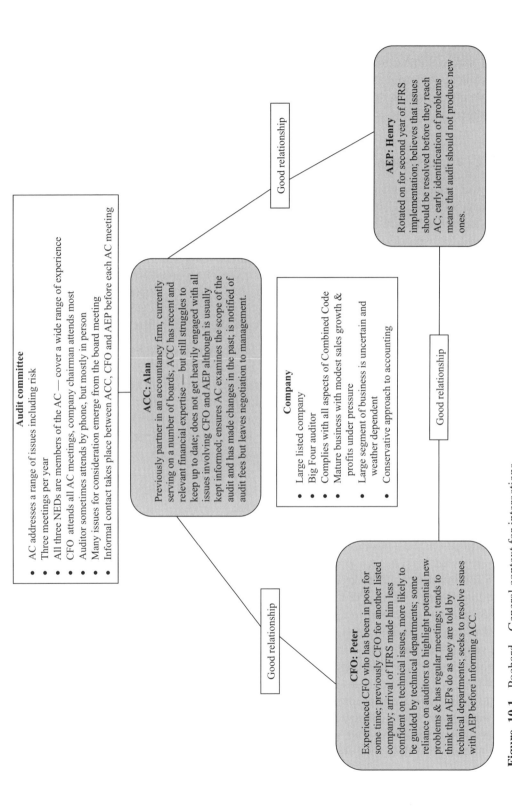

Audit committee

- AC addresses a range of issues including risk
- Three meetings per year
- All three NEDs are members of the AC — cover a wide range of experience
- CFO attends all AC meetings, company chairman attends most
- Auditor sometimes attends by phone, but mostly in person
- Many issues for consideration emerge from the board meeting
- Informal contact takes place between ACC, CFO and AEP before each AC meeting

ACC: Alan

Previously partner in an accountancy firm, currently serving on a number of boards; ACC has recent and relevant financial expertise — but still struggles to keep up to date; does not get heavily engaged with all issues involving CFO and AEP although is usually kept informed; ensures AC examines the scope of the audit and has made changes in the past; is notified of audit fees but leaves negotiation to management.

AEP: Henry

Rotated on for second year of IFRS implementation; believes that issues should be resolved before they reach AC; early identification of problems means that audit should not produce new ones.

Company

- Large listed company
- Big Four auditor
- Complies with all aspects of Combined Code
- Mature business with modest sales growth & profits under pressure
- Large segment of business is uncertain and weather dependent
- Conservative approach to accounting

CFO: Peter

Experienced CFO who has been in post for some time; previously CFO for another listed company; arrival of IFRS made him less confident on technical issues, more likely to be guided by technical departments; some reliance on auditors to highlight potential new problems & has regular meetings; tends to think that AEPs do as they are told by technical departments; seeks to resolve issues with AEP before informing ACC.

Good relationship

Good relationship

Good relationship

Figure 10.1 Pochard – General context for interactions

he considered to be the most helpful way. Henry had argued for his firm's 'house style' and was uncertain as to how significant this departure was without reference to technical departments. The issue is an example of an audit firm trying to impose its own interpretation of a standard on a client and failing, although the outcome was compliant.

10.4.2   Financial Reporting Interaction: Inventory Valuation

This was a significant annual interaction specifically focused on one of Pochard's products with highly seasonal demand and a market price which is uncertain at the time the accounts are signed off. Peter reported that Pochard has a conservative approach to inventory valuations and although there were protracted discussions on the matter, there was no indication of disagreement. This was a judgement issue and all the key parties used the available evidence to reach an appropriate judgement.

10.4.3   Financial Reporting Interaction: Contingent Liabilities

This interaction resulted from an EC investigation which could have resulted in the company receiving a very substantial fine. Furthermore, the investigation process could take up to five years to resolve. Interactions focused on the wording of the disclosure that would need to be included in the accounts given the high level of uncertainty involved. This necessitated obtaining as much relevant information as possible right up to the point at which the accounts were signed off. This was a disclosure judgement issue, considered sufficiently important that Henry included a reference to it in his audit report.

10.4.4   Financial Reporting Interaction: Fair Value on Acquisition

Pochard purchased a business based overseas, but fairly late in the acquisition process they received legal advice which made it clear that the form of the deal (proposed by a foreign merchant bank) was illegal and needed to be restructured. Peter made sure that Henry was involved as the revised deal was being finalized to ensure that there were no accounting pitfalls. A number of aspects were discussed such as the need to value separable intangibles and whether an external valuer was required to fair value a building lease. Some aspects, notably the lease, required further work but since the issues had been identified in good time, this was not a problem. Alan was kept informed as to the issues and their progress. Specifically, with respect to the fair value of the lease, Peter proposed a value based on local conditions, then Henry asked his audit team in the country to give an opinion. Following further discussions, an agreement was reached. This was a valuation judgement issue and by demonstrating that he had gone through a rigorous process, Peter was able to gain agreement from Henry without too much difficulty.

10.4.5   Financial Reporting Interaction: Restructuring Costs

Restructuring is a perennial feature of Pochard's business and the accounting focus is on the nature of disclosure. For example, whether the restructuring is sufficiently significant for inclusion on the face of the income statement, or whether it may be treated as a note. While as a board member Alan would already be aware of any major restructuring issues, Peter ensured that Henry was kept up to date to ensure that they were agreeing on disclosures. This was another disclosure judgement issue.

10.4.6   Financial Reporting Interaction: Segmental Reporting

IFRS 8 brought in a new approach to external segmental reporting based on the segments used for internal reporting. It was not mandatory for the year under review but had been widely adopted by listed companies. Although the company had never previously reported any segments, Henry challenged Peter as to whether this was appropriate under the revised standard. Peter gave a reasoned response in the form of a paper and an agreement was reached with Henry after further discussions. This was another disclosure judgement issue prompted by changing IFRS requirements.

10.4.7   Corporate Governance Interaction: Control Weakness

Following the centralization of IT at one site, a risk assessment identified a control weakness with respect to the disaster recovery plan. The matter was discussed at the audit committee. Since the weakness had not been resolved at the year-end, they believed that the matter should be disclosed in the corporate governance report. This was a good outcome as the audit committee were actively involved in reviewing the company's controls in accordance with the Combined Code (FRC, 2008a).

10.5   CONCLUSIONS

The interaction based on the presentation of the cash flow statement is a particularly interesting one as it is illustrates how sometimes auditors are inclined to be over cautious in their interpretation of standard. In this case, illustrative cash flow statements in the appendices were adopted as 'house style' and attempts were made to impose this on a client as if it were an integral part of the standard. In other words, the standard was being interpreted in a more rigid, rules-based way than was strictly necessary. Peter, who had seen different approaches to presentation in company accounts, was sufficiently experienced and technically competent to challenge this and, in the second year of IFRS, the company reverted to its previous approach to presentation.

Most of the other issues were judgemental rather than compliance issues. The inventory valuation issue was an annual recurring problem, while the contingent liability interaction was a very large and uncertain one-off issue. In both cases Peter adopted the approach of obtaining as much recent evidence as possible and this facilitated agreement with Henry (although its potential magnitude required him to refer to it in the audit report). The segmental reporting interaction was prompted by a new standard and Peter again adopted a well researched and reasoned approach to the issue which made resolution easier. Restructuring costs was another disclosure judgement issue where Peter and Henry were in communication at an early stage.

The fair value on acquisition interaction became more complex when it was apparent that some of the initial advice that the company had received was wrong and the transaction needed to be restructured. Peter ensured that Henry was involved in this process as he did not want any unpleasant accounting implications turning up after the transaction had been finalized. The valuation of the building lease, another judgement matter, was resolved using an evidence-based approach.

Finally, the internal control interaction demonstrated the involvement of the audit committee in such matters and the willingness to report them externally.

11

Case 7 — Woodpecker plc

There have got to be barriers there and everybody has got to be comfortable but I think we view them more as a partner, someone we can bounce ideas off and with their experience they can help the business. *(Richard, finance director)*

11.1 BACKGROUND TO THE CASE

The Woodpecker Group plc is a FTSE small engineering company that manufactures its own range of products and produces spare parts for other companies. Recently the group has diversified into a wider range of products and is now expanding its overseas market. Turnover and profit before tax have in recent times declined year on year. There has been an increased reliance on the market in one particular country [Country H] and the volatility of exchange rates has impacted on results.

The company was founded by its current chairman. Following expansion into overseas markets, it was floated to permit more capital to be raised, although control remains with the chairman's family. Consequently, the shares are not particularly liquid and there is, therefore, little analyst following, although there are some fairly significant institutional shareholders. The view was expressed that they were still attractive to shareholders who wanted a strong dividend and who valued the freedom that management have to take longer-term decisions which might not necessarily produce a short-term gain.

The chief executive, Charles, and a number of managers are based in [Country H], although the accounting function is based in the UK. The group finance director is George who is a qualified accountant with a Big Four background and based in [Country H]. Richard (aged in his 30s), the UK finance director responsible for the preparation of the accounts, was interviewed for this project.

Horace (in his 60s) is the audit committee chair. He is a qualified accountant who was previously a partner with a medium sized firm of accountants and joined the board eight years ago. Unfortunately, Horace was not available to be interviewed at the time this project was carried out.

Edward (in his mid-40s), a partner in a non-Big Four firm, is the current audit engagement partner, having taken over in the year following IFRS adoption. Woodpecker have a policy of regularly putting the audit out to tender and Edward's firm won the audit from a Big Four firm a few years ago.

The culture of the company is one of regulatory compliance partly because of the listing but also because of the brand. The main focus of the discussion was Edward's first year as audit engagement partner.

11.2   CORPORATE GOVERNANCE

The relevant annual report states that the group board consists of four executive directors (including an executive chairman) and five non-executive directors, four of whom are considered independent.

11.2.1   Attendees at the Audit Committee

The audit committee consisted of Horace, a professionally qualified accountant, plus two other independent non-executive directors. One of these had experience of the City, while the other was an expert in the industry. Although based in [Country H], the group finance director normally attended all audit committee meetings which were timed to coincide with board meetings. Richard also attended. The chairman and chief executive did not attend:

> They would be more than welcome to. But it isn't Charles's style. They leave it all to George basically. He [Charles] and George have got a very strong relationship so I think if George is there . . . George will go back to the chairman and the chief executive and get things agreed. That is the link really. The audit committee is there probing away and challenging and pushing on Richard and on George. (**Edward**)

Edward confirmed that he had the opportunity to meet the non-executive members alone:

> Richard and George come along, but we are allowed access just to the audit committee if we so desire. So they will give us time. (**Edward**)

Edward disclosed that, since he had been appointed engagement partner, one of the audit committee meetings was only attended by himself and the audit committee chair. He also believed there to be substantial communication between the members outside of the formal meetings:

> I get the impression that there is quite a bit of email communication throughout the year and we are not involved in that. Bear in mind that they are well spread. Horace and [another audit committee member] are two hours travel distance apart so it is not the easiest thing to get them to come together. (**Edward**)

11.2.2   Cycle of Meetings

Richard describes the content of the audit committee meetings held each year:

> Typically the audit committee meets at least two times a year. It is normally three. It is normally a meeting during the last week of May which is our May board meeting. So that is a pre-board meeting. Then there will be the feedback post-audit in . . . this year it was in August. Last year it was in July and then there will be a half year audit committee meeting. So, really three times a year the audit committee meet. (**Richard**)

Edward's view was that the audit committee was fulfilling its role:

> They do keep quite an independent stand and lay down markers and challenges to the main management basically . . . That is what they are there for from our point of view. They get the full information and then they will say they want to focus on an [accounting issue] or whatever. Right, then they will focus on the detail of what is published and so on. They have got a free rein and they will go off and do what they want to do and challenge the finance director and Richard and then into the board. **(Edward)**

Richard explained how the audit committee related to the main board:

> They will feed back into the main board any findings from the audit committee meeting. Where the board, the chief executive in particular, will have an involvement, the auditors produce an audit highlights document at each year and half year. That is a fairly comprehensive document of their findings and issues. That will always be reviewed by the chief executive before it is circulated more widely and before it is formally sent to the audit committee. So from that point of view he would get to see that and any issues they would then raise before the audit committee would see it. It is always our aim to make sure there are 'no surprises'. **(Richard)**

As the executive management have prior sight of the audit highlights document they have sometimes intervened before the document is circulated more widely:

> We have had instances where, in the audit highlights memo, the way an issue has been worded has been changed to ensure it fairly represents the matters raised. The auditors have the final say in how far they are prepared to amend the report but really it has been fairly small things and so no real concern. In the cases that have happened here they have been more than happy to amend the wording to accurately reflect the position. **(Richard)**

Richard explained that if a potential accounting issue arose during the year, the first point of contact would be with the audit director who reports to Edward rather than the audit committee:

> We would resolve with the auditors about how to technically deal with that issue. We would deal with that issue and the auditors would normally in their highlights memo, as succinctly as they could, inform the audit committee of what the area was, how we were going to cope with it. **(Richard)**

He further clarified the extent of the audit committee involvement:

> Horace would be aware of the areas that were due for change. We might not necessarily have discussed with him exactly how we were going to deal with it . . . The audit committee are also responsible for policy, for policies, so if we were looking to change an accounting policy or even a basis for a policy, we wouldn't do that without putting it through the board first. No policies would be changed without the audit committee, and actually the board, ratifying that change. **(Richard)**

Richard explained the precise mechanism for this:

> At the pre-audit [May audit committee] the agenda will be — there is very little change in the accounting treatment, and at that stage the auditors will discuss what is new and how they are expecting us to deal with it and then they will report back afterwards with their confirmation that we have dealt with whatever the changes were. **(Richard)**

Edward outlined the process of agreeing the audit fee. After the initial agreement with the finance director the proposal goes to the board and the audit committee:

> We don't get challenged again. Once it has been negotiated that is it. May get a challenge with the board, not the audit committee. Strictly you would hope that the audit committee are making sure that the fee is adequate. Their drive must not be to do it as cheap as possible but to make sure that we are doing a good job. **(Edward)**

11.2.3   The Chair's Management of the Audit Committee and Key Relationships

Richard believed that the audit committee chair possessed the necessary qualities to lead the committee:

> Horace used to be with [a medium sized firm]. Very briefly several years ago he was finance director at Woodpecker just as a temporary period. Horace has been involved with the group on and off for a number of years ... Horace is the member with the relevant financial background. I think he retired from practice a couple of years ago ... He normally puts out the agenda a week or two ahead of the meeting and then he will send out draft minutes after the meeting and invite comments on the minutes and then they will get finalized. **(Richard)**

Edward commented:

> Horace's background was from a small to medium sized audit practice and [he] had developed his own way of running the audit committee, and we worked with him to ensure that the company fully complied with corporate governance regulations. **(Edward)**

Both interviewees thought that there was sufficient expertise to ensure that the audit committee was effective:

> I would say they are all involved. [John] who is on the audit committee has the industry knowledge. Then you have got [William], he seems to have the more regulatory and accounting knowledge so he is quite a technical person. And they complement quite well with Horace who is an ex-chartered accountant. I would say Horace is perhaps less technical ... The audit committee composition is fine. [William] in particular knows his stuff. **(Edward)**

Richard emphasized that the audit committee tended to function as a team:

> I wouldn't say that one person drives it really; I would say that all three equally have their own sort of areas where they tend to be stronger. (**Richard**)

Edward was clear that Richard was his main point of contact with Woodpecker:

> Richard in terms of getting the accounts done and the audit done and then we plan our audit with Richard ... Because they have done several acquisitions ... We have assisted in some of the due diligence work. And we also had a meeting with Richard just recently talking about planning and new accounting standards that are coming in and other changes that are going on. (**Edward**)

However, he did not believe that the separation of the group finance director from the accounting function caused any major problems:

> We had a meeting here two or three weeks ago, where basically Richard and his financial controller updated on acquisitions they had just done and we then updated on changes in IFRS, etc. We met at half past three and then updated [George] on the meeting and we were able to feedback to him. He is the [group] finance director and he makes the decisions ... And he is here then for the final audit committee meeting and board meeting, and then they go off to the City and present to the financial institutions and so on. (**Edward**)

11.2.4   Tendering

The company had a strategy of going out to tender every three years. Edward gave his understanding of the rationale:

> It is their process. Making sure they are getting value but also that they are not missing something I guess. So in terms of the auditor, how are [Edward's firm] going to approach the audit? And is anybody else approaching this in a way that would be even better for us in terms of the audit committee and the board? So the tender process was one where we had meetings with the executive board and then the audit committee. You get through one board and then you have to get through the audit committee. (**Edward**)

Richard was not convinced that the policy was producing the benefits that it was supposed to:

> I think when you go to the market place every three years you get audit firms saying — they are coming round again. How much effort are we going to put into this because they didn't change last time? Whereas I think five years, with partner rotation after five years, to me seems a more sensible review period. (**Richard**)

This was in line with Edward's perception of the impact of the policy:

> Management are not overly keen because they build a relationship with the auditors but as there is audit partner rotation every five years you know, the independence aspect ... it is only really what can somebody else bring to the party? (**Edward**)

Reflecting on the experience, Edward dismissed the suggestion that the company chose its auditor purely on cost grounds:

> And I don't think anybody does really. I think their first thing is ... they will always negotiate the fee, clearly. But it is what can you bring to the audit? And they were saying our approach, our enthusiasm for work going back, four years ago, made them think — these guys really want this work — and they got to the point with [previous auditor firm] where it was a bit stale. **(Edward)**

Richard confirmed that other factors were also relevant:

> Cost was a criteria, as it always is ... We had beauty parades with all of the four ... One of them in particular ended up on the day, the lead audit partner, the way he acted, his eyes, his reaction to questions immediately put everybody's back up. It was just a personality thing. We were going to have to work with these people. **(Richard)**

The need for an international network to service the needs of the group was also a key factor in their considerations:

> The reason why we could knock off two of the mid tier quite easily was because whilst we liked the people we met, their international presence just wasn't strong enough for our group ... [Edward's firm] had [name of another firm] in the [name of another country] so whilst they are franchised the same they are actually separate companies and the profit sharing is different etc. But to the outside world and to us they are the same firm. That is how they operate. **(Richard)**

11.2.5   Nature of the Relationship with the Auditor

Richard first explained that it was Woodpecker's philosophy to deal with as much as they could themselves rather than relying on third parties:

> We generally feel we have the in-house capability to do most things. So we will try and do it ourselves, but let us have a meeting to address what is new that we need to consider for this financial year-end. Once we have got that we will go away and do the work. If we have got any problems we will give them a call and then they will come in and review it. I don't want really to outsource it. I would rather have the expertise because I think it is important for us to know ... to understand it. **(Richard)**

Edward's firm had taken responsibility for the audit of the entire group. Richard explained how their approach fitted in with the expectation at Woodpecker that an audit firm can actually add value to the business as well as covering compliance issues:

> They can actually be a pseudo adviser and you know, there have got to be barriers there and everybody has got to be comfortable but I think we view them more as a partner, someone we can bounce ideas off and with their experience they can help the business ... and we felt that [Edward's firm] had that approach. One of the things that they portrayed at the meetings when you deal with us you deal with a partner whereas with the bigger firms we would have dealt with a senior manager or a senior. **(Richard)**

Edward described how responsibilities were allocated within his firm:

> [Partner A] is down as relationship partner for this job. Previously it was [Partner B] and a guy called [Partner C] who passed away unfortunately. [Partner C] and now [Partner A] have got quite a big [Country H] client base and they are both relationship partners because they have that knowledge. Woodpecker seemed to quite like that in terms of being able to have somebody focusing on the [Country H] and some in the UK. **(Edward)**

Richard's view was that they have sufficient in-house capacity to tackle most accounting problems, however, his experience in applying IFRS for the first time led him to buy some external support:

> There were certain of the standards that seemed to be causing most of the issues with the bigger companies that weren't really affecting us, but actually when you got into the detail of doing it, disclosure wise, there was a lot that needed to be done. Because you actually had to go through and review every standard to be able to say why it wasn't an issue for us . . . We did commission a separate part of [Edward's firm]. They have got an International Standards section and we employed them on a separate project fee to help advise us and to help review the standards but we did any work that was involved . . . That was fairly complicated. **(Richard)**

11.3   KEY INTERACTIONS BETWEEN RICHARD, HORACE AND EDWARD

During the course of the audit the following issues prompted interactions between Richard, Horace and Edward:

1. Inventory valuation.
2. Breach of internal controls in an overseas subsidiary.
3. Valuation of intangible assets on acquisition of a subsidiary.

11.3.1   Inventory Valuation

Richard considered this to be a routine but important area in the business and, therefore, one that was always discussed at both the half year and full year:

> We have a stock policy, we adhere to that very strictly, and the auditors . . . and the audit committee would rightly ask the auditors to confirm that . . . there were no additional provisions that they felt were warranted because the stock was slow moving, or whatever. And we were always fairly robust and prudent in the way that we provided for the stock anyway. So I mean, when I say there were issues in a subsidiary. There were audit issues that needed to be addressed, but they were only in the run of normal. It was ratification from the audit committee's point of view that we had been prudent in the way we provided and they were looking for the auditors to confirm that was the case. **(Richard)**

Richard explained how the basic provision[1] was calculated:

> We won't provide for a product within the first two years of its life because at that point if a product's sales slow down . . . there are still things that management can do to move it on. But beyond two years, it is then sales driven, so . . . it is very formulaic depending on the number of sales, percentage of sales. We have a provision that if a product hasn't sold in the last six months we provide a percentage of its costs. **(Richard)**

He agreed that they will sometimes make additional provisions over and above the formulaic provisions, and that for some items waiting two years before a provision is made is inappropriate. However:

> The auditors are predominantly coming and saying, 'Have you applied your formulaic provision?' So, that is really the approach we take where we can. **(Richard)**

While Richard stated that the auditors were satisfied with the approach taken to provisioning, Edward had a slightly different take:

> They looked at the old stock and I said they should look at the excess stock . . . They are looking to change their policy. **(Edward)**

He explained the potential problems of the current policy:

> You have got something that might have been around for [some] years but actually the rate at which they are selling it, it is going to take [longer] to clear . . . so should there be a write down for that? . . . There are so many items that the actual materiality is very low but it could be . . . So they have changed the way they monitor that and value it forward. **(Edward)**

The process by which the policy was changed for subsequent years was then described by Edward. The matter was first raised with management:

> Management weren't overly concerned about it . . . They didn't think they had an issue . . . If they are not selling something they will bundle it with another product. So if you buy this you'll get this other product cheaper. So that clears their stock . . . There are also a couple of companies that will soak up the extra at base cost which is not less than cost. So it is not really an issue because there is a market for even the oldest products. **(Edward)**

However, the matter was raised at the next meeting of the audit committee:

> So we produce a document with all the issues that we would like to take to audit committee . . . Management convinced the audit committee that there was not an issue to worry about in that report. There could be an issue going forward with excess and

---

[1] IAS 2 (paragraph 28) states that cost may not be recoverable if inventories are damaged, if they have become wholly or partially obsolete, or if their selling prices have declined. The practice of writing inventories down below cost to net realizable value is consistent with the view that assets should not be carried in excess of amounts expected to be realized from their sale or use.

as their range of products is continuing to expand . . . they have agreed to procedures to better identify any issues. **(Edward)**

Edward explained that it was important that the audit committee were made aware of all significant matters and made their decisions based on a full discussion of the facts:

> If the audit committee said that it is fine then as far as I am concerned I have brought it to their attention, they have considered its impact. **(Edward)**

11.3.2 Breach of Internal Controls in an Overseas Subsidiary

While this issue was not material to the accounts it did expose some different expectations among the key parties regarding how a minor fraud should be handled at Woodpecker.[2] Richard explained:

> The only time where I can think where there were any raised eyebrows between the audit committee, management and the auditors was what management would have deemed to be a very small issue. There was some stock that had been scrapped . . . and there was a procedure for dealing with scrapped stock, but one employee had not adhered to the procedure at the time and had put them in the bin, and another employee had come along, taken them out of the bin and had sold them on eBay. And so this had been . . . identified by the company. Disciplinary action had been taken and had been discussed with the board at a previous board meeting, I think it may have even been in the minutes . . . The auditors picked up on this. **(Richard)**

The auditors had been told of the problem by somebody in the management team. Edward agreed that it was not an issue of great significance:

> It was very minor and in fact in that particular case, management had told us and hadn't expected to tell the audit committee . . . Not a loss for the company by any means, not substantial. **(Edward)**

But it was a failure of internal controls and:

> It shouldn't have happened. **(Edward)**

Given that the amounts involved were not material, Richard was somewhat disgruntled at the way the auditors raised this issue at the audit committee:

> In their audit highlights memo they had pretty much two pages on it and certainly the management's view was certainly that this did not warrant two pages in the audit

---

[2] Provision C.3.2 of the Combined Code (FRC, 2008a) sets out the role and responsibilities of the audit committee. These include 'to review the company's internal financial controls, and unless expressly addressed by a separate board risk committee, or by the board itself, to review the company's internal financial control and risk management systems.' Provision C.3.4 requires the audit committee to review arrangements by which staff of the company may, in confidence, raise concerns about possible improprieties in matters of financial reporting and other matters. The audit committee's objective should be to ensure that arrangements are in place for the proportionate and independent investigation of such matters and for appropriate follow up action.

highlights memo. It was an issue that had been identified by management, had been discussed with the board, had been dealt with and therefore the audit committee were fully aware of it and therefore why the auditors needed to then pick it up and make an issue of it was just not felt to be appropriate. In the end, that point was kept in there because they felt it was something that had happened during the year and needed to be in their document to the audit committee but it was a much briefer statement. **(Richard)**

Edward accepted that all the directors knew of the incident and he was aware that management thought they were making something out of nothing. It led to clearer guidance as to the type of issues to be considered by the audit committee in future:

> If it is a minor breach of internal controls the audit committee have said they don't need to know. So we are quite clear on that. **(Edward)**

11.3.3   Valuation of Intangible Assets on Acquisition of a Subsidiary

Richard explained that the company was regularly involved in acquisitions and, therefore, was affected by the IFRS 3 requirement to value separable intangible assets.[3] He was not enamoured of this particular feature of IFRS:

> The provisions of the standard are conceptually difficult to come to terms with. I have grown up through a period where it has been companies trying to put intangible assets on the balance sheet ... and the profession has fought against it. Now you have to do that. **(Richard)**

Edward also had his reservations:

> This is a tricky area, it is all very subjective to my mind. **(Edward)**

Richard was strongly of the view that the accountancy profession were the main beneficiaries of the requirement to value intangibles:

> We worked out the minimum fee for a review would be about £25,000 if we wanted them to do it ... We did it ourselves and we probably paid about £5,000. It is just every acquisition has to have it now. It is just an absolute way of making money. And because you have to have an annual impairment of the intangibles you then have to bring in valuation specialists it is ... I just find it very frustrating. **(Richard)**

Edward outlined the support provided by his firm:

> Richard asked us for some advice ... We gave Richard access to people ... who have got that expertise. So he went and had a coaching/training session on the issues around

---

[3] IFRS 3 *Business Combinations* requires that all identifiable assets should be recognized in the balance sheet at fair value. This includes all intangible assets that meet the definition of an intangible asset in IAS 38 *Intangible Assets* and whose fair value can be measured reliably and must be amortized each year. The excess of the cost of the business combination over the acquirer's interest in the net fair value of the identifiable assets, liabilities and contingent liabilities is recognized as goodwill (IASB, 2004, paras. 36–37; 45; 51). IAS 36 specifies that goodwill has an indefinite useful life and is subject to an annual impairment test. The rules are far more stringent than UK GAAP was in requiring intangible assets to be recognized and amortized rather than being subsumed into goodwill.

how to fair value a business and they looked at the value of the customer relationship and they looked at the brand that they had bought and gave them the template as to how to put these things together and then he went away and did that and then we discussed it at audit committee. That sort of helped. **(Edward)**

Given that the group was aiming to be acquisitive, Richard applied the full model to the acquisition of a relatively small foreign company.

When we bought [name of company] we paid the net asset value ... We then had to go in and increase the value of that business so creating a profit to the profit and loss account that went through other income last year because we are deemed to have got more than we paid for it and then we need to annually review those assets, it just seems ludicrous to me, it really does. **(Richard)**

Richard explained that the acquisition was completed just after the year-end (although it featured in the previous year's audit highlights) and outlined the way in which the matter would be handled by the audit committee:

This year there is the acquisition and the accounting for it and the intangible asset review. The auditors will report to the audit committee. The audit committee will know that we have to do this review, that we need to make sure that we have done our intangible asset review, and they will be looking for the auditors to confirm that we have done that, and the valuations we have come up with, they are comfortable with and so that will happen again this year. **(Richard)**

Edward was satisfied that the audit committee was fully engaged with the issue:

So we had those discussions and [name of audit committee member] in particular piped up and asked for the detail of what we had done and how we had dealt with it. The two that are involved are quite professional, they have a good understanding. So quite rightly so when you audit these things you do want some comfort that they are taking matters seriously. **(Edward)**

Edward did not care for the requirement to undertake an impairment review on goodwill and intangibles with an indefinite life:

You can have an indefinite life on an asset. Just because you don't know how long it is going to live so therefore you don't depreciate it ... Bizarre. IFRS takes you down a route and then stops and you are left hanging. **(Edward)**

Richard also had problems with IFRS 3:

And you try and explain that to non-financial people, to the chairman, the chief executive and it is very hard to try and explain something where you really don't understand it or believe in it. **(Richard)**

11.4 CONTEXTUAL FACTORS AND ANALYSIS OF THE INTERACTIONS

The general contextual factors in Woodpecker are drawn together in Figure 11.1. The company is seen as well managed and the audit committee works reasonably effectively as a team.

Richard was a competent finance director who nevertheless found IFRS implementation something of a challenge and disliked many of its requirements. He did accept that he needed some additional external support for the changeover and turned to Edward's firm. He expected his auditors to be generally available to provide some level of business advice and support.

Horace, the audit committee chair, undertook the role dutifully but appeared to not lead strongly when technical accounting issues were under review. He did not have experience of applying IFRS and to some extent appeared to rely on other members of the audit committee when accounting matters were being discussed.

Edward was the newly appointed audit partner. He attended all audit committee meetings and tried to be constructive in his dealings with management. Edward considered Richard to be his main point of contact in the company. He was technically competent although unenthusiastic about IFRS.

11.4.1 Financial Reporting Related Interaction: Inventory Valuation

The company has a conservative but formulaic policy for writing down obsolete items of inventory, although on occasions additional *ad hoc* provisions were made. Edward became concerned that the policy might not be adequate as it focused on the age of the inventory and he considered the company might have some excess stock which could take many years to sell.

Edward raised this with management who believed that they could dispose of excess stock without too much difficulty via special deals. Edward reported his concerns to the audit committee. They agreed with the management view, but new procedures were implemented to ensure that any problems were identified. Edward stated that he was satisfied that the audit committee had considered the impact of the policy, but he did not believe the matter was sufficiently material to take any further.

This issue was a matter of judgement, particularly with respect to materiality. Edward was satisfied that the issue had been raised both with management and the audit committee and that both groups had considered the implications. While the existing approach to inventory provisions was still considered valid, the new procedures would pick up any shortcomings in the approach.

11.4.2 Corporate Governance Related Interaction: Breach of Internal Controls in an Overseas Subsidiary

There had been a fraud in a subsidiary where some inventory had been scrapped and then stolen by an employee and sold on eBay. It was reported to the board and dealt

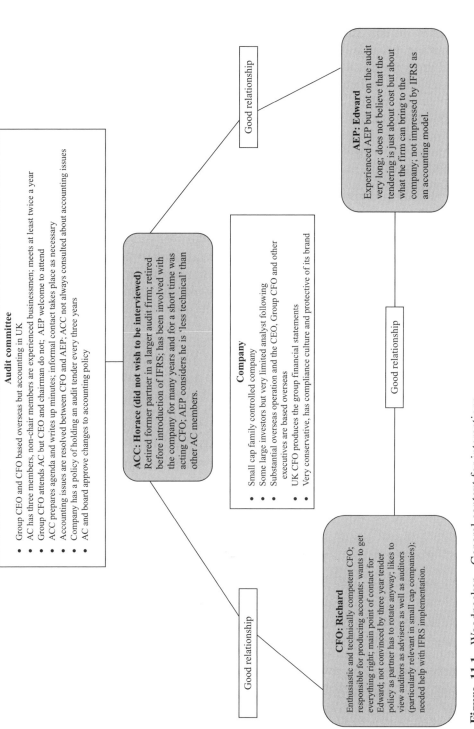

Audit committee

- Group CEO and CFO based overseas but accounting in UK
- AC has three members, non-chair members are experienced businessmen; meets at least twice a year
- Group CFO attends AC but CEO and chairman do not; AEP welcome to attend
- ACC prepares agenda and writes up minutes; informal contact takes place as necessary
- Accounting issues are resolved between CFO and AEP; ACC not always consulted about accounting issues
- Company has a policy of holding an audit tender every three years
- AC and board approve changes to accounting policy

ACC: Horace (did not wish to be interviewed)
Retired former partner in a larger audit firm; retired before introduction of IFRS; has been involved with the company for many years and for a short time was acting CFO; AEP considers he is 'less technical' than other AC members.

Company

- Small cap family controlled company
- Some large investors but very limited analyst following
- Substantial overseas operation and the CEO, Group CFO and other executives are based overseas
- UK CFO produces the group financial statements
- Very conservative, has compliance culture and protective of its brand

Good relationship

AEP: Edward
Experienced AEP but not on the audit very long; does not believe that the tendering is just about cost but about what the firm can bring to the company; not impressed by IFRS as an accounting model.

Good relationship

CFO: Richard
Enthusiastic and technically competent CFO; responsible for producing accounts; wants to get everything right; main point of contact for Edward; not convinced by three year tender policy as partner has to rotate anyway; likes to view auditors as advisers as well as auditors (particularly relevant in small cap companies); needed help with IFRS implementation.

Good relationship

Figure 11.1 Woodpecker – General context for interactions

with, but then the auditors found out about it. Although he knew the matter had been discussed by the board already, Edward raised it with the audit committee in his audit memorandum, because it was a breach of internal control and had happened during the year. Richard was annoyed because he thought the auditors were making too much fuss by including the item in their memorandum to the directors as the directors were already familiar with the issue. Subsequently, the audit committee decided not to have minor frauds reported to them. This is not a good outcome as best practice suggests that all frauds should be reported to the audit committee. Arguably, an overreaction from Edward led to the audit committee making a sub-optimal decision.

11.4.3   Financial Reporting Related Interaction: Valuation of Intangible Assets on Acquisition of a Subsidiary

The company had a policy of making acquisitions and, therefore, had to apply IFRS 3 which requires intangibles bought as part of an acquisition to be separately identified on the balance sheet. Richard thought that the whole approach was a waste of time, provided no useful information and was a money-making scheme for accountants. In the end, Richard decided they would do the valuations themselves rather than pay £25,000 to somebody else.

Despite feeling hostile towards the process, Richard sought advice from Edward's firm who gave him a training session in how to value different types of intangible assets. He applied these principles to the latest acquisition and the approach was discussed at the audit committee. This helped to defuse the problem, although a further difficulty arose about future adjustments when the value of the intangible was increasing.

The outcome was compliant, although Richard could not see the point of the exercise and Edward was also unenthusiastic towards the regulatory requirements. While Edward's firm helped Richard understand the correct approach to the intangible valuations, they could not do the work themselves as they would have breached ethical standards (APB, 2004c).

11.5   CONCLUSIONS

This chapter illustrates the scenario of a competent finance director in a small company seeking support within the current regulatory framework, combined with a somewhat disengaged ACC who nevertheless leads a competent audit committee, and an experienced non-Big Four audit partner.

The first interaction arose when Edward questioned the approach taken towards inventory provisions, suggesting that it was based around the age of stock and tended to ignore the potential problem of excess stock. This was a judgement based around whether an alternative approach would make any material difference to the accounts.

The second interaction focused on whether a fraud, which had already been reported to the board, should also be considered by the audit committee. The audit committee decided that small breaches of internal control did not need to be considered by them. This sub-optimal outcome may have been the result of management being indignant and defensive towards Edward. In both interactions, management, having been challenged, had the final word.

In the third interaction, recognition of intangibles was a compliance issue and although Richard was dismissive of the relevant standard, he accepted there was no alternative. The valuation of the intangibles was a judgement issue and Richard applied a model to produce an acceptable answer. Edward worked in partnership with Richard to come to a successful conclusion.

Case 8 — Raven plc

12.1 BACKGROUND TO THE CASE

Raven is a large international technology group. The company reporting policy is conservative and driven by a desire to protect its reputation and get its financial reporting right. The audit committee chair, Norman, is a former finance director and is technically up to date and knowledgeable. The audit engagement partner, Ivan, is a senior member of his firm. The finance director, Trevor, is a former auditor and highly competent in accounting requirements. All three are professionally qualified accountants. The interviews related to Raven's second year of IFRS implementation.

The audit committee is run effectively and the finance director, audit committee chair and the auditor work together professionally to achieve the board's reporting objectives. Norman is determined to ensure that the audit committee does not have any late surprises in the financial reporting cycle.

During the course of the interviews, Trevor and Ivan discussed financial reporting interactions but Norman did not refer to these in detail. However, he did explain how he managed the audit committee.

12.2 CORPORATE GOVERNANCE

According to the relevant financial statements there were more non-executive directors on the board than executive directors. There were no disclosures which indicated the company did not comply fully with the Combined Code. The audit committee had three members.

12.2.1 Cycle of Meetings and Attendees

Norman explained that the audit committee normally met at least six times during the year and the auditors attended every meeting. He believed there should be an open relationship and auditors should be able to attend any audit committee meetings.

There was a range of attendees at the audit committee from within the company which frequently resulted in more attendees than members. The attendees included: the head of internal audit; the head of compliance; the finance director; and the group financial controller. Norman thought it was important for the financial controller to be present as she was involved with both the management accounts and the external reporting.

Others could also be called in to attend if there were particular matters requiring discussion or explanation. If a major issue was coming to the audit committee, particularly from a subsidiary, Norman considered it was essential for the committee to hear directly from the executive responsible for it. Those asked to attend were given clear instructions about what was expected of them and the time allowed for presentation of the issue.

Norman referred to the membership of Raven's audit committee and the importance of having non-financial experts on the committee. They could stand back from the accounting issues and at times express a different view.

Ivan agreed that having non-financial experts on the audit committee was important. They raised wider issues associated with risk and disclosures rather than the detail of the accounts. They were interested in the implications for the business of accounting and disclosure issues such as those involving potential litigation and contingencies.

Audit planning, an important agenda item for the audit committee, was a bottom up process which addressed matters needing attention within divisions and subsidiaries before the plan was pulled together at group level. Trevor explained that discussions were held with management before the auditors compiled their planning document. Among matters covered in the planning document were: the auditors' view of risk in the company; audit coverage; scope; and materiality. The planning document did not include the fee proposal.

Norman explained that the audit planning process continued throughout the year. There was an agenda item at every audit committee about audit planning. As the audit progressed, outcomes were reported to the committee and, where necessary, the planning was adjusted to take account of what came up. Ivan presented his fee estimates to Trevor at the same time as the planning document.

In common with many companies, the detailed discussion on the fee took place between Trevor and Ivan, with Trevor then making a recommendation to the audit committee. There was always a lot of discussion about the planning and the fee. Questions were asked of Ivan by the audit committee about such matters as: changes in scope; the volume of work that was needed in particular areas; and whether external auditors were working with the internal auditors effectively.

Norman, as audit committee chair, was more concerned about getting the scope of the audit right than trying to knock the audit fee down. He wanted to be sure a sufficient audit was being done and if he thought the fee was too high this could readily be dealt with by Trevor or by the audit committee.

12.2.2   The Chair's Management of the Audit Committee

A prime focus for Norman was that he did not want any late surprises arising at audit committee meetings, or just before, as surprises left no time for adequate discussion. He was sure that the audit committee did not want them either. He had regular discussions with Trevor about matters as they developed and also met with him before audit committee meetings. In addition to this, Norman held pre-audit committee meetings with Ivan and Trevor and others from the company, including the internal auditors and the risk managers. The purpose was to consider items that were under discussion, so they could all be better informed about what was coming up on the audit committee agenda. The pre-meetings were particularly important before the year end as this was the time when major accounting judgements were reviewed. Norman considered that late surprises were a particular problem if they came up close to the year end.

Trevor emphasized that the pre-meetings had no formal status; describing them as a *rehearsal* for the main meetings. Despite their lack of formal status, he thought the meetings were useful for him and particularly for Norman as it helped him, as chair of the audit committee, to plan the meeting and to identify the topics where discussion needed to take place.

Ivan also valued the pre-meetings as they were able to run through the agenda to decide how to make best use of the time spent at the audit committee. It was also an opportunity for Norman to ensure he was fully briefed about difficult areas and the progress being made.

As some problems could require discussion at more than one meeting before they were accepted by the audit committee, Norman made sure that the audit committee was informed of emerging contentious issues well before final decisions had be taken. This was necessary to ensure that the non-financial members of the audit committee had the chance to brief themselves. Both Norman and Trevor made themselves available, as needed, to the non-financial experts on the audit committee if they required explanation about any complex accounting matters that were coming up.

Although Trevor had regular communication with Norman about issues as they arose, he was clear on his role in relation to the audit committee itself. He regarded it as a failure to take an unresolved problem between himself and Ivan to the audit committee for them to decide upon. He did not believe the audit committee should act as a referee between himself and Ivan. Ivan fully agreed with this view. The audit committee should have the opportunity to question the judgements, not decide between different ones.

Norman was aware that Raven was an important client to Ivan's firm and he would challenge both Ivan and Trevor on contentious matters to be sure that they were both genuinely in agreement and both fully supported any proposals that were made to the audit committee. Ivan agreed that Norman did grill both himself and Trevor on various topics. Ivan considered that Norman was particularly good at identifying key sensitivities and assumptions.

Prior to Norman becoming chair of the audit committee, Trevor and Ivan had both presented reports on key judgements made during the year and their opinion of the judgements. Norman felt it was not helpful to the committee to have two reports on what were similar issues and requested that they were combined in a way that enabled the key subject matter to be clear and the relevant views to be seen together and, therefore, in context, allowing a more effective review by the audit committee.

12.2.3 Communication with the Auditors

Ivan considered that the relationship with Raven was very open. The relationship had become a bit strained during the IFRS conversion as there had been a tremendous amount to do which had led to inevitable stress between two teams with tight deadlines. To improve relations, he set up regular meetings with Trevor even if there were no specific matters to discuss. These meetings had worked well and had helped him and his team to keep up-to-date with emerging issues and any possible accounting, control or disclosure matters that Raven was dealing with.

The team itself frequently carried out audit work at Raven which provided them with the opportunity to pick up issues as they arose. Norman had four formal meetings every year with the auditors but there were also informal communications. Norman had made it clear that Ivan was welcome to meet up with him at any time he felt the need.

Trevor felt that his relationship with Ivan became challenged if Ivan brought something up at the audit committee without notice. He thought it was because of late briefings within Ivan's firm. When this happened, Trevor made sure he communicated his views strongly to Ivan. He did not think that it helped Ivan to raise matters at the audit committee when it was apparent to the committee that he had not discussed it with Trevor first. This did not happen often.

Norman made an interesting observation on Ivan and Trevor. He thought the combination of two different personalities provided a good combination for effective review and challenge. Trevor was technically very strong and determined to do the best for Raven and Ivan was very experienced and statesmanlike in his handling of the relationship.

12.2.4 Nature of the Auditor Client Relationship

None of the three parties was critical of the working relationship itself, although each commented on it. Ivan thought that Norman was a good audit committee chair because he had kept up-to-date on accounting and financial developments. He prepared for meetings and raised very good questions. Ivan got more job satisfaction engaging with an audit committee chair who was up to speed and challenging.

On the subject of non-audit services, the audit committee set a pre-approved budget and within that budget every separate assignment was approved. Trevor felt that the restrictions on the provision of non-audit services had improved the auditor/client relationship as the partner was not focussing so much on selling other services. As a former auditor, Trevor was aware that, before this change had been introduced, audit firms had maximizing revenues as the key measure on their balanced scorecard. He believed it was much better for the partner to be judged on client retention.

Trevor looked back regretfully to the times in the 1990s when doing the best possible financial audit was the key measure on the balanced scorecard, and if that was achieved the belief was that fees would follow.

12.2.5 Satisfaction with Auditors and Partner Changes/Tendering

Although the Combined Code expects audit committees to be concerned about audit quality, Trevor did not consider the FRC's definition of audit quality was of much use to an audit committee, although it might help the Audit Inspection Unit. He thought the audit committee made judgements about audit quality in an unstructured way, based on their opinion of the audit partner. He did not think there were adequate guidelines for audit committees to work to in judging audit quality.

Trevor organized a process himself every year to assess auditor performance. An exercise was carried out at one of the finance group conferences and the whole subject was debated. This provided useful information for the audit committee about the views of Raven's staff who worked closely with Ivan's firm.

Ivan knew that assessment took place and had been concerned that after the IFRS stresses Raven might go out to tender. He thought it had now settled down and the relationship had improved. There had been problems in a couple of locations but this had also been sorted out. He thought it was right for Raven to explore the market to find out which firms would be independent if they were minded to change.

Norman was convinced that the company should keep an eye on competitors in the audit market and go out to tender, where appropriate, to be sure that the reasons they originally chose their incumbent auditor still applied. It also gave them the opportunity to compare what the incumbent firm was offering with what other firms could offer. He was also very clear that the decision to go out to tender belonged to the audit committee not the finance director.

Ivan was due to rotate off shortly as audit partner. He thought that five years was too short a period for an engagement partner to stay with a large client, as taking on large clients took a lot of personal resource in getting to grips with what the client was about. Norman and Trevor also considered that five years' incumbency was too short a time because of the problems of getting familiar with the client.

12.3 KEY INTERACTIONS BETWEEN TREVOR, NORMAN AND IVAN

Norman did not talk about any of the interactions in detail. However, as chair of the audit committee, he did not expect to be engaged with the detail of reaching agreement unless Trevor and Ivan were not able to do so. Nevertheless, he expected to be made aware of the matters being discussed and whether there were potential problems.

There were three main matters which were the subject of interactions:

1. Accounting for a complex transaction.
2. Disclosures relating to potential future losses in a subsidiary, Chestnut.
3. Business Review disclosures.

12.3.1   Accounting for a Complex Transaction

Early in the financial year, Raven had engaged in a complex transaction with a large international company and there were some challenges with accounting for it. Initially, there was a disagreement between Ivan and Trevor as to how it should be treated, as it was a judgement issue and there was no clear guidance in IFRS to cover it.

The matter was raised up front with the auditors by Trevor's staff as a matter for discussion, because it was a key area of judgement and Trevor expected his staff to raise matters with him at an early stage. Because the transaction was significant, it was referred to Ivan and Trevor by their subordinates.

As the deal had been completed in the first half of the year, Trevor and Ivan had to get agreement in principle from the audit committee about the accounting treatment before the half year results were announced.

Initially, there were conflicting views between Trevor and Ivan about how to account for it and Trevor took a hard line indicating that he was unwilling to shift unless Ivan came up with a very strong case. The point of contention was about how much profit should be recognized on the transaction for the current year's accounts and going forward. Trevor favoured a greater recognition of profit than Ivan.

Norman was aware that there was a disagreement between Ivan and Trevor as this was discussed at a pre-audit committee meeting. After the meeting, Trevor prepared a much more detailed paper justifying his proposal and providing evidence of other cases where the same treatment had been used. He thought Ivan was being cautious because his firm had not come across a similar transaction before.

Having received Trevor's more detailed paper, Ivan went back to his firm and consulted again with senior technical partners and the other partners involved with the Raven audit. They carefully checked out the additional data that Trevor had provided to ensure it was correct and then, after further debate, they decided that they could accept Trevor's proposal.

Having agreed the treatment with Trevor, Ivan then met with Norman on two occasions to explain to him what the options were and what the solution was that Trevor and he proposed. Ivan wanted to be sure that, before the proposal went to the audit committee, Norman fully understood it so that, if necessary, he could support the position taken.

When the proposal was taken to the audit committee, Trevor and Ivan presented the case together. They had to convince the committee, who were conservative and concerned to ensure that the proposal would not result in profits being overstated. The committee wanted to be sure that the accounting would stand up both to internal and external scrutiny.

Both Ivan and Trevor reflected on the situation afterwards. Ivan had accepted the accounting treatment in the end based on the additional evidence that Trevor had produced, although he had not agreed with it initially. He did not consider that he had been persuaded to accept something that he was not comfortable with. Trevor was slightly uncomfortable as he was concerned that he might have been too intransigent in his stance and this might have dominated the discussions and the outcome. However, he did acknowledge that Ivan and Norman had taken a lot of convincing.

12.3.2   Disclosures Relating to Potential Future Losses in a Subsidiary, Chestnut

Early in the year, Raven had acquired an overseas subsidiary, Chestnut, at the instigation of one of the directors. Later in the year, it emerged that Chestnut had taken out a large number of long-term fixed rate contracts for purchase of certain commodities and the price of the commodities had since fallen and was continuing to do so. There were protracted discussions as the yearend approached about how this should be disclosed, particularly in relation to the assumptions on future prices. Trevor, who was interviewed first, did not refer to this matter. Norman commented briefly and it was Ivan who described it in some depth.

Ivan explained that the key problem would be how long it would take for the price gap to be eliminated. In order to get a better understanding of this issue, Ivan's firm employed a specialist in the area to give a view on future prices and how they were expected to trend. The issue was twofold — how to account for it and what needed to be disclosed. Trevor did not take a position on the accounting treatment as both he and Ivan were seeking a resolution of it.

Based on the additional evidence provided by Ivan's expert, Ivan and Trevor resolved the accounting problem, but reaching agreement on disclosure was more difficult. The big question was how much should be disclosed about it.

Because a board member was involved, Trevor took over drafting the disclosures and it went to the main board. Trevor was aware that the transaction would have to be explained at meetings with analysts and investors and was, therefore, sensitive about it.

Ivan told them that what they were proposing to disclose was not enough to satisfy the accounting disclosure requirements and suggested increasing the disclosure. Initially there was challenge from the board and the audit committee to Ivan's proposal. He had worried a bit about the possibility of a qualification if it all got stuck, but it did not come to that because the accounting requirements made the choices clear. However, the board did discuss the commercial sensitivity of more disclosure and whether it could damage the business.

Overall, Ivan felt that, if there had been an impasse, Norman would have supported him.

12.3.3   Business Review Disclosures

Compliance with the Business Review[1] requirements had proved quite challenging for Raven because of the size of the business. The group had originally included an

---

[1] The Enhanced Business Review was brought in by the Companies Act 2006, becoming effective for yearends beginning on or after 1 October 2007. It requires companies to include in their annual reports discussion of a number of issues such as a review of the business, objectives and strategies, risks and uncertainties and include an analysis using financial and non-financial key performance indicators (KPIs). However, companies had been prepared for a previous change by the Operating and Financial Review which had been withdrawn at a late stage. Having already done the work, a number of companies decided to go ahead with the additional disclosures anyway.

Operating and Financial Review with its annual report and a late change of government policy required a different report. This had not been helpful for Trevor's team.

He believed that the matter was not contentious and all parties had worked together and had a lot of discussion to reach the best outcome. The main area of difficulty was agreeing the KPIs they should include, as there were so many which were used within the group.

The standard required a lot of disclosure which Trevor felt was unnecessary. The overall view taken on this was to include what was needed to explain the business to shareholders and analysts. Trevor expressed the view that standard setters did not sufficiently consider the consequences of what they asked companies to do.

12.4 CONTEXTUAL FACTORS AND ANALYSIS OF THE INTERACTIONS

The contextual factors are shown in Figure 12.1. Raven is a large and complex institution with a strong compliance culture. The audit committee chair, Norman, runs the committee effectively and makes it clear he wishes to be informed of significant matters as they arise but does not expect to be involved in the decision-making unless it is essential. He also holds pre-audit committee meetings to ensure there are no surprises coming up at the audit committee itself. He is experienced, competent and up-to-date with accounting developments. Trevor, the finance director, is technically very competent and forceful. He is prepared to challenge the auditor on accounting interpretations to ensure the outcomes are the best for the company and is also aware of the importance of the client to his auditors. He also feels that the relationship and audit focus has improved since the auditors' ethical standards prevented partners promoting non-audit services to Raven. The auditor, Ivan, is an experienced senior partner in his firm who is also aware of the need to maintain the relationship which suffered during the IFRS changeover. Ivan is also aware of the importance of the client to his firm. All three thought that with a client as complex as Raven the five year rotation for audit partners was too short.

12.4.1 Financial Reporting Interaction: Accounting for a Complex Transaction

This transaction was recognized as complex and significant at an early stage and was passed up by Raven and audit staff to Trevor and Ivan for resolution. Trevor took a firm stance at the outset by stating how he wanted to account for it and making it clear he would have to be convinced by Ivan if the auditors wanted a different outcome. Trevor's proposed outcome was more advantageous for the company. Ivan initially took a different view. Norman was made aware that there was a disagreement between Trevor and Ivan. In order to support his case, Trevor produced more information, including evidence of other situations where his proposed approach had been adopted.

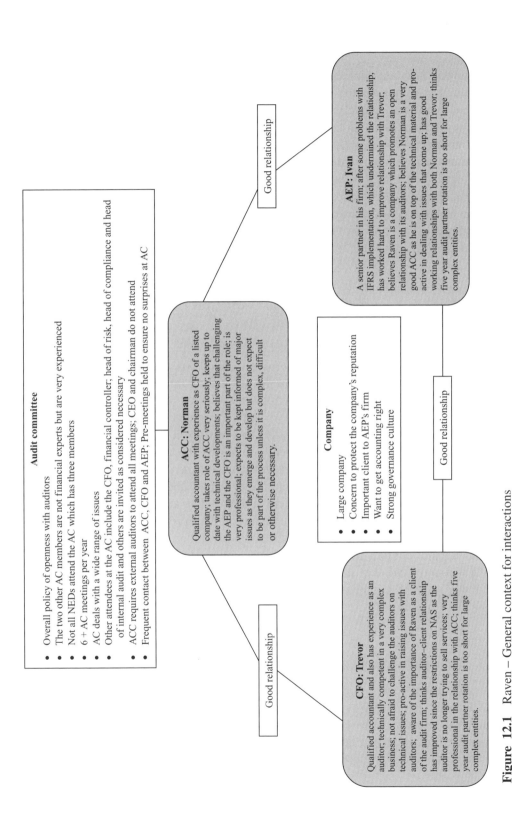

Audit committee

- Overall policy of openness with auditors
- The two other AC members are not financial experts but are very experienced
- Not all NEDs attend the AC which has three members
- 6 + AC meetings per year
- AC deals with a wide range of issues
- Other attendees at the AC include the CFO, financial controller; head of risk, head of compliance and head of internal audit and others are invited as considered necessary
- ACC requires external auditors to attend all meetings; CEO and chairman do not attend
- Frequent contact between ACC, CFO and AEP; Pre-meetings held to ensure no surprises at AC

ACC: Norman

Qualified accountant with experience as CFO of a listed company; takes role of ACC very seriously; keeps up to date with technical developments; believes that challenging the AEP and the CFO is an important part of the role; is very professional; expects to be kept informed of major issues as they emerge and develop but does not expect to be part of the process unless it is complex, difficult or otherwise necessary.

AEP: Ivan

A senior partner in his firm; after some problems with IFRS implementation, which undermined the relationship, has worked hard to improve relationship with Trevor; believes Raven is a company which promotes an open relationship with its auditors; believes Norman is a very good ACC as he is on top of the technical material and pro-active in dealing with issues that come up; has good working relationships with both Norman and Trevor; thinks five year audit partner rotation is too short for large complex entities.

Good relationship

Company

- Large company
- Concern to protect the company's reputation
- Important client to AEP's firm
- Want to get accounting right
- Strong governance culture

Good relationship

CFO: Trevor

Qualified accountant and also has experience as an auditor; technically competent in a very complex business; not afraid to challenge the auditors on technical issues; pro-active in raising issues with auditors; aware of the importance of Raven as a client of the audit firm; thinks auditor–client relationship has improved since the restrictions on NAS as the auditor is no longer trying to sell services; very professional in the relationship with ACC; thinks five year audit partner rotation is too short for large complex entities.

Good relationship

Figure 12.1 Raven – General context for interactions

Ivan discussed the material that Trevor had produced with his technical department and in the end Ivan and his advisors from the technical department were persuaded that Trevor's solution was the right answer. The situation then moved to the audit committee where, interestingly, Trevor and Ivan together convinced first Norman and then the audit committee that the proposed treatment was right. After the event, both Trevor and Norman felt slightly nervous about the outcome. Norman felt it necessary to say he had not been persuaded to accept an outcome he was not comfortable with and Trevor also wondered whether his initial tough stance had been too aggressive.

The main factor that influenced this outcome was the determination of Trevor to get acceptance of his proposed accounting treatment although he subsequently wondered if he might have been a bit too intransigent and pushed too hard. This was a judgement issue and not directly related to IFRS.

12.4.2   Financial Reporting Interaction: Disclosures Relating to Potential Future Losses in a Subsidiary, Chestnut

This interaction was particularly sensitive because one of the directors was originally involved in the acquisition and did not want to be exposed to criticism about the current position. The issue was not about the accounting treatment itself, which had already been agreed, but about the additional disclosures required by IFRS, which could embarrass the director with investors and be commercially sensitive. This was a key influence on the interaction. Initially, Trevor wanted minimal disclosure but, because of the sensitivity, the issue went straight to the main board, and Trevor drafted the proposed disclosures. Ivan was not satisfied and presented two arguments to convince the board that they had to do more. He warned about the risk of inadequate disclosure which could come back at them at a later date and it was better to be up front about it. He then told them that to comply fully with IFRS, they had to do what he recommended. This was discussed at the audit committee and Ivan felt that if there had been a major conflict Norman would have supported him. Interestingly, Norman thought that in the end they had disclosed too much.

This was an IFRS compliance issue greatly influenced by commercial sensitivity and the interest of the director. In the end, the outcome complied with IFRS.

12.4.3   Financial Reporting Issue: Business Review

All three parties worked together to bring about the change in disclosures from the OFR to the Business Review. There was some difficulty in deciding what KPIs should go in and also concern about the reaction of the analysts and investors to it. Trevor raised an interesting question as to whether the standard setters and regulators understood the potential consequences of what they asked preparers to do.

12.5 CONCLUSIONS

Raven had a strong governance and compliance culture, with a well run audit committee and a capable audit committee chair who was prepared to get engaged with major issues where necessary. The finance director was expert in his subject and assertive and the audit partner was a senior partner in his firm.

One accounting issue was judgemental where Trevor strongly influenced the outcome by stating his position up front and producing evidence of previous examples of the treatment he wanted, which was in the best interests of the company. Ivan and his colleagues convinced themselves it was acceptable and then supported Trevor in convincing Norman and the audit committee that this was the way to go.

In the second accounting issue, which was sensitive because it related to a transaction originally set up by one of the current directors, Ivan won the day by making it clear that the accounting standard required the disclosures.

This chapter shows that an assertive and technically competent finance director can convince an auditor and the technical advisors to change the initial view by providing strong evidence to support the case. However, in the second interaction the prescriptive requirement of IFRS left the company with little choice despite the director's sensitivity. Trevor raised an interesting point about the Business Review disclosures in questioning whether the standard setters considered the consequences of their efforts.

Case 9 — Ostrich plc

13.1 BACKGROUND TO THE CASE

Ostrich plc is a small manufacturing group which has grown by the acquisition of smaller companies in the same sector. The finance director, Matthew, and the audit committee chair, Victor, are qualified accountants. The audit engagement partner, Luke, has been involved with the client for a couple of years. All three were interviewed for this project but decided that they did not want a detailed case to be published. We have therefore provided a broad overview of the case to underpin the analysis of the interactions.

13.2 CORPORATE GOVERNANCE

A number of executive directors attended audit committee meetings including the CEO, who takes a keen interest in financial reporting. Victor considered this was necessary for the audit committee to gain a better understanding of the operational issues. There were at least three audit committee meetings per year dealing with audit planning, interim results, final results and other issues. The audit committee engaged with the audit planning process. The audit fee was primarily negotiated between Matthew and Luke, with some input from the other members of the board. The audit committee then approves the audit fee. Matthew believed that the main focus of the audit committee was on the audit although Victor was concerned that broader issues (e.g. risk assessment) should be given adequate consideration.

Victor expected all accounting issues to be resolved between the finance director and the auditor before they became an agenda item for the audit committee. He considered the task of the audit committee was to understand the judgements applied by management and their impact on the accounts. He did not like surprises and, therefore, he contacted Luke and Matthew before the meeting (and at other times when necessary) to ensure that he was adequately briefed.

Victor believed that regulation and external pressures had changed non-audit services purchasing behaviour, although he still believed there were advantages in accounting related services (e.g. tax) being provided by the auditor.

13.3 KEY INTERACTIONS BETWEEN MATTHEW, VICTOR AND LUKE

During the course of the audit the following issues were discussed by Matthew, Victor and Luke:

1. Recognition of intangible assets on acquisition.
2. Share-based payments.
3. Business Review.
4. Segmental reporting.

13.4   CONTEXTUAL FACTORS AND ANALYSIS OF THE INTERACTIONS

The principal contextual factors impacting on decisions in Ostrich are pulled together in Figure 13.1. All three parties interviewed were competent and experienced. Victor was able to bring recent relevant financial reporting experience to the ACC role. Matthew was an experienced and technically competent CFO, however, working in a small company in a relatively small finance function, he was appreciative of Victor's support on accounting issues. As he was responsible for the investor presentations, the CEO considered it essential for him to understand the financial reporting and he therefore attended the audit committee meetings. Victor believed that the presence of executives on the audit committee was necessary for a better understanding of the business issues.

Luke, the audit partner, was experienced in listed company work. However, since the introduction of IFRS he had found it necessary to consult with his firm's technical department as matters arose. He attended all audit committee meetings (sometimes by phone) and welcomed the executive attendance at the meetings.

13.4.1   Financial Reporting Interaction: Valuation of Intangibles on Acquisition

This was the most significant interaction in Ostrich. The IFRS 3 requirement to recognize all identifiable assets (including intangibles) on acquiring a new company was a major change from practice under UK GAAP.[1] One company had been bought in the first year of IFRS implementation but no intangibles had been recognized on the balance sheet as the auditors did not consider it material. A larger acquisition took place in the second year of IFRS. Matthew believed that an overall principle on not valuing intangibles had been established in year one of IFRS. He was also convinced that the additional information would be of no interest to the users of accounts. Luke's view was that the specific acquisitions that took place in year one of IFRS did not produce significant and material intangibles, but that future acquisitions would require separate consideration.

---

[1] IFRS 3 *Business Combinations* requires that all identifiable assets should be recognized in the balance sheet at fair value. This includes all intangible assets that meet the definition of an intangible asset in IAS 38 *Intangible Assets* and whose fair value can be measured reliably. The excess of the cost of the business combination over the acquirer's interest in the net fair value of the identifiable assets, liabilities and contingent liabilities is recognized as goodwill (IASB, 2004, paras. 36–37; 45; 51). The rules are far more stringent than UK GAAP was in requiring intangible assets to be recognized rather than being subsumed into goodwill.

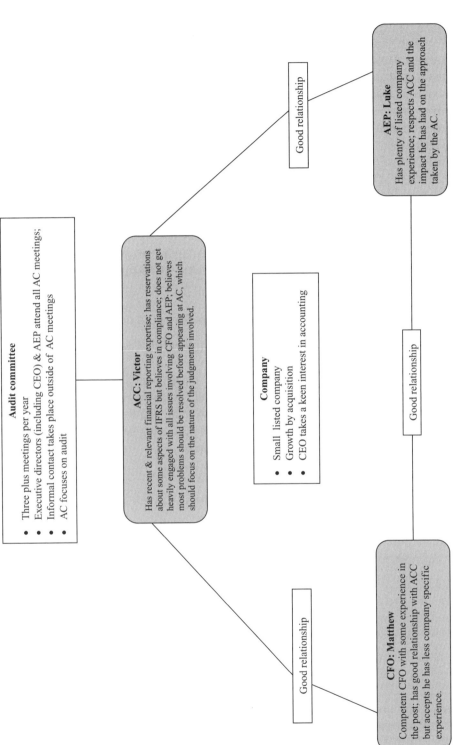

Audit committee

- Three plus meetings per year
- Executive directors (including CEO) & AEP attend all AC meetings;
- Informal contact takes place outside of AC meetings
- AC focuses on audit

ACC: Victor

Has recent & relevant financial reporting expertise; has reservations about some aspects of IFRS but believes in compliance; does not get heavily engaged with all issues involving CFO and AEP; believes most problems should be resolved before appearing at AC, which should focus on the nature of the judgments involved.

Company

- Small listed company
- Growth by acquisition
- CEO takes a keen interest in accounting

AEP: Luke

Has plenty of listed company experience; respects ACC and the impact he has had on the approach taken by the AC.

CFO: Matthew

Competent CFO with some experience in the post; has good relationship with ACC but accepts he has less company specific experience.

Good relationship

Good relationship

Good relationship

Figure 13.1 Ostrich – General context for interactions

This misunderstanding did not emerge until a late stage in the accounting cycle, a surprise which was not welcomed by Matthew. As a result, there was a late adjustment when Luke insisted that the intangibles had to be valued. Matthew was then unhappy about the cost of an external valuation and in the end the valuation was done in-house. Luke conceded that, while he was uncompromising on the principle of recognizing the intangibles, he was prepared to discuss the assumptions behind the valuation as this required a judgement based on knowledge of the business. Everyone agreed that there was no alternative to compliance, so the matter was resolved before it reached the audit committee, although Victor was kept informed of progress and the committee reviewed how the issue had been dealt with. This late surprise put a strain on the relationship and consideration of auditor change but the auditors survived the test.

The main problem was one of communication breakdown between Luke and Matthew, causing the issue to arise late in the audit. However, compliance was achieved at Luke's insistence. The outcome was compliant with respect to recognition of intangibles, although their valuation was a judgement issue.

13.4.2   Financial Reporting Interaction: Share-based Payments

This issue was also brought about by the introduction of IFRS. Matthew sought advice from Luke on how he should account for the early release of shares to staff under a share scheme.[2] Luke consulted with his technical department and informed Matthew that he needed to estimate how many shares would be released early. Matthew was surprised that he could make the number whatever he wanted. This was clearly a judgement issue and illustrates that overly complex judgements may give preparers considerable freedom in respect of some valuations.

13.4.3   Financial Reporting Interaction: Business Review

This interaction took place between Luke and the CEO, who was unenthusiastic about the requirement to disclose key performance indicators (KPIs)[3] as part of the Enhanced Business Review. This reflected concerns about commercial sensitivity but also irritation from the company regarding yet more costly change.

---

[2] IFRS 2 *Share Based Payments* requires all share such transactions to be recognized in the financial statements at fair value. In the case of payment for employee services fair value is determined with respect to the value of the equity instruments (determined by an appropriate valuation model) granted. All transactions involving share-based payments are recognized as expenses over any vesting period. The charge to the income statement requires estimates of such matters as whether the targets will be met and whether the employees will leave and is, therefore, quite judgemental.

[3] The Enhanced Business Review was brought in by the Companies Act 2006, becoming effective for yearend beginning on or after 1 October 2007. Therefore it did not have a direct impact on the year under discussion in this chapter. It requires companies to include in their annual reports discussion of a number of issues such as a review of the business, objectives and strategies, risks and uncertainties and include an analysis using financial and non-financial key performance indicators (KPIs).

13.4.4   Financial Reporting Interaction: Segmental Reporting

Victor recalled that Luke had raised the question of whether Ostrich had identified a sufficient number of business segments for external reporting purposes.[4] Following a discussion it was agreed that no change was required. This was a judgement issue.

13.5   CONCLUSIONS

The first interaction in this case was discussed at length by all three interviewees and unfortunately was a late surprise. While communications between the three parties were generally good, they were strained over this issue. Matthew believed a precedent had been set whereas Luke did not. Recognition of intangibles was a compliance issue, although the valuation was a judgement issue.

Issue two involved Luke providing some very broad parameters within which Matthew could arrive at a valuation. Matthew was surprised at the amount of leeway he was permitted for this task.

Issues three and four were both judgement areas with respect to disclosure. In both these cases, Luke was constructively challenging the status quo and ensured compliance with the requirements.

---

[4] IFRS 8 *Segment Reporting* was issued in November 2006 to replace IAS 14. It was effective for periods beginning after 1 January 2009, but early adoption was permitted. An operating segment is defined as a component of an entity, identified as based on internal reports on each segment that are regularly used by the entity's chief operating decision maker to allocate resources to the segment and to assess its performance. An operating segment becomes a reportable segment if it exceeds predetermined quantitative thresholds. IAS 14 *Segment Reporting*, still in force for the accounting periods covered by these interviews, requires an entity to look to its organizational structure and internal reporting system for the purpose of identifying its segments.

Part III

Cross-Case Analysis and Conclusions

14

Views of Interviewees on the Regulatory Framework

At the end of the day what we are saying is that the rules actually allow for a contrived structure, which, in certain circumstances, will collapse *(ACC 3, Large Co.)*

We now get as part of the audit planning process that we have to do all this because of the international auditing standards, which doesn't really answer the question for the layman which is — shouldn't you do them because they are right or wrong not because somebody tells you to do them? And if they are the right things to do why weren't you doing them before and if they are the wrong things to do why are you doing them now? *(ACC 1, Large Co.)*

14.1 INTRODUCTION

The interviews with the CFOs, ACCs and AEPs covered wider regulatory issues in addition to the interaction issues. This occurred in two ways. At times, the discussion on a specific interaction issue broadened out such that views were expressed on aspects of the current regulatory framework. Also, if time was available, the interviewees were invited to express their thoughts on various aspects of the regulatory framework covering financial reporting, auditing and corporate governance. These responses provide further insights into the views of our interviewees in these three key areas of regulation.

As some comments were made by interviewees who did not wish to be reported verbatim in the case studies, in order to ensure their comments are not identified to any particular case, we have labelled all quotes by interviewee job title and company size and changed the case reference numbers so that interviewees are not matched to cases. FTSE 100 plus FTSE 350 companies are referred to as large, and the others are small. Audit partners are designated Big Four or non-Big Four. We include a summary of views at the end of the chapter.

14.2 FINANCIAL REPORTING ISSUES

In this section we report comments on IFRS, other regulation relating to disclosures in the annual report disclosures and the FRRP.

14.2.1   International Financial Reporting Standards (IFRS)

Many of the interviewees made comments about the impact of IFRS which were of a more general nature than those specific to the interaction issues. There were some supportive comments, for example CFO 1 was quite positive:

> Maybe because I did an economics degree. (**CFO1, Small Co.**)

Frequently, however, positive comments about the concept of common global standards were accompanied by reservations. For example, in the view of one AEP:

> Just to be clear, I am a fan of IFRS but very frustrated with some of the focus within it. (**AEP 8, Big Four**)

The main criticism was the excessive complexity introduced by IFRS (see sub-section 2.3.2 in Chapter 2 for a discussion of the complexity debate). One AEP was particularly concerned about the impact on clients:

> I think there are aspects of it that are sensible and are good but it is just so over complicated. A lot of companies I find, and I am sure many of my colleagues are in the same boat, they are just so detailed that trying to keep on top of it ... I am struggling, and I get conferences every year that bring me back up to speed. I get constant bulletins coming in, regular calls, all sort of stuff. What it is like for a poor finance director who doesn't have any of those things, it just becomes so difficult. The trouble is, it just becomes more and more esoteric. So I haven't really changed my view. The concept of it, I am absolutely in favour of it, absolutely. It is just when you get into it. The idea of having a global financial statement is so right. (**AEP 8, Big Four**)

This view was to some extent affirmed by an ACC struggling to see the value of some of the requirements:

> I think it is good and bad at various levels. I think the concept is good. The idea of having a standard set of financial principles across the world is good. Then you can compare one with another. I think removing subjectivity's good. However, the flip side is ... I think a lot of the rules, which have been designed just to fit all, don't add a lot of value and cost money. You end up with a lot of additional cost and the auditors are getting a lot of money for doing things that ultimately don't make anybody better informed. But I am not quite sure what the solution is to it, because once you go down that path you have to continue down that path. (**ACC 2, Small Co.**)

Another ACC expressed the view that the added complexity put strains on their finance function but that they were reluctant to put in additional resource for financial reporting:

> I think it all depends on the size of the company. If you are an HSBC then you have a great big team. In [name of company] we are a cost conscious company and every hundred thousand pounds matters. So there is a limit on how much resource you want to put into producing a load of stuff that people are inclined to think doesn't really matter a row of beans. (**ACC 6, Large Co.**)

Some interviewees expressed the opinion that since the implementation of IFRS their own confidence in technical matters has been eroded leaving them more reliant on technical departments of audit firms. For example:

> I think it has made it much more difficult for finance directors, I was certainly very comfortable with UK GAAP and we knew how to interpret UK GAAP and I had been in various companies that had interpreted things differently, so you knew the range of acceptable ways to do it ... We allow ourselves to be guided by the technical departments of the auditing firms. There is a load of rubbish in the accounts that I wouldn't put in the accounts because the disclosures don't mean anything for our company. I think under UK GAAP we would have left it out on the basis that it was irrelevant and didn't add to it. But now I probably err on the side of caution, and if [name of audit firm] feel that it should go in, I put it in. And I don't think it helps anybody. (**CFO 3, Large Co.**)

Even audit partners were prepared to admit that they found the new standards challenging:

> It is interesting because it is new. There is a lot in there. You don't feel quite as relaxed discussing technical matters. I don't feel quite as relaxed as I did three or four years ago ... You have got to prepare more for meetings, do more reading, do more consultation. (**AEP 2, Big Four**)

A more positive view expressed by one AEP was that such technical difficulties were a short-term phenomenon which would disappear with greater familiarity:

> I think the clients are largely comfortable. I think the auditors and the accountants are generally now on top of it. I think, generally, now they understand it. I think some of the investor community are quite sophisticated and understand it, particularly those that have industry focus, they will understand what impairments mean, etc. (**AEP 9, Big Four**)

An alternative view was that IFRS was just inherently too complex:

> Well, complexity and judgement and relying on estimation. There is a lot of that around. I think that understanding the financial statements and all the notes is only possible if you are a qualified practitioner. You cannot understand those things. And I defy an accounting team, my divisional finance directors, my controllers, to understand what they are putting in those notes. They just don't understand it. (**CFO 8, Small Co.**)

Financial statements produced under IFRS are supposed to meet the needs of users. A commonly expressed view was that they failed to achieve this:

> Because the numbers are not that transparent. That is the problem. They are not transparent, they get lost in gobbledegook. And that is the real danger with IFRS reporting ... you actually end up with numbers that no one really signs up to. They are doing it because they have to. Lots and lots of disclosure but it doesn't actually help you know what is going on. (**CFO 2, Large Co.**)

The same CFO explained how he did manage to communicate with investors:

> The system works as long as you are able to do investor relations presentations that allow management to interpret the numbers. If IFRS or regulations started to invade management interpretation of numbers then the system would fall down because then you would have numbers that are gibberish. (**CFO 2, Large Co.**)

An ACC made a similar point about the value of a set of accounts suggesting another means of communication:

> My problem is that they have got so complex to try to ensure that no one does anything wrong that you have now created a set of accounts that no one can read . . . When anyone says to me, 'what should I be reading as users of the accounts?', I say — well actually you might as well just read the OFR because frankly that is the best review you are going to get of the business . . . You never find the things you need to know. Why does it have to be so complicated? (**ACC 7, Large Co.**)

One AEP admitted that a lot of time and energy was focused on aspects of the accounts which were of no interest to analysts:

> A disproportionate amount of time is spent on things like intangible accounting and fair values of intangibles which analysts ignore entirely because they focus on headline numbers. They focus on EBITDA; they focus on before amortization or whatever and I don't think that has been picked up. A lot of effort is being focused on an area which the analysts, by and large, are discounting. (**AEP 8, Big Four**)

This view was supported by other interviewees:

> Yes, there are too many numbers you don't want there. You have to strip it out and reassemble it. That is what a lot of the analysts do, to be fair. What you want to know is what the net debt is and it is all focused on cash as opposed to net debt. If you look at most finance directors, in the financial review, they restate the cash flow to a meaningful cash flow. (**ACC 9, Large Co.**)

Another AEP considered that the excessive complexity just brought the whole system of standards into disrepute:

> They have massively over complicated things to the extent that the number of people out there who really do think they understand a set of accounts is tiny. Your average investor in the market wouldn't have a clue . . . I know in the early days of IFRS we were going round talking to analysts and they didn't have a clue . . . There are so many things that people say, 'Obviously that is a nonsense, it is an IFRS thing, it is a technicality, don't worry about it, take that out', and you end up with a lot of things like that in your accounts. (**AEP 9, Big Four**)

A minority view expressed by one ACC was that complexity was already present in UK GAAP and that the introduction of IFRS made little difference:

> I don't think it is any less understandable than if we had stayed with UK GAAP. A lot of the changes have come from us anyway so whether we had stood alone or gone for international we would probably have had the same issues. (**ACC 9, Small Co.**)

One CFO doubted that his accounts were actually read by investors:

> Who reads them? How many people actually read financial statements? I have had two enquiries from shareholders in the last six years on our statutory accounts. (**CFO 8, Small Co.**)

Another CFO thought that the sheer volume of disclosure would discourage potential readers:

> I think there are huge amounts of worthless disclosure that nobody ever reads. I have never had a question from analysts on any of the detailed disclosures, so who is it for if it is not for the analysts? (**CFO 2, Large Co.**)

One of the ACCs suggested that the move to more extensive disclosures was being pushed by auditors concerned about their potential liabilities:

> Insurance liabilities are driving them to look at what they are going to get sued on. The fact that there is a page in here that says the directors are responsible for the accounts. We used to do it in one line, I think, and now it is a whole page and the audit report is now two pages long, whereas it used to be four lines in my day ... Disclosure is a wonderful get out ... You can get obsessed with technical disclosure over letting people know what they need to know. I have never looked at HSBC, 400 pages that sort of thing, who would read it? (**ACC 1, Large Co.**)

Other aspects of IFRS were criticized by interviewees. One ACC considered that the extensive use of fair values in IFRS undermined the original purpose of accounts, which was to assess stewardship on the part of directors:

> Because I think it has forgotten what the purposes of financial statements are and this obsession with marking to market is wrong. It is a stewardship report, particularly with this type of company. What actually happens as opposed to what the market does ... You only need to look at stock market volatility to know that the market is not right. The market has a drunken man's stagger towards the right answer over time, but, at any point in time the market is wrong. And this assumes the opposite. (**ACC 1, Large Co.**)

Another CFO believed that IFRS had, in some respects, increased subjectivity which could undermine the position of the auditors:

> Well, what I don't like is subjectivity, because the problem with it is, it could be what we want it to be. It doesn't mean it is right ... With historic accounting, we all understood it ... There were some judgements in it, but we all knew what those judgements were. We knew what the weaknesses were. It was basically simple. Now with IFRS it is very complicated, there are lots of judgements. You need to bring other people in to provide

you with some assistance. I could go and get a property expert to give me some advice. I could get the right number from him. What can the auditor do? They just have to accept that there is some third party evidence. If they get their own third party evidence which is different from the third party evidence that I have got, how could they really insist that we take their evidence? **(CFO 8, Small Co.)**

Although the IASB claim that their standards are principles-based, a number of interviewees dispute this claim:

> I think that is an illusion. The principles are not reflected in the detailed standards. The detailed standards are very rules-based. And I suppose if you say you are trying to get 160 or whatever countries to try and adopt this, it is understandable, but in Britain you have got a very well developed profession where you really have to exercise judgement. **(AEP 4, Big Four)**

Other AEPs were also prepared to criticize IFRS on the same grounds:

> If we take IFRS to start with, as I understand it they are quite rules-based . . . There are times I will get tripped up in IFRS because it is so rules- not necessarily logic-based . . . You have to go through the volumes from cover to cover. It is going to take it away into the real technical process. I suppose that is fine to try and keep some companies in line but invariably I don't think it works very well. So I am not the greatest fan of IFRS. I am all for consistency, that is great. If you get that, that is fantastic. But the depths that they are going to is just unreal . . . I've been told — you don't understand, it's a rule, not logic — that is ridiculous so I don't like that very much. **(AEP 5, Non-Big Four)**

ACCs were also unhappy with this aspect of IFRS:

> I have issues with IFRS because it seems to be taking the profession down a much more academic [route] . . . IFRS will prescribe a balance sheet at the end where this is a rule about how you produce every number in the balance sheet and you follow that rule and that is accurate . . . It is too prescriptive and takes away judgement when judgement is valuable. **(ACC 5, Small Co.)**

Another referred back to Enron to support his argument for principles-based standards and highlighted what he considered a deficiency in current reporting:

> I suppose, perhaps I'm old fashioned but, I do believe that truth and fairness is, should be the overriding principle . . . it means that Enron can't happen . . . I think that the truth and fairness is the one thing that says regardless of the fact that you had all these special vehicles when you cut through the crap basically you should be consolidating . . . And actually one of the questions I have asked a number of colleagues who sit on bank audit committees is why special investment vehicles are not the same as Enron and no one has been able to answer the question yet. I think again we are in risk of someone saying they don't need to be consolidated because blah, blah, blah, blah and therefore they trip through all these clever little paragraphs, and not someone saying, 'Is the end risk, on either profit or liquidity, yours or not?'. And if it is, it is in? **(ACC 1, Large Co.)**

This theme was also picked up by another experienced ACC who pointed out that companies like Enron always tend to produce compliant audited accounts, however:

> At the end of the day what we are saying is that the rules actually allow for a contrived structure, which, in certain circumstances, will collapse. (**ACC 3, Large Co.**)

He was also in no doubt that it was the IASB's agenda of convergence with the US's FASB that was driving IFRS towards rules-based standards:

> The SEC says that US companies can report by IFRS and not produce reconciliations. All that is happening is that, because IFRS is so close to what they find acceptable anyway, they are saying — OK we can use this. We are heading across the Atlantic anyway. That is why they say it is acceptable. The Americans have got their rules, a lot of that comes from their history and really it is in their genes. (**ACC 3, Large Co.**)

One AEP expressed the view that US influence over IFRS would increase if they took the decision to adopt international standards:

> The other looming problem is that once the Americans ditch US GAAP and go for IFRS we are going to have another version of IFRS. The SEC will impose its view on the rest of the world as to what IFRS means. (**AEP 2, Big Four**)

Those interviewees familiar with US GAAP still tended to consider that IFRS was superior and feared that IFRS would be further affected by convergence:

> If you ask me to compare IFRS with US GAAP, I would accept IFRS without hesitation. I find US GAAP truly arbitrary in many, many ways and more than that, the way in which the financial information is presented. If you take any annual report in the US it's very, very difficult to comprehend, because of the way in which the balance sheet and the income statement is structured . . . I think it would be much more healthy to just say North America can have its own standard and the rest of the world can have theirs because the convergence agenda, actually, is overriding some sensible compromises. (**AEP 8, Big Four**)

However, one ACC was able to identify one aspect of US GAAP that he considered to be superior to IFRS:

> I am a huge fan of IAS versus US GAAP in accounting terms but [US GAAP's] insistence on identifying risks for the reader of the accounts upfront . . . you could argue that if you have got a heavy risky model you would have to say something. You know, like Northern Rock would have had to say 'We rely on borrowing short term in the financial markets'. (**ACC 8, Large Co.**)

Finally, some interviewees expressed the view that certain problems of IFRS were a consequence of the IASB being largely composed of full time standard setters who, therefore, produced impractical 'academic' standards:

> There is a difference between academia and reality when you have been on the inside. And the people who devised these things should have done the job, I think . . . When I was in the profession, which was in the 70s, people would rotate through professional

standards, but not get stuck in it because it wasn't a job anybody wanted to do, but it was a good job to do for a bit because it was seen as a good career step. (**ACC 1, Large Co.**)

14.2.2   Other Regulation Relating to Disclosures in the Annual Report

The ACCs were particularly sceptical about the proposals for an enhanced Business Review. The main concern was the requirement to discuss future strategy:

> Future events, I think is the issue ... company finance directors are scared stiff about it and it feels to be wrong that company finance directors are scared around it. I am not sure they ought to be but the reality is that they are. We don't describe well enough what happens yet, it seems to me ... And I would rather have KPIs about fiscal numbers looking backwards ... rather than trying to predict what is going to happen. (**ACC 1, Large Co.**)

Another ACC could see two main problems with reporting KPIs. Firstly, disclosing commercially sensitive information which might be of interest to competitors. Secondly, it raised the whole issue of managing expectations:

> I want to be ambitious and I will set this target but it is that sort of managing expectations. If I tell you I am going to do 100 and I do 90 I am clobbered. If I tell you I'm going to do 80 and I do 90, great, but I was going to say 80 but my goal is 100. How do you get proper consistency in the reporting in the business review with different people, and different approaches? (**ACC 5, Small Co.**)

Another considered the change unlikely to produce better informed investors because of the tendency of regulation to stifle real communication:

> The danger is that it won't help transparency. It will have a retrograde effect. It will produce more boilerplate. The idea that you can sit down and spell out honestly what you think the prospects for your business are, god, come on, get real. Why would you ask anyone, in a published document, to put their hands up to say what their plans are for the future? I know there is a balance to be struck ... you have got to say something, of course you have, but people will say more formulaic things and less interesting things if there is more pressure to follow a model ... They will say well, 'How many KPIs have you put up? Well I'm going to put up 375, now pick the bones out of that!' (**ACC 3, Large Co.**)

14.2.3   Financial Reporting Review Panel (FRRP)

Since the FRRP changed its terms of reference to become a proactive enforcement agency, it is now communicating more frequently with more companies. One AEP agreed that the FRRP was more visible than in the past, but was generally positive about the process of dealing with them:

> We get a lot more letters from them. It is virtually normal now, I mean three years ago if you got a letter from the Financial Reporting Review Panel it was a crisis, career

threatening type thing ... It seems so serious, if you read the language. It is all very civil but it is very formal and if you are not familiar with it, the first time you read one of them you think — oh my God, what is going on? But once you actually get into the process you realize you are dealing with reasonable people and they are asking reasonable questions and you just deal with it on that basis. But I think people are a lot more comfortable with the process now ... But then I personally have never been involved in anything that has gone further than an exchange of letters. So, maybe my view reflects that. **(AEP 1, Big Four)**

This AEP thought that the FRRP had gained respect by focussing on the important issues and keeping the smaller ones in proportion. Typically, minor issues might appear in the appendix to the main letter to the company with an invitation by the FRRP to review its future treatment in the accounts:

We don't want to hear back from you, we just want you to consider this next time you prepare your accounts. Which is the type of thing which maybe three years ago they would have put in the main letter, so that is actually helpful. **(AEP 1, Big Four)**

He was keen to stress that a letter from the FRRP was still treated with the utmost seriousness and that his firm had set up internal processes to deal with problems that might arise.
One CFO had had prior experience of an FRRP investigation and was not anxious to repeat the experience:

I think everyone is running scared of a Financial Reporting Review Panel investigation ... I have had experience of them before in a company where I was finance director. I walked in to a set of accounts which had just been signed by the previous finance director and there was an investigation and it is an unpleasant experience ... It was a long time ago ... It is to be avoided if you possibly can ... They are looking at everything over a period of time, so you know you are going to be looked at, but it is still the same issue. You would rather they didn't find anything. **(CFO 3, Large Co.)**

An ACC agreed that the general view was that it was preferable to adopt policies which would keep you clear of the FRRP:

I think it has certainly kept people on their toes. I mean, in all the audit discussions one of the things that comes up is things that the Financial Reporting Review Panel are looking at and likely to look at, so we have got to stay one jump ahead ... We look to the audit firms to look ahead, tell us what is going to happen, what is coming down the track. **(ACC 2, Large Co.)**

One of the AEPs confirmed that the firms were up to speed with the latest thinking from the FRRP so that they could share this intelligence with clients:

Yes, we know what is going on in terms of reviews of our clients — to understand the approach, that helps us. **(AEP 2, Big Four)**

Another AEP drew on a personal example to demonstrate that he occasionally talked up the threat of FRRP intervention to strengthen his own negotiating position when the client is being stubborn:

> I had a conversation with the audit committee chair. I pointed out that, if we qualified it, the likelihood of the Financial Reporting Review Panel not picking it up was almost nil, so he said, 'alright, I'm not bothered'. So I said, 'the Financial Reporting Review Panel will generally pick on the qualified accountants on the board and will publicly discipline them for doing this'. The audit committee chair is a chartered accountant and suddenly things changed. They left it until right at the end. That is because we tried to do it through persuasion, before we got to the big stick ... Occasionally we use the Financial Reporting Review Panel as the big stick. **(AEP 9, Big Four)**

The same AEP believed that active regulatory enforcement agencies were now a feature of the framework and that this had changed behaviour:

> My impression of the whole environment is that things are becoming more and more regulated and prescriptive and it is not going to get any less. The resources that seem to be available for these regulators and these reviewers, whether it is the Financial Reporting Review Panel or AIU or whoever, they all seem to get greater rather than less, so it is just not worth the risk from anyone's point of view. **(AEP 9, Big Four)**

An ACC agreed that the risk of being caught was now so great that compliance was the only sensible option:

> I am sure that everything now is much more public or potentially much more public; not only have you got the published accounts but you have got the scrutiny of the auditors which wasn't there before, the Audit Inspection Unit ... You have got the Financial Reporting Review Panel as well, not just the threat but the certainty for a FTSE company. I mean, the idea that somebody is going to say — well we sat there and said if you give me that I'll give you two of those, is just ludicrous. It may be a bit more subtle than that in some places, but I see no sign of it. **(ACC 3, Large Co.)**

14.3   AUDITING ISSUES

In this section we report comments on Ethical Standards, International Standards of Auditing (ISAs) and the Audit Inspection Unit (AIU).

14.3.1   Ethical Standards

The interviewees had varied views about the provision in ethical standards requiring the audit engagement partner to rotate every five years (APB, 2004a). A positive view was expressed by this CFO:

> It can become too cosy as a relationship. I don't want an auditor that just agrees to everything we do. I want an audit and I do want to be audited otherwise it is a total waste of everybody's time, in my view. I think the audit partner potentially needs to continue in some sort of capacity, maybe as an advisor during a hand over period, but [I] do think it is important. I genuinely want accounts which are right. **(CFO 8, Small Co.)**

Others replied in the affirmative when asked if the rule might impact on audit quality:

> It probably does because you build up a huge amount of experience and I just think ... [Name of AP] has done well but it takes a while to get to the level that [Name of previous AP] had. I think there are other ways to manage that. I think seven years would be better than five. (**CFO 4, Large Co.**)

Another CFO, while essentially happy with a five year rotation period, pointed out that every audit partner change was a critical moment in the audit firm's relationship with the company:

> I want to make sure [of] the quality of the replacement. A couple of organizations ago we had a partner change and he wasn't that good, I would rather have somebody who gives me a tough time, who I can respect. I want to make sure of the quality of the replacement. (**CFO 1, Small Co.**)

AEPs were also concerned about the rule's potential impact on audit quality:

> I think the five year rotation rule has undermined an audit partner's ability to do his job, absolutely no question about that, and I am staggered that there wasn't more pushback on it. Because that was definitely done to solve a problem that wasn't there. (**AEP 8, Big Four**)

He explained the practical problems associated with such a short rotation period:

> You will probably attend the audit committee for the previous year-end, I do that just to hear what is going on and get a sense of tone, etc. And then you get involved in engagement ... the first year you are trying to find out what is going on. With a complex engagement like this you probably need to have relationships with about 20 people ... You need to know and understand the chief executive. You need to know and understand the finance director and a number of other key people, audit committee chair and they change sometimes. After year three, year four, next year, people will want to know what is happening, who is your successor ... So year one is a wipe out in relation to your ability to really get in there and challenge things. Year two and three you are refining and developing and year four onwards you are working out how to exit and transition. So it is definitely not a help to doing your job. (**AEP 8, Big Four**)

Another AEP thought the practicality of the rotation period depended on the complexity of the client:

> Is five years the right answer? Probably not ... Five is fine if you are dealing with something small ... If you are dealing with something bigger and complicated, over the years you acquire a lot of expertise and understanding and knowledge of the people, and changing brings risk so you have to manage the change effectively ... but I think it is right. You don't want people on a job for 25 years and that has happened in the past so, yes, you should have rotation, but it needs to be a little more flexible. (**AEP 1, Big Four**)

He also noted that the risk levels rose when other key parties such as the CFO or ACC were also new to their jobs:

> If you all change at the same time that is very risky. If you change at different times there is no continuity. **(AEP 2, Big Four)**

Some AEPs were completely dismissive of the idea that greater restrictions on the supply of non-audit services to audit clients brought in by Ethical Standards had changed their degree of independence but the restrictions had resulted in additional administration, for example:

> I think the independence guidance that has come with it on non audit services . . . is just tedious to administrate. To me none of this particularly matters because it doesn't affect my independence . . . I will probably spend two hours trying to work out whether some tax services fee is an issue or not, when it can't be an issue because it is not something which bothers me. So I think there is too much detail there and extra refinement. **(AEP 8, Big Four)**

Another AEP was equally firm pointing out the relevant risks and rewards:

> I don't care what sort of fee my client is paying someone else in my business. I am not going to jeopardise my professional position. My personal career, I am not going to throw that away just so some other person in my organization is getting a big fat fee. I couldn't care less. It isn't important to me; it is not going to make me do something that I wouldn't want to do . . . Most auditors will do what is right, regardless of anything else. I don't actually think it responds to an issue that was really there. It was an external perception that it was there. The fact that it does that is a good thing. I don't mind the extra disclosure; that makes good sense. **(AEP 9, Big Four)**

However, he did regret that one consequence of the rule tightening was that younger auditors had a much narrower experience and clients received less practical assistance:

> The ethical guidelines force you down a narrow route. If the ethical guidelines didn't force us down quite such a narrow route, it is possible to be a bit of a business adviser to your clients as well as the auditor. But for a while anybody who was trained in those five years post-Enron will have had it banged into them. You are auditor. Don't be anything else. It is too dangerous. Actually most clients don't want that at all. Certainly at the mid-market and downwards clients want more than that from their auditors. **(AEP 9, Big Four)**

14.3.2   International Standards of Auditing (ISAs)

The views of our interviewees on ISAs to some extent mirrored their views on IFRS. There was a level of support for the concept of a single set of global auditing standards:

> To arrive at one set that would be great. That would just take away so much pain. So that would be good. We do more and more internationally so anything that harmonized things would be great. **(AEP 3, Non-Big Four)**

Such views supporting the general concept were not confined to APs:

> I think that is important, actually. It is certainly important outside the UK. I happen to think the UK audit profession is pretty good. But ... I think it will have an impact on some of the work that is done outside the UK. **(CFO 9, Large Co.)**

However, there was considerably less enthusiasm for the particular approach currently adopted in ISAs:

> International standards, there are just too many of them, too much detail ... I'm not sure that is helpful, to have loads and loads of different things we have to do; it is a hostage to fortune and I'm not sure it adds to quality frankly ... I suppose what I am saying is that too many rules is the wrong approach. It is this whole debate around principles. Those principles are far less likely to fail and are far easier to understand. **(AEP 3, Big Four)**

Even AEPs who could see that ISAs were raising standards in some respects also criticized them for bureaucratic overkill:

> Turning to ISAs: that was a bigger change than people gave it credit for. Actually it changed the whole approach ... There is extra rigour now, and it is a good thing that people are willing to talk about it. And there are a whole load of other things that are probably good, but a lot of it is bureaucracy ... But at the end of the day somebody has got to pay for it and fine ... but this isn't adding anything for me, so why should I pay for it? It is a bit like Health and Safety requirements ... I think we just have to lump it. I can't see how you can push back and get it changed. **(AEP 4, Big Four)**

He acknowledged that this made a visible difference to the audit approach:

> The problem with it is ... the way firms respond ... You have to draw up a checklist to make sure you have got everything done and at the end of the day there is some poor unfortunate sitting with his laptop at the end of the table. If this is the audit room we will all be sitting round here with laptops, and I always say when I walk into an audit room 'Is anyone out there talking to the client? Anyone doing some auditing?' You just get into this process of completing forms. **(AEP 3, Big Four)**

Another AEP admitted that although ISAs had been good for business he was doubtful that anyone had benefitted:

> It has been good for our business, because we have had to do more work. It is always a funny situation where everyone talks about audits going on forever. Who benefits most, well that will be the accountants. But there are things that now have to be done, and they have to be done in a way they were never done before. And the client has to pay for it. Does the client receive any value out of it? In a lot of cases probably not, but that is now deemed to be what an audit is and therefore you do it. You don't have a lot of choice. **(AEP 9, Big Four)**

While understandably the main impact of ISAs was on the auditors, at least one ACC perceived that there were additional bureaucratic requirements:

> I see it as bureaucracy ... We now get as part of the audit planning process that we have to do all this because of the international auditing standards which doesn't really answer the question for the layman which is — shouldn't you do them because they are right or wrong not because somebody tells you to do them? And if they are the right things to do why weren't you doing them before and if they are the wrong things to do why are you doing them now? But you know, it is just a fruitless discussion because for the guy sitting opposite it isn't an issue anyway. (**ACC 1, Large Co.**)

14.3.3   Audit Inspection Unit (AIU)

Some of our AEP interviewees had direct experience of a review by the AIU and had formed some firm opinions on their approach as a consequence:

> I have been done over by them, the AIU ... I was absolutely amazed at the detail they went into. It really was staggering really having never come across them before ... I lost some faith in that, some trust. This isn't their job to be involved in this basically. Of course the lead guy was quite reasonable; the guy doing the work on the file was ridiculous ... He just got into too much detail. It didn't endear me to the whole process really ... I don't think that it is about improving audit quality. (**AEP 5, Non-Big Four**)

Another AEP, perhaps having heard adverse reports of other partners' experiences, was more positive:

> I have recently been through an AIU review and I was reasonably impressed by it because it wasn't quite as picky as I thought it was going to be ... But actually what I felt was that it helped in the quality. It was done in respect of the audit for a prior year, and we are now engaged with, just about finished, the follow up audit and there has been a step change in the quality of that audit. It is not all down to the AIU ... it was an impetus, the senior manager and me really forced through an improvement in, not so much the quality of the audit, more the documentation of the audit. I have found over the last two or three years that the quality and volume of evidence that is going into the files is much, much better than it has ever been. (**AEP 1, Big Four**)

However, even this AEP acknowledged that such an improvement comes at a cost:

> If you spend all your time writing up you spend less time thinking about it. So, if I have a concern it is that there is perhaps too much emphasis on what is on the papers, and that is because of the very existence of the AIU and the threat of a review by a regulator ... The other downer is, because you are spending too much time writing it up, you are not spending as much time talking to the client about issues and going back and asking that follow up question, and going back again ... The risk is you will go into an audit room and it will be full of people and it shouldn't be, they should be out there. We should be out at clients. (**AEP 1, Big Four**)

Other AEPs were also prepared to question the AIU's emphasis on documentation:

> Their approach is very much a US standard setting ... it is a box ticking. If you haven't got a piece of paper there is a fault, even if there is nothing wrong with the opinion or judgement that was taken ... If you have documented that your procedures will be X, Y, Z and you go X miss out Y and go to Z and you still have a conclusion that everyone is comfortable with, you still have a failure ... What happens then is that you have to be very careful what you document. It does seem to be a very much form filling type of approach. **(AEP 9, Big Four)**

Some were prepared to go further in their criticisms and argue that audit judgement was not as central to the inspection regime as it should have been:

> I think the emphasis is still compliance with auditing standards rather than audit judgement, which I think is a mistake. Certainly whilst I have not had direct experience of the AIU, I talk to all my partners who have. None of them have enjoyed it, but none of them have come out of the process saying that they learnt much out of the process other than they are now more familiar with certain auditing standards that they hadn't previously ... so that is a real concern ... And because it has not been centred around judgement, it has been centred around mere compliance ... a lot of work, certainly effort, is spent on making sure that bits of paper are there because once you start on — if I cannot see a piece of paper which explains very clearly your reasoning, you haven't done it. **(AEP 4, Big Four)**

One AEP thought the contribution of the AIU was more rigorous than his firm's approach to internal peer review:

> It is a much [more] effective review than the firm's internal processes in my view. Because it actually sits down and works out whether the firm has done the audit properly, whereas the internal processes don't do that ... They tend to focus on whether you have done this or that and also they don't have anything like as much time. The firm's own processes ... a senior manager will get a small number of days and he or she will focus on the key issues that we happen to have raised on the file, and the whole process of whether we have followed the firm's requirements, and what goes on to the file. The AIU spend months, they spend more time than I suspect the audit team does in preparing an external audit. **(AEP 1, Big Four)**

Despite any misgivings they might have had about the AIU's approach, interviewees were clear that a poor report could have a highly undesirable outcome for an individual:

> I know some perfectly good auditors in our business who are no longer auditors because they have been looked at — is that the right sort of environment to have? **(AEP 1, Big Four)**

Another admitted that the possibility of falling foul of a regulatory inspection affected his whole approach to the job:

> Over the last 12 months the Financial Reporting Review Panel and the AIU have been there. If you fall foul, it is not great for your career in [name of firm] to be quite honest.

So there is a fear factor I guess. We have got good risk management and we do use it. You back everything off and you get opinion on it and you get clearance on it. (**AEP 5, Non-Big Four**)

Neither CFOs nor ACCs had direct experience of the AIU's processes, indeed some were scarcely aware of its existence, although some thought that its presence must improve audit quality:

I think it does because the firms have to focus on things that are important and they have to make sure that it is properly documented. It must do. (**CFO 9, Large Co.**)

Another shared the scepticism of many of the AEPs:

The Audit Inspection Unit, yes. So of course what you get is, 'The files must be in order'. That doesn't necessarily mean the audit has been done properly. I can't say that the audit has been done properly. (**CFO 8, Small Co.**)

One of the ACCs, while broadly familiar with the work of the AIU, considered that strength of character of the individuals involved in a particular situation was a more important factor:

Every big audit firm has got a pretty good audit approach. You could have the best audit approach in the world independently reviewed ... you know, and have a weak audit partner, so that when it really comes to it, he buckles. (**ACC 8, Large Co.**)

At the time of the interviews the AIU was only publishing a single generic annual report providing a very broad overview of the results of their inspections. While some of our company interviewees had read them, nobody had found them particularly informative:

I have read them ... I don't think I thought there was anything in the AIU public report that is relevant to me, to tell the truth, but I can't precisely remember why now. (**ACC 5, Large Co.**)

However, one CFO derived some level of general comfort from the message delivered in the report:

It landed on my desk recently. I can't say I read every page of it, but I did look through to get a feel of the quality of audits. I think the general view was that audits were pretty good. (**CFO 2, Large Co.**)

14.4 CORPORATE GOVERNANCE

In this section we report interviewees' comments about audit committees and other aspects of corporate governance.

14.4.1   Audit Committees

A number of the interviewees, particularly the ACCs and AEPs, talked more generally about the enhanced role of audit committees, drawing on their experiences with other companies. The consensus view was that the changes brought in post-Enron had greatly improved this aspect of corporate governance:

> They were around before but they have been given more teeth and they are taking their responsibilities more seriously. I had a number of clients in the days before Enron where the audit committee consisted of a couple of cronies of the chairman and the CEO and they were just buddies … And they were totally ineffective. I haven't got any clients like that now. **(AEP 9, Big Four)**

Another AEP confirmed audit committees now played a central role in the audit process:

> There were some pretty average audit committees and some pretty average audit committee members, you know, here we go, after lunch … I used to regard audit committees as a waste of time because it made no difference. Whereas now they are the thing that drives the audit more than anything else, it is preparation for that committee. The interaction with the non-executive directors, the importance of the audit committee chair, it has moved. The audit committee chairs are much more important persons now in the organization in my view than they were. They get paid more. They have more formal responsibility. **(AEP 1, Big Four)**

An ACC was able to spell out why he considered audit committees were valuable:

> Because you have got a combination of execs and non-execs focusing on the audit and the accounts in ways that a board never would … I think the nature of it means that you will actually dig into issues that a board wouldn't. Because if there is a complexity or a technical point, a board will never get into that … I think it actually means that you have got people on the board who have got an understanding of that sort of issue and the accounts. **(ACC 4, Small Co.)**

One AEP, while accepting the value of audit committees, suggested that the standard was still not uniformly high in all companies:

> I think the way we have got it now is fine. It is good. I think I have been lucky with my audit committees … I hear anecdotally that there are some useless audit committees out there, not up to the job and not interested. **(AEP 5, Non-Big Four)**

Another AEP suggested that the quality of the audit committee was not a result of regulation but dependent on the quality of the people appointed to it:

> There is no regulatory requirement to have one even today and I think that custom and practice has evolved. It is all down to the quality of the individual member and whether they are willing to engage when they should engage. And I think nowadays they tend to be pretty active and if they don't understand something, they will ask. That definitely has made a difference. **(AEP 8, Big Four)**

One of the ACCs interviewed thought that it was vital that any appointed ACC should have suitable qualifications and experience:

> I think you have got to be a lot tougher about what qualifications you think your audit committee chair should have. I am sorry, there are just far too many people out there dragging very old qualifications through. They could still be incredibly savvy and therefore very good audit committee chairs, so there are always exceptions. But you can sit there sometimes and have a discussion with other audit committee chairs about what their responsibility for risk management is and be shocked, shocked at the breadth of answer. Either no idea at all, or it is an operational area, or fail to understand the difference between oversight and management. **(ACC 8, Large Co.)**

Other ACCs described their work as increasingly demanding to the extent that it restricted their ability to take on other roles:

> Non-exec directors have got equal responsibility as executive directors but they are not expected to work twenty four seven in the company understanding every single last detail and every single last risk. So you take that responsibility, which is a bit frightening sometimes to focus on, and you add to it the fact that you have got to, as audit committee chair, you have got to maintain a level of technical understanding at least to a degree where you can deal with issues. It is starting to make it difficult to be able to do that. **(ACC 4, Large Co.)**

Another ACC confirmed that they had never worked harder at keeping up to date on technical accounting developments:

> The biggest part of my current job, on paper, would appear to be audit committee chair ... because I regard that as a small bit of my job of being a non-exec director, I find it comparatively easy. I have been a FTSE 100 finance director. I have stayed up to date. I actually work quite hard staying up to date. I read Accountancy more now than I ever did when I was a finance director and I go to things that are run by professional accounting firms. So I work at that, but I work at that because I am interested in financial reporting and I do believe that financial reporting is important to shareholders. **(ACC 1, Large Co.)**

14.4.2   Other Aspects of Corporate Governance

While discussions on changes to corporate governance tended to focus on the audit committee, one ACC picked another improvement — clarity of directors' responsibilities:

> Directors are a lot more conscious of their responsibilities and that they have to take them seriously. That was less prevalent ten years ago, so I think you have got people's attention. **(ACC 2, Small Co.)**

This view was echoed by one of the AEPs as part of a raft of changes which had, in his opinion, improved UK corporate governance:

> Do I think the various changes that have come across as a result of the realization of the importance of corporate governance have made a difference? I think they have made a tremendous difference. There is much greater clarity around who does what and why. I think that has been one of the features of the last 15 years as a result of the debacles in the late 80s . . . It has just so much greater character about it. The emphasis on fraud, the emphasis on independent chairman, independent directors, audit committees, their role, the role of the board, tremendous actually. A much better system than I think the Americans have got. And it is a British system in the best sense of the word. (**AEP 1, Big Four**)

He then proceeded to spell out a list of specific improvements:

> What I think is better is that, actually, governance of public companies is very much better. You have audit committee chairs who know what they are doing. You have directors who take their finance director responsibility seriously. It varies from company to company even today but there is just a step change improvement in governance and the time that is given to these issues. (**AEP 1, Big Four**)

14.5 SUMMARY

In this section we summarize the interviewees' comments and refer back to our literature review in Chapter 2.

While global harmonization of financial reporting is viewed as a worthy objective, the introduction of IFRS is not generally seen as an initiative which has improved the quality of UK financial reporting. It is seen as excessively complex, particularly for smaller listed companies, and many senior people with years of experience of UK GAAP are less confident about their technical knowledge, deferring to the technical departments based in the audit firms. The high volume of disclosure required under IFRS is seen as an impediment to effective communication and it is believed that users, the supposed beneficiaries of the new accounting standards, do not engage sufficiently with corporate annual reports due to their complexity and volume. These comments support the concerns expressed by the FRC (2009a) and others that since the introduction of IFRS, financial reporting has become overly complex (see sub-section 2.3.2, Chapter 2).

The increased use of fair values has introduced more subjectivity in some areas of accounting, but generally IFRS is seen as a rules-based system where compliance has tended to replace judgement (see sub-section 2.3.1, Chapter 2). The widely held view is that the convergence project with the US standard setter is responsible for the emphasis on rules rather than principles. The academic literature in this area indicates a range of views about the problems of the distinctions between rules and principles. Bennett et al. (2006) find that a relatively more principles-based system requires more professional judgement both at the transaction level (substance over form) and at the financial statement level (true and fair view). Thus, the more a system is rules-based, the higher the likelihood that professional judgement will be diminished in favour of compliance with rules.

Despite the long and convoluted history of the Enhanced Business Review described in sub-section 2.3.3 of the literature review in Chapter 2, our interviewees express concerns that it will not improve communications.

The FRRP, described in sub-section 2.5.1 of Chapter 2, is seen as a very visible institution and is also generally well respected. All parties prefer to keep clear of it and compliance is seen as the best way to achieve that objective. Audit partners use it as a threat to persuade difficult clients to fall into line to avoid a spat with the FRRP. An adverse criticism from the FRRP was seen by audit partners as career damaging. These findings reconfirm the findings of Hines *et al.* (2001) and Fearnley *et al.* (2002) that the FRRP is feared by both directors and auditors.

There were mixed views about the effect of the change to audit ethical standards (see sub-section 2.2.4, Chapter 2) that, at the time of our interviews, required audit partners to rotate at five yearly intervals. While some thought that it prevented relationships from becoming too cosy, there were also concerns that there could be an adverse impact on audit quality, particularly where a client was large and complex or if the rotation took place when key directors in the company had also moved on. These comments reflect the range of findings in the literature about the impact of rotation.

The other major change to ethical standards was greater restriction of non-audit services which could be provided to an audit client. Audit partners were dismissive of the idea that such activity had ever impaired their independence, while at the same time regretting that they could no longer add value to an audit client by offering business advice. A particular problem about the need for advice was perceived to exist in smaller companies. Beattie *et al.* (2009a) find that NAS fees have significantly fallen since the regime change and identify resistance among preparers to further change to the NAS regime because of inconvenience and additional cost. There is no appetite among our interviewees for further restrictions, consistent with the views expressed by respondents to the APB's consultation paper (APB, 2010a).

There was little comment about ISAs and the AIU from the ACCs and the CFOs as the impact on them was limited other than an observance that auditors spent time in the audit room ticking boxes. The change was more significant for the auditors as ISAs, introduced in 2005 alongside IFRS (see section 2.2.3) were a major change from UK auditing standards, introducing more detailed and prescriptive requirements. Many auditors were concerned that the enforcement of these standards by the AIU was leading audit teams to spend a lot of time in the audit room filling in forms and completing documentation rather than engaging with the client's staff. Many were sceptical that the emphasis on documentation added value. This situation of rules potentially undermining audit effectiveness has some similarities to the impact of rules-based accounting systems identified by Bennett *et al.* (2006) where substance over form and true and fair are put at risk. Global auditing standards were seen as desirable in principle but in a similar vein to their attitude to IFRS, auditors were less comfortable with the quality of the standards themselves.

Similarly, the approach of the AIU (see sub-sections 2.2.3, 2.2.4 and 2.5.2, Chapter 2) in inspecting public interest audits was criticized by some for its concern with detail, documentation and compliance at the expense of judgement, particularly in relation to the more prescriptive ISAs. Other interviewees believed it to be driving up standards. However, it was considered a formidable enforcement agency and audit partners getting an adverse AIU report could find that their career prospects were seriously damaged. There is no extant UK research about the impact of the AIU and studies carried out in other countries find differing evidence about the impact on the audit market of audit inspection regimes. Other studies have produced no evidence about the impact on individual partners.

There was agreement that the quality of corporate governance (see section 2.6, Chapter 2) has greatly improved over the last ten years or so. Audit committees, in particular, are believed to have improved considerably and now play a central role in the audit and financial reporting process. It is considered that their success is dependent on the quality of people appointed to serve on them, especially the audit committee chair, a role which is now seen as demanding in itself and requiring a high level of accounting competence since the introduction of IFRS. However, there is a view expressed that not all audit committee chairs are up to speed with current requirements. Research about audit committees generally confirms the growing importance of the role of the audit committee in interacting with the external auditor and management, for example, Sabia and Goodfellow (2005), and the importance of continuing communication. Coffee (2006) also emphasizes the role of the audit committee as gatekeeper. However, existing research makes little distinction between the role of audit committee and that of the audit committee chair. It is perceived that there have been advances in other aspects of corporate governance, notably the clarification of directors' responsibilities.

These comments on the regulatory framework were made towards the end of 2007 and in 2008 when most of the changes, such as the introduction of IFRS and ISAs in 2005, were relatively recent. It is possible that views may have mellowed since as preparers become more used to the regime. However, some of the concerns about a rules-based system bringing complexity and box ticking may not diminish with familiarity. Little has changed in the framework since this time, although more change is planned, but it is worth pointing out that the AIU adopted a more targeted approach on specific issues rather than going through a whole audit in every case selected for inspection (Audit Inspection Unit, 2010. p. 9). The AIU is also issuing more specific reports available to firms for them to disclose to ACCs of their clients (AIU, 2010, p. 28).

15

Attributes and Procedures of the Audit Committee and the Audit Committee Chair: Evidence

15.1 OVERVIEW

In this chapter we review the attributes and activities of the audit committee and of the ACC which emerge from the survey reported in Chapter 3 and from the more detailed information about audit committee attributes and procedures provided by our interviewees in each of the case studies. Selected attributes of the nine audit committees in our case studies are shown in the overview of cases in Table 4.1 (Chapter 4). A particular issue which emerges from the literature is the limited research into the process and detailed procedures of audit committees and about the specific role of the ACC as opposed to the audit committee itself. In this chapter, companies have not been referred to by name as some of the material comes from the abbreviated case in Chapter 13.

15.2 THE AUDIT COMMITTEE

15.2.1 Membership and Attendance

The audit committee membership in the case studies ranged from three to five members, which is in line with the survey findings of an average audit committee membership of 3.4. The number of meetings reported by the interviewees ranged from a minimum of three to more than six. This is also compatible with the survey which shows a mean of four meetings. Unsurprisingly, the larger companies held more audit committee meetings. Meetings were scheduled in advance to fit in with the cycle of main board meetings and were normally held before the main board meeting took place. Extra meetings were arranged as needed.

As shown in the survey results, there are other attendees at audit committees over and above the membership of the committee itself, which is small. The attendees at the audit committee meetings included the CEO (75% respondents reported attendance), CFO (94% respondents reported attendance), other directors and executives as appropriate and, in some cases, the company chairman. The survey results do not, of course, offer an explanation as to *why* other directors and executives who were not members of the audit committee attended; however, the stories reveal two overriding reasons for their attendance. First, directors who were not members of the audit committee did not wish to miss anything of importance which was relevant to their role and responsibilities in the company. Second, the audit committee members themselves, who were non-executive directors, frequently required the more knowledgeable input from the executive directors on the audit committee business discussed. This applied particularly to the CFO and the financial controller, whose detailed knowledge was deemed necessary for the understanding of some of the accounting issues which came up. In one case, the ACC himself insisted that all the directors attended so they all knew what was happening. The attendance of the chairman was viewed differently by the interviewees. In two cases, the chairman had accounting experience and challenged accounting issues. There was an explicit recognition in one company that the presence of the chairman changed the dynamic of the meeting. There were only two case companies, one small cap and one very large company, where neither the CEO nor the chairman attended the audit committee meetings. One CEO attended to ensure he was familiar with the accounting issues so that he could respond to any questions raised at meetings with analysts. In one company the ACC had a policy of inviting directors and other senior executives to present on issues so the information came directly to the audit committee from those directly responsible for the particular issue.

In all the case companies the auditor attended some if not all of the audit committee meetings and in three companies the auditor's attendance at the audit committee was expected by the ACC. All audit committees met with the auditor without executives present.

15.2.2 Financial Experience and Understanding

All the ACCs we interviewed had recent and relevant financial experience. All except one, who was very experienced in financial matters, held a recognized accountancy or other financial qualification. The survey respondents indicated that most audit committees had at least one member with recent and relevant financial experience as expected by the Combined Code (FRC, 2005), but this would not necessarily be the ACC. In one of our case studies the ACC was not considered by the CFO to be the most technically up-to-date member of the audit committee. The survey respondents report an average of more than one audit committee member with recent and relevant experience (1.6 individuals on average) but reveal a very small number of small cap companies where this experience is lacking on the audit committee.

15.2.3 Interviewees' Views on IFRS

An interesting issue emerges from the interviews about the changeover to IFRS from UK GAAP. Most of the interviewees acknowledged that ACCs and audit committees found IFRS difficult to understand and believed that IFRS accounts were unhelpful to the business and the shareholders. Interviewees reported three specific issues of concern. First, the complexity of IFRS created a greater dependence by the company accountants on the AEP and the audit firm's technical department for up-to-date knowledge and interpretation of what was required. Second, some company interviewees also thought that the AEP's reliance on the audit firm technical department undermined the AEP's authority. Third, concerns were expressed that audit committee members without recent and relevant financial experience may become detached from accounting numbers and be less able to engage with the issues which came up.

Because of the complexity of IFRS, even those who were technically up-to-date found the accounts difficult. Thus, the accounting complexity created a dilemma for the audit committees. It was not considered desirable for all members of the audit committee to be accountants because members with wider business experience were believed to be necessary for a balanced audit committee, but an accountancy qualification was believed to be necessary for the understanding of IFRS. IFRS was not generally liked by the interviewees reinforcing the findings of Beattie *et al.* (2009a). Two cases reported serious tensions between the company and the auditor over the IFRS conversion and one reported a tripling of audit fees in the first year.

15.3   THE ROLE OF THE AUDIT COMMITTEE CHAIR

15.3.1   Dealing with Accounting Problems

None of the ACC interviewees considered it the role of the ACC or the audit committee to resolve disputes between the AEP and the CFO, nor did they wish to opine on how to deal with complex accounting issues which arose in the business. ACCs did not see it as the role either of the audit committee or the ACC to make executive decisions and expected the CFO and AEP to present an agreed proposal on accounting issues to the audit committee for them to challenge and/or approve. However, ACCs wanted to know about emerging issues which needed to be resolved between the CFO and AEP and expected to be kept informed about progress. In most cases this procedure operated smoothly, however, the cases did produce two interactions where the audit committee became a forum for problem resolution (this is discussed further in sub-section 16.6.3, Chapter 16).

There was regular communication outside the audit committee meeting between the ACC, the AEP and the CFO and between the ACC and the audit committee. All ACC interviewees were adamant that they did not want late surprises, before or at the audit committee meetings, coming either from the AEP or the CFO. Some audit committees held pre-audit committee meetings with the CFO and the AEP to ensure that the audit committee meeting, which would be attended by various others, went smoothly. Seven out of the nine ACCs interviewed referred to holding separate meetings with the AEP without the involvement of the CFO.

15.3.2   Level of Engagement

There were different levels of engagement between ACCs, CFOs and AEPs. Some ACCs were far more willing to get involved in the detail of the accounting problems than others, as they wanted to understand fully what the issues were and what recommendations the CFO and the AEP would make to the audit committee. Some CFOs saw it as a poor reflection on their own ability if they could not reach agreement with their AEP about the accounting treatment of a particular problem.

However, there were two exceptions. In one small company, which had limited resources in its accounting function, the ACC was regularly consulted by the CFO about how to deal with problems. Ironically, in this smaller company the ACC preferred a more hands-off role but found that it was not possible. In another particularly interesting case the CFO took an accounting issue to the audit committee himself as he felt very strongly that what was required under IFRS made no sense and he wanted to be sure that this was understood by the audit committee. Another very capable ACC felt that he was not in a position to act as arbiter in an accounting disagreement as his knowledge base was less than that of the CFO and the AEP.

Interestingly, in one smaller company the ACC drew up the agenda and wrote the minutes of the meetings.

15.4   ISSUES DISCUSSED AT AUDIT COMMITTEE MEETINGS

15.4.1   Range of Issues

Some audit committees had a much wider range of activity than others. In the smaller companies the agendas were limited to audit and accounting matters as they had smaller main boards and much of the company business was dealt with at the main board meetings. Risk was only referred to by interviewees from five companies, but this does not mean that risk was not considered by the others as it could have been dealt with by a risk committee or at the main board.

15.4.2   Audit Planning

All the interviewees reported that audit planning was presented to the audit committee by the AEP (as required by ISA (UK and Ireland) 260 (APB, 2004b)) and discussed at the audit committee. Of the survey respondents, 96% referred to discussing planning. In most cases the planning proposal was first discussed with the CFO but in one case it was discussed with the ACC first. In the larger companies, the planning process began at manager level in both the company and the audit firm and was then submitted to the CFO and ACC. The CFO was heavily involved in the preparation of the audit plan. In each company the audit committee itself engaged with the audit plan and was prepared to make changes to it. In one small company the whole audit committee went through the plan in detail. In one of the larger companies, the audit plan was discussed at every audit committee meeting as the audit progressed and changes were made as considered appropriate.

15.4.3   Audit Fees

In the seven cases where interviewees referred to fees, the initial negotiation of the fee was carried out between the CFO (or financial controller) and the AEP, and in all but one case an agreed position was presented to the audit committee for approval. Most ACCs were prepared to leave the fee negotiation to the CFO and were not interested in encouraging the audit committee to try and reduce the fee. They were more concerned that the fee should be sufficient for an adequate audit to be carried out. In one company the CFO took a fee proposal he did not accept to the audit committee as he wanted them to support him to go back to the auditor and get it reduced. In this case the ACC was a cost cutter so the CFO had support. In another case the CFO wanted to keep the fee down by placing extra reliance on internal audit, but the ACC still wanted to be sure a proper job was done. Thus, there were different views and possible tensions between the ACC and the CFO about fees relating to their own roles and responsibilities within the company.

15.5   CONCLUSIONS AND CONTRIBUTION TO THE ACADEMIC LITERATURE

Some interesting issues emerge from this analysis. The most significant finding is the high level of engagement of the ACC with the financial reporting and auditing process. ACCs expect to be kept informed by AEPs and CFOs about accounting and auditing problems as they arise and they also act as a filter for the audit committee itself, ensuring that they are informed about emerging issues. As ACCs do not want late surprises or to be asked to resolve accounting disagreements between the AEP and the CFO, the AEP and CFO are put under pressure to reach agreement between themselves before the proposed resolution of the issue goes to the audit committee for discussion and approval.

This model significantly changes the predominant dynamic which existed before the regulatory changes of a dyad relationship between the CFO and the AEP, which could lead to a power struggle between the two (Beattie *et al.*, 2001). The relationship is now very firmly a triad relationship. Both the CFO and AEP are accountable to the ACC, who is responsible for managing the AC. The AC finally approves the financial statements, the audit plan and the audit firms' fees before they go to the main board. A further interesting dynamic is the presence of other senior directors at audit committee meetings, a practice considered essential for informed decision-making but which may influence behaviour if not outcomes. Neither a CFO nor an AEP would wish to expose an unresolved disagreement to such a group, as this would generally be seen to result in loss of face and damage their personal reputation and respect. These findings support those of Cohen *et al.* (2008) and Gibbins *et al.* (2007) that audit committees play a passive role in dispute resolutions in the sense that resolution is sought before the matter comes to the audit committee's attention. However, neither Cohen *et al.* (2008) nor Gibbins *et al.* (2007) explore the role of the ACC.

Much of the literature about audit committees is set in the US and Canada where the legal and governance regimes differ. Both Bush (2005) and ICAEW (2006b) report significant differences between the UK and US regimes. Although the Canadian legal and governance regime is closer to that of the UK (Chartered Accountants of Canada, 2001), the unitary board, where executives (i.e. management) and non-executives work together, operates differently under the Canadian and the US regimes (Wyman, 2002). There is very little in the literature which distinguishes the role of the ACC and the role of the audit committee.

Sabia and Goodfellow (2005) refer to relationships between management, the auditor, the audit committee and the board. However, the UK unitary board model, where both management and non-executive directors work together, changes this dynamic as board members other than the CFO attend the audit committee meetings as a matter of course and are, therefore, informed of audit committee business and decisions. Interestingly, Sabia and Goodfellow (2005) report that the audit committee is reluctant to resolve problems but can prevent escalation. However, in our study, the role of preventing escalation lies more with the ACC. In the UK context, the role of the audit committee itself has developed into one of reviewing decisions and discussing judgements that have already been made under the watchful eye of the ACC. However, procedures may differ in smaller companies where limited accounting resources may force some decision-making into the audit committee and where the main board itself deals with a wider range of business.

Gibbins et al. (2007), a Canadian study which does not encompass the role of the ACC, find that the CFO may not keep an AEP informed of accounting issues at the decision-making stage, because of feelings of ownership of the financial statements. They find that this situation is more likely to lead to a negotiation. In our study, we find that the engagement of the ACC changes behaviour as both parties need to keep the ACC informed and the CFO no longer has sole ownership of the financial statements. As ACCs do not want late surprises, withholding of information would reflect badly on a CFO in the triad nexus of relationships as the AEP would inform the ACC of any difficulty.

The role of the audit committee and the ACC as a mechanism to control the relationship between the CFO and AEP is consistent with the findings of Beasley et al. (2009) who refer to a monitoring and a ceremonial role for the audit committee. However, there are UK nuances to this. Our findings suggest that the ceremonial role, that is, the importance of the audit committee's existence and its ability to challenge, remains with the audit committee but some of the monitoring is carried out by the ACC.

The complexity of IFRS raises some problems for ACCs and audit committee members. Although interviewees report audit committee members having recent and relevant financial experience, some interviewees report a divide in understanding the accounting numbers between ACC members who are accountants and those who are not. At the time of these interviews, companies were either in their first or second year of IFRS implementation. It is possible that some of these IFRS pressures may have diminished as directors and auditors become more familiar with the regime. However, difficulties with the complexity of IFRS are likely to remain for audit committee members who are not qualified accountants, thus making the presence of qualified accountants on audit committees essential.

Pomeroy and Thornton (2008) conclude from a review of mainly US studies that audit committees have a greater impact on audit quality than financial reporting quality (see sub-section 2.8.6, Chapter 2). However, this is not reflected in the present study, as it is clear that audit committees do monitor complex or material financial reporting decisions as well as audit matters, although there will be a greater contribution from the more financially literate members of the audit committee. These findings also support Coffee's analysis (2006) that the audit committee acts as a gatekeeper. However, this study extends this analysis by indicating that the ACC is also a gatekeeper for the audit committee.

Overall, this chapter has shown how the ACC and the existence of an audit committee has changed the behaviour of both the AEP and the CFO and supports the findings of Beasley *et al.* (2009) regarding the AC's monitoring and ceremonial roles and Coffee's gatekeeping role. However, we extend this to the ACC as a separate party from the audit committee with an enhanced and different role to the audit committee itself. These insights form an integral part of the analysis of the financial reporting interaction in the next chapter and of the revised grounded theory which emerges from this analysis.

16

Cross-case Analysis and Theory Development

16.1 INTRODUCTION

This chapter draws upon the grounded theory of financial reporting interactions developed by Beattie *et al.* (2001) which is explained in more detail in sub-section 2.8.5, Chapter 2. This theory is used as a starting point for the present study, together with knowledge of other extant theory and the current regulatory setting. The theory of Beattie *et al.* (2001), which is summarized in sub-section 2.8.5, Chapter 2, is tested using the fieldwork evidence collected for the present study and analysed in the within-case analyses presented in Chapters 5–13. Section 16.2 begins by summarizing and commenting upon the interaction attributes identified in Chapter 4. Section 16.3 summarizes the cross-case analysis, using a tabulated analysis of the 50 interactions as a key analytical tool. An overview of the revised grounded theory is presented in section 16.4. It is apparent that new concepts have emerged, the significance of established concepts has changed and relationships have altered. Sections 16.5–16.9 discuss in detail the five main category groups in the model: general company/audit firm context; specific interaction context; international regulatory regime; national regulatory regime; and the interaction itself. The key influences on the outcome of the interactions (in terms of the quality and ease of agreement of the outcome) are explored in section 16.10. This is achieved by examining the similarities and differences between outcome clusters in relation to context and interaction process. Finally, section 16.11 offers a comparison of the findings of this study with those of the extant literature, particularly the previous UK study of Beattie *et al.* (2001).

16.2 SUMMARY OF INTERACTION ATTRIBUTES

Table 4.1 in Chapter 4 itemized the 50 interactions described across the nine cases. Of these, three are audit fee negotiations (S1, M1 and F1) and two are solely corporate governance discussions (K6 and W2). One interaction (P7) concerned both corporate governance and a financial reporting judgement. Thus, there are a total of 45 financial reporting interactions analysed in depth this chapter. The other five interactions are referred to as relevant in the context of our consideration of governance and audit fees. The 45 financial reporting interactions are summarized in the first five columns of Table 16.1 by issue type and interaction type, that is, discussion or negotiation. Recognition/measurement issues and disclosure issues are the most frequent issue

Table 16.1 Analysis of financial reporting interactions by issue type, interaction type and decision type (n = 45)

Issue type	Code	Interaction type			Decision type			
		Discussion	Negotiation	Total	Compliance	Judgement	Compliance/ judgement	Total
Fundamental principle	FP	1	–	1	–	1	–	1
Recognition	R	–	1	1	1	–	–	1
Measurement	M	8	2	10	–	9	1	10
Classification	CL	3	3	6	2	4	–	6
Disclosure	DI	11	–	11	1	10	–	11
Recognition/measurement	R/M	6	5	11	–	4	7	11
Measurement/disclosure	M/DI	–	3	3	1	1	1	3
Recognititon/measurement/ disclosure	R/M/DI	–	1	1	–	1	–	1
Measurement/corporate governance	M/CG	1	–	1	–	1	–	1
Total		30 (66%)	15 (34%)	45	5 (11%)	31 (69%)	9 (20%)	45

type (equal top rank), followed by measurement issues. Together, these account for the majority (70%) of the financial reporting interactions. The recognition/measurement category is split approximately equally between discussions and negotiations. The disclosure issues were all discussion interactions, as were most of the measurement interactions.

Within these broad categories, several specific issues arose in more than one case. Five case companies had an interaction concerning the identification/valuation of intangible assets on acquisition. In the survey reported in Chapter 3, 'intangible assets/goodwill' was the top ranked discussion issue for two of the three respondent groups and the third ranked negotiation issue for two of the three groups, while 'fair value on acquisition' was in the top ten discussion and negotiation issues for all three groups. Four case companies had interactions concerning inventories, which was the eighth ranked negotiation issue for the ACC respondent group.

The Business Review, which five case companies reported having discussion interactions about, was also in the top ten discussion and negotiation issues for all three groups (with the exception of ACC's negotiation rankings). Similarly, segmental reporting, about which three case companies reported having discussion interactions, was also in the top ten discussion and negotiation issues for all three groups. Two case companies reported interactions surrounding share-based payments (one discussion and one negotiation); this issue appeared only in the top ten discussion issues for AEPs.

Intangible assets, goodwill and acquisitions represent common business activities. Although IFRS changed the accounting for goodwill and intangibles, interactions about these items did appear in Beattie *et al.* (2001). Segmental reporting, Business Review and share-based payments were not reported as interactions in Beattie *et al.* (2001) as the requirements did not exist at the time.

Accounting for a complex transaction (two case companies) did not feature in the survey list of issues, as the nature of such transactions cannot be specified *ex ante*. All other issues were represented once only in the case companies. Overall, it seems fair to conclude that the case company interactions are fairly representative of the interactions reported in the large-scale survey.

Table 16.1 (columns 6–9) also offers an analysis of the interactions by issue type and decision type, the decisions being classified into one of three categories (compliance, judgement and combined compliance/judgement). It can be seen that judgements are the most frequent decision type (69%), most often involving measurement or disclosure issues. Combined compliance/judgement decisions tend to involve recognition/measurement issues. Matters of fact are compliance issues, whereas matters of judgement are judgement issues. Some interactions incorporated both elements. For example, the recognition of intangible assets on the acquisition of a subsidiary would be a compliance issue, but the valuation of those intangibles would be a matter of judgement. It is much more difficult to evaluate the quality of outcome for a judgement issue.

Table 16.2 presents an analysis of decision type by interaction type. From Table 16.1 we can see that most interactions (69%) involved judgements without any compliance aspect. Of particular interest in Table 16.2 is the finding that the more intense interactions which led to negotiation were more likely to occur where compliance decisions were involved. Three out of five compliance issues (60%) led to a negotiation, whereas only seven out of 24 judgement issues (23%) led to a negotiation. We return to the significance of this finding later in the chapter.

Table 16.2   Analysis of decision type by interaction type

Decision type	Discussion	Negotiation	Total
Compliance	2 (40%)	3 (60%)	5
Judgement	24 (77%)	7 (23%)	31
Compliance/judgement	4 (44%)	5 (56%)	9
Total	30 (60%)	15 (34%)	45

Interaction type spans Discussion and Negotiation.

16.3   SUMMARY OF CROSS-CASE ANALYSIS

In order to test the original grounded theory of interaction outcomes we have undertaken a cross-case analysis in this chapter of the nine cases and 50 interactions presented in Chapters 5–13, focussing on the 45 financial reporting interactions. Table 16.3 serves as a key analytical tool in this stage of the study. This summary table reports the findings from a review of the within-case analysis to identify, for each interaction, the following:

• key interaction attributes;
• general case contextual factors;
• specific features of the interaction process (including key events, tactics employed and strategy adopted);
• involvement of the audit firm technical department, ACC and AC; and
• outcome attributes.

As in Beattie *et al.* (2001), the outcome has been defined in terms of two dimensions. First, in terms of quality, compliance issues are classified as either compliant or non-compliant (although there are no actual cases of non-compliance), while judgement issues are classified as acceptable or unacceptable (although again there are no instances of an outcome being unacceptable). The second dimension is ease of agreement, which classifies each interaction as easy, slightly difficult or difficult. Any interaction which escalates to a negotiation is classified as either slightly difficult or difficult.

16.4   A REVISED GROUNDED THEORY OF FINANCIAL REPORTING INTERACTIONS — OVERVIEW

During the analytical process (which was outlined in Chapter 4), a similar set of categories and category groups emerged to those identified by Beattie *et al.* (2001) and shown in Figure 2.1 in Chapter 2. However, the degree of influence of the category groups, together with the specific categories within each group, has changed very significantly. Before looking at each category individually, it is useful to present an overview of the theory in the form of a 'conditional matrix' (Corbin and Strauss, 2008, pp. 95–97). The groups are shown in Figure 16.1 as a series of embedded rectangles. Each group of categories represents a set of conditional features acting upon the core category (the interaction).

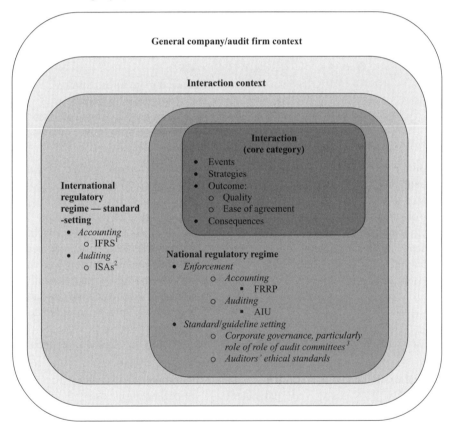

Figure 16.1 Principal analytical categories in the revised grounded theory of financial reporting interactions

Notes:

[1] IFRS are issued by the IASB.

[2] ISAs are issued by the IAASB, with minor changes to adapt for the UK environment.

[3] The UK national governance code is issued by the FRC, and compliance (on a 'comply or explain' basis) is a stock exchange listing requirement. Enforcement is therefore market-based.

Table 16.3   Cross-case analysis of interactions

		Interaction attributes		
ID	Issue	Decision type[1]	Nature of issue	Interaction context, form of interaction & tactics adopted
Sandpiper, Case 1				Large stable company; Cost conscious, ACC a fee grudger; Poor relationship AEP & CFO; satisfactory relationship AEP & ACC; good relationship CFO & ACC; Conservative but don't like aspects of IFRS; like some leeway.
S1	Audit fees	N/A	Audit	AEP proposed fee, CFO could not get reduction, so escalated; Proposal to AC without endorsement of CFO; Required more information & re-negotiation required; Both sides used external evidence; AC considered possibility of a tender; Fees were reduced.
S2	Accounting treatment of costs associated with a major change in computer system	C/J	Established judgement issue	CFO concerned excessive costs could have been capitalized; CFO's paper went to AC who imposed cap on spend in each location; AEP informed & agreed approach; Concerns re-emerge as system went live, possible impairment considered; CFO believed AEP gave misleading advice & discovered the standard was less conservative, so no write down necessary; Face-saving re. original investment from some AC members.
S3	Re-organization costs	J	IFRS judgement issue	CFO proposed presentation for re-organization costs; AEP produced a counter proposal; CFO found external evidence to support his argument (i.e. another audit client using his preferred approach) & his proposal was accepted based on this precedent; CFO concerned about presentation to analysts.

Involvement of:			Outcome attributes	
Technical Dept	ACC	AC	Quality	Ease of agreement
None	As part of AC	Reviewed initial proposal & involved in fee reduction strategy	N/A	Difficult
Not known	Aware of the issue & advice given by AEP	Reviewed CFO's paper & proposed a policy	Acceptable	Difficult
Not known	Aware of the issue	Not known	Acceptable	Difficult

(*Continued*)

Table 16.3   *(Continued)*

		Interaction attributes		
ID	Issue	Decision type[1]	Nature of issue	Interaction context, form of interaction & tactics adopted
Sandpiper (Continued)				
S4	Inventory provisions	J	Established judgement issue	New legislation impacted on value of non-compliant stock; CFO made assumptions re. future demand to estimate provision, discussed with AEP & AC — provision accepted; Following year demand higher than anticipated — AEP suggested provision too high; CFO obtained internal & external evidence to support current provision; AEP accepted the view — then AC.
S5	Dividends from sub-sidiaries	C	Established legal compliance issue	AEP raised issue with company; Company realised another mistake provided a solution; Time pressure.
S6	Pension liabilities	J	Recent judgement issue	AEP questioned mortality rates used in calculating pension deficit; CFO produced evidence to support assumptions; Following year discussion between co & firm pension experts; Co. pension manager involved.
Kestrel, Case 2				Large company but growth hit by recession; Competent CFO with strong views on IFRS; Effective AC.
K1	Valuation of intangibles	C/J	IFRS imple-mentation	AEP stated position clearly, preferred external valuation; CFO dubious of value & feasibility — push back; Unresolved issue to AC who required compliance; Valuation performed in-house; Auditors unhappy with approach; Revised valuation accepted & process established for future; CFO believes analysts ignore valuation; AEP wants to establish a future principle.

Involvement of:			Outcome attributes	
Technical Dept	ACC	AC	Quality	Ease of agreement
Not known	As part of AC	Original provision & assumptions considered by AC; Reconsidered the following year	Acceptable	Slightly difficult
Not known	Informed before resolution	Informed after resolution	Compliant	Easy
Pension experts asked questions	Aware of issue	Not known	Acceptable	Slightly difficult
Not known	As part of AC	Forum for resolution	Compliant	Difficult

(*Continued*)

Table 16.3   (*Continued*)

		Interaction attributes		
ID	Issue	Decision type[1]	Nature of issue	Interaction context, form of interaction & tactics adopted
Kestrel (Continued)				
K2	Impairment reviews	J	Established judgement issue	AEP noted one acquisition performing below expectations & questioned whether write down required; CFO produced evidence suggesting business case intact; Agreed — but disclosure amended; Impact on executive bonus; Face-saving (i.e. directors responsible still in post).
K3	Financial instruments — preference share	C	IFRS implementation	First year of IFRS CFO proposed treatment, AEP initially accepted but then insisted on alternative treatment; Issue taken to AC & debated, accepted view of AEP; Subsequent year, AEP admitted they were wrong & company correct.
K4	Financial instruments — hedging	C/J	IFRS implementation issue	AEP raised issue with the company; Processes were changed to provide a solution; Initially raised by subsidiary auditors.
K5	Reorganization costs	J	IFRS judgement issue	AEP questioned the proposed presentation with CFO & ACC; CFO argued for the proposed treatment; AEP accepted as compliant; Information needs of analysts.
K6	Fraud & illegal acts	N/A	Corporate governance	Discovered within the company & reported to AC.
Mallard, Case 3				Large capital intensive company; Results subject to fluctuations in commodity markets, previous going concern issues; Well managed company with competent AC.
M1	Audit fee	N/A	Audit	CFO & AEP agree fee; Proposal to AC for approval.

Involvement of:			Outcome attributes	
Technical Dept	ACC	AC	Quality	Ease of agreement
Not known	Discussed before AC with AEP & CFO to ensure close to agreement	Reviewed judgements & decision	Acceptable	Difficult
Insisted on initial treatment	As part of AC	Forum for resolution in first year	Compliant	Difficult
Not known	As part of AC	Solution discussed	Compliant	Easy
Not known	Aware of the issue & approved the treatment	Not known	Acceptable	Easy
Not known	As part of AC	Internal control implications considered	N/A	Easy
None	As part of AC	Reviewed fee & all changes pre-approved	N/A	Difficult

(Continued)

Table 16.3 (*Continued*)

		Interaction attributes		
ID	Issue	Decision type[1]	Nature of issue	Interaction context, form of interaction & tactics adopted
Mallard (Continued)				
M2	Accounting for a complex transaction	J	Unique transaction — solution seeking	CFO recognized unique complexity & engaged second firm of accountants to provide advice; Audit firm (not AEP) proposed a solution but CFO considered results of applying it perverse; Further discussions between key parties produced an agreed solution; Proposal reviewed by AC; Second firm of accountants technical dept.
M3	Business Review	J	Early adoption of new legal requirement	Tone & coherence considered by AC.
M4	Financial instruments — hedging	C/J	IFRS implementation & ongoing compliance issue	CFO proposed that a contract constitutes a hedge; AEP challenged this, keen to ensure that they can demonstrate compliance; Market risk department documenting decisions.
M5	Going concern	J	Established judgement issue	CFO submits twice yearly paper to AC & auditors comment on it.
M6	Impairment of assets	J	Established judgement issue	Solution seeking between AEP, CFO & ACC re. future approach; All parties accept no current need for impairment write down.
Finch, Case 4				Small listed company; Newly appointed audit firm following tender & newly appointed CFO; Strong entrepreneurial culture but conservative accounting style; Effective AC
F1	Audit fees following a tender	N/A	Audit	AEP pitched in tender process; ACC involved in negotiating fee down; AEP managed to re-negotiate higher fee in light of many restatements; Tender process indicated market rate.

Involvement of:			Outcome attributes	
Technical Dept	ACC	AC	Quality	Ease of agreement
Fully involved in discussing treatment — AEP peripheral	As part of AC	Proposed solution reviewed by AC	Acceptable	Difficult
Not known	As part of AC	Annual review	Acceptable	Easy
Specialist IAS 39 director advised the AEP	Aware of issue	Not known	Compliant	Difficult
Not known	As part of AC	Regularly review papers on the issue	Acceptable	Easy
Not known	Discussions regarding the future approach	Not known	Acceptable	Easy
Not known	Tender process & negotiations	Approve all fees	N/A	Slightly difficult

(Continued)

Table 16.3 *(Continued)*

		Interaction attributes		
ID	Issue	Decision type[1]	Nature of issue	Interaction context, form of interaction & tactics adopted
Finch (Continued)				
F2	Notional interest on deferred consideration	C/J	IFRS implementation	Previous auditor advised treatment adopted by company in first year of IFRS; New AEP advised this was incorrect & proposed new treatment; CFO supported change & considered by AC; Form of adjustment discussed; Chairman & CEO had view on form of re-statement; Previous auditors involved.
F3	Earnings per share	C	IFRS implementation	AEP discovered an error in previous years accounts; Reported to CFO then AC, who accepted that a restatement was appropriate; Previous auditors involved.
F4	Share-based payments	C	IFRS implementation	AEP advised appropriate treatment; Founders considered the proposal did not reflect substance of the transaction; ACC accepts it is necessary for compliance; Founders donated shares.
F5	Treatment of tax credits on options	C	IFRS implementation	Previous auditors advised on treatment in first year of IFRS; AEP suggested this was wrong in second year of IFRS & proposed new treatment; Accepted by CFO & discussed at AC; Previous auditors.
F6	Revenue recognition & provisioning on contracts	J	Established judgement issue	Regular review of major contracts between AEP & CFO, & then at AC & possibly the Board; The Board will discuss large contracts.
F7	Valuation of intangible assets on acquisition	C/J	IFRS implementation	Following acquisitions, CFO performed valuations; Reviewed by auditors, then raised at AC; Analysts unlikely to understand per CFO.

Involvement of:			Outcome attributes	
Technical Dept	ACC	AC	Quality	Ease of agreement
Not known	As part of AC	Approved original treatment & reviewed need for subsequent change	Compliant	Slightly difficult
Not known	As part of AC	Considered error and restatement	Compliant	Easy
Not known	Fully aware of issue — insistence on compliance	Not known	Compliant	Difficult
Not known	As part of AC	Need for & wording of restatement discussed	Compliant	Slightly difficult
Not known	As part of AC	Reviews state of major contracts & accounting implications	Generally acceptable	Easy
Valuations Dept. review valuations	Identified as key issue at audit planning meeting	Reviewed approach agreed by CFO & AEP	Compliant	Easy

(Continued)

Table 16.3 (*Continued*)

			Interaction attributes	
ID	Issue	Decision type[1]	Nature of issue	Interaction context, form of interaction & tactics adopted
Finch (Continued)				
F8	Segmental reporting	J	IFRS implementation (early adoption)	AEP challenged approach to segmental reporting — no change; Also related issue raised by AEP, restatement agreed by CFO.
F9	Business Review	J	Early adoption of legal requirement	Reviewed by AEP and AC for coherence with financial statements.
Cormorant, Case 5				Small company with large family holding; Strong compliance culture; CFO is a resource-seeker; ACC takes hands-off approach; Non-Big Four auditor.
C1	Identification of intangibles on acquisition	C/J	IFRS implementation	Following acquisition, AEP stated position clearly despite doubts from CFO; CFO engaged an external valuer for the work; Valuation considered by AEP, then technical dept. & AC; AEP questioned valuation, so AC agreed to revise downwards.
C2	Impairment of goodwill on acquisition	J	Established judgement issue	Issue considered by CFO when acquisition reported losses — prepared forecasts supporting decision not to write down; Accepted by AEP.
C3	Deferred tax asset	J	IFRS implementation	Issue raised at pre-audit committee meeting; ACC came up with solution, accepted by AEP and approved by AC.
C4	Provision on inventories	J	Established judgement issue	CFO applied standard formulaic provision to inventories; Challenge raised by AEP concerned about possible excess stock; Considered by other parties, inc. Chairman — agreed no change; Impact on executive bonus.
C5	Business Review	J	Early adoption of new legal requirement	CFO considered possibility of moving to an enhanced Business Review early but decided not to.

Involvement of:			Outcome attributes	
Technical Dept	ACC	AC	Quality	Ease of agreement
Not known	Not known	Not known	Acceptable	Easy
Not known	As part of AC	Considered if accounts sufficiently advanced	Acceptable	Easy
Provided advice to AEP on suitabil-ity of values	Consulted at an early stage by CFO re. suitable approach	Valuation reviewed	Compliant	Easy
Not known	Not known	Not known	Acceptable	Easy
Not known	Initiated the solution to the problem	Confirmed ACC solution	Acceptable	Easy
Not known	Aware of the issue	Not known	Acceptable	Easy
Not known	Reviews narrative reports	Not known	Acceptable	Easy

(Continued)

Table 16.3   *(Continued)*

		Interaction attributes		
ID	Issue	Decision type[1]	Nature of issue	Interaction context, form of interaction & tactics adopted
Cormorant (Continued)				
C6	Misreporting in subsidiary	J	Established judgement issue	Concerns raised when subsidiary failed to meet forecasts; CFO & another director visited & found accounting errors; Reported to AC; Subsidiary newly acquired.
Pochard, Case 6				Large mature company; Conservative approach to accounting; Experienced CFO; Effective AC.
P1	Presentation of cash flow statement	J	IFRS implementation	AEP proposed presentation based on guidelines included in relevant standard for first year of IFRS; Company accepted in first year but did not like the format — so adopted alternative for subsequent year; AEP warned CFO of risk of regulatory action & discussed with ACC; CFO & AC adopted revised format — subsequently discovered other companies had also used this format.
P2	Inventory valuation	J	IFRS implementation	Annual review of inventory when market price & demand uncertain involved CFO, AEP & ACC.
P3	Contingent liabilities	J	Established judgement issue	Annual review of adequacy of disclosure conducted by CFO, AEP & ACC, informed by latest legal advice; Lawyers involved.
P4	Fair value of lease on acquisition	J	IFRS implementation	Acquisition deal was re-structured with help from auditors; Paper prepared by CFO outlining issues presented to ACC — agreed need to fair value lease; Company used relevant market values as a basis & presented valuation to AEP who consulted with their partner firm in the relevant country & agreement reached; AEP's firm in country of acquisition involved.

Involvement of:			Outcome attributes	
Technical Dept	ACC	AC	Quality	Ease of agreement
Not known	Informed of problem just before AC	Lack of controls discussed	Acceptable	Easy
Consulted on company's preferred format	Pre-meetings with AEP & sought clarification on whether a qualification issue	Accounting treatment considered	Acceptable	Difficult
Not known	Debate re. adequacy of provision	Not known	Acceptable	Easy
Not known	Debate re. adequacy of disclosure	Not known	Acceptable	Easy
Not known	Kept up to date with progress	Informed of transaction	Acceptable	Easy

(Continued)

Table 16.3   (*Continued*)

		Interaction attributes		
ID	Issue	Decision type[1]	Nature of issue	Interaction context, form of interaction & tactics adopted
Pochard (Continued)				
P5	Re-organization costs	J	IFRS implementation	CFO needed to consider accounting disclosure following plant closures; Possible treatment discussed with AEP and agreement reached; Presentation to analysts.
P6	Segmental reporting	J	IFRS implementation (early adoption)	CFO presented paper as to how new standard should be applied, agreement reached with AEP.
P7	Control weakness	N/A/J	Corporate governance/ Established judgement issue	Control weakness prompted the need to consider how this should be disclosed; Discussions involved CFO, AEP & ACC.
Woodpecker, Case 7				Small listed company; Compliance culture; CFO is a resource-seeker; Non-Big Four auditor.
W1	Inventory valuation	J	Established judgement issue	Existing basis of provision challenged by AEP; CFO prepared paper supporting current policy, submitted to AC.
W2	Breach of internal controls in overseas subsidiary	N/A	Corporate governance	Fraud discovered & relevant employee disciplined; Issue reported to the Board; AEP noted the item in the Board minutes & reported to AC for consideration; AC decide no longer to be informed of minor breaches of internal controls; The Board considered the fraud before the AC.
W3	Valuation of intangibles on acquisition	C/J	IFRS implementation	Following acquisition CFO sought advice from the auditors on the valuation of intangibles; Auditors passed him on to someone able to give a coaching session; CFO did valuation in-house; Accepted by AEP & reported to AC.

Involvement of:			Outcome attributes	
Technical Dept	ACC	AC	Quality	Ease of agreement
Not known	Informed at an early stage in the process	Not known	Acceptable	Easy
Not known	Not known	Not known	Acceptable	Easy
Not known	Involved in discussions re. disclosure	Eradication of control weakness considered	Acceptable	Easy
Not known	As part of AC	Considered paper from CFO, approved existing policy	Acceptable	Easy
Not known	As part of AC	Considered report from AEP	Not best practice	Easy
Not known	As part of AC	Report on accounting implications of acquisition provided by AEP; Reviewed valuation	Compliant	Easy

(Continued)

Table 16.3 (*Continued*)

		Interaction attributes		
ID	Issue	Decision type[1]	Nature of issue	Interaction context, form of interaction & tactics adopted
Raven, Case 8				Large international group; Conservative accounting policy; Experienced CFO prepared to challenge; Effective AC; Important client to auditor.
R1	Accounting for a complex transaction	J	Unusual transaction — solution seeking	Passed up by more junior staff for discussion by CFO & AEP but no initial agreement; ACC aware of problem at pre-AC meeting; CFO acquired more evidence to support his view based on similar cases elsewhere; AEP checked with technical dept. & accepted the proposal; Following agreement between AEP & CFO met with ACC to ensure he supported it; CFO & AEP jointly presented solution to AC who asked questions before accepting.
R2	Disclosures relating to potential future losses in a subsidiary	J	Established judgement	CFO & auditor's adviser agreed accounting treatment; CFO drafted proposed disclosures; Board wanted disclosures minimised because director involved; AEP wanted more disclosure; Resistance from AC & board — argued commercially sensitive, but finally accepted accounting requirements left them with little choice; Face-saving because of risk of analysts' questions.
R3	Business Review	J	Early adoption of new legal requirement	New format considered by CFO.

Involvement of:			Outcome attributes	
Technical Dept	ACC	AC	Quality	Ease of agreement
Fully con-sulted at each stage	Aware of issue at pre-AC meeting and thereafter discussed proposed solution with CFO & AEP	Reviewed the final proposed solution	Acceptable	Difficult
Specialist adviser on market em-ployed engaged by auditors	Fully involved with discussions over disclosure	Reviewed disclosure proposals & initially argued against AEP	Acceptable	Difficult
Not known	Not known	Not known	Acceptable	Easy

(*Continued*)

Table 16.3 (*Continued*)

	Interaction attributes			
ID	Issue	Decision type[1]	Nature of issue	Interaction context, form of interaction & tactics adopted
Ostrich, Case 9				Small listed company; Effective AC.
O1	Valuation of intangibles	C/J	IFRS implementation	Acquisition previous year had not resulted in intangibles being recognized; After further acquisitions in following year AEP stated analysis necessary to ascertain whether intangibles acquired; CFO thought principle of non recognition had been established; Misunderstanding persisted until close to year-end, CFO then annoyed at cost of valuation; CFO obtained a valuation methodology & arrived at a valuation; Assumptions behind valuation discussed with AEP, who accepted them, reviewed by AC; Big Four firm provided valuation advice; Time pressure.
O2	Share-based payments	J	IFRS implementation	CFO raised query on valuation of new share scheme with AEP; AEP responded after consulting technical dept.; CFO produced valuation which was accepted.
O3	Business Review	J	Early adoption of new legal requirement	AEP discussed content & raised query re. chosen KPIs with CEO; CEO strong views on KPIs.
O4	Segmental reporting	J	IFRS implementation (early adoption)	AEP challenged choice of reported segments & subsequently debated with management. No change.

[1]Note: C = compliance; J = judgement.

Involvement of:			Outcome attributes	
Technical Dept	ACC	AC	Quality	Ease of agreement
Not known	As part of AC	Reviewed the process & final valuation	Compliant	Difficult
Consulted by AEP	Not involved in resolving problem	Not known	Acceptable	Easy
Not known	Not known	Not known	Acceptable	Easy
Not known	Aware of debate	Not known	Acceptable	Easy

A notable feature of this matrix is the proximity of the category groups to the core interaction, which shows how the key influences on interaction outcomes have changed significantly since Beattie *et al.* (2001) as shown in Figure 2.1 (Chapter 2).

In Figure 2.1 (Chapter 2) the outermost, peripheral level contains categories which have the weakest and most indirect influence on the interaction. This group relates to the general context of the company and the audit firm. Moving towards the core, we come to the specific context of the interaction, that is, features of the interaction that can vary from interaction to interaction and which can be moderated by the general contextual factors.

In our revised interaction model, however, the categories impacting most directly on the core category of the interaction itself relate to the regulatory regime, both the standard-setting regime and the enforcement regime. The accounting and auditing standards are essentially international over which the UK has influence but limited control; whereas the enforcement, together with the corporate governance regime (particularly relating to the role of the audit committee), is specific to the UK. The evidence from the interactions in this study indicates that it is the national enforcement regime which lies closest to the core category group, that is, the interaction itself. The interaction category group comprises four categories: events, strategies, outcome and consequences.

The national enforcement regime now has three main activities, which have been greatly enhanced since our previous study. The two enforcement agencies are the FRRP, which is now pro-active in its review of company accounts, and the AIU, which regularly inspects public interest audits and issues public and private reports. The activities of these two bodies have greatly increased the risk to companies and auditors of getting found out if they do not comply with the regulatory regime. The result of non-compliance is the time and cost taken in responding to the regulators' queries or criticisms, together with the risk of personal and corporate reputation damage. The corporate governance regime, with its 'comply or explain' model is market-driven and companies which do not comply may find themselves being subject to market criticism.

In the next section, we offer a detailed examination of each principal category in the revised model.

16.5 GENERAL COMPANY/AUDIT FIRM CONTEXT

16.5.1 Quality of Primary Relationships

Table 2.1 (Chapter 2) set out the concepts that are grouped into this and other categories, drawing on Beattie *et al.* (2001). The influence of this category was not particularly strong on the nature and outcomes of interactions. The enhanced role of ACCs has resulted in three primary relationships rather than one. The added complexity has meant that all parties have to engage with each other and make sure that the relationships work. Concepts such as compatible personalities and age gap did not seem to be significant in this revised model of corporate governance. Only in two cases (Sandpiper and Cormorant) were there relationships between key parties which were classified as less than 'good', although in Cormorant's case the difference was slight. This did not have a discernible effect on the quality of the outcomes, although it may have impacted on the ease of agreement.

The strong enforcement environment has reduced the likelihood of key parties having hugely different objectives, with compliance now accepted as the prime objective in order to avoid being criticized by a regulator. This is discussed further in sub-section 16.6.2. Different levels of professional integrity of key parties are unlikely to produce different outcomes because of the strength of the imperative to comply. This is discussed further in sub-section 16.5.3. The tightening of the auditors' ethical standards has impacted on other concepts linked to the quality of the primary relationship, particularly length of relationship. Given that ACCs and CFOs move on regularly from companies it is unlikely that an AEP will be working with the same ACC and CFO for as long as five years.

The relationships between the three key parties are represented in Figure 16.2. Compared with the simple dyad that was the norm in the late 1990s in the UK, this more complex set of relationships has, in conjunction with the regulatory regime, resulted in changes to the power, authority and role of each of the three key parties, with the ACC (and audit committee) having gained more power on accounting and auditing matters at the expense of the other two parties. It has also resulted in a change in the character of interactions, which now tend to be characterized to a greater extent by problem-solving behaviour between the three parties and less by disagreement and confrontation. The regulatory framework has restricted the scope for the latter types of behaviour, largely because of the enhanced role of the ACC and the audit committee who are both overseeing how the AEP and the CFO interact with each other on reaching agreement on problem issues.

16.5.2 Company Circumstances

Most of the concepts underpinning this category in the original model had no influence on the interaction outcomes. Reporting style differences were difficult to discern within the prevailing culture of detailed rules in IFRS and compliance. CFOs, being acutely aware of being monitored by ACCs, audit committees and the wider regulatory framework, were concerned with accounting compliance, although they were frustrated when this impeded communication with investors (e.g. Kestrel). All of the audit committees included in the cases were effective in their roles. The interviews for the cases were conducted in a comparatively benign financial environment so factors like financial position, growth position and bid risk did not affect outcomes. Companies, however, wish to avoid FRRP inquiries and some AEPs acknowledged that they use the FRRP as a threat to achieve accounting compliance from clients.

The complexity of IFRS was particularly challenging for CFOs in smaller listed companies (e.g. Cormorant and Woodpecker) which tend to have limited in-house

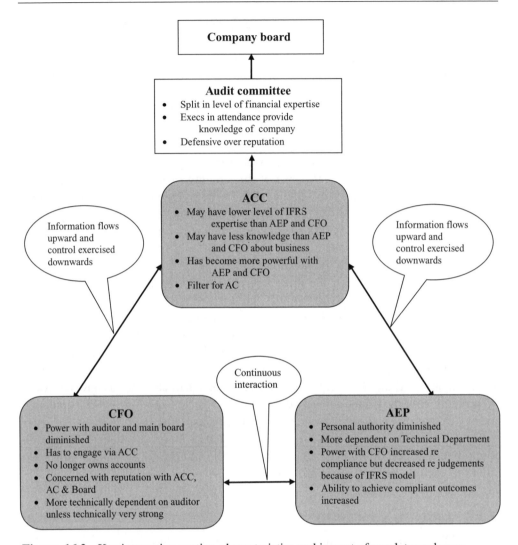

Figure 16.2   Key interaction parties, characteristics and impact of regulatory change

accounting support. Such companies can be classified as 'resource-seekers' in terms of their buyer type. Ethical standards (APB, 2004c) now restrict the provision of many non-audit services to clients and consequently CFOs have not had the accounting support from their auditors that would previously have been available. Again, while this affected the process, it did not affect the quality of the outcome, although it added extra stress to the process.

16.5.3   Audit Firm Circumstances

Unfortunately, the interviews do not provide much detail regarding the audit firm circumstances. However, concepts such as the nature of the support and monitoring infrastructure (e.g. second partner review; technical review; peer review) are now mandatory for audit firms and, therefore, not subject to significant variation, as was the case at the time the original model was developed. The AIU has reinforced the culture of compliance for audit firms and FRRP inquiry can be equally damaging for the firm and the individual AEP. Factors previously considered important, the personal and professional integrity of the AEP, have become subsumed within this compliance culture. Personal integrity, defined as behaviour that goes beyond the standard required by professional ethics, was rarely evident in the cases. Whenever an AEP attempted to go beyond the strict requirements of an accounting standard (e.g. P1) they met resistance and generally backed down as the enforcement regime brings double jeopardy from the FRRP and the AIU.

AEP (seller) types were explained in sub-section 2.8.5 of Chapter 2. In the present study, very little variation in AEP type was observed, with all nine AEPs matching most closely the descriptor for the 'safe pair of hands' type. It can be concluded that the increasing dominance of the regulatory regime, which sets rules and strictly enforces them, has had a very significant homogenizing effect on AEP behaviours. Provided the rules are high quality, the financial reporting will, therefore, also be high quality.

There was some evidence to suggest that non-Big Four firms might have adopted a more flexible approach to offering advice despite the non-audit services requirements to meet the needs of their smaller clientele (e.g. Cormorant).

16.5.4   Company Buyer Types

Company buyer types were explained in sub-section 2.8.5 of Chapter 2. The ACCs were all comfort-seekers with the exception of the Sandpiper ACC who was a comfort-seeker and also a fee grudger, as was the CFO. The CFOs were also all comfort-seekers and those employed in smaller listed companies (Cormorant and Woodpecker), having limited resources, were also at times resource-seekers. They tended to consult more with the ACC or AEP. Although these characteristics could affect the audit fee negotiations (e.g. S1 and F1) they had no impact on financial reporting interaction outcomes.

16.6   SPECIFIC CONTEXT

16.6.1   Interaction Issues

The interaction attributes were examined in section 16.2. IFRS has introduced more complex judgements into a number of key issues such as intangible valuations and share-based payments, of which a number of our interviewees were highly critical, as shown in Chapter 14. These cases were based on interactions which arose in the first two years after the implementation of IFRS in the UK, so inevitably some of the interactions were not just about resolving a one-off current issue, they were also about establishing future practice (e.g. O1). This did not change the quality of the outcome but in some cases made the agreement more difficult to obtain. The extent of visibility in the financial statements and materiality were other relevant dimensions along with impact of the recently changed regulatory framework for accounting governance and enforcement.

16.6.2   Goals and Objectives of Parties

The primary goal of all parties appeared to be ensuring compliance with the regulatory regime and hence keep out of trouble. There seemed to be a reputational aspect to this primary goal, although there was scope in some cases for business considerations to conflict with compliance. Many of the more specific objectives of individuals who took part in the interactions identified in Table 2.1 in Chapter 2 were still in evidence. Face-saving was sometimes evident when an investment was being reviewed for impairment and the director who championed it was still with the company (e.g. S2 and R2). This tended to make it more difficult to obtain agreement. Conversely, when one or more key parties were new to their role (e.g. Finch) agreement was easier as there was no need to defend previous actions. CFOs were mindful of the impact of accounting disclosures on investors and analysts and sometimes wanted to minimize the effect (e.g. P5) without straying outside of compliance. ACCs see it as their role to resolve differences between AEPs or CFOs and their strategy for achieving this was to discourage unresolved issues being presented at the audit committee. With the exception of Sandpiper, ACCs also were less willing than CFOs to reduce audit fees as they were concerned to get a proper job done, whereas some CFOs wanted to keep costs down. Thus, different objectives about audit costs emerge. It was pointed out in a couple of cases (K2 and C4) that the outcome of an interaction which could have material effect on the results would affect executive bonus payments, but there was no suggestion that it influenced the outcome of any of the interactions.

16.6.3   Third Parties

In addition to the three key parties interviewed a number of individuals and groups were influential in the interactions (see Table 16.3). Prominent among these were the technical departments of the audit firms. To our knowledge they were directly involved in ten of the interactions and were strongly influential in the outcome to the extent that, in a compliance culture where there was a rule rather than a judgement to be enforced, they had the final word. It would appear that the arrival of IFRS with its complexity and increased emphasis on rules has increased the power of technical departments, but at the same time, there was a more process-driven attitude to judgements, such as valuation of intangibles where, if the company had followed due process and the valuation appeared reasonable, it was accepted (e.g. Woodpecker and Cormorant). Interestingly, the ACC and the AEP thought that the valuation would produce unhelpful results for the company going forward and a compromise agreement was reached.

The audit committee was also frequently involved in the interaction. The nature of their involvement is known for 28 of the 45 interactions and unknown for the remaining 17. In general, this group featured only in the final stage of the interaction and 'reviewed', 'discussed' or 'considered' proposed solutions and 'approved' these. In two cases (S5 and P4), one where time pressure featured, the audit committee was merely 'informed' of the interaction outcome. Of particular note are the three cases where the audit committee had a more active role in the interaction. In K1 and K3 the audit committee, which included a high level of financial expertise and was very effective, was used as a forum for resolving the issues. In R2 the audit committee initially argued against the proposed treatment on the grounds of the commercial sensitivity of proposed disclosures but were persuaded of the need to ensure compliance.

Other directors were sometimes influential, either individually (usually the Chairman or CEO, as in F2 and O3, and unusually the founders, as in F4) or as a group (the Board, as in F6, W2 and R2). This involvement, occasionally direct, was more frequently indirect and stemmed from their reaction to reported outcomes anticipated by key parties. Other company managers were drawn into a few specific issues (e.g. the company pension manager in S6). CFOs were also mindful of the impact of the financial statements on analysts (e.g. K1, K5, F7 and P5). Previous auditors (F2, F3 and F5), subsidiary company auditors, a partner firm in another country (P4) and other audit firms (M2) were occasionally involved. Lawyers were involved in one interaction (P3). Accounting practices in other companies were also influential to the point of being a deciding factor in some interactions (e.g. S3) as they provided a precedent.

16.6.4   Other Specific Contextual Factors

Time pressure was rarely an issue as all the ACCs adopted a policy of 'no surprises' at the AC, meaning that issues were raised in good time which tended to reduce confrontation and make agreement easier. The exceptions were O1 and S5. The impact on future accounting periods (either in terms of the earnings impact or the establishment of a reporting precedent) was a feature in several interactions — C1, K1, M4 and O1. A factor to emerge from the cases which has not previously been identified was poor communication by a key party. This was a feature of two interactions (K3 and O1) and resulted in difficult (albeit compliant) outcomes.

16.7   INTERNATIONAL REGULATORY REGIME

Given that interactions are driven by the need for compliance with the regulatory framework, the quality of the final outcomes will depend on the quality of the standards and regulations being enforced. In contrast with enforcement, which is under UK control, the accounting and auditing standards are either directly set by an international organization (e.g. IFRS set by the IASB) or strongly influenced by one (e.g. ISAs effectively set by the International Auditing and Assurance Standards Board but with minor amendments to meet UK company law introduced by the APB). Both are considered to be rather more detailed and rules-based than the UK standards they replaced. In a number of interactions based on IFRS, the outcome was compliant for all the reasons previously discussed, but interviewees protested that the impact on the financial statements was misleading (e.g. F4). In other transactions, notably those involving recognition and valuation of intangible assets on acquisition of a subsidiary (e.g. K1), the interviewees argued that the additional cost incurred did not benefit anyone as users of accounts ignored the additional information generated.

The complexity of the standards impacted on the interactions. AEPs were considered by CFOs to be increasingly reliant on their technical departments for solutions. This trend is likely to have been exacerbated by the robust enforcement regime. Despite this support there were a number of interactions where the auditors had made an error in the first year of IFRS implementation (K3, F2, F3 and F5) which then required correction in the following year. In the first year of IFRS implementation CFOs would have been more reliant on their auditors for interpretation of IFRS and less confident about challenging an AEP's position on an interaction. There were exceptions to this (e.g. CFO at Kestrel who was highly technically competent). More detail of the interviewees' comments on the international regulatory regime is provided in Chapter 14.

If CFOs found it difficult to keep up to date with technical issues, this was even more of a challenge for ACCs. In most cases they played an important role in guiding the audit committee through the accounting technicalities and the presence of the CFO at the audit committee meeting would help. However, the complexity of the accounting has made it very difficult for non-accountants to understand the accounting numbers and made it essential for the ACC to have a high level of accounting competence.

16.8   NATIONAL REGULATORY REGIME

The FRRP is the UK institution responsible for enforcing accounting standards. It is clear from both the cases and sub-section 14.2.3, in Chapter 14, that the FRRP was perceived as an active enforcement agency liable to pick up on any cases of non-compliance. The risk of being caught was considered by CFOs, ACCs and AEPs to be so high that it has changed behaviour and placed severe limitations on the extent to which the key parties were prepared to negotiate, providing a contrast with the findings of Beattie et al. (2001). While CFO and ACC interviewees independently expressed an awareness of the FRRP, it was apparent that AEPs were prepared to reinforce the message if they thought it would help to bring resolution (e.g. P1). While those with experience of dealing directly with the FRRP considered the process fair and reasonable, CFOs and ACCs wanted to keep clear of the FRRP because of concerns about the time and cost of an investigation, personal and organizational reputation and the risk of adverse publicity upsetting investors. AEPs would want to keep their clients clear of the FRRP to preserve their firm's reputation as well as their own standing within the firm. ACCs and audit committees are specifically charged with monitoring the integrity of the financial statements of the company (FRC, 2008a), so they would wish to avoid public criticism of their accounts.

The other enforcement agency in the UK regulatory environment is the AIU, which is responsible for inspecting public interest audits. While few comments were made in the cases, it is evident from sub-section 14.3.3 (Chapter 14) that the AEPs take risk of inspection very seriously such that it influences their approach to auditing, as a poor review could impact on an individual's career prospects. The CFO and ACCs do not have direct contact with the AIU and, therefore, had less to say about it, although a number were aware of its broad approach. The overall consensus was that it reinforced a process-driven approach to auditing and hence reporting.

The combined effect of these two influential UK enforcement agencies has been to increase the risk that cases of non-compliance with accounting, auditing or auditors' ethical standards will be discovered, bringing adverse consequences for the offenders. While AEPs face the twin threats of the FRRP and AIU, both CFOs and ACCs face sufficient threats from the FRRP to encourage compliance.

The corporate governance regime is also part of the UK regulatory framework. As the previous chapter has demonstrated, the audit committee is seen as an effective monitoring mechanism and has had a major impact changing the behaviour of both the AEP and the CFO. Non-compliance with the Combined Code can bring market pressure on directors.

16.9 INTERACTIONS (CORE CATEGORY)

16.9.1 Interaction Events

Interaction events are those which take place during an interaction. They can be distinguished from interaction strategies which are planned high-level tactics. In our cases all the events listed in Table 2.1, in Chapter 2, occurred. Provision of information justifying the accounting numbers was frequently used to support judgements by the CFO and not normally challenged by the AEP. Third party opinions were sought where there was a high degree of uncertainty involved (e.g. lawyers in P3). A joint seeking of a solution was a particular feature of some complex and unique issues (e.g. M2). There was also an example of an AEP admitting they had been wrong previously (K3) and rather more of an AEP pointing out that another audit firm had been wrong (Finch).

16.9.2 Interaction Tactics and Strategies

In matters of compliance AEPs often stated their position firmly at the outset of an interaction (assertiveness). Regarding sanctions, while the option of tendering the audit was considered following a difficult interaction (O1) this was never raised as a negotiation strategy, although if the relationship became tense the auditor would be aware of the risk. (e.g. sub-section 12.2.5, Chapter 12). In the current regulatory framework it is more difficult for a CFO to make such threats because the decision to change would require the approval of the audit committee. The threat of an audit qualification was used as a sanction in one case (again O1) by an AEP when other methods of communication had apparently failed.

While there was no evidence of ingratiation being employed, reason was a commonly used strategy. A key tactic was the use of evidence to support a reasoned argument. Another was to argue that an accounting treatment used by another company established a precedent, particularly if the treatment was accepted by the same audit firm. In the prevailing culture of compliance there was no evidence of the reciprocity-based strategy (i.e. strategic give and take concessionary strategy) identified by Hatfield *et al.* (2008) and Sanchez *et al.* (2007) in the US environment. The ACC ensured that the audit committee was rarely in a position of arbiter, but occasionally (e.g. K1) it was placed in the position of a 'court of appeal' judging between cases presented by the AEP and CFO (coalesce). As already discussed, both these parties frequently appealed to a higher authority to confirm their position (e.g. their own technical department or somebody else's).

16.9.3   Interaction Outcome

In Table 2.1 (Chapter 2) two dimensions of the outcome of the interaction are identified as being of critical importance and these are still relevant for the cases currently under review. What is of primary interest to external parties is the *quality* of financial reporting by the company, that is, does the outcome reflect 'good' or 'bad' accounting from a public interest perspective? This is essentially a dichotomous variable for compliance issues (matters of fact), but it is a continuous variable for matters of judgement.

In addition, for the parties involved directly in the interaction, the ease with which the agreed outcome is reached is important. For a given outcome, it is rational to prefer an easy interaction to a difficult one. This outcome dimension is also a continuous variable. It captures issues like the number of parties involved, the number of interaction stages,and the extent to which strategies were used that undermine ongoing relationships.

These two dimensions of outcome (quality and ease of agreement) capture the effectiveness and efficiency of the audit, respectively.

However, a key issue is the level of dissatisfaction reported in Chapter 14 about the quality of the accounting regime. Whereas the outcome would comply with the regime there was a lot of disquiet in the interviews as to whether compliance with the accounting regime delivered a quality output.

16.9.4   Interaction Consequences

Interactions can have a number of consequences, most obviously on ongoing accounting interactions (e.g. S2) or future accounting periods (e.g. O1). They can also impact on audit fee negotiations (e.g. F2, F3 and F5) or affect the quality of a primary relationship (e.g. S3).

16.10   OUTCOME DETERMINANTS

The aim of this section is to understand those factors that are most influential in determining the two dimensions of the final outcome, including the identification of critical moderating variables. The 45 financial reporting interactions cluster into six outcome groups, shown in Figure 16.3. Using Table 16.3 once again as an aid to analysis, in conjunction with Figure 16.3, the critical contextual factors and strategies in each cluster are explored. The objective is to understand the extent and nature of the linkages between context, interaction process and outcome.

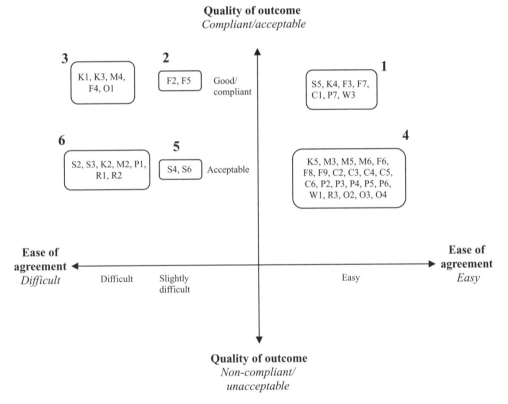

Figure 16.3 Visual representation of financial reporting interaction outcomes in two dimensions

Cluster 1: Compliant Outcome, Attained Easily

The six outcomes in this cluster (S5, K4, F3, F7, C1 and W3) come from five cases. Typically, the AEP's tactic was to state his position firmly at the start of the interaction process. Given the backing of relatively clear regulatory guidance, this produced a compliant outcome. S5 was the consequence of the auditors discovering that the company had overlooked an aspect of company law and was not therefore contested. F3 resulted in a fairly minor restatement as a consequence of the newly appointed AEP discovering an error which had not been picked up by the previous auditors. Three of the interactions (F7, C1 and W3) related to a single issue, recognition and valuation of intangible assets on acquisition of a subsidiary. While the question of recognition is clearly a matter of compliance, the issue of valuation involves a high degree of judgement. In all three cases the CFOs were unenthusiastic about the value of the process they were required to follow but accepted it was necessary for compliance. All complained about the cost of obtaining a valuation and two (F7 and W3) did the work themselves. The valuations were presented to the AEP (and subsequently the ACs), who reviewed them to ensure that the process was acceptable but were apparently reluctant to seriously challenge the assumptions on which they were based. In C1, the CFO, a resource-seeker, was frustrated by the lack of support from the AEP, who could not offer advice because of the restrictions on non-audit services. However, having obtained a valuation from a local valuer and presented it for review at the AC, the AEP from a non-Big Four firm questioned the valuation, not because of doubts about the underlying assumptions, but on the grounds that it might adversely impact on the results of subsequent years.

In these cases the regulatory context was the dominant influence on the outcome — the AEP could point to relatively clear rules in the accounting standards and all parties were aware of strong monitoring and enforcement mechanisms underpinning the accounting and audit aspects of financial reporting. The AEPs used an assertiveness strategy in relation to the compliance issues, while CFOs used a reasoning strategy (the use of evidence and reasoned argument) in relation to the valuations.

Cluster 2: Compliant Outcome, Attained with Slight Difficulty

The two outcomes in this cluster (F2 and F5) come from just one case (Finch) where both the CFO and the AEP were newly appointed. Both interactions related to restatements to the previous year's accounts which were based on the advice of the previous auditor. The changes, initially raised by the AEP, were supported by the CFO who had no stake in the previous decision. The audit committee, who had approved the previous treatment and, therefore, might have had a face-saving agenda, understandably wanted to ensure that the new approach was compliant and that the change was portrayed appropriately in the accounts. The complaint outcome can be attributed to the strength of the regulatory regime. The slight difficulty associated with the outcome can be attributed to the lack of congruence in the objectives of the key parties — the CFO and AEP had no face-saving agenda whereas the ACC and audit committee did.

Cluster 3: Compliant Outcome, Attained with Difficulty

The five outcomes in this cluster (K1, K3, M4, F4 and O1) are drawn from four different cases. In all of these interactions, although the requirements of the relevant accounting standard were fairly clear, the CFO (in the case of K1, K3 and O1) or others in the company were prepared to challenge the rationale and impact of that standard. Two of the interactions related to the recognition and valuation of intangible assets on acquisition. A further two related to the treatment of financial instruments, and the other interaction involved share-based payments. Accounting practice in each of these areas was radically altered when IFRS was introduced. It would appear that some of the interactions (e.g. K1, M4 and O1) were about establishing principles and practices for future years, and that this was a factor in the difficulty achieving agreement, one that may have become less significant in subsequent years. However, the CFO at Kestrel disagreed with the relevant standard on K1 so strongly that he wanted to escalate the issue so that he could argue the case against at the audit committee, even though he did not expect to win the argument. Two of the interactions (K3 and O1) were particularly difficult because the AEP was not perceived by the CFO to have communicated clearly on the issue and for O1 introduced time pressure to obtain a resolution. Another (F4) became difficult because the directors directly involved in the problem transaction found it difficult to accept the rationale for the required treatment of that transaction in the financial statements. However, while particular circumstances might have resulted in an outcome taking longer to agree, non-compliance was not considered a serious option in any of the cases. In two cases (K1 and K3), the audit committee was the forum for resolution, in another (F4) the audit committee chair insisted on a compliant outcome and was closely involved in the process for the other interactions. The compliant outcome can be attributed to the strength of the regulatory regime.

Cluster 4: Acceptable Judgement Outcome, Attained Easily

This is the cluster with the most outcomes, 23 with eight of the nine cases represented (K5, M3, M5, M6, F6, F8, F9, C2, C3, C4, C5, C6, P2, P3, P4, P5, P6, P7, W1, R3, O2, O3 and O4). Although a wide range of issues are included there are recurring themes. Valuations feature frequently with inventory valuation particularly prominent (C4, P2 and W1). The AEP would question the adequacy of the existing provision; the CFO would undertake more work and present evidence to the audit committee that the status quo was satisfactory. Impairments (M6 and C2) tended to follow the same pattern with the AEP questioning and the CFO providing forecasts to support the initial valuation which is then accepted by AEP and AC. Sometimes although it was relatively easy to gain agreement between the three key parties, the valuation itself might be subject to considerable uncertainty and require the assistance of an independent expert (P3). C3 followed a more unusual route with the ACC proposing a solution to the valuation problem.

In other interactions the judgement was focused on the nature of disclosures where IFRS provided little guidance, for example, reorganization costs (K5 and P5) where the AEP challenged the proposed disclosure framed with investors presentations in mind and an agreement was reached. Segmental reporting occured in three interactions (F8, P6 and O4). Typically the AEP questioned whether the existing reported segments were appropriate and the CFO engaged in a debate but there was no change in reporting practice. Business Review was the subject of five interactions (M3, F9, C5, R3 and O3) where sometimes there was tension between the AEP's concern to ensure consistency with the financial statements and compliance with new legislation the company's desire to communicate appropriately with investors.

Cluster 5: Acceptable Judgement Outcome, Attained with Slight Difficulty

The two interactions in this cluster (S4 and S6) came from one case characterized by less good relationships between the AEP and both the CFO and ACC. In both cases the AEP challenged the CFO's judgement with respect to a valuation and in both cases the CFO produced external evidence to support his valuation which was then accepted by the AEP and (in the case of S4) the audit committee.

Cluster 6: Acceptable Judgement Outcome, Attained with Difficulty

There were seven interactions in this cluster (S2, S3, K2, M2, P1, R1 and R2) derived from five cases. Two of the interactions (M2 and R1) involved complex and unique transactions for which there was little guidance in the regulatory framework. In both interactions the audit firm's technical department was fully involved, while in M2 the CFO engaged another firm of accountants to provide technical support. The process essentially involved reviewing a number of proposed solutions until one was found that all parties felt comfortable with.

The impairment interactions (S2 and K2) were particularly sensitive because of the presence of directors on the boards who had championed the original investment being reviewed. In both cases, the CFO was able to provide evidence to support the valuations. Face-saving was also a feature of R2 where the directors argued their case for reduced disclosure based on commercial sensitivity, but gave in when the AEP argued that the standard required greater disclosure.

P1 was a disclosure issue resolved with some difficulty because the AEP was taking an ultra-cautious approach to application of accounting standards by interpreting guidelines as if they were an integral part of the standard. In this interaction the CFO and audit committee agreed to ignore the AEP's warnings and adopted their preferred format, subsequently discovering that other companies had used the same format in their accounts. S3 was another interaction where the CFO and AEP had traded proposals when the CFO discovered another client of the same audit firm had been permitted to use his preferred treatment.

Clusters 1–6

The most striking aspect of the entire set of 45 financial reporting outcomes was that none of them was considered non-compliant or unacceptable. This confirms that the strongest influence on interactions was regulation and, in particular, regulatory enforcement.

As Table 16.1 illustrates, a high proportion of the interactions were not compliance issues but matters of judgement and, therefore, the quality of the outcome is more difficult to evaluate. Reaching agreement on the judgement issues fell into different types. There were two cases where there were unusual transactions. In one case all the parties worked together to find an appropriate solution and also took third party advice (M2). In the second case (R1) the CFO set out his position immediately, which was then challenged by the AEP who was not initially prepared to accept the proposal until more evidence justifying the argument, including precedent in another case, convinced him and his technical advisors in the firm that the accounting treatment was appropriate. Interestingly in this case, both parties wondered whether they had got it right. Regarding the inventory valuations, constructive interactions took place between CFOs and AEPs to reach a reasonable outcome with the auditor raising challenges and requiring the client to justify the position (S4). However, there was different behaviour regarding the valuation of intangibles on acquisition. Some CFOs thought the IFRS requirement to split the valuation between goodwill and other intangibles was a waste of time and money and was of little value externally as intangibles were ignored by analysts. In these cases, the AEPs were more minded to accept the company valuations provided they had followed due process and complied with the standard (e.g. K1, F7, W3 and O1). A similar situation appeared in accounting for share-based payments (F4 and O2). In other cases, the AEP might make an initial challenge, then the CFO would usually respond by obtaining more business-specific data to support the valuation and its underlying assumptions (S6).

The relationships between the four main influence categories and the outcome characteristics are summarized diagrammatically in Figure 16.4. In this figure, the

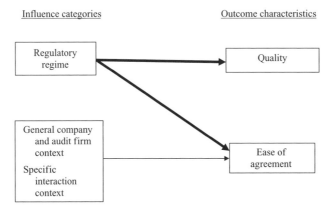

Figure 16.4 Relationships between influence categories and outcome characteristics

weight of the arrow lines gives an indication of the relative strength of the influence. It can be seen that it is the regulatory framework that is the only significant influence on outcome 'quality', and is the dominant influence on ease of agreement. Local contextual factors have no discernible impact on 'quality' and only a minor impact on ease of agreement.

16.11 COMPARISON WITH EXTANT LITERATURE

16.11.1 Beattie *et al.* (2001)

A crucial comparison is between the findings of the present study, set in the post-IFRS UK environment before the financial crisis took hold, with that of Beattie *et al.* (2001), set in the late 1990s. As discussed in detail in Chapter 2, the major change in the environment is in terms of the regulatory regime. It is apparent that the nature of interaction issues has changed. In line with the comparison of findings from the large-scale surveys discussed in Chapter 3, the interview evidence indicates that the number of interactions has risen (45 financial reporting interactions over nine cases compared to 22 financial reporting interactions over six cases previously). However, true negotiations appear to have become more infrequent. The interaction issues involved often concerned IFRS standards which introduced significant change.

The nine case studies presented here were used to test the grounded theory model of interactions proposed by Beattie *et al.* (2001) and summarized in Figure 2.1, Chapter 2. It became clear to us that the 2001 model did not provide an appropriate theoretical framework to explain interactions occurring in the changed regulatory environment. The model fit was poor. Comparing the revised model of Figure 16.1 with the original model, there may appear to be a superficial similarity — broadly the same category groups are represented. However, the relative importance of these groups in relation to the interactions (the core category) is radically altered. Bearing in mind that the proximity of the group to the central category reflects its level of influence, it can be seen that the crucial influences relate to the regulatory regime, leaving the general and specific contextual categories at the periphery. In other words, the influence of local interaction context (general and specific) and regulatory regime are now inverted. While these contextual factors still exist in relation to interactions, their influence upon interactions has been suppressed by the dominating influence of enforcement.

In relation to the tactics and strategies adopted, there has been a decrease in the range observed. Table 2.1 (Chapter 2) lists eight generic strategies observed in the Beattie *et al.* (2001) study. In the present study, we found examples of only five of these: assertiveness (AEP stating their position firmly at the outset); sanction (audit qualification threat); reason (CFO or AEP using evidence to support their argument); coalescing (ACC using the audit committee to secure agreement); and higher authority (usually an audit firm technical department). In the prevailing culture of compliance there was no evidence of ingratiation, conditions being attached to acceptance or bargaining strategies. In particular, the reciprocity-based bargaining strategy (i.e.

strategic give and take concessionary strategy) identified by Hatfield *et al.* (2008) and Sanchez *et al.* (2007) in the US environment is not found.

One aspect of the model that warrants detailed examination is the interaction outcome. The two outcome attributes are represented visually in Figure 16.3. A similar analysis was undertaken in Beattie *et al.* (2001) and a comparison of both sets of findings, in terms of the boundaries of the observed outcome domain which classifies outcome quality from compliant/acceptable to non-compliant/unacceptable and classifies the ease of agreement of the outcome from easy to difficult. This is shown in Figure 16.5. Several observations can be made regarding this figure. First, the overall size of the outcome domain has shrunk, especially in relation to the outcome quality dimension. This shows that changes in the interaction environment have acted to reduce the variability of outcomes, especially outcome quality. Provided this small variation is around a high quality mean, this can be considered good. Indeed, this appears to be the case, as there are no unacceptable outcomes in the present study, whereas there were four unacceptable outcomes in Beattie *et al.* (2001).

However, a slight caveat is warranted and suggests that the improvement may not be entirely successful. As explained in sub-section 16.5.3, regulatory changes have had a very significant homogenizing effect on AEP behaviours and all case AEPs were considered a safe pair of hands (see section 2.4.5 for a description of the Beattie et al. (2001) classification of AEPs). This means that the framework has made it very difficult for AEPs of lesser quality (the accommodators, trusters and incompetents) to operate in the current environment. It also means, however, that the 'crusader' (two out of the six AEPs were of this type in Beattie *et al.* (2001)) can no longer thrive either in the current environment. This is because there are significant disincentives to 'go beyond' the accounting and auditing standards as they are written, particularly in the 2007/2008 environment where true and fair was deemed to mean compliance with IFRS and there was little scope to apply an override. Thus, in Figure 16.5 the lowering of the domain leaving a gap at the top represents the loss of the true and fair view override and the principles of substance over form and prudence which are not part of the IFRS accounting model.

Turning now to the ease of agreement dimension in Figure 16.5, there is much less change indicated. A slight reduction in the scope for very difficult outcomes is shown. This change can be attributed, once again, to regulatory changes. In particular, the enhanced role of the audit committee, discussed in the previous chapter, has produced a fairly standard (and simpler in some cases) 'pattern' to interactions — the CFO and AEP are under pressure to agree issues and present this agreed solution to the ACC, and then to the audit committee. The scope for the involvement of other executive directors, which often characterized difficult interactions in Beattie *et al.* (2001), has been substantially reduced by the audit committee's enhanced role. In addition, the existence of accounting standards which are more rules-based has limited the scope for disagreement. However, the valuation judgements still remain in a number of areas, such as intangibles. Finally, the more rigorous enforcement regime means that the primary goal of all parties is to comply with the standards, irrespective of their

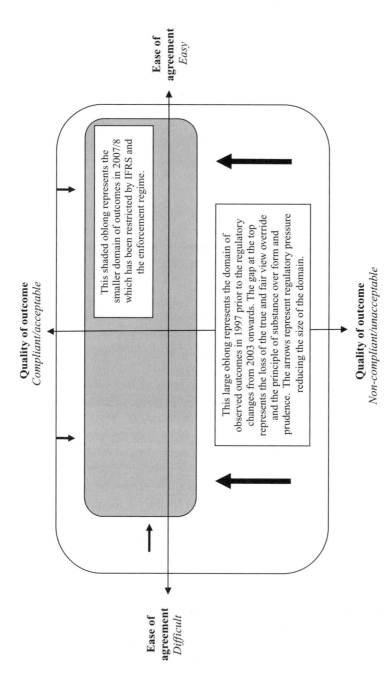

Quality of outcome
Compliant/acceptable

Ease of agreement
Easy

This shaded oblong represents the smaller domain of outcomes in 2007/8 which has been restricted by IFRS and the enforcement regime.

This large oblong represents the domain of observed outcomes in 1997 prior to the regulatory changes from 2003 onwards. The gap at the top represents the loss of the true and fair view override and the principle of substance over form and prudence. The arrows represent regulatory pressure reducing the size of the domain.

Quality of outcome
Non-compliant/unacceptable

Ease of agreement
Difficult

Figure 16.5 The shrinking interaction outcome domain between 1997 and 2007

perceived merits. This increase in goal congruency has, not surprisingly, reduced the extent of disagreement and conflict and, in turn, the difficulty of interactions. It has, however, undermined the ability of the AEP to go beyond the framework to press for a true and fair view and the primacy of substance over form.

16.11.2   Other Literature

In relation to the other academic literature reviewed in Chapter 2, we make the following observations on the wide range of research in this area.

While it is indeed the case that accounting and auditing standard-setting is increasingly global (Cooper and Robson, 2006), our study points to the importance of the enforcement regime in relation to financial reporting and auditing outcomes. It is important to note that this is, at present, effectively national and is likely to continue as such because of the difficulty establishing global enforcement regimes.

There is a wealth of evidence throughout the case studies that Wade's (2007) 'standards-surveillance-compliance' system of regulation based on transparency and calculable standards and outcomes pervades financial reporting and auditing activity. This increased drive for transparency in the audit process and in financial reporting disclosure is the profession's and government's response to scandals and to adverse reports on audit practice (AIU, 2010) and is continuing virtually unchecked. This is creating increasingly lengthy and complex financial statements which both users and preparers have criticized heavily, including our own interviewees as reported in Chapter 14. The recent debate on auditor scepticism (FSA/FRC, 2010; APB, 2010b) suggests that auditors are once again being identified as scapegoats, consistent with the ideas of Hirschleifer (2008) and Guénin-Paracini and Gendron (2010). Our evidence from a number of interactions does indicate that auditors are primarily concerned under this regime with compliance where there are clear rules in IFRS and with process and/or evidence gathering where judgements are concerned. Process involves ensuring that the client has followed an IFRS mandated process with regard to such issues as valuations. Evidence gathering can involve requiring more information from the client to justify an accounting treatment and the audit firm's own research. In some cases, this evidence can be the identification of a precedent where another company has accounted for an item in a particular way. In this study there are no judgement issues where the auditor was seriously uncomfortable about the outcomes, therefore, we cannot predict the behaviour if this was the case.

Interview evidence reported here indicates a considerable level of concern among key participants in the financial reporting process regarding the quality of IFRS and the consequent integrity of financial reporting in the UK. This is consistent with the findings of Beattie *et al.* (2009a; 2008a) and others. The detailed evidence presented here, set in the context of specific interactions, explains the nature of these concerns.

As noted in section 2.3 of Chapter 2, the true and fair view override has effectively disappeared from UK reporting under IFRS, as has a clear statement of substance over form. Certainly there was no mention of either of these concepts by the interviews in the present study. In one of the few cases where the override was applied and the reporting outcome was consequently not compliant with IFRS (the French bank Société Générale's trading loss incident in 2008), the auditors faced criticism and difficulty. Since then, auditors and other key parties in the financial reporting process have been most concerned to ensure compliance above all else. A further consequence of this has been the disappearance of the AEP type characterized by the highest level of integrity — the *crusader* (sub-section 2.4.5, Chapter 2).

In line with our conclusions from Chapter 14, the evidence from the detailed financial reporting interactions is consistent with the view that the more a system is rules-based, the higher the likelihood that professional judgement will be diminished in favour of compliance with rules (Bennett *et al.*, 2006).

The five interactions concerning the Business Review (M3, F9, C5, R3, and D3) indicated concerns with regard to the commercial sensitivity of disclosures and the potential for misunderstanding by investors and analysts. Thus, the interactions focussed upon disclosure disincentives, rather than incentives.

The issue of non-audit service provision by the incumbent auditor is now very restricted and there was no hint in our evidence from the specific interactions that the remaining provision threatens auditor independence. The substantive issue to emerge from the case studies is that the existing regulation (i.e. ES 5 and the monitoring and enforcement of this ethical standard) is creating a severe problem for some small companies (also identified from the evidence in Chapter 14). This is because they can no longer access accounting advice in an environment where the standards have become more complex. These findings complement those of Beattie *et al.* (2009b), in relation to the inconvenience and added cost of seeking alternative service providers.

In relation to the ethical requirement for AEPs to rotate every five years (the period extant at the time of the study, though now likely to increase to seven years in certain circumstances), relevant evidence is provided in the initial context section of each case write-up. This shows that, in an environment where there are now three key parties to interactions, that parties in this triad seldom stay the same for long. While the quality of the auditor–client relationship has a greatly reduced influence on interactions in the modified grounded theory model, a change of AEP, CFO or ACC can impact behaviour, especially the face-saving objective. If relevant parties to a transaction are no longer involved with the company there is less concern about face-saving, while there is more concern about face-saving if a current board member has particular sensitivities about a specific matter.

We do not find evidence of heterogeneity of audit partner types, such as found by Beattie *et al.* (2001) and Van Buuren (2009). Both of these studies were conducted in the pre-IRFS European setting. Post-IFRS, only the 'safe pair of hands' AEP type was in evidence. The general tenor of the interview evidence is that AEPs now regard the quality of their judgements as something to be regulated and verified through inspection systems, consistent with the findings of Gendron *et al.* (2006) in the Canadian context. There is, therefore, no incentive to go beyond this requirement, although we do find some partners may be over dependent on their own technical departments and whilst remaining a safe pair of hands become too process-driven themselves.

The body of evidence presented here in relation to financial reporting interactions confirms the view of Menkel-Meadow (2009) that 'one size will not fit all' in negotiation research. In particular, the audit committee, especially the ACC in this study, has a crucial role in the negotiation process and the impact of the regulatory regime, particularly enforcement of a rules-based system, is fundamental in the audit setting. The ACC is a key third party in the negotiation. The audit committee acts, not as a conflict resolution body, but as a means of encouraging AEPs and, particularly, CFOs to resolve disputes before they are taken to the audit committee, in order to avoid loss of face.

In relation to the developing (mainly North American) literature on negotiation tactics in audit settings (see sub-section 2.8.2, Chapter 2), we do not find evidence of the reciprocity-based strategy (i.e. strategic give and take concessionary strategy) identified by Hatfield et al. (2008) and Sanchez et al. (2007) (see sub-section 16.9.2). We attribute this to the UK enforcement regime under which such reciprocity is likely to be identified by the inspection regime.

The case studies afford limited insight into the role of the full audit committee (sub-section 2.8.3, Chapter 2). In particular, we are unable to comment meaningfully on the impact that the audit committee's knowledge that a negotiation took place had on the nature of the audit committee's investigation of the decision (Pomeroy, 2010), as it is not clear from the case studies how much information was passed to the audit committee by the ACC. Nor can we comment on the relationship between trust and the degree of professional scepticism shown and the quality of the relationships (e.g. Rose, 2007), except to observe that the dominating influence of the regulatory regime suppressed the impact of the more personal aspects of interactions. However, there is some useful evidence on the role and effectiveness of audit committees beyond the general views reported in Chapter 14.

In particular, our findings offer important nuances to Turley and Zaman's (2007) conclusions that the audit committee in the UK setting has a significant influence on power relations between key organizational participants and that the audit committee may be used as a threat, ally or arbiter in resolving issues and conflicts (sub-section 2.8.5, Chapter 2). Our findings indicate that the primary party to have this influence and serve these uses is the ACC rather than the full audit committee.

Despite the significant changes in the regulatory regime, which have arguably reduced the extent of judgement exercised by auditors in the production of financial statements, comfort remains a central concept for the key parties. This is evident from the frequent use of this term by interviewees as they told the interaction stories and supports the significance of this concept identified in the literature (e.g. Pentland, 1993; Power, 1999; Carrington and Catasús, 2007).

Company buyer types, as with AEP types, also exhibited less variation than previously observed in the UK context (Beattie and Fearnley, 1998; discussed in sub-section 2.8.5, Chapter 2). Previously it did seem possible to identify a buyer type associated with the company as a distinct entity (driven mostly by the views of the Chairman, CEO and CFO) (Beattie *et al.*, 2001). In the environment of the late 2000s, the CFO and ACC views take precedence and the influence of other directors is substantially reduced. Only two buyer types were in evidence. All ACCs were comfort-seekers and one was also an audit fee grudger. All CFOs were also comfort-seekers although two were also resource-seekers due to the small size of the company.

Of particular relevance to the present study are the interview finding of McCracken *et al.* (2008) who conduct eight matched interviews of the CFO — AEP dyad in the 2001 Canadian setting (see sub-section 2.8.5, Chapter 2). They conclude that it is the CFOs who define the relationship and the roles — with the AEP being cast in the role of either 'expert advisor' or 'police officer'. In both situations the audit partner had responsibility for managing the relationship in order to keep the client happy. As discussed above, the expert advisor role has been heavily affected by the introduction of IFRS and by NAS restrictions. We also find that the ACC in many cases plays a key role in managing the relationships within the triad as they are in a powerful position and effectively oversee the CFO and AEP.

17

Conclusions

17.1 OVERVIEW

In this final chapter we begin by summarizing the regulatory setting for this study (17.2). We then set out the evidential base that this chapter draws upon and the overall structure of our presentation of the findings and conclusions (17.3). The five interlinked sets of findings and conclusions are then reported (17.4–17.8). The following section (17.9) derives policy recommendations. Finally, we consider the implications for future research and regulatory interest both in the UK and in other countries, particularly the EU (17.10).

A brief summary of our conclusions is also included in the introductory chapter (1.6)

17.2 THE REGULATORY SETTING

The setting for this UK study is characterized by the introduction of a range of changes made in the UK after the collapse of Enron and the 2005 introduction, at EU level, of IFRS for the group accounts of listed companies. The post-Enron changes made in the UK comprise: the changes to the UK Corporate Governance Code by the FRC; the introduction of ISAs and Auditors' Ethical Standards by the APB; and the strengthening of the enforcement regime by (a) extending the role of the FRRP from a reactive role of investigating non-compliance in public interest financial statements to one of pro-actively monitoring financial statements for non-compliance and (b) the creation of the AIU, a body responsible for the inspection of public interest audits. At the time our research was carried out, in 2007 and early 2008, the economic crisis had not fully manifested itself and our evidence, therefore, relates to a relatively benign pre-financial crisis economic environment.

The corporate governance changes relating to the role of the audit committee and the ACC served to shift the predominant dynamic in financial reporting interactions of a dyad relationship between the CFO and the AEP to a triad relationship where both the CFO and AEP are accountable to the ACC, who manages the AC.

17.3 EVIDENTIAL BASE AND STRUCTURE OF FINDINGS

Our findings emerge primarily from the nine case studies reported in Chapters 5–13, together with our grounded theory analysis of the 45 financial reporting interactions in Chapter 16. We also draw upon the 26 interviewees' views regarding the regulatory framework reported in Chapter 14 and the details of the attributes, activities and procedures of the audit committee and of the ACC reported in Chapter 15. The

interview material in Chapters 14 and 15 is supported by reference to our survey results in Chapter 3.

The key issues to emerge from this body of evidence are grouped under the following five headings: the nature of financial reporting interactions (section 17.4); the interaction process (section 17.5); interaction outcomes (section 17.6); the regulatory framework (section 17.7); and the ACC and the audit committee (section 17.8).

17.4   THE NATURE OF FINANCIAL REPORTING INTERACTIONS BETWEEN FDS, ACCS AND AEPS

A total of 45 financial reporting interactions (Table 16.1 in Chapter 16) were identified across the nine case companies, many more than emerged in the Beattie *et al.* (2001) study (22 interactions across six cases). We attribute this increase to the increased complexity of IFRS compared to UK GAAP as well as the 'newness' of IFRS. Of these 45 interactions, 70% involve disclosure issues, measurement issues or a joint recognition/measurement issue. The recognition/measurement category is split approximately equally between discussions and negotiations. The disclosure issues were all discussion interactions, as were most of the measurement interactions.

Specific interaction issues that occurred more than once were: the identification/valuation of intangible assets on acquisition (five case companies); inventories (four case companies); the Business Review (five case companies); segmental reporting (three case companies); share-based payments (two case companies); and accounting for a complex transaction (two case companies). The case company interactions were fairly representative of the interactions reported in the large-scale survey.

Judgements (Table 16.2, Chapter 16) were the most frequent decision type (69%), most often involving measurement or disclosure issues, followed by combined compliance/judgement decisions (20%), which tended to involve recognition/measurement issues, with the remaining 11% of interactions being compliance issues. The more intense interactions which led to negotiation were more likely to occur where compliance decisions were involved. Three out of five compliance issues (i.e. 60%) led to a negotiation whereas only seven out of 24 judgement issues (23%) led to a negotiation. One third of all interactions were classed as negotiations, however, intense negotiations (involving disagreement and conflict) appear to have become less frequent since the Beattie *et al.* (2001) study. Negotiation issues often concerned IFRS standards which introduced significant change.

17.5   THE INTERACTION PROCESS

The within-case analysis of the financial reporting interactions (Chapters 5–13) revealed that the interactions had, compared to Beattie *et al.* (2001), become much less complex and varied in nature. In general, interactions were characterized by fewer events, fewer stages and fewer parties involved. Different aspects of the regulatory framework dominated various dimensions of the interactions: the goals and objectives of the key parties as well as the interaction process.

The cross-case analysis of interactions (Chapter 16) tested the grounded theory model of Beattie *et al.* (2001) (Figure 2.1). Although a similar set of concepts, categories and category groups emerged to those identified by Beattie *et al.* (2001), the model 'fit' to the current study was generally poor, as the degree of influence of the category groups, together with the specific categories within each group, had changed very significantly. New concepts had emerged, the significance of established concepts had changed and relationships had altered. The original interaction model was, therefore, modified.

In the revised grounded theory interaction model (represented in Figure 16.1, Chapter 16), the main influences on the interaction are local context (in the form of general company/audit firm context and specific interaction context) and the regulatory regime (encompassing the international regulatory regime and the national regulatory regime). Each group of categories represents a set of conditional features acting upon the core category (the interaction), with the proximity of the category group to the core interaction indicating the level of influence upon the interaction. In this model, local contextual factors lie at the periphery of the interaction and represent relatively weak influences on the interaction. The categories impacting most directly on the core category relate to the regulatory regime, both the (mainly international) standard-setting regime and the (national) enforcement regime. Of these, the national enforcement regime lies closest to the core category, representing the most powerful influence on the various aspects of the interaction (events, strategies, outcome and consequences).

The UK's legal enforcement regime has two main activities which have been greatly enhanced since the Beattie *et al.* (2001) study was conducted — the changed, now pro-active role of the FRRP and the AIU. The activities of the FRRP and the AIU have greatly increased the risk to companies and auditors of getting found out if they do not comply with the regulatory regime, with such discovery bringing attendant adverse consequences for the parties involved in terms of time, cost and reputation damage (organizational and personal). The high risk associated with non-compliance has changed behaviour and restricted the extent to which the key parties were prepared to negotiate. The corporate governance code has no regulatory backing as such, however non-compliance with the 'comply or explain' model was considered likely to bring market criticism.

The accounting and auditing standards that were being so effectively enforced by the national framework were considered to be more detailed, rules-based and process-driven than the UK standards they replaced. In a number of interactions based on IFRS, the compliant outcome was considered by the key parties either to result in misleading financial statements or to be unjustifiably costly (resulting in information that users disregarded anyway). Clearly, under an effective enforcement regime, it is the quality of the standards and regulations being enforced that will determine the quality of the final outcomes. The complexity of the standards impacted on the interaction process, rendering AEPs increasingly reliant on their audit firm's technical departments for solutions and so reducing their personal power. This trend is reinforced by the robust enforcement regime.

The local context category group which appeared to have the greater influence on the core category was the specific interaction context, rather than the general company/audit firm context. The specific interaction context included: the nature if the interaction issue; the goals and objectives of the key parties; third parties and any other specific factors. In relation to the nature of the interaction issues to emerge in the case studies, it should be noted that IFRS has introduced more complex judgements into a number of key accounting areas such as intangible valuations and share-based payments. The IFRS accounting treatment was criticized by several interviewees. The primary goal of all parties appeared to be to ensure compliance with the regulatory regime (whether this involved complying with a rule or with the process underpinning a judgement, including evidence gathering in support of a judgement). The overall objective was to keep out of trouble with regulators and avoid market criticism. Subsidiary specific objectives included: face-saving (which tended to make it more difficult to obtain agreement, whereas newness to role tended to make agreement easier as there was no need to defend previous actions to save face); and desire to minimize effect due to impact of accounting disclosures on investors and analysts.

The technical departments of the audit firms and the company audit committee were influential and prominent third parties. The technical departments have assumed a more powerful position due to the complex, rules-based nature of IFRS, the process-driven approach to judgements and the compliance culture. Audit committees generally featured only in the final stage of the interaction and 'reviewed', 'discussed' or 'considered' proposed solutions and 'approved' these. Exceptionally, the audit committee was merely 'informed' of the interaction outcome or acted as a forum for resolving the issue. Less frequent third parties included other directors, senior company managers, previous auditors, subsidiary company auditors, partner firm in another country, other audit firms, lawyers and other companies (in relation to their accounting practices acting as a precedent). Other specific interaction context factors included time pressure, impact on future accounting periods and poor communication by a key party.

General local context relating to the company/audit firm has the least influence on the interaction in the revised model. This category group includes: quality of primary relationships, company circumstances, audit firm circumstances and company buyer type. The single primary relationship in the original model (CFO–AEP) has increased to three primary relationships due to the enhanced role of ACCs. The ACC has gained power on accounting and auditing matters at the expense of the other two parties. This triad relationship is shown diagrammatically in Figure 16.2 (Chapter 16).

In the regulatory regime of the present study, interactions tended to be characterized by problem-solving behaviour between the three parties, with little evidence of disagreement and confrontation. The increased relationship complexity has served to dampen the impact of concepts such as compatible personalities and age gap. The strong compliance-driven enforcement environment has also impacted indirectly on the quality of relationships by reducing the likelihood of key parties having hugely different objectives or significantly different levels of professional integrity. Jointly, these influences have not only reduced the significance of relationship quality on interactions, but they have also reduced the incidence of poor relationships as resolution processes are more clearly defined and there is greater goal congruency.

The engagement of the ACC has changed CFO behaviour as they no longer have the same degree of 'ownership' of the financial statements. Withholding information would reflect badly on a CFO in the triad nexus of relationships as the AEP would inform the ACC of any difficulty. This has served to increase the extent of early interaction between CFOs and AEPs, and is one factor acting to reduce the incidence and seriousness of negotiations (the other key factor being regulation).

Company circumstances, which were influential in the original model, had no discernible influence on the interaction outcomes in the present study. Reporting style differences were masked by the prevailing culture of detailed rules in IFRS and compliance. In terms of company buyer types, the ACCs and CFOs were all comfort-seekers, with CFOs employed in smaller listed companies also being resource-seekers. Audit firm procedures (e.g. second partner review; technical review, peer review) have become greatly standardized due to regulatory changes and so this influence has effectively disappeared. Similarly, the compliance culture has resulted in very little variation in AEP (seller) types — the 'safe pair of hands' AEP type is now standard. Although the regulatory regime has effectively eradicated AEP types of lesser quality, it has also produced an environment where a higher AEP quality type (the crusader) is unlikely to survive.

The core category (the interaction) comprises several categories: interaction events; tactics and strategy, outcome and consequences. Observed interaction events included the provision of information justifying the accounting numbers proposed by the CFO; third party opinions in situations of high uncertainty; joint solution seeking (for complex and unique issues); AEP admission of previous error; and AEP noting error of another audit firm. The tactic used frequently by AEPs in matters of compliance was to state their position firmly at the outset (an assertiveness strategy). Reason was a commonly used strategy in matters of judgement, often involving the use of evidence to support a reasoned argument or citation of a reporting precedent established by another company. Appeal to a higher authority (technical department) was another commonly used strategy. Less frequently, a coalescing strategy (using the audit committee to judge between cases presented by the AEP and CFO) or a sanction (tender threat or audit qualification threat) was used. In the prevailing culture of compliance neither ingratiation strategies nor reciprocity-based strategies were observed. Interactions consequences relate to ongoing accounting interactions, future accounting periods, impact on audit fee negotiations and effect on the quality of a primary relationship.

17.6   INTERACTION OUTCOMES

The two interaction outcome dimensions are the quality of financial reporting by the company and the ease of agreement with which the outcome is reached. This is shown diagrammatically in Figure 16.3 (Chapter 16) with the interactions labelled according to the first letter of the company name in the relevant case study. The quality of compliance issues (classified as compliant or non-compliant) was judged based on whether the outcome complied fully with the regulatory framework ruling at the time of the relevant transaction and did not make any judgement as to the quality of that framework. The *inherent* quality of a judgement issue is not possible to evaluate, and was classified as either acceptable or unacceptable in terms of compliance with the *process* of reaching the judgement. These two dimensions reflect the effectiveness and efficiency of the audit, respectively. Cluster analysis was used to identify which categories were most influential in determining these two dimensions of the final outcome, including the identification of critical moderating variables.

Easily attained compliant outcomes frequently resulted from the AEP stating his position firmly at the start of the interaction process or CFOs using a reasoning strategy in relation to the valuations — successful tactics where clear regulatory guidance exists and enforcement is robust. The two compliant outcomes attained with slight difficulty arose where the CFO and AEP were both newly appointed and related to restatements to the previous year's accounts. The slight difficulty was due to the face-saving agenda of the ACC and audit committee. The difficulty may have been greater but for the strong enforcement regime. Compliant outcomes, attained with difficulty, arose where the CFO or others in the company challenged the rationale and impact of an accounting standard, despite the requirements of the standard being fairly clear. The accounting issues involved were intangible assets on acquisition, financial instruments and share-based payments, areas where accounting practice had changed radically under IFRS. Once again, the compliant outcome was attributable to the strength of the compliance regime.

The majority of outcomes were acceptable judgements, attained easily. Frequent issues were valuations (often inventory or impairments) and disclosures where IFRS provided little guidance (re-organization costs, segmental reporting or Business Review). In the case of valuations, the common pattern was for the CFO to propose a figure based on evidence; this would be questioned by the AEP and the CFO would undertake more work and present further evidence, possibly based on advice from an independent expert.

In the case of disclosure judgements, companies sometimes proposed disclosures with investor presentations or commercial sensitivity in mind and the AEP challenged this. The two acceptable judgement outcomes attained with slight difficulty arose from a case characterized by less good relationships between the AEP and both the CFO and ACC. The AEP's challenge to the CFO's valuation judgement resulted in the CFO producing external supporting evidence which was then accepted. The acceptable judgement outcomes attained with difficulty were typically either complex, unique transactions for which there was little guidance in the regulatory framework or interactions rendered sensitive by the presence of directors on the boards who had a face-saving agenda. Generally with judgements the company would justify its position by providing more evidence if faced with a challenge from the auditors. The most successful challenges were where evidence was provided of a precedent for the accounting treatment, particularly if it was agreed by auditors' own firm.

Of the four main influence categories, the only significant influence on the financial reporting outcome quality is the regulatory framework (Figure 16.4 in Chapter 16). This is also the dominant influence on ease of agreement. Local contextual factors have no discernible impact on 'quality' and only a minor impact on ease of agreement. Comparing the revised grounded theory interaction model of the present study, set in the post-IFRS UK environment before the financial crisis took hold, with the original model of Beattie *et al.* (2001), set in the late 1990s, it is clear that the relative importance of the four categories has radically altered. The dominant influences relate to the regulatory regime, leaving the local contextual categories as minor influences. This is an inversion of the original model, where local contextual factors had great influence on both the outcome quality and the ease of agreement.

The pervasive influence of the regulatory regime has reduced the range of several categories which were identified in Beattie *et al.* (2001) in their original interaction model. These include relationship quality, company buyer types, AEP (seller) types and the tactics and strategies adopted. The net effect on the final range of outcomes observed in this study is, predictably, to reduce variation. The empirically-informed boundaries of the observed outcome domain from the present study and from Beattie *et al.* (2001) were compared (Figure 16.5 in Chapter 16). The overall size of the outcome domain has shrunk, especially in relation to the outcome quality dimension. This shrinkage is in both directions. The good news is that there are now no unaccept-able outcomes. The bad news is that the loss of the true and fair view override and the principles of substance over form and prudence (which are not part of the IFRS accounting model), mean that the crusader AEP, who is prepared to go beyond the rules to achieve the best possible outcome, does not thrive in the current environment.

In terms of the ease of agreement dimension, much less change is indicated, with only a slight reduction in the scope for very difficult outcomes. This is due to the enhanced role of the audit committee, the reduced scope for the involvement of other executive directors, the existence of accounting standards which are more rules-based, and the more rigorous enforcement regime.

17.7   THE REGULATORY FRAMEWORK

The introduction of IFRS is not believed to have improved the quality of UK financial reporting, due to excessive complexity and high disclosure volume. The complexity of IFRS has increased the influence of audit firm technical departments relative to CFOs, AEPs and ACCs. This complexity has also created a divide on the audit committee between those with sufficient 'recent and relevant financial experience' to follow and engage with accounting issues (normally only those with an accounting qualification and with recent experience of IFRS) and those without this knowledge and experience. The latter group of audit committee members find it extremely difficult to make informed contributions to discussions of accounting matters. This complexity also impedes effective communication with users. IFRS is generally seen as a rules-based system where compliance and box-ticking have become increasingly dominant and judgements based on process, evidence and precedent have tended to replace judgements based on principles such as substance over form and the use, where necessary, of the true and fair view override. The Enhanced Business Review (an EU initiative) was not thought to have improved communication. It is unlikely that these expressed views emanate simply from a resistance to change, as the interviewees are all intelligent business professionals who are well used to change.

The FRRP is considered an effective monitoring and enforcement body. All three key parties have incentives to avoid an FRRP challenge, particularly in terms of personal reputation damage. Thus, the FRRP is a powerful influence on compliance, used by audit partners to persuade difficult clients to accede.

There were concerns regarding the impact of some aspects of audit ethical standards. The five year rotation period was considered by many to be too short, potentially resulting in reduced audit quality, especially in the case of large, complex client companies where other key parties in the triad had also changed. Both CFOs and AEPs regretted the greater restriction on some non-audit services provision, especially accounting advice and business advice. Small cap companies with fewer accounting resources were particularly adversely affected by these restrictions. All companies also resented the fact that their auditors could no longer assist with the valuations required under certain IFRS standards. Companies either had to pay for external valuations (mostly intangibles on acquisition), creating a new market for independent valuers, or attempt to do the valuation work in-house.

ISAs were viewed as being more detailed and prescriptive than the UK auditing standards they replaced and the AIU enforcement regime was considered by many to be overly concerned with detail, documentation and compliance. With regard to judgements, which constituted the majority of the interactions, auditors were concerned to ensure that the required process had been followed and evidence supporting the decision made was obtained. This evidence could be more data from the company, third party evidence or the identification of a precedent. A consequence of this combination was thought to be that auditors were spending too much time on ensuring compliance and less time on engaging with the client and carrying out the actual audit itself. The existence and nature of the inspection process was thought to have made auditors defensive, as they seek to protect themselves against the inspectors. These rules-based standards and audit inspection procedures were, therefore, judged to have a similarly adverse impact on financial reporting as the rules-based IFRS accounting system. However, the AIU was considered a formidable enforcement body, and audit partners in receipt of an adverse AIU report suffered damage to their career prospects, with the audit firm facing public criticism in the public reports on individual firms which began in 2007/08.

There was widespread agreement among interviewees and extensive evidence from the case studies that the quality of corporate governance has improved dramatically over the last ten years or so. Audit committees, in particular, now play a central role in the audit and financial reporting process, especially the ACC.

17.8   THE ACC AND THE AUDIT COMMITTEE

Generally, we find a high level of engagement of the ACC with the financial reporting and auditing process. ACCs do not want late surprises and expect to be kept informed by AEPs and CFOs about accounting and auditing problems as they arise, so information flows to the ACC from both of the other key parties. The ACC also acts as a filter to, and manager of, the audit committee itself, ensuring that they are informed about emerging issues. As ACCs do not want to be asked to resolve accounting disagreements between the AEP and the CFO, pressure is put upon these two parties to reach agreement between themselves before the proposed resolution of the issue is presented to the audit committee for discussion and for approval. Both the survey evidence and the case study evidence show that many other senior directors attend audit committee meetings. This puts further pressure on the AEP and the CFO to reach agreement since neither would wish to damage their personal standing by taking an unresolved disagreement to such a group.

While understanding of IFRS can be expected to improve with time, the inherent complexity means that directors with professional accounting qualifications will be very much 'in demand'. Despite this constraint, audit committees were found to monitor complex or material financial reporting decisions as well as audit matters, contrary to US findings.

The UK unitary board structure, where executives (i.e. management) and non-executives work together, changes the audit committee dynamic from that of North America as board members other than the CFO attend the audit committee meetings as a matter of course and are, therefore, informed of audit committee business and decisions. As a consequence, the role of preventing escalation of disagreement lies more with the ACC in the UK than with the full audit committee (as reported in the US literature). In the UK context, the role of the full audit committee is more one of reviewing decisions and discussing judgements that have already been sanctioned by the ACC. In this setting, some of the monitoring role of the audit committee is taken on by the ACC as an individual, with the audit committee fulfilling the ceremonial role and the remaining part of the monitoring role.

17.9   POLICY IMPLICATIONS

Clearly, under an effective enforcement regime, it is the quality of the standards and regulations being enforced that will determine the quality of the final outcomes. Our study calls the quality of outcomes into question. In a number of specific interactions and in giving more general views on the regulatory regime, interviewees considered that the accounting rules (rigorously enforced) at times produced dysfunctional results or were incomprehensible to users. Given that the three parties involved are among those most knowledgeable about financial reporting and with the greatest expertise, this is extremely worrying.

This study has identified the enforcement regime as being critical in relation to financial reporting and auditing outcomes. It is important to note that this enforcement regime is, at present, effectively national and is likely to continue as such because of the difficulty in establishing global enforcement regimes where the underlying culture and legal frameworks differ. Nevertheless, this study offers important insights into the auditing and financial reporting outcomes that arise from the unique regulatory nexus formed by: (i) IFRS which are regarded as too complex and at times capable of producing counter intuitive outcomes; (ii) a robust financial reporting enforcement regime; (iii) ISAs which are also regarded as detailed and rules based; and (iv) a robust auditing practices enforcement regime which is viewed as being process-driven. These insights have relevance not only to regulators in the UK, but also to regulators in other countries, particularly within the EU (as they monitor and review the performance and impact of the regulatory regime in their own jurisdiction and consider possible revisions). The findings are particularly relevant to regulators and standard setters with aspirations to extend their remit into countries other than their own.

The study points to a range of undesirable, unintended consequences that regulation in the UK has had. First, the complexity of IFRS has led to disengagement from some accounting matters by audit committee members lacking the necessary accounting expertise and additional costs. While this means fees for accounting firms and also others providing valuation services, it is an added cost burden for reporting companies, creating unnecessary work. For example, analysts and investors are believed to ignore certain costly information in their decision-making such as valuations attributed to intangibles. Second, there is, in part, a communication failure as users do not always understand aspects of the financial reports. Third, although the AIU has reduced drastically the scope for poor quality auditing and forced compliance with auditing standards, the box-ticking, process-driven nature of the inspections, combined with the more detailed auditing standards themselves, may have helped to reduce the scope for very high quality audit as well, since partners will no longer go beyond or override the rules. Fourth, the ethical standard requiring frequent AEP rotation, combined with high natural turnover rates for the other parties in the triad, may mean that there is little continuity on accounting matters at board and auditor level and this can have detrimental effects. The ethical standard restricting non-audit service provision by the incumbent auditor has proved to be costly for companies, especially smaller listed companies seeking accounting advice.

Arising from this study, there are a number of actions that policy makers and other interested parties could consider. These relate to the accounting model and the way in which accounting standards are set. Clearly action on the IFRS complexity debate is warranted — the merits of different extant standards should be re-evaluated in light of IFRS experience to date and changes made to simplify them. More fundamentally, consideration could be given to moving towards a more *de facto* principles-based set of standards — one that would reinstate the substance over form principle and the true and fair view. Finally, the IASB could be made more accountable or, more fundamentally, consideration could be given as to who controls global standard-setting and whether the aspirations of various organizations for one global set of standards is actually desirable or achievable, given the dissatisfaction with IFRS identified by expert preparers in this study.

To a lesser extent these concerns also apply to ISAs where auditors have expressed concerns about the detailed and prescriptive nature of the standards.

17.10 LIMITATIONS AND IMPLICATIONS FOR FUTURE RESEARCH AND REGULATORY INTEREST

Existing research makes little distinction between the role of the audit committee and that of the audit committee chair. While the present study does make this distinction, the main focus is on the ACC. Further research is required to delve more deeply into the audit committee's role and engagement in financial reporting interactions and how this interacts with the ACC's role and engagement.

While this study provides indicative evidence regarding the quality of judgement interactions and has found no evidence of judgements lying outside the bounds of materiality, more detailed investigation of individual interactions of this type would permit more informed and finely grained evaluations to be made. The conduct of such research would, however, face access problems for the researchers themselves.

The evidence for this study was collected in 2007 and 2008 when most of the regulatory changes, such as the introduction of IFRS and ISAs in 2005, were relatively recent. Companies and auditors were either in their first or second year of IFRS and ISA implementation. It is possible that views may have subsequently mellowed as preparers and auditors have become more used to the regime. The concerns about a rules-based system bringing complexity and box ticking are, however, unlikely to diminish with familiarity. In addition, the full effects of the economic crisis were not apparent and findings could be different in an environment under more stress, which could further test the effectiveness of the recent changes. Ongoing research is required to investigate the impact of these issues.

This study has been carried out in the UK and, therefore, the findings reflect the influence of the UK regulatory system. Many of the accounting, auditing and governance issues which we identify are, however, of importance in other regulatory settings. Our findings will, therefore, be of value to researchers and regulators in many other jurisdictions in making useful comparisons and inferences in relation to selected aspects of the regulatory framework. Given the focus on regulatory change in the EU following the economic crisis, our findings may be of particular relevance to European regulators.

References

Agrawal, A. and Chadha, S. (2005). Corporate governance and accounting scandals. *Journal of Law and Economics*, 48(2): 371–405.

AICPA (1994). *Improving Business Reporting — A Customer Focus: Meeting the Information Needs of Investors and Creditors*, Comprehensive Report of the Special Committee on Financial Reporting (The Jenkins Report). New York, NY: American Institute of Certified Public Accountants.

AIU (2010). *2009/10 Annual Report*. (Available at http://www.frc.org.uk/images/uploaded/documents/AIU%20Annual%20Report%202009–10%20Final.pdf, accessed 10 September 2010).

Anderson-Gough, F., Grey, C. and Robson, K. (1999). *Making Up Accountants: The Organizational and Professional Socialization of Trainee Chartered Accountants*. Aldershot, Hampshire: Ashgate.

APB (2004a). *International Standards on Auditing (UK and Ireland)*. London: Auditing Practices Board.

APB (2004b). ISA (UK and Ireland) 260. *Communication of Audit Matters with Those Charged with Governance*, International Standard on Auditing (UK and Ireland) 260. London: Auditing Practices Board. (Available at http://www.frc.org.uk/images/uploaded/documents/ISA%20_UK%20and%20Ireland_%20260.pdf).

APB (2004c). *Ethical Standards 1–5*. London: Auditing Practices Board.

APB (2007). *APB Press Release*. (www.apb.org.uk.apb/press/pub1361.html, accessed 14 September 2007) London: Auditing Practices Board.

APB (2009a). *Ethical Standard 3 (revised): Long Association with the Audit Engagement*. London: Auditing Practices Board.

APB (2009b). *Revised Draft Ethical Standards for Auditors*, Consultation Paper. London: Auditing Practices Board.

APB (2010a). *The Provision of Non-audit Services by Auditors. Feedback on Previous Consultations and Consultation Paper on Revised Draft Ethical Standards for Auditor*. London: Auditing Practices Board.

APB (2010b). *Auditor Scepticism: Raising the Bar*, Discussion Paper. London: Auditing Practices Board.

ASB (1993). *Operating and Financial Review*. London: Accounting Standards Board.

ASB (1994). *Reporting the Substance of Transactions*. Financial Reporting Standard 5. London: Accounting Standards Board.

ASB (2003). *Operating and Financial Review*. London: Accounting Standards Board.

ASB (2005). *Operating and Financial Review*, Reporting Standard 1. London: Accounting Standards Board (www.frc.org.uk/asb).

ASB (2006). *Reporting Statement: Operating and Financial Review*. London: Accounting Standards Board (www.frc.org.uk/asb).

Audit Committee Chair Forum (2006a). *The Role and Function of the Audit Committee*. Audit Committee Chair Forum. (http://www.ey.com/global/Content.nsf/UK/Audit_Committee_Chair_Forum).

Audit Committee Chair Forum (2006b). *Audit Committee Regulation: 'Financial Literacy? — What Does it Mean?* Audit Committee Chair Forum. (http://www.ey.com/global/Content. nsf/UK/Audit_Committee_Chair_Forum).

Audit Committee Chair Forum (2007). *Audit Committee Communication: What is Said, Why, How and to Whom?* Audit Committee Chair Forum. (http://www.ey.com/global/ Content.nsf/UK/Audit_Committee_Chair_Forum).

Ball, R. (2006). International Financial Reporting Standards (IFRS): pros and cons for investors. *Accounting and Business Research*, Special Issue: International Accounting Policy Forum, 36: 5–27.

Bame-Aldred, C.W. and Kida, T. (2007). A comparison of auditor and client initial negotiation positions and tactics. *Accounting, Organizations and Society*, 32(6), 497–511.

Barth, M., Landsman, W.R. and Lang, M.H. (2008). International accounting standards and accounting quality. *Journal of Accounting Research*, 46(3): 467–498.

Beasley, M.S., Carcello, J.V., Hermanson, D.R. and Neal, T.L. (2009). The audit committee oversight process. *Contemporary Accounting Research*, 26(1), 65–122.

Beattie, V. and Fearnley, S. (2002). *Auditor Independence and Non-Audit Services: A Literature Review*. London: Institute of Chartered Accountants in England and Wales.

Beattie, V.A. and Fearnley, S. (1998). *What Companies Want (and Don't Want) From their Auditors*, Research Report. London: Institute of Chartered Accountants in England and Wales.

Beattie, V., Fearnley, S. and Brandt, R. (1998). Auditor independence and the expectations gap: some evidence of changing user perceptions. *Journal of Financial Regulation and Compliance*, 6(2): 159–170.

Beattie, V., Fearnley, S. and Brandt, R. (1999). Perceptions of auditor independence: UK evidence. *Journal of International Accounting, Auditing and Taxation*, 8(1): 67–107.

Beattie V.A., Fearnley, S. and Brandt, R. (2000). Behind the audit report: a descriptive study of discussion and negotiation between auditors and directors. *International Journal of Auditing*, 4(2): 177–202.

Beattie, V., Fearnley, S. and Brandt, R. (2001). *Behind Closed Doors: What Company Audit is Really About*. Basingstoke, Hampshire: Palgrave.

Beattie, V., Fearnley, S. and Brandt, R. (2004). A grounded theory model of auditor-client negotiations. *International Journal of Auditing*, 8(1): 1–19.

Beattie, V., Fearnley, S. and Hines, T. (2008a). Does IFRS undermine UK reporting integrity? *Accountancy*. December: 56–57.

Beattie, V., Fearnley, S. and Hines, T (2008b). *Auditor/Company Interactions in the 2007 UK Regulatory Environment: Discussion and Negotiation on Financial Statement Issues Reported by Finance Directors, Audit Committee Chairs and Audit Engagement*

Partners. Briefing. London: Institute of Chartered Accountants in England and Wales. (http://www.icaew.com/index.cfm?route=156997).

Beattie, V., Fearnley, S. and Hines, A. (2009a). The accounting standards debate: the academics. *Finance Director Europe*, 2: 16–17.

Beattie, V., Fearnley, S. and Hines, T. (2009b). *The Impact of Changes to the Non-audit Services Regime on Finance Directors, Audit Committee Chairs and Audit Partners of UK Listed Companies*. Briefing. London: Institute of Chartered Accountants in England and Wales.

Beattie, V., Fearnley, S. and Hines, T. (2010). Factors affecting audit quality in the 2007 regulatory environment: perceptions of Chief Financial Officers, Audit Committee Chairs and Audit Engagement Partners, Working Paper.

Bédard, J. and Gendron, Y. (2010). Strengthening the financial reporting system: can audit committees deliver? *International Journal of Auditing*, 14(2): 174–210.

Bennett, B., Bradbury, M. and Prangnell, H. (2006). Rules, principles and judgments in accounting standards. *Abacus*, 42(2): 189–204.

Benston, G.J., Bromwich, M. and Wagenhofer, A. (2006). Principles- versus rules-based accounting standards: The FASB's standard setting strategy. *Abacus*, 42(2): 165–188.

Bhimani, A. (2008). The role of crisis in reshaping the role of accounting. *Journal of Accounting and Public Policy*, 27(6): 444–454.

BIS (2010). *The Future of Narrative Reporting: A Consultation*. London: Department for Business Innovation and Skills. (Available at http://www.bis.gov.uk/assets/biscore/business-law/docs/n/10–1057-future-narrative-reporting-consultation.pdf, accessed 3 August 2010).

Black, J., Hopper, M. and Band, C. (2007). Making principles-based regulation a success, *Law and Financial Markets Review*, 1(3): 191–206.

Boone, J.P., Khurana, I.K. and Raman, K.K. (2010). Do the big 4 and the second-tier firms provide audits of similar quality? *Journal of Accounting and Public Policy*, 29(4): 330–352.

Brandt, R., Fearnley, S., Hines, T. and Beattie, V. (1997). The Financial Reporting Review Panel: an analysis of its activities, in *Financial Reporting Today: Current and Emerging Issues, 1998*. London: Accountancy Books.

Brass, D.J. and Burkhardt, M.E. (1993). Potential power and power use: an investigation of structure and behaviour, *Academy of Management Journal*, 36(3): 441–470.

Broadley, P. (2007). Discussion of financial reporting quality: is fair value a plus or a minus? *Accounting and Business Research*. Special Issue: International Accounting Policy Forum, 37: 45–48.

Brown, H.L. and Johnstone, K.M. (2009). Resolving disputed financial reporting issues: effects of auditor experiences and engagement risk on negotiation process and outcome. *Auditing: A Journal of Practice and Theory*, 28(2): 65–92.

Brown, S.M. (1992). Cognitive mapping and repertory grids for qualitative survey research: some comparative observations. *Journal of Management Studies*, 29(3): 287–307.

Bush, T. (2005). *Divided by Common Language. Where Economics Meets the Law. US versus non-US Financial Reporting Models*. London: Institute of Chartered Accountants in England and Wales.

Bush, T. (2009). Is the view true and fair? *Accountancy*, May: 20.

Buthe, T. and Mattli, W. (2008). *Assessing the IASB: Results of a Business Survey about International Financial Reporting Standards and IASB's Operations, Accountability, and Responsiveness to Shareholders*. (Available at http://www.standards-project.com).

Cadbury Report (1992). *Report of the Committee on the Financial Aspects of Corporate Governance*. London: Gee and Co.

Carcello, J.V., Hermanson, R.H. and McGrath, N.T. (1992). Audit quality attributes: the perception of audit partners, preparers and financial statement users. *Auditing: A Journal of Practice and Theory*, 11(1): 1–15.

Carrington, T. and Catasús, B. (2007). Auditing stories about discomfort: becoming comfortable with the numbers. *European Accounting Review*, 16(1): 35–58.

Casterella, J.R., Jensen, K. and Knechel, R.W. (2009). Is self-regulated peer review effective at signalling audit quality? *The Accounting Review*, 84(3): 713–735.

Center for Audit Quality (2008). *Report on the Survey of Audit Committee Members*. (http://www.thecaq.org).

CGAA (2003). *Final Report to the Secretary of State for Trade and Industry and the Chancellor of the Exchequer*. Co-ordinating Group on Audit and Accounting Issues. London: Department of Trade and Industry.

Chartered Accountants of Canada (2001). *Beyond Compliance: Building a Corporate Governance Culture*. (Available at http://www.ecgi.org/codes/documents/beyond_compliance.pdf, accessed 1 September 2010).

Chung, J.O.Y., Cohen, J.R. and Monroe, G.S. (2008). The effect of moods on auditors' inventory valuation decisions. *Auditing: A Journal of Practice & Theory*, 27(2): 137–159.

Cianci, A.M. and Bierstaker, J.L. (2009). The impact of positive and negative mood on the hypothesis generation and ethical judgments of auditors. *Auditing: A Journal of Practice & Theory*, 28(2): 119–144.

Coffee, J.C. (2006). *The Professions and Corporate Governance*. Oxford: Oxford University Press.

Cohen, J., Gaynor, L.M., Krishnamoorthy, G. and Wright, A.M. (2007). Auditor communications with the audit committee and the board of directors: policy recommendations and opportunities for future research. *Accounting Horizons*, 21(2): 165–187.

Cohen, J., Hayes, C., Krishnamoorthy, G. Monroe, G.S. and Wright, A. (2009). The impact of the Sarbanes-Oxley Act on the financial reporting process: experiences of directors. International Symposium on Audit Research.

Cohen, J., Krishnamoorthy, G. and Wright, A.M. (2002). Corporate governance and the audit process. *Contemporary Accounting Research*, 19(4): 573–594.

Cohen, J., Krishnamoorthy, G. and Wright, A.M. (2004). The corporate governance mosaic and financial reporting quality. *Journal of Accounting Literature*, 23: 87–152.

Cohen, J., Krishnamoorthy, G. and Wright, A. (2008). Corporate governance in the post Sarbanes-Oxley era: auditors' experiences.

Cooper, D.J. and Robson, K. (2006). Accounting, professions and regulation: locating the sites of professionalization. *Accounting, Organizations and Society*, 31(4–5), 415–444.

Corbin, J. and Strauss, A. (2008). *Basics of Qualitative Research: Techniques and Procedures for Developing Grounded Theory*, 3rd edition. London: Sage Publications.

Creswell, J. (2009). Editorial: mapping the field of mixed methods research. *Journal of Mixed Methods Research*, 3(2): 95–108.

Dal Bo, E. (2006). Regulatory capture: a review. *Oxford Review of Economic Policy*, 22(2): 203–225.

Dart, E. (2009). UK investors' perceptions of the threats to auditor independence. University of Cardiff, Accounting and Finance Working Papers, A2009/1.

DeAngelo, L.E. (1981). Auditor size and audit quality. *Journal of Accounting and Economics*, 3(3): 183–199.

DeFond, M.L. (2010). How should the auditors be audited? Comparing the PCAOB inspections with the AICPA peer reviews. *Journal of Accounting and Economics*, 49(1–2): 104–108.

Deloitte (2007). *iGAAP 2007 in Your Pocket*. London: Deloitte Touche Tohmatsu.

Devalle, A., Onali, E. and Magarini, R. (2010). Assessing the value relevance of accounting data after the introduction of IFRS in Europe. *Journal of International Financial Management and Accounting*, 21(2): 85–119.

DeZoort, F.T., Hermanson, R.R., Archambeault, D.S. and Reed, S.A. (2002). Audit committee effectiveness: a synthesis of the empirical audit committee literature. *Journal of Accounting Literature*, 21: 38–75.

DeZoort, F.T., Hermanson, D.R. and Houston, R.W. (2003). Audit committee member support for proposed audit adjustments: a source credibility perspective. *Auditing: A Journal of Practice and Theory*, 22(2): 189–205.

DeZoort, F.T., Hermanson, D.R. and Houston, R.W. (2008). Audit committee member support for proposed audit adjustments: Pre-SOX versus post-SOX judgments. *Auditing: A Journal of Practice and Theory*, 27(1): 85–105.

DTI (2002). *Modernising Company Law*, White Paper, Cmnd 5553. London: Department of Trade and Industry.

DTI (2004). *Draft Regulations on the Operating and Financial Review and Directors' Report: A Consultative Document*. London: Department of Trade and Industry.

DTI (2005). *Guidance on the Changes to the Directors' Report Requirements in the Companies Act 1985*. (Available at http://www.dti.gov.uk/bbf/financial-reporting/business-reporting/page21339.html).

Duff, A. (2004). *Auditqual: Dimensions of Audit Quality*. Edinburgh: Institute of Chartered Accountants in Scotland.

Dunne T., Fifield S., Finningham G., Fox A., Hannah G., Helliar C., Power D. and Veneziani M. (2008). *The Implementation of IFRS in the UK, Ireland and Italy*. Edinburgh: Institute of Chartered Accountants of Scotland.

Eisenhardt, K.M. (1989). Building theories from case study research. *Academy of Management Review*, 14(4): 532–550.

European Commission (2002). *Recommendation on Auditor Independence*. Brussels. European Commission.

European Commission Green Paper (2010). Audit Policy: Lessons from the Crisis. European Commission. (Available at: http://ec.europa.eu/internal_market/consultations/docs/2010/audit/green_paper_audit_en.pdf).

European Union (2002). *Regulation (EC) 1606/2002 of the European Parliament and of the Council on the Application of International Accounting Standards*. Brussels: European Union.

Evans, L. (2003). The true and fair view and the 'fair' presentation override of IAS 1. *Accounting and Business Research*, 33(4): 311–325.

Fargher, N., Lee, H-Y. and Mande, V. (2008). The effect of audit partner tenure on client managers' accounting discretion. *Managerial Auditing Journal*, 23(2): 161–186.

Fearnley, S., Hines, T., Brandt, R. and McBride, K. (2002). The impact of the Financial Reporting Review Panel on aspects of the independence of auditors and their attitudes to compliance in the UK. *British Accounting Review*, 34(2): 109–139.

Fearnley, S. and Sunder, S. (2007). Pursuit of convergence is coming at too high a cost. *Financial Times Accountancy Column*, August 23.

Fellingham, J.C. and Newman, D.P. (1985). Strategic considerations in auditing. *The Accounting Review*, 60(4): 634–650.

Financial Accounting Standards Board and International Accounting Standards Board (2006). *A Roadmap for Convergence between IFRS and US GAAP — 2006–2008 Memorandum of Understanding between the FASB and the IASB*. 27 February 2006. Norwalk, Connecticut: FASB & IASB.

Fisher, J., Schatzberg, J.W. and Shapiro, B.P. (1996). A theoretical and experimental examination of strategic auditor-client interaction. *Advances in Accounting*, 14: 135–160.

Francis, J.R. (2004). What do we know about audit quality? *British Accounting Review*, 36(4): 345–368.

Francis, J.R. (2006). Are auditors compromised by non audit services? Assessing the evidence. *Contemporary Accounting Research*, 23(3): 747–760.

Frankel, R.M., Johnson, M.F. and Nelson, K.K. (2002). The relation between auditors' fees for non-audit services and earnings management. *The Accounting Review*, 77(1): 71–105.

FRC (1998). *The Combined Code on Corporate Governance*. London: Financial Reporting Council.

FRC (2003). *The Combined Code on Corporate Governance*. London: Financial Reporting Council.

FRC (2005). *Guidance on Audit Committees* (The Smith Guidance). London: Financial Reporting Council.

FRC (2006a). *The Combined Code on Corporate Governance*. London: Financial Reporting Council.

FRC (2006b). *Promoting Audit Quality*, Discussion Paper. London: Financial Reporting Council.

FRC (2006c). *The UK Approach to Corporate Governance*. London: Financial Reporting Council.

FRC (2008a). *FRC Launches Complexity Project*, FRC PN 236. London: Financial Reporting Council.

FRC (2008b). *The Combined Code on Corporate Governance*. London: Financial Reporting Council.

FRC (2008c). *The Audit Quality Framework*. London: Financial Reporting Council.

FRC (2009a). *Louder than Words: Principles and Actions for Making Corporate Reports Less Complex and More Relevant*. London: Financial Reporting Council.

FRC (2009b). *Audit Inspection Unit, 2008/9 Audit Quality Inspections: An Overview*. (Available at http://www.frc.org.uk/images/uploaded/documents/Public%20Report%20an%20overview.pdf, accessed 18 June 2010).

FRC (2010). *The UK Corporate Governance Code*. (Available at http://www.frc.org.uk/documents/pagemanager/Corporate_Governance/UK%20Corp%20Gov%20Code%20June%202010.pdf, accessed 21 June 2010).

FRRP (2006). *Preliminary Report — IFRS Implementation*. London: Financial Reporting Council.

FSA and FRC (2010). *Enhancing the Auditor's Contribution to Prudential Regulation*. London: Financial Services Authority & Financial Reporting Council.

Gendron, Y. (2009). Discussion of "The audit committee oversight process": advocating openness in accounting research. *Contemporary Accounting Research*, 26(1): 123–134.

Gendron, Y. and Bédard, J. (2006). On the constitution of audit committee effectiveness. *Accounting, Organizations and Society*, 31(3): 211–239.

Gendron, Y., Suddaby, R. and Lam, H. (2006). An examination of the ethical commitment of professional accountants to auditor independence. *Journal of Business Ethics*, 64(2): 169–193.

Gibbins, M., McCracken, S.A. and Salterio, S.E. (2005). Negotiations over accounting issues: the congruency of audit partner and chief financial officer recalls. *Auditing: A Journal of Practice and Theory*, 24(Supplement): 171–193.

Gibbins, M., McCracken, S.A. and Salterio, S.E. (2007). The Chief Financial Officer's perspective on auditor-client negotiations. *Contemporary Accounting Research*, 24(2): 387–422.

Gibbins, M., Salterio, S. and Webb, A. (2001). Evidence about auditor-client management negotiation concerning client's financial reporting. *Journal of Accounting Research*, 39(3): 535–563.

Gilbertson, D.L. and Herron, T.L. (2009). PCAOB enforcements: a review of the first three years, *Current Issues in Auditing*, 3(2): A15–A34.

Glaser, B.G. and Strauss, A. (1967). *Discovery of Grounded Theory: Strategies for Qualitative Research*. Sociology Press.

Gold, A., Hunton, J.E. and Goman, M.I. (2009). The impact of client and auditor gender on auditors' judgments. *Accounting Horizons*, 23(1): 1–18.

Grajzl, P. and Murrell, P. (2007). Allocating lawmaking powers: self-regulation vs government regulation. *Journal of Comparative Economics*, 35(3): 520–545.

Guénin-Paracini, H. and Gendron, Y. (2010). Auditors as modern pharmakoi: legitimacy paradoxes and the production of economic order. *Critical Perspectives on Accounting*, 21(2): 134–158.

Gulliver, P.H. (1979). *Disputes and Negotiations: A Cross-Cultural Perspective*. New York: Academic Press.

Hampel Report (1998). *Committee on Corporate Governance — Final Report*. London: Gee and Co.

Hansen, C.D. and Kahnweiler, W.M. (1993). Storytelling: an instrument for understanding the dynamics of corporate relationships. *Human Relations*, 46(12): 1391–1409.

Hatfield, R.C., Agoglia, C.P. and Sanchez, M.H. (2008). Client characteristics and the negotiation tactics of auditors: implications for financial reporting. *Journal of Accounting Research*, 46(5): 1183–1207.

Hecimovic, A., Martinov-Bennie, N. and Roebuck, P. (2009). The force of law: Australian Auditing Standards and their impact on the auditing profession. *Australian Accounting Review*, 19(1): 1–10.

Hilary, G. and Lennox, C. (2005). The credibility of self-regulation: evidence from the accounting profession's peer review program. *Journal of Accounting and Economics*, 40(1–3): 211–229.

Hines, T., McBride, K., Fearnley, S. and Brandt, R. (2001). We're off to see the wizard: an evaluation of directors and auditors' experiences with the Financial Reporting Review Panel. *Accounting, Auditing and Accountability Journal*, 14(1): 53–84.

Hirshleifer, D. (2008). Psychological bias as a driver of financial regulation. *European Financial Management*, 14(5): 845–874.

HMSO (2005). *Companies Act 1985 (Operating and Financial Review and Directors' Report etc) Regulations 2005*, Statutory Instrument 2005/1011 (www.opsi.gov.uk/si/si2005/20051011.htm).

Humphrey, C. (2008). Auditing research: a review across the disciplinary divide. *Accounting, Auditing and Accountability Journal*, 21(2): 170–203.

Humphrey, C. Loft, A. and Woods, M. (2009). The global audit profession and the international financial architecture: understanding regulatory relationships at a time of financial crisis. *Accounting, Organizations and Society*, 34(6–7): 810–825.

IASB (2004). *International Accounting Standard 38, Intangible Assets*. London: IASB.

ICAEW (1997). *Financial Reporting of Risk: Proposals for a Statement of Business Risk*. London: Institute of Chartered Accountants in England and Wales.

ICAEW (2006a). *Effective Corporate Governance Frameworks*. London: Institute of Chartered Accountants in England and Wales.

ICAEW (2006b). *Emerging Issues: How Differences Between the US and UK Securities Markets Create Pressures and Point to Opportunities for International Policy, Investment, Business and Accounting*. London: Institute of Chartered Accountants in England and Wales.

ICAEW (2007). *EU Implementation of IFRS and the Fair Value Directive*. London: Institute of Chartered Accountants in England and Wales.

ICAEW (2009). *Developments in New Reporting Models*, Report. London: Institute of Chartered Accountants in England and Wales.

ICAS (1999). *Business Reporting: The Inevitable Change?*, Beattie, V. (ed.), Edinburgh: Institute of Chartered Accountants of Scotland.

ICAS (2006). *Principles Not Rules: A Question of Judgement*. Edinburgh: Institute of Chartered Accountants of Scotland.

ICAS (2010a). *Making Corporate Reports Readable — Time to Cut to the Chase*, Discussion Paper. Edinburgh: Institute of Chartered Accountants of Scotland.

ICAS (2010b). *The Provision of Non-audit Services by Audit Firms to their Listed Audit Clients*, Working Group Report. Edinburgh: Institute of Chartered Accountants of Scotland.

Isaac, W.M. (2009). *Testimony of William M. Issac, Chairman, The Secura Group of Lecg. Former Chairman, Federal Deposit Insurance Corporation before the Subcommittee on Capital Markets, Insurance and Government Sponsored Enterprises*. US House of Representatives Committee on Financial Services. 12 March 2009. (Available at http://www.finreg21.com/content/testimony-william-m-isaac-chairman-the-secura-group-of-lecg-former-chairman-federal-deposit-).

Jackson, A.B., Moldrich, M. and Roebuck, P. (2008). Mandatory audit firm rotation and audit quality. *Managerial Auditing Journal*, 23(5): 420–437.

Jenkins, D.S. and Velury, U. (2008). Does auditor tenure influence the reporting of conservative earnings? *Journal of Accounting and Public Policy*, 27(2): 115–132.

Jermakowicz, E. and Gornik-Tomaszewski, S. (2006). Implementing IFRS from the perspective of EU publicly traded companies. *Journal of International Accounting, Auditing and Taxation*, 15(2): 170–196.

Johnson, V., Khurana, I. and Reynolds, J.K. (2002). Audit firm tenure and the quality of financial reports. *Contemporary Accounting Research*, 19(4): 637–660.

Kelle, U. (2005). 'Emergence' vs. 'forcing' of empirical data? A crucial problem of 'grounded theory' reconsidered. *Forum: Qualitative Social Research*, 6(2). (Available at http://www.qualitative-research.net/index.php/fqs/article/view/467, accessed 7 September 2010).

Kinney, W.R. (2005). Twenty-five years of audit deregulation and re-regulation: what does it mean for 2005 and beyond? *Auditing: A Journal of Practice & Theory*, 24(Supplement): 89–109.

Kipnis, D. and Schmidt, S.M. (1983). An influence perspective on bargaining within organizations, ch. 17 in Bazerman, M.H. and Lewicki, R.J. (eds.), *Negotiating in Organizations*. Beverly Hills, CA: Sage Publications.

Kipnis, D., Schmidt, S.M. and Wilkinson, I. (1980). Intraorganizational influence tactics: exploration in getting one's way. *Journal of Applied Psychology*, 65(4): 440–452.

Kleinman, G. and Palmon, D. (2001). *Understanding Auditor-Client Relationships: A Multi-faceted Analysis*. Princeton: Markus Wiener Publishers.

Kolb, D.M. (2009). Gender and negotiation research over the past twenty-five years. *Negotiation Journal*, 25(4): 515–531.

Kolb, D.M. and Williams, J. (2000). *The Shadow Negotiation*. New York: Simon & Schuster.

KPMG (2006). *The Audit Committee Journey: A Global View*. London: KPMG.

Larcker, D.F., Richardson, S.A. and Tuna, I. (2007). Corporate governance and accounting outcomes. *The Accounting Review*, 83(4): 963–1008.

Leary, K. (2004). Critical moments in negotiation. *Negotiation Journal*, 20(2): 143–145.

LeBlanc, R. and Gillies, J. (2005). *Inside the Boardroom: How Boards Really Work and the Coming Revolution in Corporate Finance*. Mississauga, Ontario: John Wiley & Sons.

Lennox, C. (2009). The changing regulatory landscape, Editorial. *International Journal of Auditing*, 13(2): 79–85.

Lennox, C. and Pittman, J. (2010). Auditing the auditors: evidence on the recent reforms to the external monitoring of audit firms. *Journal of Accounting and Economics*, 49(1–2): 84–103.

Lev, B. (2001). *Intangibles: Management, Measurement and Reporting*. Brookings Institution Press.

Li, D. (2010). Does auditor tenure affect accounting conservatism? Further evidence. *Journal of Accounting and Public Policy*, 29(3): 226–241.

Lin, J.W. and Hwang, M.I. (2010). Audit quality, corporate governance, and earnings management: a meta-analysis. *International Journal of Auditing*, 14(1): 57–77.

Livne, G. and McNichols, M. (2009). An empirical investigation of the true and fair override in the United Kingdom. *Journal of Business Finance and Accounting*, 36(1&2): 1–30.

Mastenbroek, W. (1989). *Negotiate*. Oxford: Basil Blackwell.

McCracken, S., Salterio, S. and Gibbins, M. (2008). Auditor-client management relationships and roles in negotiating financial reporting. *Accounting, Organizations and Society*, 33(4–5): 362–383.

McCreevy, C. (2009). *The Credit Crisis — Looking Ahead*. Speech by Charlie McCreevy, European Commissioner for Internal Markets and Services. Institute of International and European Affairs. Dublin .9 February. (http://europa.eu/rapid/pressReleasesAction.do?reference=SPEECH/09/41&format=HTML&aged=0&language=EN&gui Language=en).

Menkel-Meadow, C. (2009). Chronicling the complexification of negotiation theory and practice. *Negotiation Journal*, 25(4): 415–429.

Millman, G. (2009). Execs Hail Mary Schapiro for Folding IFRS Roadmap. *Roadmap*. 26 January. (Available at http://www.ifrsreporter.com/index.php?option=com_content&view=article&id=52:-execs-hail-mary-schapiro-for-folding-ifrs-roadmap&catid=36:sec&Itemid=53, accessed 4 July 2010).

Myers, J.N., Myers, L.A., and Omer, T.C. (2003). Exploring the term of the auditor-client relationship and the quality of earnings: a case for mandatory auditor rotation? *The Accounting Review*, 78(3): 779–799.

Nelson, M.W. (2005). A review of experimental and archival conflicts-of-interest research in auditing. In Moore, D.A. Cain, D.M. Loewenstein, G. and Bazerman, M.H. (eds.), *Conflicts of Interest: Problems and Solutions in Law, Medicine, and Organizational Settings*. Cambridge: Cambridge University Press.

Nelson, M.W. (2009). A model and literature review of professional scepticism in auditing. *Auditing: A Journal of Practice & Theory*, 28(2): 1–34.

Nelson, M. and Tan, H.-T. (2005). Judgment and decision making research in auditing: a task, person, and interpersonal interaction perspective. *Auditing: A Journal of Practice and Theory*, 24(Supplement): 41–71.

Nobes, C. (2009). The importance of being fair: an analysis of IFRS regulation and practice — a comment, *Accounting and Business Research*, 39(4): 415–427.

O'Fallon, M.J. and Butterfield, K.D. (2005). A review of the empirical ethical decision-making literature: 1996–2003. *Journal of Business Ethics*, 59(4): 375–413.

Oxley, M.G. (2007). The Sarbanes-Oxley Act of 2002 — restoring investor confidence. *Current Issues in Auditing*, 1(1): C1–C2.

Page, M. and Whittington, G. (2007). The price of everything and the value of nothing. *Accountancy*, September, 140(1369): 92–93.

PCAOB (2004). *Standing Advisory Group Meeting: Potential Standard Communications and Relations with the Audit Committee*. Washington DC: Public Company Accounting Oversight Board.

Penman. S.H. (2007). Financial reporting quality: is fair value a plus or a minus? *Accounting and Business Research*, Special Issue: International Accounting Policy Forum, 37: 33–44.

Pentland, B.T. (1993). Getting comfortable with the numbers: auditing and the micro-production of macro-order. *Accounting, Organizations and Society*, 18(7/8): 605–620.

Pickering, J., Aisbitt, S., Gray, S.J. and Morris, R. (2007). Preparers' perceptions of the costs and benefits of IFRS adoption in Australia: 'Regulation gone mad'. Paper presented at the 19th Asian Pacific Conference on International Accounting Issues, Kuala Lumpur, Malaysia.

Plantin, G., Sapra, H. and Shin. H.S. (2005). Marking to market, liquidity and financial stability. *Montary and Economic Studies (Special Edition)*, October:133–164.

Pomeroy, B. (2010). Audit committee member investigation of significant accounting decisions. *Auditing: A Journal of Practice & Theory*, 29(1): 173–205.

Pomeroy, B. and Thornton, D.B. (2008). Meta-analysis and the accounting literature: the case of audit committee independence and financial reporting quality. *European Accounting Review*, 17(2): 305–330.

Power, M. (1999). *The Audit Society: Rituals of Verification*. Oxford: Oxford University Press.

Putnam, L.L. (2004). Transformations and critical moments in negotiations. *Negotiation Journal*, 20(2): 275–295.

PwC (2009). *IFRS Pocket Guide*. London: PwC.

Quick, R., Turley, S. and Willekens, M. (2007). *Auditing, Trust and Governance: Developing Regulation in Europe*. Oxford: Routledge.

Rennie, M.D., Kopp, L.S. and Lemon, W.M. (2010). Exploring trust and the auditor-client relationship: factors influencing the auditor's trust of a client representative. *Auditing: A Journal of Practice & Theory*, 29(1): 279–293.

Rest, J.R. (1986). *Moral Development: Advances in Research and Theory*. New York: Praeger.

Rose, J.M. (2007). Attention to evidence of aggressive financial reporting and intentional misstatement judgments: effects of experience and trust. *Behavioral Research in Accounting*, 19(1): 215–229.

RSA (1998). *Sooner, Sharper, Simpler: A Lean Vision of an Inclusive Annual Report*. London: Royal Society of Arts.

Sabia, M.J. and Goodfellow, J.L. (2005). *Integrity in the Spotlight: Audit Committees in a High Risk World*, 2nd edn. Toronto, Ontario: Canadian Institute of Chartered Accountants.

Sanchez, M.H., Agoglia, C.P. and Hatfield, R.C. (2007). The effect of auditors' use of a reciprocity-based strategy on auditor-client negotiations. *The Accounting Review*, 82(1): 241–263.

Sarbanes-Oxley Act (2002). (www.sarbanes-oxley.com).

Schipper, K. (2005). The introduction of International Accounting Standards in Europe: implications for international convergence. *European Accounting Review*, 14(1): 101–126.

Schneider, A., Church, B.K. and Ely, K.M. (2006). Non-audit services and auditor independence: a review of the literature. *Journal of Accounting Literature*, 25: 69–211.

SEC (2003). *Strengthening the Commission's Requirements Regarding Auditor Independence: Final Rules*, Release No. 33–8183. Washington, DC: Securities and Exchange Commission.

SEC (2007). *Acceptance from Foreign Issuers Financial Statements Prepared in Accordance with International Financial Reporting Standards Without Reconciliation to US GAAP*. RN 33–8879. 34 457 06. File no S7 13 07. (http://www.iasplus.com/usa/sec/0712reconciliationfinalrule.pdf).

SEC (2008). *Roadmap for the Potential Use of Financial Statements Prepared in Accordance with International Financial Reporting Standards from US Issuers*. Rl. 33–8982; 34–58960; File No. 57–27–08. (http:// www.sec/gov/news/rules/proposed/2008/33–8982.pdf/).

Smith Committee (2003). *Audit Committee Combined Code Guidance*. London: Financial Reporting Council.

Sunder, S. (2010). Adverse effects of uniform written reporting standards on accounting practice, education and research. *Journal of Accounting and Public Policy*, 29(2): 99–114.

Tomorrow's Company (2007). *The Future of Corporate Reporting*. London: Tomorrow's Company.

Trotman, K., Wright, A. and Wright, S. (2009). An examination of the effects of auditor rank on pre-negotiation judgments. *Auditing: A Journal of Practice & Theory*, 28(1): 191–203.

Turley, S. and Zaman, M. (2007). Audit committee effectiveness: processes and behavioural effects. *Accounting, Auditing and Accountability Journal*, 20(5): 765–768.

Turner, A. (2009). *The Financial Crisis and the Future of Financial Regulation*. Speech by Adair Turner, chairman, FSA. The Economist's Inaugural City Lecture. 21 January 2009. (www.fsa.gov.uk/pages/Library/Communications/Speeches/2009/0121_at.shtml).

UK Treasury Committee (2009). *Banking Crisis: Reforming Corporate Governance and Pay in the City*, House of Commons Treasury Select Committee, Ninth report of session 2008/09,

HC 519, The Stationery Office Ltd. (Available at http://www.publications.parliament.uk/pa/cm200809/cmselect/cmtreasy/519/519.pdf, accessed 28 June 2010).

United Nations Conference on Trade and Development (2008). *Review of the Practical Implementation Issues Relating to International Financial Reporting Standards; Case Study of the United Kingdom of Great Britain and Northern Ireland*. United Nations Conference on Trade and Development. TD/B/C. II/ISAR/48.

Van Buuren, J.P. (2009). *On the Nature of Auditing: The Audit Partner Effect*, PhD Thesis, Nyenrode Business Universiteit.

Van de Poel, K., Opijnen, M.V., Maijoor, S. & Vanstraelen, A. (2009). Public oversight and audit quality: evidence from public oversight of audit firms in the Netherlands. Working Paper.

Wade, R. (2007). A new global financial architecture? *New Left Review*, 46(July–August): 113–129.

Walker Report (2009). *A Review of Corporate Governance in UK Banks and Other Financial Industry Entities — Final Recommendations*. (Available at http://webarchive.nationalarchives.gov.uk/+/http://www.hm-treasury.gov.uk/d/walker_review_261109.pdf, accessed 21 June 2010).

Wang, K. and Tuttle, B. (2009). The impact of auditor rotation on auditor-client negotiation: the role of political costs and the market for audit. *Accounting, Organizations & Society*, 34(2): 222–243.

Watrin, C., Lindscheid, F. and Pott, C. (2009). The effect of audit engagement and review partner rotation on audit quality. Paper presented at the 5th EARNET Symposium, Valencia.

Which? (2010). (Available at http://commission.bnbb.org/banking/sites/all/themes/whichfobtheme/pdf/commission_report.pdf, accessed 28 June 2010).

Wyman, P. (2002). *Peter Wyman's speech on Corporate Governance at the OCAI / ICAEW Joint Conference*. 2 September 2002. (Available at http://www.icaew.com/index.cfm/route/107498/icaew_ga/en/Home/Press_and_policy/Peter_Wyman_s_Speech_on_Corporate_Governance_at_the_ICAI_ICAEW_Joint_Conference_-2_September_2002, accessed 1 September 2010).

Yin, R.K. (2008). *Case Study Research: Design and Methods*, 4th edn. Newbury Park, CA: Sage Publications.

Index

AADB *see* Accountancy and Actuarial Discipline Board
abnormal accruals 31–2
academic literature *see* relevant academic literature
accountabilities, corporate governance provisions 27–8
Accountancy and Actuarial Discipline Board (AADB) 13
Accountancy Foundation 13
   see also Financial Reporting Council
accounting qualifications 8, 44–5, 49–50, 59–67, 93–4,
   99–100, 145–51, 164–71, 173, 193, 213, 229,
   265–6, 272–7, 331–3
accounting and reporting commentary, Kestrel plc 101–2,
   286–7
accounting standards
   see also Financial Reporting Review Panel
   concepts 13, 15, 17, 307–319
Accounting Standards Board (ASB) 13, 15, 17
   see also FRS . . .
accruals, abnormal accruals 31–2
ACCs *see* audit committee chairs
acquisitions 8, 10, 16, 33–4, 46–50, 63, 65, 67, 99–127,
   160–2, 166–7, 169–70, 171, 173–92, 203–5, 210,
   211–12, 217, 222–7, 242, 244–5, 281–2, 286–9,
   292–7, 302–3, 307–10, 313–17, 326–35
   fair value accounting 46–50, 65, 102, 107–12, 122–7,
     160–2, 169–70, 171, 179–82, 190, 192, 203–5, 210,
     211–12, 222–7, 242, 244–5, 281–2, 292–7, 302–3
   identification of pre/post acquisition expenses 47–50,
     281–2
   impairment reviews 63, 112–15, 124–7, 160–2, 182–3,
     288–9, 313–17, 330–5
   valuation of acquisition intangibles 8, 10, 63, 65, 67,
     107–15, 122–7, 156–2, 169–70, 171, 179–82, 190,
     192, 203–5, 210, 211–12, 222–7, 242, 244–5,
     281–2, 286–9, 292–7, 302–3, 307–10, 313–17,
     326–35
adjustments
   financial statements 40–1, 48–50
   negotiations 33–41, 43–50
agency theory 27, 39
agendas 129–34, 148
aggressive accounting choices 19, 31–2, 41, 92, 94, 98,
   189
   see also earnings management
aggressive reporting style 59–67, 92, 94, 98, 189
AIU *see* Audit Inspection Unit

alternative accounting treatments 39
American Institute of Certified Public Accountants 17
amortization 109, 115, 119–24, 161–3, 181–4, 190–2,
   222–7
analysis of the interactions
   see also Cormorant plc, Finch plc, Kestrel plc, Mallard
     plc, Ostrich plc, Pochard plc, Raven plc, Sandpiper
     plc, Woodpecker plc
   concepts 55–67, 93–8, 122–7, 141–4, 277, 279–324
   cross-case analysis of interactions 55–7, 247–335
Andersen 3, 20
annual general meetings (AGMs) 195
annual reports 16–17, 72–3, 249–58, 267–9, 271–7
   see also financial reporting; financial statements;
     narrative reports
   ICAS Short Form Annual Report and Results 16
APB *see* Auditing Practices Board
appraisals, auditors 78
archival studies using public data, concepts 31–2
ASB *see* Accounting Standards Board
assertiveness, negotiation influences 29, 38, 311–12,
   314–16, 318–24, 329–35
assets 6, 8–9, 10, 17–18, 25, 33–4, 46–50, 63, 84–5,
   87–9, 100, 107–15, 124–7, 141, 144, 160–2, 182–4,
   190, 192, 219–21, 222–7, 286–9, 290–1, 292–3,
   298–7, 313–17, 330–5
   see also intangibles
   carrying values 84, 141
   write-downs 33–4, 82–5, 87–9, 161, 219–21, 224,
     286–7, 290–1, 298–9
associates 49–50
audit committee chairs (ACCs) 3, 5–10, 19, 24, 28, 31,
   39–40, 43–50, 53–67, 69–98, 99–107, 120, 249–69,
   271–7, 281–324, 325–35
   see also interactions, Cormorant plc, Finch plc, Kestrel
     plc, Mallard plc, Ostrich plc, Pochard plc, Raven
     plc, Sandpiper plc, Woodpecker plc
   appointment criteria 28, 78, 272–4
   attributes/procedures overview 59–67, 271–7,
     279–300
   auditing quality survey 24
   case studies' overview 53–67, 281–300
   critique 8–10, 39–40, 265–7, 269, 271–7, 322–4,
     332–5
   future research 334–3

audit committee chairs (ACCs) (*Continued*)
  key findings and conclusions 3, 6, 8–10, 44–50, 57–67,
    235, 249–69, 271–7, 281–324
  objectives/goals 8, 9, 19, 28, 35–40, 120, 265–7,
    271–7, 305–6, 308–9, 322–4, 325–5
  outcome determinants 313–24, 330–5
  powers 9, 265–7, 275–7, 304–7, 321–4, 325–35
  research background 6, 39–40, 44–50, 53–67, 271–7,
    318–24, 325–35
  revised grounded theory model 279, 284–324, 325–35
  roles/responsibilities 8, 19, 35–40, 120, 129–34,
    265–7, 271–7, 304–24, 325–35
  survey summary 43–50
  top ten issues 46–50, 281
  types 39–40
  views on regulatory framework 8–10, 55, 57, 60, 94–5,
    96–8, 122–7, 136–7, 142–4, 174–6, 192, 198–200,
    206–8, 233, 249–69, 272–3, 332–5
audit committees 3, 5–10, 23–8, 31–3, 38–50, 59–67,
  107, 120–1, 122–7, 129–34, 141–4, 146–51,
  164–71, 173–9, 188–92, 193–7, 207, 208–12,
  214–19, 224–7, 229–33, 236–9, 241–4, 265–9,
  271–7, 281–324, 325–35
see also interactions; internal controls; risk management,
  Cormorant plc, Finch plc, Kestrel plc, Mallard plc,
  Ostrich plc, Pochard plc, Raven plc, Sandpiper plc,
  Woodpecker plc
  attributes/procedures overview 59–67, 271–9, 279–300
  auditing quality 23–4, 31, 40–1, 133–4, 277
  case studies' overview 59–67, 281–300
  critique 8–10, 26–8, 38–9, 40–1, 49–50, 265–9, 271–7,
    332–5
  effectiveness assessments 39–40, 265–9, 323–4,
    334–5
  evolution 26–7
  financial reporting quality 40–1, 277
  future research 334–5
  ISA 260 *Communication of Audit Matters*... 4, 13
  key findings and conclusions 3, 6, 8–10, 44–50, 57–67,
    249–69, 271–7, 281–324, 325–35
  meetings 44–5, 59–67, 69–78, 93–5, 99–107, 122–7,
    129–34, 141–4, 146–51, 164–71, 173–9, 188–92,
    193–7, 208–12, 214–19, 224–7, 229–33, 236–9,
    241–2, 243–4, 271–7
  objectives/goals 8, 9, 26–8, 31, 35–41, 44–5, 49–50,
    120–1, 193–7, 207, 214–15, 265–9, 271–7, 308–9,
    321–4, 325–35
  outcome determinants 313–24, 330–5
  powers 9, 26–8, 33, 39, 265–9, 275–7, 304–7, 321–4,
    325–35
  processes 38–41, 61–7, 69–78, 99–107, 129–34,
    141–4, 145–51, 164–71, 173–9, 188–92, 193–7,
    208–12, 213–19, 224–7, 229–33, 236–9, 265–9
  reforms 26–8, 39, 44–5, 265–9
  relevant academic literature 6–7, 11–41, 275–7
  research background 4–6, 31–41, 44–50, 53–67,
    271–7, 318–24, 325–35
  revised grounded theory model 279, 284–324, 325–35
  roles/responsibilities 8, 26–8, 31, 32–3, 35–41, 120,
    129–34, 193–7, 207, 214–15, 265–9, 271–7, 308–9,
    321–4, 325–35
  structure 27–8, 39–40, 44–5, 49–50, 59–67, 69–78,
    93–5, 99–107, 122–7, 271–7, 305–7

survey statistics 44–50, 53, 59–67, 271–7
survey summary 43–50
types of members 39–40, 49–50, 265–9
UK system 26–8, 265–9
views of others on audit committees 265–9, 332–5
views on regulatory framework 8–10, 55, 57, 60, 94–5,
  96–8, 122–7, 136–7, 142–4, 174–6, 192, 198–200,
  206–8, 233, 249–69, 272–3, 332–5
audit engagement partners (AEPs) 3–10, 13–14, 21–3,
  24, 31–41, 43–50, 53–67, 69–98, 120, 150–1,
  164–71, 217–18, 233, 249–69, 272–3, 275–7,
  281–324, 325–35
see also auditors; interactions, Cormorant plc, Kestrel
  plc, Mallard plc, Sandpiper plc, Woodpecker plc
  appraisals 78
  case studies' overview 53–67, 281–300
  changes 4, 10, 13–14, 21, 24, 32–3, 58, 77–9, 82, 94,
    97–8, 150–1, 164–71, 217–18, 233, 272–1,
    284–307, 324
  'crusader' AEPs 22, 319, 322, 329, 331
  ease of agreement 9, 279, 282–300, 284–304, 305–24,
    329–35
  ES 3 rotation requirements 4, 10, 13–14, 107, 268,
    322–3, 332, 334
  key findings and conclusions 3, 6, 8–10, 44–50, 57–67,
    249–69, 275–7, 281–324, 325–35
  objectives/goals 8, 9, 35–40, 120, 305–7, 308–9, 324,
    325–35
  outcome determinants 313–24, 330–25
  powers 9, 275–7, 304–7, 321–4, 325–25
  research background 6, 31–41, 44–50, 53–67, 275–7,
    318–24, 325–35
  revised grounded theory model 279, 284–324, 325–35
  rotation requirements 4, 10, 13–14, 21, 24, 32–3, 58,
    107, 129, 132, 141, 143, 209, 217–18, 233, 259–60,
    268, 322–3, 332, 334
  sensitive issues 58
  survey summary 43–50
  tenders 61, 79, 82, 95, 150–1, 152–3, 164–6, 170–1,
    213, 217–18, 233, 284, 290–1
  top ten issues 46–50, 281
  types 21–3, 319, 322, 329
  views on regulatory framework 8–10, 55, 57, 60, 94–5,
    96–8, 122–7, 136–7, 142–4, 174–6, 192, 198–200,
    206–8, 233, 249–69
audit firm characteristics category, grounded theory
  model 34–40, 62–7, 284–307, 317–18, 327–35
Audit Inspection Unit (AIU) 3–4, 9, 10, 18–19, 25–6, 81,
  107, 258, 262–4, 268–9, 284–304, 311, 321,
  325–34
see also Professional Oversight Board
  auditing quality definition 18–19
  box-ticking procedures 10, 107, 263–4, 332, 334, 335
  critique 10, 25–6, 107, 262–4, 268–9, 284–304, 311,
    332–4
  key findings and conclusions 10, 258, 262–4, 268–9,
    284–304, 311, 325–34
  objectives/goals 3, 25–6, 304, 311, 325, 332
  relevant academic literature 25–6
  responsibilities 3, 25–6, 304, 311, 325, 332
  revised grounded theory model 284–304, 311
  views on regulatory framework 258, 262–4, 268–9,
    332

audit planning and scope 13, 59–67, 100–1, 132, 148, 195–6, 217, 230, 241, 243, 249, 260–2, 274–7, 305, 334
Audit Quality Framework, FRC 19
Auditing Practices Board (APB) 4, 5, 13–14, 21, 106, 258–60, 306, 310, 325
    see also Ethical Standards; International Standards on Auditing
    discussion paper in 2010 5
    objectives/goals 4, 13–14, 310, 325
auditing quality 5, 7, 10, 11, 18–24, 25–6, 31, 40–1, 133–4, 259–60, 267–9, 277, 312, 325–35
    see also Audit Inspection Unit
    audit committees 23–4, 31, 40–1, 133–4, 277
    critique 10, 40–1, 259–60, 267–9, 333–5
    definition 18–19
    gender factors 22–3
    individual partner effects 18, 21–3
    key findings and conclusions 10, 312, 325–35
    psychological factors 21–3, 40–1
    relevant academic literature 18–24, 40–1
    research background 18, 19, 23–4, 40–1
    surveys 23–4
    tenure issues 21
auditor–client relationships 6–7, 11–41, 59–67, 69–78, 93–8, 99–107, 122–7, 129–34, 141–4, 173–9, 188–92, 193–7, 208–12, 213–19, 224–7, 229–33, 236–9, 273–7, 322–4
    see also quality of . . .
    case studies' overview 59–65, 279–300, 326–33
    relevant academic literature 6–7, 11–41, 275–7, 322–4
auditors 3–10, 13–14, 21–3, 24, 31–41, 43–50, 53–67, 69–98, 120, 133–4, 150–1, 164–71, 217–18, 233, 249–69, 272–3, 275–7, 281–324, 325–35
    see also audit engagement partners
    appraisals 78
    changes 4, 10, 13–14, 21, 24, 32–3, 58, 77–9, 82, 94, 97–8, 133–4, 150–1, 164–71, 217–18, 233, 272–3
    critique 4–6
    engagement terms 13
    fees 20–1, 25–6, 31–2, 63, 69, 79–82, 94, 95, 97–8, 101–2, 135, 142–4, 152–3, 166, 170–1, 176, 189, 196, 216–19, 222, 230, 232, 241, 268, 275, 279–82, 284, 288–9, 290–1, 308, 313, 329, 334
    global financial crisis from 2008 4–6, 12, 15, 20–1, 28, 317–18, 335
    independence needs 13–14, 18–24, 120, 147–51, 164–71, 217–18, 260, 267
    integrity needs 13–14, 22, 305, 306–7, 322, 329
    key findings and conclusions 3, 6, 8–10, 44–50, 57–67, 249–69, 281–324, 325–35
    objectives/goals 5–6
    objectivity needs 13–14
    Registered Auditor Status 23
    relevant academic literature 6–7, 11–41, 275–7
    resignations 31
    types 21–3
audits
    case studies' overview 59–67, 279–300, 326–35
    critique 5–6, 258–66, 268–9
    findings 13
    grounded theory model 11, 34–41, 277, 279–324, 325–35

ISA 260 Communication of Audit Matters . . . 4, 13
    key findings and conclusions 3, 6, 8–10, 44–50, 57–67, 249–69, 271–7, 281–324, 325–35
    negotiations/interactions 7, 11, 30–41
    regulatory changes 3–10, 12–41, 43–50, 55, 133–4, 176, 249–69, 272–3, 284–324, 325–35
    research background 4–6, 18, 19, 23–4, 30–41, 44–50, 53–67, 271–7, 318–24, 325–35
    revised grounded theory model 279, 284–324, 327–35
    value added 152–3
    views on regulatory framework 258–66, 268–9
Australia 21, 23

balance sheets 64, 84, 107, 112–17, 125–7, 157–60, 179–92, 198
balanced scorecards 232
banks
    The Future of Banking Commission 5
    global financial crisis from 2008 4–6, 12, 15, 20–1, 28, 317–18, 335
bargaining
    see also negotiations
    concepts 29–41
Barnier, Michel 5
Beattie et al 5–6, 8–9, 12, 15, 20–4, 33–8, 43–4, 48–9, 55–67, 279, 281–2, 304, 310, 317–23, 326–31
Behind Closed Doors: What Company Audit is Really About (Beattie et al) 5–6, 8–9, 55–6
benchmarks, audit fees 81–2
best practice guidelines, concepts 12
biases, psychological aspects of regulation 12
Big Four professional firms 12, 19, 39, 44, 59–67, 69–98, 99, 106–7, 123, 145, 151, 165, 179, 180, 193–7, 208–12, 213, 226, 249–69
boards of directors 26–8, 39–40, 45, 69–78, 93–5, 99–107, 122–7, 130–4, 148–50, 156, 160, 166, 168, 195–6, 215–16, 266–7, 269, 271–7, 305–6, 330–5
    see also audit committees; directors . . . ; finance directors
    structures 26–7, 39–40, 45, 69–70, 99–107
    survey statistics 45
bonds 92–3, 116
bonuses 113, 308
box-ticking procedures 10, 107, 263–4, 331–40, 334, 335
brands 46–50
business combinations 8, 10, 16, 33–4, 49–50, 89–91, 107–12, 122–7, 160–2, 169–70, 171, 179–83, 190, 192, 222–7, 242, 244–5, 286–7, 292–3, 302–3, 307–9
    see also acquisitions; groups
business reviews 8, 17–18, 46–50, 63, 65, 67, 137–8, 143–4, 164, 170–1, 186–7, 191, 192, 235–6, 238–9, 244–5, 256, 268, 281–2, 290–1, 292–3, 294–5, 302–3, 302–3, 313, 316–17, 322–3, 326–35
    critique 256, 268, 313, 316–17, 322–3, 326, 332–5
    sensitive issues 256, 322–3, 330–5

Cadbury Report 27–8
Canada 23, 26–7, 33, 35, 39, 276–5, 322
capitalization of expenditure 16, 33–4, 69, 82–5, 95–6, 98, 135–6, 284–5, 290–1
capitalization of R&D costs 16
carrying values 84, 141

case studies 3–10, 39, 51–245, 279–324, 325–35
see also individual cases; interviews
    coding scheme 57–65
    cross-case analysis of interactions 55–7, 279–324, 327–35
    descriptive concepts 58–65
    grounded theory model 7, 55–67, 279–324, 325–35
    interactive concepts 58–67
    introduction 53–67
    labels 58–67
    overview 53–67, 279–300, 325–35
    preliminary analysis of context 59–67, 69–78, 93–5, 99–107, 122–7, 129–34, 145–51, 173–9, 188–92, 193–7, 208–11, 213–19, 224–7, 229–33, 236–9
    research background 6, 53–67, 325–35
    selection/approach criteria 7, 53–5
    sensitive issues 57–8
    within-case analysis 55–7, 60, 282–300
    writing-up the cases 54–5, 57–8
cash flow hedges, concepts 117, 138–40
cash flow statements 65, 135–6, 198–200, 208, 210, 211–12, 252–3, 296, 313, 316
cash flows from investing, concepts 198–200, 296
cash generating units (CGUs), concepts 84, 112, 141, 161
categories, grounded theory model 34–40, 58–67, 284–324, 326–35
CCAB 61–3, 94
Center for Audit Quality 23
CEOs *see* chief executive officers
CFOs *see* chief financial officers
CGAA *see* Co-ordinating Group on Audit and Accountancy Issues
chairman
    see also audit committee chairs
    concepts 28, 39–40
Chestnut 235–7
chief executive officers (CEOs)
    attendance at meetings 45, 59–67, 69–78, 93–5, 129–34, 141–4, 146–51, 164–71, 173–9, 188–92, 193–7, 208–12, 214–19, 224–7, 229–33, 236–9, 241–4, 243–4, 271–7, 309
    sign-offs 23
chief financial officers (CFOs) 3, 6, 9–10, 23–4, 31–41, 43–50, 53–67, 69–98, 99–107, 120, 122–7, 129–34, 141–4, 146–51, 164–71, 173–9, 188–92, 193–7, 208–12, 213–19, 224–7, 229–33, 236–9, 241–4, 243–4, 271–7, 281–324, 325–33
see also finance directors, Cormorant plc, Finch plc, Kestrel plc, Mallard plc, Ostrich plc, Pochard plc, Raven plc, Sandpiper plc, Woodpecker plc
    auditing quality survey 24
    case studies' overview 53–67, 281–300
    critique 8–10, 275–7, 328–35
    key findings and conclusions 8–10, 44–50, 57–67, 249–69, 275–7, 281–324, 325–35
    outcome determinants 313–24, 330–5
    powers 9, 275–7, 305–7, 321–4, 328–35
    relevant academic literature 31–41, 275–7
    research background 4–6, 31–41, 44–50, 53–67, 271–9, 318–24, 325–35
    sign-offs 23
    survey summary 43–50

top ten issues 45–50, 281
views on regulatory framework 8–10, 55, 57, 60, 94–5, 96–8, 122–7, 136–7, 142–4, 174–6, 192, 198–200, 206–8, 233, 249–69
classification in primary statements 59–67, 82–98, 107–27, 134–44, 151–71, 179–92, 197–212, 219–27, 233–9, 241–5, 279–82, 326–35
Co-ordinating Group on Audit and Accountancy Issues (CGAA) 3, 13
    see also Financial Reporting Council
coalitions, negotiation influences 29–30, 38, 312, 318–24, 329–35
coding scheme, case studies' overview 57–67
Combined Code for Corporate Governance 4, 13, 27–8, 44–5, 69, 94, 99–100, 105–6, 121, 123, 129–30, 147–8, 174, 193–4, 207, 211, 221–2, 229, 233, 272, 311, 327
    see also Corporate Governance Code
comfort factors, negotiations 34–41, 323–4, 329
comfort-seeker company buyer-type, grounded theory model 34–40, 307, 323–4, 329
community issues 18
Companies Act 1985 17
Companies Act 2005 89
Companies Act 2006 14, 18, 186, 235, 244
company buyer-type category, grounded theory model 34–40, 305–6, 307, 323–4, 328–35
company circumstances category, grounded theory model 34–40, 44–50, 59–67, 282–300, 284–307, 317–18, 327–35
company reporting styles 59–67, 72–8, 129–44, 173–9, 210, 284–7, 329–30
company secretaries 100–1, 123
company sizes, case studies' overview 59–67
competence requirements, auditing quality 18–24
complex transactions 61, 63, 135–6, 143–4, 234–5, 236, 238, 239, 281–2, 290–1, 300–1, 313, 316, 326–35
see also Mallard plc, Raven plc,
complexity concerns about IFRSs 4, 8–9, 16–17, 147–51, 174–9, 249–58, 267–9, 272–3, 276–7, 305–6, 307–10, 321–2, 326, 328–35
compliance factors 8–9, 13, 15–16, 59–67, 78–98, 99–127, 134–44, 147–71, 173–92, 193–212, 213–27, 229–39, 241–5, 254–8, 267–8, 279–324, 325–35
    case studies' overview 59–67, 279–300, 326–7
    critique 254–8, 267–8, 321–4
    definition 59
    ease of agreement 313–24, 329–35
    key findings and conclusions 8–9, 254–8, 279–324, 325–35
    outcome determinants 313–24, 326–35
'comply or explain' statements, corporate governance 27–8, 284, 327–8
conclusions 3, 6, 7, 8–10, 44–50, 57–67, 271–7, 279–324, 325–35
'conditional matrix', revised grounded theory model 284–304
conflicts of interest 31–2, 150–1
    see also non-audit services
consequences category, grounded theory model 35–40, 67, 282–300, 284–304, 312–13, 327–35

conservative reporting style 59–67, 129–44, 173–9, 210, 284–7
consolidations 89–91, 97, 98, 286–7
    see also groups
contextual factors 33–41, 58–67, 69–78, 93–8, 99–107, 122–7, 129–34, 141–4, 145–51, 164–71, 282–300, 284–324, 327–35
    case studies' overview 58–67, 282–300, 327–35
    grounded theory model 34–40, 58–67, 282–300, 284–324, 327–35
    outcome determinants 313–24, 330–3
contingencies 65, 153–4, 166–7, 170–1, 180, 200–2, 210, 211–12, 292–3, 296
contingent liabilities, Pochard plc 65, 200–2, 210, 211–12, 296
contracts, revenue recognition 63, 158–60, 169, 170–1, 292–3
control weaknesses, Pochard plc 65, 207, 211, 212, 296–7
convertibles 117
Cormorant plc 64–5, 173–92, 294–7, 305, 307, 308, 313–17, 322
    analysis of the interactions 65, 188–92, 294–5, 313–17
    business reviews 65, 186–7, 191, 192, 294–5, 313, 316–17, 322
    conclusions 192
    contextual factors 173–9, 188–92, 294–5, 307, 308, 313–17
    corporate governance 65, 173–9, 188–92
    deferred tax assets resulting from Eagle losses 65, 184, 191, 192, 294–5
    identification/valuation of acquisition intangibles 65, 179–82, 190, 192, 294–5, 313–17
    impairment of goodwill on acquisition of Eagle 65, 182–4, 190, 192, 294–5, 308, 313–17
    interactions 179–92, 294–5, 313–17
    meetings 62, 173–9, 188–92
    misreporting in Eagle 65, 187–8, 191, 192, 296–7
    overview 62, 173, 188–92, 294–5
    provisions on inventories 65, 185–6, 191, 192, 294–5
    quality of the relationships 173–9, 188–92, 294–5, 305, 313–17
corporate governance 3–10, 11, 13–41, 44–5, 55, 59–67, 69–78, 94–5, 97–8, 133–4, 176, 264–9, 272–3, 279–82, 284–324, 325–35
    see also audit committee . . . , Cormorant plc, Finch plc, Kestrel plc, Mallard plc, Ostrich plc, Pochard plc, Raven plc, Sandpiper plc, Woodpecker plc
    case studies' overview 59–67, 279–82
    'comply or explain' statements 27–8, 284, 327–8
    directors' responsibilities 266–7, 269
    provisions 27–8
    regulatory changes 3–10, 13–41, 44–5, 55, 133–4, 176, 264–9, 272–3, 325–35
    relevant academic literature 7, 11, 26–8, 40–1
    revised grounded theory model 284–324, 327–35
    views on regulatory framework 264–9, 332
Corporate Governance Code 4, 13, 27–8, 44–5, 69, 94, 99–100, 105–6, 121, 123, 129–30, 145–8, 174, 193–4, 207, 211, 221–2, 229, 233, 272, 311, 327
    see also Combined Code for Corporate Governance
    concepts 4, 13, 27–8
    FRC 27–8, 284–304
credit crunch see global financial crisis from 2008

credit rating agencies 5
critical moment, negotiation concepts 30
cross-case analysis of interactions 55–7, 247–335
    grounded theory model 55–7, 279–324, 327–35
    summary 282–300
'crusader' AEPs 22, 319, 322, 329, 331
cultural issues 30, 94, 328–35
customer lists 46–50, 109–11, 122–4
customers, segmentation strategies 16, 46–50, 63, 85–7, 162–4, 170–1, 292–3

de-regulation trends, US 12–13
decisions see key financial reporting decisions
deferred consideration, notional interest 63, 153–4, 166–7, 170–1, 292–3, 313–17
deferred tax assets/liabilities 46–50, 63, 163–4, 184, 191, 192, 294–5
defined benefit pension schemes 91–93, 97, 98, 286–7
    see also pension . . .
Deloitte/American Accounting Association Wildman Medal 5
derivatives 6, 16, 143–4
    see also forward contracts
descriptive concepts, case studies' overview 58–67
dilution 155, 168
directors
    see also finance directors
    remuneration 27–8, 46–50, 70, 113–15, 156–8, 168–9, 244, 281–2, 302–3, 307–8, 313–17, 326–35
    responsibilities 266–7, 269
directors' reports
    see also finance directors
    concepts 17–18, 24–5
disaster recovery plans, IT systems 65, 207, 211, 212
disclosures 8, 17–18, 33–4, 46–50, 59–67, 69, 86, 96, 98, 112–27, 137–8, 143–4, 156–7, 163–71, 179–92, 197–212, 235–9, 244–5, 249–69, 279–82, 290–1, 292–3, 294–5, 302–3, 302–3, 313, 316–17, 322–3, 326–35
    case studies' overview 59–67
    complexity issues 4, 8–9, 16–17, 147–51, 174–9, 249–58, 267–9, 272–3, 276–7, 305–6, 307–10, 321–2, 326, 328–35
    top ten changes 48–50, 281
    views on regulatory framework 249–69
discontinued operations 16
discounts, time value of money 153, 161, 167, 183
discussions 43–50, 54–67, 78–98, 107–27, 134–44, 151–71, 179–92, 197–212, 219–27, 233–9, 241–5, 274–7, 279–82, 326–35
    see also interactions
    case studies' overview 54–67, 279–300, 326–35
    definition 43–4
    survey summary 43–50
disposals of assets 119–20, 288–9
distributable reserves, concepts 89–91, 286–7
dividends, subsidiaries 63, 89–91, 97, 98, 286–7
due diligence 203–5

Eagle 173–92
earnings management 15, 19, 40–1, 46–50
    see also aggressive accounting choices
earnings misstatements 40–1

earnings per share (EPS)
  concepts 63, 154–5, 167, 170–1, 292–3
  definition 154
ease of agreement
  compliance factors 313–24, 329–35
  key findings and conclusions 9, 279, 282–300,
    284–304, 305–24, 325–35
  outcome determinants 313–24, 326–35
EBITDA 252
EBRs see enhanced business reviews
EC 20, 36, 46
EFRAG see European Financial Reporting Advisory
    Group
enforcement regimes 7, 9–10, 11, 12, 24–6, 256–8,
    268–9, 284–324, 325–35
  see also Audit Inspection Unit; Financial Reporting
    Review Panel
  critique 10, 12, 256–8, 268–9, 321–4, 331–5
  key findings and conclusions 9–10, 256–8, 268–9,
    284–324, 325–35
  relevant academic literature 7, 11, 24–6, 321–4
  revised grounded theory model 284–324, 327–35
engagement terms, auditors 13
enhanced business reviews (EBRs) 8, 17–18, 48–50, 63,
    65, 67, 137–8, 143–4, 164, 170–1, 186–7, 191, 192,
    235–6, 238–9, 244–5, 256, 268, 281–2, 290–1,
    292–3, 294–5, 302–3, 313, 316–17, 326–35
  critique 256, 268, 316–17, 326–35
  sensitive issues 256, 322–3
  views on regulatory framework 256, 268, 332–5
Enron 3–4, 9, 12–13, 16, 20, 21–3, 79–80, 254–5, 265,
    325
environmental issues 18
EPS see earnings per share
ES see Ethical Standards
ethical standards 4, 10, 13–14, 20–1, 30, 57, 166,
    258–60, 268–9, 284–304, 305–7, 322–4, 325–35
  critique 10, 258–60, 268–9, 322–4, 332–5
  gender factors 30
  key findings and conclusions 10, 258–60, 268–9,
    284–304, 305–7, 322–4, 325–35
  negotiations 30
  psychological factors 22–3
  relevant academic literature 13–14, 322–4
  views on regulatory framework 258–60, 268–9, 332,
    334
Ethical Standards (ES) 4, 13–14, 20–1, 166, 258–60,
    268–9, 284–304, 305–7, 322–4, 325–35
  ES 3 rotation requirements 4, 10, 13–14, 107, 259,
    268, 322–3, 332, 334
  ES 5 Non-audit Services Provided to Audited Entities
    4, 10, 14, 20–1, 106, 260, 268, 322, 332, 334
  objectives/goals 4
ethnicity, case studies 57
European Financial Reporting Advisory Group (EFRAG)
    11, 16
European Union (EU) 4, 5–6, 11, 13, 14, 18, 36, 200–1,
    334, 335
  see also International Accounting Standards Board
  8th Statutory Audit Directive 14
  Accounts Modernization Directive 17
  green paper on the role of auditors 5
  SOX 13

events category, grounded theory model 35–40, 67,
    282–300, 284–304, 311–12, 326–35
evidential base, key findings and conclusions 325–6,
    335
exceptional items 46–50, 119–20, 288–9
executive directors 26–8, 49–50, 59–67, 70–78, 93–5,
    146–51, 164–71, 266, 271–9
  see also directors
experimental studies, negotiations 32–3, 335
expert advisers 38–9, 324
external national climate, grounded theory model 34–40

fair value accounting 4, 15, 25, 46–50, 65, 84, 91, 102,
    107–12, 117–18, 122–7, 138–40, 156–62, 169–70,
    171, 179–82, 190, 192, 200, 203–5, 210, 211–12,
    222–7, 242, 244–5, 252–6, 267–8, 281–2, 288–9,
    290–1, 292–303
  see also International Financial Reporting Standards;
    mark-to-market principles
  acquisitions 46–50, 63, 65, 102, 107–12, 122–7,
    160–2, 169–70, 171, 179–82, 190, 192, 203–5, 210,
    211–12, 222–7, 242, 244–5, 281–2, 292–7, 302–3
  critique 15, 46–50, 252–6, 267–8
  leases 63, 203–5, 210, 211–12
  share-based payments 156–7, 168, 244, 307–8
fair value hedges, concepts 117, 138–40
FASB see Financial Accounting Standards Board
fees, audits 20–1, 25–6, 31–2, 63, 69, 79–82, 94, 95,
    97–8, 101–2, 135, 142–4, 152–3, 166, 170–1, 176,
    189, 196, 216–19, 222, 230, 232, 241, 268, 275,
    279–82, 284, 288–9, 290–1, 308, 313, 329, 334
fictitious invoices 121–2, 288–9
finance directors 3–10, 23–5, 69–98, 99–107, 266–7,
    269, 325–35
  see also chief financial officers, Cormorant plc, Finch
    plc, Kestrel plc, Mallard plc, Ostrich plc, Pochard
    plc, Raven plc, Sandpiper plc, Woodpecker plc
  key findings and conclusions 3, 6, 8–10, 44–50, 57–67,
    249–69, 281–324, 325–35
  objectives/goals 8, 120
  outcome determinants 313–34, 330–5
  relevant academic literature 6–7, 11–41, 275–7
  research background 4–6, 44–50, 53–67, 271–7,
    318–24, 325–35
  revised grounded theory model 279, 284–324, 327–35
  views on regulatory framework 8–10, 55, 57, 63, 94–5,
    96–8, 122–7, 136–7, 142–4, 174–6, 192, 198–200,
    206–8, 233, 249–69
Financial Accounting Standards Board (FASB)
  see also US GAAP
  concepts 4, 16
  IASB convergence 4, 14–15, 16–17, 255–6, 267–8,
    273
financial crisis from 2008 see global financial crisis from
    2008
financial instruments 6, 16, 46–50, 63, 115–18, 125–7,
    138–40, 143–4, 288–91, 313–17
financial reporting
  case studies' overview 59–67, 279–300
  key findings and conclusions 8–10, 44–50, 57–67,
    249–58, 267–9, 271–7, 281–324, 325–35
  quality issues 6, 10, 11, 15, 24–5, 40–1, 277, 284–304,
    312, 327–35

regulatory changes 3–10, 12–41, 43–50, 55, 133–4, 176, 249–69, 272–3, 281–2, 284–324, 325–35
views on regulatory framework 249–58, 263–4, 267–9, 272–3, 276–7, 305–6, 307–10, 317, 321–2, 331–5
Financial Reporting Council (FRC) 3, 5, 13, 16–19, 198, 267, 284–304, 325
see also Audit Inspection Unit; Auditing Practices Board; Corporate Governance Code; Professional Oversight Board
Audit Quality Framework 19
auditing quality definition 18–19
consultation paper on reducing complexity 16–17
creation 13
discussion paper of June 2010 5
objectives/goals 3, 13, 284, 325
financial reporting decisions *see* key financial reporting decisions
financial reporting outcomes of interactions 3, 6, 8–10, 11, 15, 19, 24–5, 31–41, 59–67, 277, 279–324, 325–35
case studies' overview 59–67, 279–300, 313–17, 325–35
ease of agreement 9, 279, 282–300, 284–304, 305–24
key findings and conclusions 8–10, 279–324, 325–35
policy implications 333–4
quality issues 6, 10, 11, 15, 19, 24–5, 40–1, 277, 284–304, 312, 327–35
Financial Reporting Review Panel (FRRP) 4, 9, 10, 13, 23–5, 36, 47, 57, 117, 125, 199, 206, 208, 256–8, 263–4, 268–9, 284–304, 307, 310–11, 325–32
see also accounting standards
creation 24, 325
critique 10, 24–5, 117, 256–8, 263–4, 268–9, 284–304, 310–11, 332
key findings and conclusions 10, 256–8, 268–9, 284–304, 307, 310–11, 325–32
objectives/goals 4, 24–5, 256–8, 304, 310–11, 325, 332
referrals 23, 307, 310–11
relevant academic literature 24–5
revised grounded theory model 284–304, 307, 310–11, 327–32
views on regulatory framework 256–8, 263–4, 268–9, 332
Financial Services Authority (FSA)
concepts 5, 19, 24, 25–6, 27–8
discussion paper of June 2010 5
financial statements 3–10, 23–6, 40–1, 43–50, 65, 72–3, 86–7, 145, 154–8, 163–6, 169–70, 198–200, 205, 208, 210, 211–12, 271–7, 290–1, 296–7, 313, 314, 316
see also balance sheets; cash flow . . . ; P&L
CEO/CFO sign-offs 23
formats 86, 119, 198–200, 296
presentation issues 46–50, 65, 86, 198–200, 205, 208, 210, 211–12, 296, 313, 316
restatements 40–1, 48–50, 145, 154–8, 163–6, 169–70, 290–1, 314
views on regulatory framework 249–69
Finch plc 61–2, 145–71, 290–5, 308, 313–15, 322
analysis of the interactions 62–3, 164–71, 290–2, 313–17
audit fees following a tender 63, 152–3, 166, 170–1, 290–1

business reviews 63, 164, 170–1, 294–5, 313, 316–17, 322
conclusions 170–1
contextual factors 63, 145–51, 164–71, 290–2, 308, 313–17
corporate governance 63, 145–51, 164–71
earnings per share 63, 154–5, 167, 170–1, 292–3
interactions 63, 151–71, 290–2, 313–17
meetings 63, 146–51, 164–71
notional interest on unwinding deferred consideration 63, 153–4, 166–7, 170–1, 292–3, 313–17
overview 63, 145, 164–71, 290–2
quality of the relationships 63, 145–51, 164–71, 290–2, 308, 313–17
revenue recognition and provisioning on contracts 63, 158–60, 169, 170–1, 292–3
segmental reporting 63, 162–4, 170–1, 294–5, 313, 316–17
share-based payments 63, 155–8, 168–9, 170–1, 292–3, 313–17
tax credits on exercise of share options 63, 157–8, 168–9, 170–1, 292–3, 313–17
valuation of acquisition intangibles 63, 160–2, 169–70, 171, 292–3
Fledgling stock market index 44
forward contracts, concepts 143–4
fraud risks 63, 71–2, 121–2, 126–7, 267, 288–9, 298–9
FRC *see* Financial Reporting Council
FRRP *see* Financial Reporting Review Panel
FRS 5 *Reporting the Substance of Transactions* 14–15
FSA *see* Financial Services Authority
FTSE
100 40, 44, 249, 266
250 44, 129
Small-Cap 44, 145, 173, 213, 225
fundamental accounting principles 59–67, 140, 141, 144, 279–82
The Future of Banking Commission 5
future research 334–5

game theory 30, 32–3
gender factors
auditing quality 22–3
case studies 57
ethical standards 30
Germany 21
global financial crisis from 2008 4–6, 12, 15, 20–1, 28, 317–18, 335
global regulatory climate, grounded theory model 34–40, 321, 327–35
going concerns 25, 59–67, 91, 130, 140, 141, 144, 290–1
goodwill 25, 46–50, 62, 107–27, 160–2, 179–92, 242, 281–2, 292–3, 302–3, 317
see also intangibles
grounded theory model 7, 11, 34–41, 53–67, 277, 279–324, 325–35
broad approach 55–7, 282–300
case studies' overview 7, 55–67, 279–300
categories 34–40, 58–67, 284–324, 326–35
'conditional matrix' 284–304
cross-case analysis of interactions 55–7, 279–324, 327–35
definition 34, 55–6, 284–324

grounded theory model (*Continued*)
    revised model 279, 284–324
    testing/modifying grounded theory 55–7, 279–324
    within-case analysis 55–7, 60, 282–300
groups 89–91, 97, 98, 99–127, 286–7
    see also business combinations
grudger company buyer-type, grounded theory model
    34–40, 307, 323–4

Hampel Report 27
Health and Safety regulations 261
hedge accounting 61, 117–18, 125–7, 138–40, 143–4,
    288–9, 290–1, 313–17
hedge funds 5, 16, 125–7
hedging 63, 117–18, 125–7, 138–40, 143–4, 288–9,
    290–1, 313–17
heuristics 12
higher authorities, negotiation influences 29–30, 38, 312,
    318–24, 329–35

IAASB *see* International Auditing and Assurance
    Standards Board
IASB *see* International Accounting Standards Board
ICAEW 16, 17–18, 27, 46, 48, 55, 276
ICAS
    non-audit services 21
    Short Form Annual Report and Results 16
identification of pre/post acquisition expenses 47–50,
    281–2
IFAC 11, 14
IFIAR *see* International Forum of Independent Audit
    Regulators
IFRSs *see* International Financial Reporting Standards
impairment of assets 63, 65, 84–5, 100, 110, 112–15,
    124–7, 141, 144, 160–2, 182–4, 190, 192, 220–1,
    222–7, 288–9, 290–1, 292–5, 313–17, 330–35
impairment reviews, Kestrel plc 63, 112–15, 124–7,
    160–2, 182–3, 288–9
independence needs, auditors 13–14, 18–24, 120,
    147–51, 164–71, 217–18, 260, 267
indexed bonds 92–3
individual partner effects, auditing quality 18, 21–3
inflation rates 92–3
ingratiation, negotiation influences 29–30, 38, 312,
    318–19, 329–35
institution theory 24–5, 39
institutional shareholders, corporate governance
    provisions 27–8
intangibles 6–10, 17–18, 25, 46–50, 63, 65, 67, 107–15,
    122–7, 160–4, 169–70, 171, 179–82, 190, 192,
    203–5, 210, 211–12, 222–7, 242, 244–5, 252,
    281–2, 286–9, 292–9, 302–3, 307–10, 313–17,
    326–35
    see also goodwill
    critique 8, 10, 334–5
    definitions 107–9, 160, 179–80
    impairment reviews 63, 112–15, 124–7, 160–2, 182–3,
        288–9, 313–17
    key findings and conclusions 8, 10, 46–50, 281–2, 334
    valuation of acquisition intangibles 8, 10, 63, 65,
        107–15, 122–7, 160–4, 169–70, 171, 179–82, 190,
        192, 203–5, 210, 211–12, 222–7, 242, 244–5,
        281–2, 286–9, 292–9, 302–3, 307–10, 313–17,
        326–35

integrity needs, auditors 13–14, 22, 305, 306–7, 322, 329
interactions
see also discussions; negotiations; outcome . . . ,
    Cormorant plc, Finch plc, Kestrel plc, Mallard plc,
    Ostrich plc, Pochard plc, Raven plc, Sandpiper plc,
    Woodpecker plc
    analysis of the interactions 55–67, 93–8, 122–7,
        141–4, 277, 279–324
    audit settings 30–41
    case studies' overview 54–67, 279–300, 326–35
    comfort factors 34–41, 307, 323–4, 329
    concepts 3–10, 28–41, 54–67, 271–7, 279–324,
        326–35
    critique 8–9, 28–41, 271–7, 326–35
    cross-case analysis of interactions 55–7, 249–335
    ease of agreement 9, 279, 282–300, 284–304, 305–24,
        329–35
    experimental studies 32–3, 335
    future research 334–1
    grounded theory model 11, 34–41, 277, 279–324,
        325–35
    interview studies 34–41, 279–324
    issue types 59–65, 279–324, 326–5
    key findings and conclusions 3, 6, 8–10, 44–50, 57–67,
        271–7, 279–324, 325–35
    outcome determinants 313–24, 326–35
    policy implications 333–5
    quality concerns 333–5
    questionnaire surveys 3–10, 31, 33–4, 43–50, 53–5,
        326–35
    relevant academic literature 28–41, 56, 275–7, 317–24
    revised grounded theory model 279, 284–324, 327–35
    survey summary 45–50, 281
    top ten issues 45–50, 281
    types 59–65, 279–324, 326–35
interactive concepts, case studies' overview 58–67
interim statements 176
internal audits 20, 45, 132, 142, 193–4, 230–1, 275
internal controls 23–4, 65, 69–78, 121–2, 193–7, 207,
    211–12, 221–7, 288–9, 296–7, 298–9
    see also audit committees
International Accounting Standards Board (IASB) 4,
    14–18, 115, 254–6, 284, 309–10, 334
    see also International Financial Reporting Standards
    FASB convergence 4, 14–15, 16, 255–6, 267–8, 273
    IAS 1 *Presentation of Financial Statements* 86, 119,
        126–7, 140, 205
    IAS 2 *Inventories* 87, 185, 200, 220
    IAS 7 *Cash Flow Statements* 198, 208
    IAS 11 *Construction Contacts* 158
    IAS 12 *Income Taxes* 157, 184
    IAS 14 *Segment Reporting* 48, 162, 206, 245
    IAS 16 *Plant, Property and Equipment* 83
    IAS 17 *Leases* 204
    IAS 18 *Revenue* 158, 187
    IAS 19 *Employee Benefits* 91
    IAS 32 *Financial Instruments: Disclosure and
        Presentation* 116
    IAS 33 *Earnings per Share* 154, 167
    IAS 36 *Impairment of Assets* 84, 112–15, 141, 161,
        183, 222
    IAS 37 *Provisions and Contingencies* 153, 167, 201
    IAS 38 *Intangible Assets* 107, 109, 160, 179–80, 242

IAS 39 *Financial Instruments: Recognition and Measurement* 115–16, 117–18, 125–7, 138–40, 143–4, 290–1
recommendations 334
International Auditing and Assurance Standards Board (IAASB) 4, 13, 284, 309–10
see also International Standards on Auditing
'clarity project' 13
International Financial Reporting Standards (IFRSs) 4, 7, 8–10, 11, 14–18, 22, 46, 47–8, 50, 63, 65, 74–6, 94–5, 96–8, 107–9, 115–16, 120, 122–7, 136–7, 142–4, 147–51, 166–71, 174–93, 198–200, 206–8, 210, 211–12, 236–9, 249–58, 267–7, 281–2, 284–307, 318–24
cash flow statements 65, 198–200, 208, 210, 211–12, 252–3, 296
complexity concerns 4, 8–9, 16–17, 147–51, 174–9, 249–58, 267–9, 272–3, 276–7, 305–6, 307–10, 321–3, 326, 328–35
critique 4, 8–10, 14–18, 63, 74–6, 94–5, 96–8, 107–9, 122–7, 136–7, 142–4, 147–51, 174–9, 192, 198–200, 206–8, 236–9, 249–69, 272–3, 276–7, 305–24, 331–35
fair value accounting 4, 15, 252–6, 267–8
IFRS 2 *Share-based Payment* 156–7, 168–9, 244, 307–8
IFRS 3 *Business Combinations* 46, 107–9, 122–5, 160–1, 169–70, 173, 179–84, 190, 203, 222–3, 226, 242, 307–9
IFRS 8 *Segment Reporting* 48, 162, 170, 206–7, 245
key findings and conclusions 8–10, 249–69, 284–324, 325–35
'present fairly' requirement 14–15
recommendations 333–5
relevant academic literature 7, 11, 14–18
revised grounded theory model 284–324, 327–35
subjectivity concerns 253–6
US GAAP convergence 4, 14–15, 74–5, 255–6, 267–8, 273
views on regulatory framework 249–58, 267–9, 272–3, 276–7, 305–6, 307–10, 317, 321–2, 331–35
International Forum of Independent Audit Regulators (IFIAR) 11
International Standards on Auditing (ISAs) 4, 10, 13, 24, 260–2, 268–9, 274, 284–304, 309–10, 325–35
critique 10, 260–2, 268–9, 309–10, 335
ISA 260 *Communication of Audit Matters with those Charged with Governance* 4
key findings and conclusions 10, 260–2, 268–9, 284–304, 309–10, 325–35
objectives/goals 4, 13, 325
relevant academic literature 13
views on regulatory framework 260–2, 268–9, 335
interviews 7, 8–10, 34–41, 44–50, 53–67, 94–5, 96–8, 122–7, 136–7, 142–4, 174–6, 192, 193, 198–200, 206–8, 233, 249–69, 272–3, 279–324, 325–35
see also case studies
concepts 7, 8–10, 34–41, 53–67, 193, 249–69, 279–324, 325–35
key findings and conclusions 8–10, 44–50, 57–67, 249–69, 318–24, 325–35
laddering technique 55
negotiations/interactions 7, 34–41, 53–67

prompts 55
research background 5–6, 7, 31, 34–41, 53–67, 279–324, 325–35
techniques 55
views on regulatory framework 8–10, 55, 57, 63, 94–5, 96–8, 122–7, 136–7, 142–4, 174–6, 192, 198–200, 206–8, 233, 249–69, 272–3
introduction and background to the book 3–10
inventories 6, 8, 47–50, 63, 65, 87–9, 96–7, 98, 185–6, 191, 192, 200, 210, 211–12, 219–21, 224, 226–7, 281–2, 286–7, 294–5, 296, 298–9, 326–335
critique 8, 87–9, 96–7, 98
key findings and conclusions 8, 281–2, 326–35
non-compliant stock provisions 87–9, 96–7, 98, 286–7
provisions 65, 185–6, 191, 192, 294–5, 313, 316–17, 326–35
valuations 63, 65, 87–9, 96–7, 98, 185–6, 191, 192, 200, 210, 211–12, 219–21, 224, 226–7, 281–2, 294–5, 296, 298–9, 313, 317, 326–35
ISAs *see* International Standards on Auditing
issue category, grounded theory model 35–40, 279–300, 328–35
IT systems 20, 65, 69, 82–5, 95–6, 98, 152, 207, 211, 212, 284–5, 313, 316

Jenkins Report 17
joint decisions
see also negotiations
concepts 29–41
joint ventures 49–50
judgements 8–9, 15–16, 44–50, 59–67, 78–98, 107–27, 134–44, 151–71, 179–92, 198–212, 219–27, 236–9, 241–5, 254–8, 267–8, 279–324, 325–35
case studies' overview 59–67, 279–300, 313–17, 326–35
definition 59, 60, 282
ease of agreement 9, 279, 282–300, 284–304, 305–24, 329–35
future research 333
outcome determinants 313–24, 326–35

Kestrel plc 62–3, 99–127, 286–9, 305, 313–17
accounting and reporting commentary 101–2, 286–9
analysis of the interactions 63, 122–7, 286–9, 313–17
conclusions 126–7
contextual factors 63, 99–107, 122–7, 286–9, 313–17
corporate governance 63, 99–107, 122–7
financial instruments 63, 115–18, 125–7, 288–9, 313–17
fraud and illegal acts 63, 121–2, 126–7, 288–9, 298–9
hedging 63, 117–18, 125–7, 288–9
impairment reviews 63, 112–15, 124–7, 288–9
interactions 63, 107–27
meetings 63, 99–107, 122–7
overview 63, 99, 122–5, 286–9
preference shares 63, 115–17, 125–7, 288–9, 313–17
quality of the relationships 99–107, 122–7, 286–9, 305, 313–17
restructuring costs 63, 119–20, 126–7, 288–9, 313, 316–17
valuation of acquisition intangibles 63, 107–15, 122–7, 286–7

key financial reporting decisions
  compliance factors 8–9, 13, 15–16, 59–67, 279–300
  concepts 3–10, 28–41, 55, 279–300
  judgements 8–9, 15–16, 44–50, 59–67, 78–98, 107–27,
    134–44, 151–71, 179–92, 198–212, 219–27, 236–9,
    241–5, 254–8, 267–8, 279–324, 326–35
key findings and conclusions 3, 6, 7, 8–10, 44–50, 57–67,
    271–7, 279–324, 325–35
  concepts 3, 6, 7, 8–10, 44–50, 57–67, 279–324, 325–35
  evidential base 325–6, 335
key performance indicators (KPIs) 137–8, 143, 235–6,
    238, 244–4, 256
  see also non-financial performance indicators

labels, case studies' overview 58–67
laddering technique, interviews 55
leases, fair value on acquisition 65, 203–5, 210, 211–12,
    296–7
legal disputes 20
liabilities/provisions 46–50, 253–4
life expectancies, pension schemes 91–93, 97, 98, 286–7
loss recognition 15

Machiavellianism personality trait 30
Mallard plc 62–3, 129–44, 288–91, 313–17, 322
  analysis of the interactions 63, 141–4, 288–91, 313–17
  audit fees 63, 135, 142–4, 288–9
  business reviews 63, 137–8, 143–4, 290–1, 313,
    316–17, 322
  complex transactions 63, 135–6, 143–4, 290–1, 313,
    316
  conclusions 144
  contextual factors 129–34, 141–4, 288–91, 313–17
  corporate governance 63, 129–34, 141–4
  financial instruments 63, 138–40, 143–4, 290–1,
    313–17
  going concern 63, 130, 140, 141, 144, 290–1
  hedging 63, 138–40, 143–4, 290–1, 313–17
  impairment of assets 63, 141, 144, 290–1, 313–17
  interactions 63, 134–44, 288–1, 313–17
  meetings 63, 129–34, 141–4
  overview 63, 129, 141–4, 288–91
  quality of the relationships 129–34, 141–4, 288–91,
    313–17
mark-to-market principles
  see also fair value accounting
  concepts 4, 15, 253–6
market-based UK regulatory approach
  see also corporate governance
  concepts 27–8, 284–304
materiality principle 59–67, 308, 335
measurement classification 59–67, 82–98, 107–27,
    134–44, 151–71, 179–92, 197–212, 219–27, 233–9,
    241–5, 279–82, 326–35
media 12
meetings 44–5, 59–67, 69–78, 93–5, 99–107, 122–7,
    129–34, 141–4, 146–51, 164–71, 173–9, 188–92,
    193–7, 208–12, 213–19, 224–7, 229–33, 236–9,
    241–2, 243–4, 271–7
  see also Cormorant plc, Finch plc, Kestrel plc, Mallard
    plc, Ostrich plc, Pochard plc, Raven plc, Sandpiper
    plc, Woodpecker plc
  case studies' overview 59–67

misleading statements 173
misreporting, subsidiaries 65, 187–8, 191, 192, 294–5
mixed methods research design, concepts 6
mortality assumptions, pension schemes 91–93, 97, 98,
    286–7

narrative reports 17–18, 24, 63, 65, 164, 170–1, 186–7,
    191, 192, 206, 235–9, 244–5, 256, 268, 294–5,
    322–3
  see also directors' reports; enhanced business reviews;
    operating and financial review statement
NAS see non-audit services
negotiations 3, 7–11, 22–3, 28–41, 43–50, 54–67, 78–98,
    107–27, 134–44, 151–71, 179–92, 197–212,
    219–27, 233–9, 241–5, 258, 274–7, 279–324,
    325–35
  see also interactions
  audit settings 30–41
  case studies' overview 54–67, 279–300, 326–35
  coalitions 29–30, 312
  comfort factors 34–41, 307, 323–4, 329
  cultural issues 30, 94, 328–35
  definition 28–9, 43–4
  empirical studies 29–41
  ethical standards 30, 57
  experimental studies 32–3, 335
  grounded theory model 11, 34–41, 279–324, 325–35
  interview studies 7, 34–41, 53–67, 279–324
  key findings and conclusions 8–10, 44–50, 57–67,
    274–7, 279–324, 325–35
  models 29–30
  psychological factors 30, 32–3, 40–1
  questionnaire surveys 7, 31, 33–4, 43–50, 53–5,
    326–35
  relevant academic literature 28–41, 275–7
  revised grounded theory model 279, 284–324,
    327–35
  survey summary 45–50, 281
  theory 28–9, 279–324
  top ten issues 45–50, 281
net current assets/liabilities 90–1, 252–3
net debt figures 252–3
net realizable value, concepts 87, 185, 200, 220–1
Netherlands 26
non-audit services (NAS) 4, 7, 10, 11, 14, 18, 19, 20–1,
    28–30, 31–2, 44–50, 106–7, 188, 237, 260, 268,
    307, 322–4, 332–5
  bans 21
  critique 10, 19, 20–1, 28–30, 31–2, 44–5, 260, 268,
    322–4, 332, 334
  ES 5 Non-audit Services Provided to Audited Entities
    4, 10, 14, 20–1, 106, 260, 268, 322, 332
  key findings and conclusions 10, 44–50, 260, 268, 307,
    322–3, 324, 325–35
  relevant academic literature 20–1, 28–30, 322–4
  survey statistics 20, 44–50
  types 20
non-Big Four professional firms 19, 54–67, 173–92,
    213–27, 249–69, 294–5, 298–9, 307, 314–17
non-compliance factors
  case studies' overview 59–67, 282–300
  inventory provisions 87–9, 96–7, 98, 286–7
  outcome determinants 313–24, 327–35

non-executive directors (NEDs) 26–8, 45, 49–50, 59–67, 69–78, 85, 93–5, 99–107, 115, 122–7, 129–34, 137–44, 145–51, 159, 164–71, 173–9, 181, 188–92, 193–7, 208–12, 229–33, 236–9, 265–9, 271–7
see also audit committees
non-financial performance indicators
see also key performance indicators
concepts 17–18, 137–8, 143, 235–6, 238, 244–5, 290–1, 302–3
Northern Rock 255
notional interest on unwinding deferred consideration, Finch plc 63, 153–4, 166–7, 170–1, 292–3, 313–17

objectives of parties category, grounded theory model 35–40, 284–304, 308–9, 328–35
objectivity needs, auditors 13–14
OFR *see* operating and financial review statement
'one size will not fit all' views 322–3
operating cash flows, concepts 198–200
operating and financial review statement (OFR), concepts 17–18, 235–6, 252
Ostrich plc 58, 66–7, 241–5, 302–3, 313–17
business reviews 244–5, 302–3, 313, 316–17
contextual factors 67, 242–5, 302–3, 313–17
corporate governance 67, 241, 243–5
interactions 67, 241–5, 302–3, 313–17
meetings 67, 241–2, 243
overview 67, 241–2, 302–3
quality of the relationships 67, 241–2, 243–4, 302–, 313–17
segmental reporting 67, 245, 302–3, 313, 316–17
share-based payments 67, 244, 245, 302–3, 313–17
valuation of acquisition intangibles 67, 242, 244–5, 302–3
other category, grounded theory model 35–40, 327
outcome category, grounded theory model 35–40, 59–67, 279–300, 284–324, 326–35
outcome determinants, concepts 313–24, 326–35
overview of the book 3, 6–10

P&L 135–6, 156, 168–9, 206
Parmalat 13
PCAOB *see* Public Company Accounting Oversight Board
pension schemes 49–50, 63, 72–3, 91–93, 97, 98, 113–15, 194, 286–7, 313, 316
see also retirement benefits
liabilities 63, 91–93, 97, 98, 286–7
mortality assumptions 91–93, 97, 98, 286–7
percentage-of-completion revenue recognition, contracts 158
POB *see* Professional Oversight Board
Pochard plc 64–5, 193–212, 296–9, 313–17
analysis of the interactions 65, 208–12, 296–7, 313–17
cash flow statements under IFRS 65, 198–200, 208, 210, 211–12, 296–7, 313, 316
conclusions 211–12
contextual factors 65, 193–7, 208–12, 296–7, 313–17
contingent liabilities 65, 200–2, 210, 211–12, 296–7
control weaknesses 65, 207, 211, 212, 298–9
corporate governance 65, 193–7, 207, 208–12
fair value of lease on acquisition 65, 203–5, 210, 211–12, 296–7

interactions 65, 197–212, 296–7, 313–17
inventory valuations 65, 200, 210, 211–12, 296–7
meetings 193–7, 208–12
overview 65, 193, 208–12, 296–7
quality of the relationships 65, 193–7, 208–12, 296–7, 313–17
restructuring costs 65, 205–6, 211, 212, 298–9, 313, 316–17
segmental reporting 65, 206–7, 211, 212, 298–9, 313, 316–17
policy implications, key findings and conclusions 8–12, 333–5
positive moods, ethical decisions 22–3
powers
of the parties 9, 26–8, 33, 39, 265–9, 275–7, 304–24, 325–35
professional accountancy associations 12
preference shares 63, 115–17, 125–7, 288–7, 313–17
preliminary analysis of context, case studies' overview 59–67, 69–78, 93–5, 99–107, 122–7, 129–34, 145–51, 173–9, 188–92, 193–7, 208–11, 213–19, 224–7, 229–33, 236–9
'present fairly' requirement, IFRSs 14–15
presentation issues
cash flow statements 63, 198–200, 208, 210, 211–12, 296, 313, 316
financial statements 46–50, 65, 86, 198–200, 205, 208, 210, 211–12, 296, 313, 316
principles-based standards 9–10, 15–16, 17–18, 76–7, 111–12, 254–6, 267–8, 269, 319–20, 327–8, 331–5
critique 9–10, 15–16, 111–12, 254–6, 267–8, 269, 334
recommendations 334
relevant academic literature 15–16, 319–20
prior year adjustments 49–50
processes, audit committees 38–41, 63, 69–78, 99–107, 129–34, 141–4, 145–51, 164–71, 173–9, 188–92, 193–7, 208–12, 213–19, 224–7, 229–33, 236–9, 265–9
professional accountancy associations, powers 12
Professional Oversight Board (POB)
see also Audit Inspection Unit; public interest audits
objectives/roles 13, 25–6
prompts, interviews 55
provisions 62, 153–4, 158–60, 166–7, 169, 170–1, 185–6, 191, 192, 292–3, 294–5, 313, 316–17, 326–35
prudence principle, concepts 9, 319–20, 331–35
psychological factors
individual audit partners 21–3
negotiations 30, 32–3, 40–1
regulation theory 12
Public Company Accounting Oversight Board (PCAOB) 25–6, 41
public interest accounts 4, 24–5, 256–8, 268–9, 304, 310–12, 325, 332
see also Financial Reporting Review Panel
public interest audits 3, 13, 25–6, 262–4, 268–9, 304, 311, 325
see also Audit Inspection Unit; Professional Oversight Board
public policy economics, concepts 11–12

qualified audit reports 19, 31, 199, 312, 318–19
qualitative interviews, concepts 34–41, 54–67, 279–324

quality of the primary relationship category 34–40,
59–67, 69–78, 93–8, 99–107, 122–7, 129–34,
141–4, 273–7, 282–300, 284–324, 325–33
see also Cormorant plc, Finch plc, Kestrel plc, Mallard
plc, Ostrich plc, Pochard plc, Raven plc, Sandpiper
plc, Woodpecker plc
case studies' overview 59–67, 282–300, 313–17
grounded theory model 34–40, 59–67, 284–324,
325–35
revised grounded theory mode 284–324, 327–35
questionnaire surveys
concepts 3–10, 31, 33–4, 43–50, 53–5, 326–35
negotiations 7, 31, 33–4, 43–50, 53–5, 326–35
summary 43–50

R&D costs 16
rational behaviour 12
Raven plc 58, 64–5, 229–39, 300–1, 313–17, 322
analysis of the interactions 65, 236–9, 300–1, 313–17
business reviews 65, 235–6, 238–9, 302–3, 313,
316–17, 322
complex transactions 65, 234–5, 236, 238, 239, 300–1,
313, 316
conclusions 239
contextual factors 65, 229–33, 236–9, 300–1, 313–17
corporate governance 65, 229–33, 236–7
disclosures of future losses in a subsidiary 65, 235,
238–9, 302–3
interactions 233–9, 300–1, 313–17
meetings 229–33, 236–9
overview 58, 65, 229, 236–9, 300–1
quality of the relationships 65, 229–33, 236–9, 300–1,
313–17
re-organization costs 48–50, 63, 65, 69, 85–7, 96, 98,
119–20, 126–7, 205–6, 211, 212, 284–5, 288–9,
296–7, 313, 316–17, 330–3
reasoning, negotiation influences 29, 38, 312, 318–24,
329–33
reciprocity-based strategy, concepts 12, 32, 312, 319,
323, 329
recognition classification 59–65, 107–27, 134–44,
151–71, 179–92, 219–27, 233–9, 241–5, 279–82,
326–5
recommendations 7, 333–5
recoverable amounts, impairment of assets 84–5, 141,
161, 183, 220
references 335–46
Registered Auditor Status 23
regulation theory, relevant academic literature 7, 11–12
regulatory economics, concepts 11–12
regulatory framework 3–41, 43–50, 55, 57, 60, 76–7,
87–9, 94–5, 96–8, 122–7, 133–4 136–7, 142–4,
174–6, 192, 198–200, 206–8, 233, 249–69, 272–3,
281–2, 296, 284–324, 325–35
see also European Union; standards; UK . . . ; US . . . ;
views . . .
changes 3–10, 12–41, 43–50, 55, 76–7, 87–9, 133–4,
176, 249–69, 272–3, 281–2, 284–324, 325–35
creators 12
critique 8–10, 11, 76–7, 249–69, 284–324, 325–35
global financial crisis from 2008 4–6, 12, 15, 20–1, 28,
317–18, 335
grounded theory model 34–40, 284–324, 325–35

key findings and conclusions 8–10, 249–69, 317–24,
325–35
market-based UK regulatory approach 27–8, 284–304
policy implications 8–12, 333–33
relevant academic literature 6–7, 11–41, 317–24
revised grounded theory model 284–324, 327–35
supranational private sector bodies 11
regulatory policy/structures, relevant academic literature
12–13
relevant academic literature
AIU 25–6
auditing quality 18–24, 40–1
CFOs 31–41, 275–7
concepts 6–7, 11–41, 56, 275–5, 317–24
corporate governance 7, 11, 26–8, 40–1
enforcement regimes 7, 11, 24–6, 321–4
ethical standards 13–14
FRRP 24–5
IFRSs 7, 11, 14–18
interactions 28–41, 56, 275–7, 317–24
ISAs 13
negotiations 28–41
non-audit services 20–1, 28–30, 322–4
regulation theory 7, 11–12
regulatory policy/structures 12–13, 317–22
rotation requirements for AEPs 21, 32–3, 322–3
remuneration committee 70
research background 4–6, 18, 19, 23–4, 30–41, 44–50,
53–67, 271–7, 318–24, 325–35
resignations, auditors 31
resource-seeker company buyer-type, grounded theory
model 34–40, 305–6, 307, 314, 323–4, 329
restatements 40–1, 48–50, 145, 154–8, 163–6, 169–70,
290–1, 314
restructuring costs 63, 65, 86–7, 119–20, 126–7, 205–6,
211, 212, 284–5, 288–9, 296–7, 313, 316–17,
330–35
retirement benefits 49–50, 63, 91–93, 97, 98, 286–7
see also pension schemes
revenue recognition 33–4, 39, 46–50, 63, 147–8, 158–60,
169, 170–1, 187–8, 191, 192, 292–3, 294–5
revised grounded theory model, concepts 279, 284–324,
327–35
risk management 63, 69–78, 121, 131–4, 142–4, 175,
193–7, 207, 211, 212, 235–6, 255–6, 264, 296–7,
302–3
see also audit committees
rotation requirements for AEPs 4, 10, 13–14, 18, 21, 24,
32–3, 58, 107, 129, 132, 141, 143, 209, 217–18,
233, 259–60, 268, 322–3, 332, 334
8th Statutory Audit EU Directive 14
critique 10, 21, 32, 107, 259–60, 268, 322–3, 332,
334
key findings and conclusions 10, 259–60, 268, 322–3,
325–35
relevant academic literature 21, 32–3, 322
rules-based process-driven standards
see also International Financial Reporting Standards;
International Standards on Auditing
critique 4, 5, 8–10, 15–16, 76–7, 111–12, 254–6,
267–8, 269, 319–20, 322–4, 327–35
relevant academic literature 15–16, 319–20, 322–4
US GAAP 4

salary inflation rates 81–2
salience effects, psychological aspects of regulation
    theory 12
sanctions
    see also enforcement . . . ; qualified audit reports
    negotiation influences 29–30, 38, 311–12, 318–24,
        329–35
Sandpiper plc 63, 69–98, 284–7, 305, 307
    analysis of the interactions 62–3, 93–8, 284–7
    audit fees 63, 69, 79–82, 94, 95, 97–8, 284, 308
    capitalization of expenditure 69, 82–5, 95–6, 98,
        284–5
    conclusions 97–8
    contextual factors 63, 69–78, 93–8, 284–7, 305, 307
    corporate governance 69–78, 94–5, 97–8
    dividends from subsidiaries 63, 89–91, 97, 98, 286–7
    interactions 63, 78–98, 284–7
    inventory provisions 63, 87–9, 96–7, 98, 286–7, 313,
        316, 317
    IT system costs 69, 82–5, 95–6, 98, 284–5, 313, 316
    meetings 63, 69–78, 93–5
    overview 63, 69, 93–5, 284–7
    pension liabilities 63, 91–93, 97, 98, 286–7, 313,
        316
    quality of the relationships 69–78, 93–8, 284–7, 305,
        307
    re-organization costs 63, 69, 85–7, 96, 98, 284–5
    satisfaction with auditors and partner changes 77–8
Sarbanes-Oxley Act 2002 (SOX) 3, 12, 13, 23, 25–6,
        32–3, 39
scapegoating, concepts 12
scepticism 23, 25, 33–4, 323–4
Securities and Exchange Commission (SEC) 14–15, 21,
        25–6, 36
segmental reporting 16, 46–50, 63, 65, 162–4, 170–1,
        206–7, 211, 212, 245, 281–2, 292–3, 296–7, 302–3,
        313, 316–17, 326–33
segmentation strategies, customers 85–7, 162–4, 292–3
self-regulation mode, concepts 12–13
sensitive issues
    case studies 57–8
    enhanced business reviews 256, 322–3, 330–5
shadow negotiations 35–41
share options, tax credits 61, 157–8, 168–9, 170–1,
        292–3, 313–17
share-based payments 16, 46–50, 63, 155–8, 168–9,
        170–1, 244, 245, 281–2, 292–3, 302–3, 307–8,
        313–17, 326–35
shareholders
    corporate governance provisions 27–8
    market-based UK regulatory approach 27–8, 284–304
Smith Report 27–8, 100–1, 133–4
social issues 18, 35–41
social positioning, concepts 35–41
Société Générale 321
SOX *see* Sarbanes-Oxley Act 2002
specific contextual factors, grounded theory model
        34–40, 284–324, 327–35
SSAP 25 48
standards
    see also International Financial Reporting Standards;
        International Standards on Auditing
    concepts 4, 5, 8–10, 11, 65, 249–69, 284–324

critique 8–10, 11, 249–69, 317–24
key findings and conclusions 8–10, 55, 249–69,
    284–324, 325–35
policy implications 8–10, 333–4
principles-based standards 9–10, 15–16, 76–7,
    111–12, 254–6, 267–8, 269, 319–20, 327–6, 331–5
revised grounded theory model 284–324, 327–35
rules-based process-driven standards 4, 5, 8–10,
    15–16, 76–7, 111–12, 254–6, 267–8, 269, 319–20,
    322–4, 327–35
views on regulatory framework 249–69
'standards-surveillance-compliance' system 12, 321–2
status-seeker company buyer-type, grounded theory
    model 34–40, 307
strategies 12, 29–41, 60, 282–300, 284–304, 311–17,
    318–24, 327–35
    see also assertiveness; coalitions; higher authorities;
        ingratiation; reasoning; reciprocity . . . ; sanctions
    case studies' overview 62–7, 282–300
    negotiations 29–41, 60, 282–300, 284–304, 311–17,
        318–24, 327–35
strategy category, grounded theory model 35–40,
    282–300, 284–304, 311–17, 318–24
subjectivity concerns, IFRSs 253–6
subsidiaries 17–18, 46–50, 63, 65, 89–91, 97, 98,
    99–127, 173–92, 221–7, 235, 238–9, 286–7, 298–9
    breach of internal controls 65, 221–7, 298–9
    disclosures of future losses 65, 235, 238–9, 302–3
    dividends 63, 89–91, 97, 98, 286–7
    misreporting 62, 187–8, 191, 192, 294–5
substance-over-form principle, concepts 9, 10, 14–16,
    319–22, 331–35
supranational private sector bodies
    see also International Accounting Standards Board;
        International Forum of Independent Audit
        Regulators
    concepts 11, 14
surveys 23–4, 31–41, 43–50, 53–5, 271–7, 281–2,
    326–35
    see also case studies; questionnaire surveys
    auditing quality 23–4
    findings 44–5, 59–67, 271–7, 281–2, 326–35
    summary 43–50
Sweden 34

tactics
    case studies' overview 62–7, 282–300, 329–35
    negotiations 29–41, 60, 282–300, 284–304, 311–12,
        318–24, 329–35
tax credits, share options 60, 157–8, 168–9, 170–1,
    292–3, 313–17
taxation 46–50, 63, 65, 104, 157–8, 163–4, 168–9,
    170–1, 184, 191, 192, 292–3, 294–5
technical departments, key findings and conclusions
    328–33
tenders, auditors 63, 79, 82, 95, 150–1, 152–3, 164–71,
    170–1, 213, 217–18, 233, 284, 290–1
tenure issues
    see also rotation . . .
    concepts 18, 21
testing/modifying grounded theory, concepts 55–7,
    279–324
theory development 279–324

third parties category, grounded theory model 35–40, 284–304, 308–9, 328–35
time value of money 153, 161, 167, 183
top ten issues, negotiations/interactions 45–50, 281
transformation moments, negotiation concepts 30
transparency issues, concepts 12, 80–2, 321–2
Treasury Select Committee on the Banking Crisis 16–17, 19, 20–1
Treasury Select Committee on the Financial Regulation of Public Limited Companies 5
'true and fair view'
   concepts 5, 9, 10, 14–15, 16, 120, 254–5, 319–22, 331–5
   override considerations 15, 16, 319–22, 331–5
trust 12, 20–1, 30, 33–4, 191–2, 319, 323–4
Tweedie, Sir David 115, 116–17

UK 3–10, 13–41, 92–3, 107, 120, 157–8, 160, 169, 176, 180, 207, 222, 242, 251, 253–6, 267, 272–3, 276–7, 292–3, 325–35
   see also Combined Code . . . ; Financial Reporting Council; Financial Reporting Review Panel; Financial Services Authority
   audit committees 26–8, 333–5
   changes 3–10, 13–41, 43–50, 55, 133–4, 176, 249–69, 272–3, 281–2, 284–324, 325–35
   GAAP 14–15, 36, 39, 107, 120, 157–8, 160, 169, 176, 180, 207, 222, 242, 251, 253–6, 267, 272–3, 326
   narrative reports 17–18, 24, 63, 164, 170–1, 186–7, 191, 192, 206, 294–5
   pension schemes 92–3
   Treasury Select Committee on the Banking Crisis 16–17, 19, 20–1
   Treasury Select Committee on the Financial Regulation of Public Limited Companies 5
UNCTAD 15
US 3–4, 12, 13, 23, 25–6, 32–3, 39, 41, 57, 276–7
   see also Financial Accounting Standards Board
   de-regulation trends 12–13
   PCAOB 25–6, 41
   SOX 3, 12, 13, 23, 25–6, 32–3, 39
US GAAP 4, 14–15, 255–6
   see also Financial Accounting Standards Board
   critique 255–6
   IFRS convergence 4, 14–15, 74–5, 255–6, 267–8, 273
   rules-based process-driven standards 4, 15–16, 267–8

valuations 8, 10, 20–3, 59, 63–7, 87–9, 96–7, 98, 107–15, 122–7, 141, 160–4, 169–70, 171, 179–82, 185–6, 190, 191, 192, 200, 203–5, 210, 211–12, 219–21,
   222–7, 242, 244–5, 281–2, 286–9, 292–7, 298–9, 302–3
   acquisition intangibles 8, 10, 63, 65, 67, 107–15, 122–7, 160–4, 169–70, 171, 179–82, 190, 192, 203–5, 210, 211–12, 222–7, 242, 244–5, 281–2, 286–9, 292–9, 302–3, 307–10, 313–17, 326–35
   customer lists 109–11, 122–4
   inventories 63, 65, 87–9, 96–7, 98, 185–6, 191, 192, 200, 210, 211–12, 219–21, 224, 226–7, 281–2, 294–5, 296, 298–9, 313, 317, 326–35
value added, audits 152–3
views on regulatory framework 8–10, 55, 57, 60, 94–5, 96–8, 122–7, 136–7, 142–4, 174–6, 192, 198–200, 206–8, 233, 249–69, 272–3, 276–7, 305–6, 307–10, 317, 321–2, 325–35
   AIU 258, 262–4, 268–7, 332
   audits 258–66, 268–9
   corporate governance 264–9, 332
   ethical standards 258–60, 268–9, 332, 334
   FRRP 256–8, 263–4, 268–9, 332
   IFRSs 249–58, 267–9, 272–3, 276–7, 305–6, 307–10, 317, 321–2, 331–5
   ISAs 260–2, 268–9, 335
vividness effects, psychological aspects of regulation theory 12

Walker Report 28
whistleblowing 100–1, 121, 126–7, 201
within-case analysis, concepts 55–7, 62–7, 282–300
Woodpecker plc 64–5, 213–27, 298–9, 305, 308, 313–17
   analysis of the interactions 65, 224–7, 298–9, 313–17
   breach of internal controls in an overseas subsidiary 65, 221–7, 298–9
   conclusions 226–7
   contextual factors 65, 213–19, 224–7, 298–9, 305, 308, 313–17
   corporate governance 65, 213–19, 224–7
   interactions 65, 219–27, 298–9, 313–17
   internal controls 65, 221–7, 298–9
   inventory valuations 65, 219–21, 224, 226–7, 298–9
   meetings 214–19, 224–7
   overview 65, 213, 224–7, 298–9
   quality of the relationships 65, 213–19, 224–7, 298–9, 313–17
   valuation of acquisition intangibles 65, 222–7, 298–9, 308
working capital 117
write-downs 33–4, 84–5, 87–9, 161, 219–21, 286–7, 290–1, 298–9
write-offs 86–7, 96, 97–8, 119–20, 288–9
writing-up the cases, concepts 54–5, 57–8

Index compiled by Terry Halliday